P9-CML-493

7-26-74

AUDUBON in FLORIDA

AUDUBON

in FLORIDA

BY *Kathryn Hall Proby*

WITH SELECTIONS FROM THE WRITINGS

OF *John James Audubon*

UNIVERSITY OF MIAMI PRESS
Coral Gables, Florida

Designed by Anne Hertz

Manufactured in the United States of America

Library of Congress Cataloging in Publication Data
Proby, Kathryn Hall, 1921-
Audubon in Florida.
Bibliography: p.
1. Audubon, John James, 1785-1851. 2. Birds—Florida. I. Audubon, John James, 1785-1851. Selections. 1974. II. Title.
QH31.A77P76 1974 598.2' 9759 72-85114
ISBN 0-87024-241-5

Illustration credits: Courtesy of Mr. & Mrs. Toby Bruce: p. 42. Jim Conway: pp. 68, 75, 78 (top), 80. Denny Cosmetto: p. 69. Florida News Bureau: pp.xxv, 55, 61, 82, 84. H. W. Hannau: p. 50. Anne Hertz: p. 81. Fred Kent: p. 67.

Charles S. McIntosh: p. 54. Courtesy of Monroe County Library: pp. 42, 85. Courtesy of Dewey Moody: p. 57. National Audubon Society: frontispiece. National Park Service: pp. 70, 78 (bottom), 79. Philip F. Prioleau, p. 56. Kathryn Hall Proby: p. 72. Dade Thornton: p. 77.

Mitchell Wolfson Family Foundation and Audubon House, Key West: pp. 86, 93, 95, 98, 101, 103, 104, 109, 118, 121, 123, 133, 134, 139, 143, 145, 148, 151, 157, 162, 169, 180, 185, 187, 188, 191, 194, 203, 211, 216, 219, 226, 231, 234, 238, 245, 247, 250, 256, 259, 264, 265, 266, 271, 274, 280, 283, 289, 290, 298, 305, 307.

Frontispiece: John James Audubon, after an engraving by H. B. Hall of portrait by Henry Inman, 1833. Said to be the portrait Audubon himself most favored.

for Lucien

Contents

Illustrations

Foreword

Audubon was a phenomenon. He was an artist, a scientist, a woodsman, and a failure at mundane commercial enterprises. Above all he was a man who looked at the wilderness that was America and saw beauty and excitement. He also saw the seeds of destruction and amid his flowery prose and ecstatic descriptions sounded some of the earliest warnings that man's stewardship of the new continent needed some revisions. His name was very properly attached, some thirty years after his death, to the awakening of our national conscience that has gathered strength and become the environmental movement of the 1970s.

Audubon was also one of the first "birdwatchers," certainly in North America and perhaps in the world. There had, of course, been many gifted ornithologists, but Audubon seems to have had the enthusiasm, the drive, and the engaging personality to inspire others with a "spirit . . . which infects all who come within it with a mania for bird killing and bird stuffing." Hardly the reaction of a modern birdwatcher but, given the differences that 140 years can make, the pattern is there. His interest and unstinting personal efforts simply rubbed off on many of his friends and acquaintances. Audubon has, at times, been criticized for shooting birds wherever he went. This is certainly a case of clouded hindsight. Before the days of museum collections, good binoculars, cameras, and field guides, there was simply no other way to study birds than to shoot them, and those collected by Audubon himself were a mere drop in the bucket to the general killing that was an accepted part of frontier America. Audubon's popularization of nature and particularly birds through his books and paintings has probably done more to preserve birds than any other single action. It can well be said that the birds that he collected died in an excellent cause.

The picture of Audubon the man and of wilderness Florida that emerges from this book is fascinating. The letters and episodes given here paint a very human picture of the enormous difficulties facing a naturalist in the 1800s, and also of the boundless energy and good humor that Audubon brought to his task. There were Indians, mosquitoes, pirates, and rattlesnakes, but Audubon was up at 3:00 A.M. and out finding places of great beauty and wildlife of all sorts every day, all day. He then gave us the benefit of his insight by writing notes and letters far into the night. We owe him a debt of thanks.

We are fortunate, too, that so many of the places that Audubon visited are still here to be seen and enjoyed today. The protection of such sites through the efforts of private persons and state and federal governments bespeaks the influence started by Audubon so long ago.

Florida is presently grappling with problems more complex than any that Audubon could conceive. Tremendous growth, shortages of water, loss of wild areas vital to both wildlife and man, and massive pollution all loom on the horizon. It is a good time to look back at the Florida that was and see it through the eyes of a perceptive and sensitive naturalist, to catch a glimpse of parts of it as they are today, and to think seriously about what it will be like tomorrow.

Alexander Sprunt IV

Acknowledgments

Many people are remembered for their kindness and valuable assistance in the research for this book. To most of them I was a stranger asking questions and seeking advice. From the beginning, countless doors were opened to me by specialists who shared their knowledge and gave generously of their time. My traveling companions, in each instance, were ideally suited to follow Audubon's trail through Florida. From our experiences, convivialities, and searches, lasting friendships have emerged and previous friendships have been strengthened. It gives me pleasure to express my deep appreciation to the following persons:

Jeff Willard, Cindy Purcell, and Elizabeth Willis of Jacksonville; Xavier and Catherine Pellicer and Rose and Ray Vinten, Saint Augustine; Jim Lucas and Bob Folks, Astor; Allen Morris, photo archivist, and the Florida Development Commission, Tallahassee; Stanley Dean, Pensacola Art Center; Eileen Butts, historian, Ormond Beach; Dr. E. Ashby Hammond, professor of history, University of Florida.

In the Miami area, John D. Pennekamp, associate editor of *The Miami Herald;* George Rosner, Associate Director for Archives and Special Collections, Otto G. Richter Library of the University of Miami; Kathleen Leathen, Florida Collection Librarian, Miami Public Library; H. Lewis Dorn, director of the Museum of Science-Planetarium; David Alexander, museum director of the Historical Association of Southern Florida; Ralph Miele, ranger-pilot, Everglades National Park; Mary Dutcher, Myrtle Rosner, Jeannie Nicoll, and Jim Conway.

In Key West, Betty Bruce, historian, Monroe County Library; Bob Reno, *Newsday,* former bureau chief of *The Miami Herald;* Steve

Boyden, curator of Audubon House, and Jessie Porter Newton, a driving force in the restoration of old Key West.

Joseph William Jackson, genealogist, New Orleans; Edward H. Dwight, Director, Museum of Art, Munson-Williams-Proctor Institute, Utica, New York; William Curry, *Philadelphia Inquirer;* Waldemar Fries, Providence, Rhode Island; Theodore E. Leach, Library of Congress; Richard Maxwell and Mark G. Eckhoff, National Archives; James J. Heslin, New-York Historical Society; Charles H. Callison, Roland C. Clement, Carl W. Buchheister, and Alexander Sprunt IV of the National Audubon Society.

Special thanks go to Stanley Stern and Gerald Whaley of Wometco Enterprises and to Colonel and Mrs. Mitchell Wolfson and the Wolfson Family Foundation for making arrangements for photographing the 52 Audubon bird portraits especially for this book from the Elephant Folios at Audubon House in Key West, as well as to Ed Thompson of Wometco Enterprises, who did such a fine job in photographing them.

I especially wish, also, to thank Charles Brookfield, Florida representative of the National Audubon Society, retired, who introduced me to the Everglades, its mysteries and its wildlife, and who provided ongoing counsel as the manuscript took shape.

Finally, I am indebted to the late Fred Shaw, professor, editor, columnist, and steadfast friend, who suggested my research on Audubon's travels in Florida and who directed most of its progress.

Introduction

John James Audubon's nineteenth-century travels cover that period in pioneer America when it was not unusual for men with curiosity and spirit to leave their families and trudge alone through the vast New World. Few of these hearty adventurers, unfortunately, kept records of their good and evil doings. Audubon, however, quite faithfully wrote his impressions day by day in a notebook. His total output in writing amounted to phenomenal proportions—an estimated million words.

Early in his journals there is mention of Audubon's eagerness to know the birds of Florida, its waters and sea life. He first glimpsed the Florida coast in 1826, when he was an unknown bird painter on board the *Delos,* which had sailed from New Orleans May 17, bound for Liverpool. He did not have the opportunity to actually explore Florida until 1831-1832.

Audubon's life prior to 1826 had been more notable for failure than success. His encounters with well-known persons of his time, his hardships, his discoveries, and his eventual rise to fame are well documented by historians, notably the late Dr. Francis Hobart Herrick, America's foremost authority on this subject, and Alice Ford, who is considered Audubon's modern interpreter. Audubon's life was complex and fascinating. He was above all faithful to his dream of drawing the birds of America, and he lived to see this dream fulfilled.

The purpose of this book is to concentrate on the Florida travels of the "American Woodsman," travels that made substantial additions to *The Birds of America,* and to present many of Audubon's writings about Florida, particularly from the *Ornithological Biography.*

Audubon's monumental work known as *The Birds of America* consists of 435 plate pages, usually called the original Audubon prints, containing 1,065 life-sized bird portraits. Reproduced from the original artwork by copper plate engravings which were printed on double-elephant (29 1/2 by 39 1/2 inches) Whatman handmade drawing paper, each print was colored by hand. Published in Edinburgh and London between 1826 and 1838, the reproductions were issued in parts, or numbers, of five plates each, which sold for two guineas. These funds, plus those solicited from subscribers to the whole set, enabled Audubon to finance the publication of the project. The complete work, published in four huge leather-bound volumes, sold in England for 182 pounds 14 shillings, for $1,000 in America.

An estimated 190 to 200 sets were completed. Although the total number of original patrons reached 284, 118 of these let their subscriptions lapse; some of them, however, were believed to have completed their sets from the engraver's residual stock. Audubon's own set, surely one of the best, was sold by Mrs. Audubon in 1862 for $1,200 to a John T. Johnson of New York. The subsequent owners of these volumes are not known. In 1863 Audubon's widow sold her collection of the original watercolors from which the engravings were made to the New-York Historical Society for $4,000. The money for this purchase was subscribed by a special committee and paid in installments to the society.

The New York Times (November 24, 1969) reported that a first edition of *Birds of America* Elephant Folio was sold to a Chicago rare book dealer for $216,000. Sotheby's of London handled the transaction, which was believed to be the highest auction price ever paid for a printed work. Fewer than 150 complete sets of the original edition are thought to remain in existence today.

In 1972-1973 a limited, facsimile Elephant Folio edition was published by Johnson Reprint Corporation of New York. The publishers have made it available in two formats, an unbound set of 435 prints in a special cabinet selling at $5,940, and a set bound in half-leather selling at $6,960.

Audubon's *Ornithological Biography, Or an Account of the Habits of the Birds of the United States of America* is not as well known. Published in Edinburgh between 1832 and 1839, it was issued in five leather-bound volumes, royal octavo size (10 by 6 1/2 inches); the

By

JOHN JAMES AUDUBON,

Fellow of the Royal Societies of London & Edinburgh and of the Linnæan & Zoological Societies of London
Member of the Natural History Society of Paris, of the Lyceum of New York, of the Philosophical Society and the Academy of Natural Sciences of Philadelphia, of the Natural History Society of Boston of Charleston.
&c. &c. &c

Published by the Author.

Vol. II.

1831. 34.

Title page, Birds of America

complete set contains over 3,000 text pages. Volumes I and II were also published in Philadelphia and Boston, respectively. Because he was aware of his limitations in speaking and writing English, Audubon hired a thirty-four-year old University of Edinburgh science professor, William MacGillivray, to edit the work. This massive treatise contains life histories and detailed accounts of all the birds depicted in *The Birds of America.*

Volumes I through III are "Interspersed with Delineations of American Scenery and Manners," discourses known as the Audubon Episodes. Of the sixty episodes, eleven are based on experiences relative to Audubon's Florida travels and are reprinted here along with the life histories of the birds selected.

Each bird history corresponds by number to each plate and tells a story of its own, beginning as a narrative. Audubon often names his companions, records the date, tells where he was, and then describes the habits and habitats of the bird involved. Following this he gives detailed technical descriptions of the bird, including such things as the number of feathers on a wing, measurements of various kinds, the sizes and weights of internal organs, etc. In addition, for some plates he describes the vegetation included in the drawing or the plate's scenic background.

In this book I have omitted the technical sections, of value and interest mainly to ornithologists. Where Audubon described several geographical habitats for the same bird, I have often included only the Florida portion of the text. Other cuts were made to enhance the flow of the description by dropping extraneous material and because of space considerations. Deletions are indicated by ellipses in the text and by the page references cited after each history. My basic aim has been to emphasize those portions of Audubon's writings that enable the reader to visualize his Florida travels and the fresh and unspoiled scenes of the 1830s.

Common and scientific names as Audubon published them in the *Ornithological Biography* are given on the left-hand heading; the currently accepted names are on the right-hand side in brackets. Captions on the *The Birds of America* plates do not always agree with the bird names used in the *Ornithological Biography.* In Plate CLXIII, for example, the name on the folio plate reads Palm Warbler, the name published in the *Ornithological Biography* was Yellow Red-Poll Warbler. In some cases, Audubon unwittingly described the habits and behavior of more than one bird, as with the Cayenne Tern, or confused two separate species as phases of one, as with the Whooping Crane and Sandhill Crane.

While certain aspects of the original typography are not followed (such as setting proper names in full caps in text, reproducing the format of the original headings, etc.), I have attempted to follow exactly the original spelling, punctuation, and capitalization, in an effort to give the present-day reader a "feel" of the text as it actually first appeared in print. Audubon's biographers have pointed out that the text is sometimes inconsistent and confusing, and where necessary I have inserted clarifications within brackets.

Some modern biographers have deleted all references to the shooting of birds; I have not done this, though some references may have been omitted for space considerations. One must remember that in Audubon's time birds were extremely abundant, were shot for sport as well as for the table, and were collected for scientific study and for wide distribution to museums for the advancement of knowledge.

This collection provides the bulk of Audubon's descriptions of Florida and its birds as they originally appeared in print. Those who wish to read more modern versions will find excellent edited editions of selections readily available. It should be noted that this text from the original *Ornithological Biography* differs somewhat from the subsequently published octavo edition, in which the text was revised and in which the sometimes altered bird portraits from *The Birds of America* appear in a different (family) order. Dover's fine paperback facsimile of the first octavo edition, reflecting these changes, is available in seven volumes.

Audubon's writing style has been compared to that of James Fenimore Cooper, an author he admired, and Herman Melville, whose tales of adventure have delighted generations. Audubon, a born storyteller, said repeatedly that writing was a dreadful task, one that he intensely disliked. He faced the endeavor, however, as a necessary part of his total undertaking of painting and describing all of the birds of America. His notebooks, journals, reports, and letters provided vital reference material for the *Ornithological Biography*.

Audubon's Florida material is not conveniently grouped chronologically, for he often referred to Florida in his descriptions of excursions to other territories. Likewise, the plates in *The Birds of America* do not follow his travels chronologically. The order of the plates and the dates given in the legends on the plates reflect the time when the engraver released the prints. The transcript of the legend engraved on Plate CCLXXXI, for example, reads "Great White Heron . . . View Key-West. 1835." We know that Audubon did the watercolor for this bird in Key West on May 26, 1832, after which the painting had to be transmitted to Havell in London, where it was then engraved, printed, colored, and eventually released, in this case three years later.

The Florida expedition, dreary at the beginning, increased *The Birds of America* plates by thirty-some drawings. Audubon stated that "The birds, almost all of them, were killed by myself, after I had examined their motions and habits . . . and were regularly drawn on or near the spot where I procured them " (*Ornithological Biography*, Vol. I, p. xii). The drawings selected for engraving were sometimes chosen from several studies of the same bird. Drawings of many birds commonly seen in Florida had been made in Louisiana and elsewhere before Audubon's Florida travels, and others were made subsequently.

S. C. Arthur's *An Intimate Life of the American Woodsman* (1937) cited thirty-two plates as originating from Audubon's Florida expedition. Edward H. Dwight, the Director of the Museum of Art, Munson-Williams-Proctor Institute, well-known for his comprehensive studies of Audubon's original work, ascribes one painting to the period when Audubon was becalmed on the *Delos* off the coast of Florida, possibly twenty-nine paintings to Audubon's Florida travels of 1831-1832, and three more sketched subsequently from specimens Audubon collected or otherwise obtained while in Florida. Others were done from specimens sent to him later from Florida. Dwight has clarified much of the speculation about those drawings in which others assisted or finished Audubon's works as well as identifying artists who supplied backgrounds for some of the plates. This information is reflected in the handsome American Heritage publication *The Original Water-Color Paintings of John James Audubon for "The Birds of America "* (1966).

My selection of material included in the present volume is based on the richness of the writings on Florida in the *Ornithological Biography* and is not a claim that Audubon painted or drew fifty-two *Birds of America* portraits in Florida. Indeed, Plate CCCVIII, Telltale Godwit or Snipe, which has a view of East Florida as background and Dwight says was done there in the winter of 1831-1832, and Plate CCCXI, American White Pelican, which Dwight says may have been done in Florida, are not included because the text in each case mainly describes the birds in other habitats. After all, it is not important whether or not exactly twenty-nine or thirty-two plates of "Florida birds" were made. It is of significance that in Florida Audubon found what he had so longed to see—the water birds. And they form an integral portion of his discoveries and his art.

Kathryn Hall Proby

PART ONE

BY KATHRYN HALL PROBY

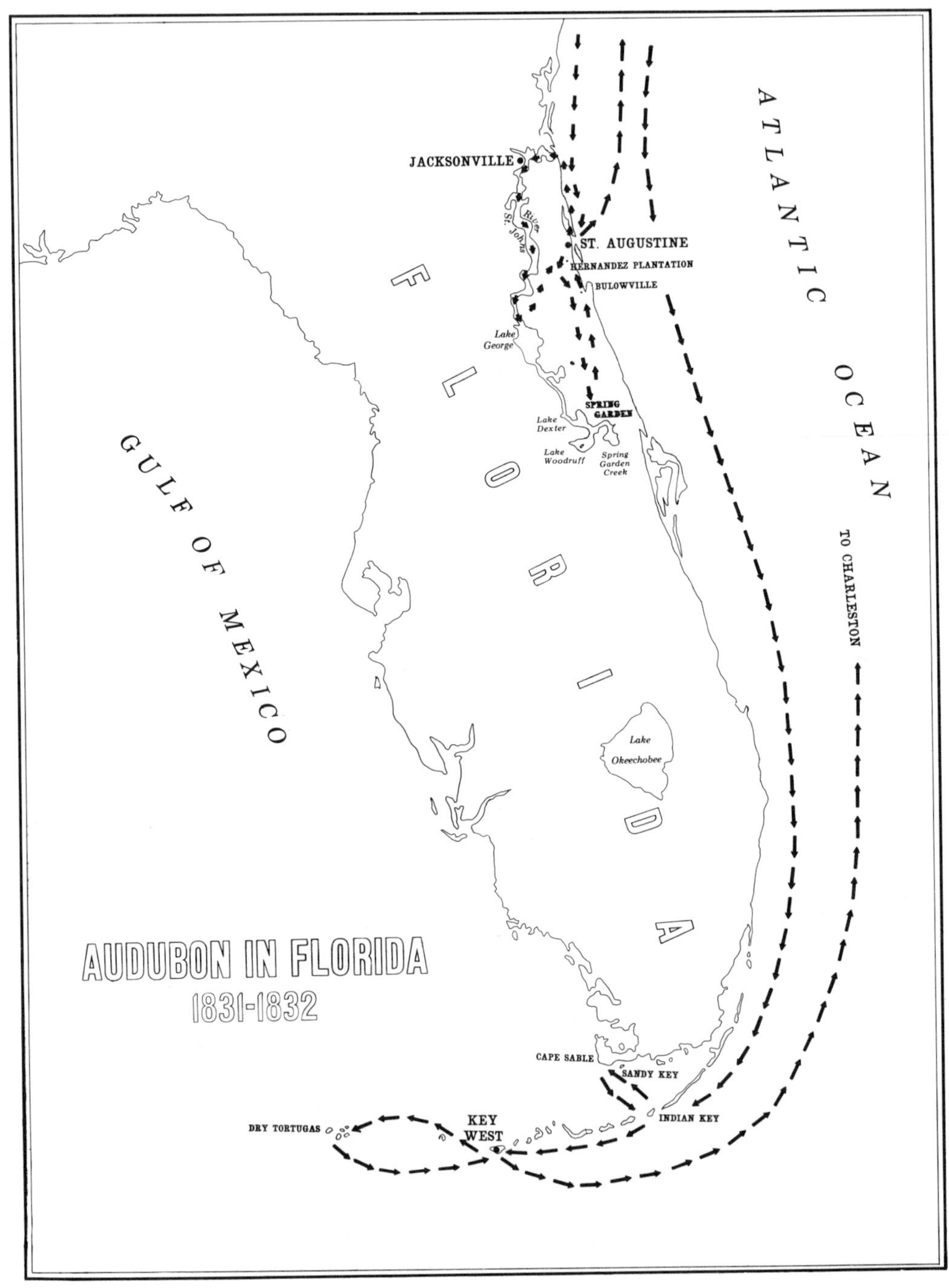
AUDUBON IN FLORIDA
1831-1832
ATLANTIC OCEAN
GULF OF MEXICO
FLORIDA
JACKSONVILLE
St. Johns River
ST. AUGUSTINE
HERNANDEZ PLANTATION
BULOWVILLE
Lake George
SPRING GARDEN
Lake Dexter
Lake Woodruff
Spring Garden Creek
Lake Okeechobee
TO CHARLESTON
CAPE SABLE
SANDY KEY
INDIAN KEY
KEY WEST
DRY TORTUGAS

Chronology

Nov. 15, 1831.	*Wednesday.* Audubon sails from Charleston toward Saint Augustine on schooner *Agnes.*
Nov. 20, 1831.	*Sunday.* Arrives at Saint Augustine.
Dec. 14, 1831.	*Wednesday.* Arrives at Hernandez Plantation, 30 miles south of Saint Augustine.
Dec. 25, 1831.	*Sunday.* Leaves Hernandez Plantation. Goes by foot 15 miles to Bulow Plantation.
Dec. 28, 1831.	*Wednesday.* Descends Halifax River to Live Oak Landing on hunting trip with Bulow. Returns the following day.
Jan. 6, 1832.	*Friday.* Rides Indian pony to Spring Garden, the plantation of Colonel Orlando Rees. Stays two days.
Jan. 14, 1832.	*Saturday.* To Saint Augustine to await passage to southern peninsula.
Jan. 25, 1832.	*Sunday.* Sails from Saint Augustine toward Jacksonville on schooner *Spark* to enter Saint Johns River. Returns because of seasickness and high seas.
Feb. 5, 1832.	*Sunday.* Leaves Saint Augustine again on *Spark* for Saint Johns River trip.
Feb. 17, 1832.	*Friday.* Leaves *Spark* and walks to Saint Augustine by Indian trail during a storm.
Feb. 25, 1832.	*Saturday.* Hunts with Live-oakers near Saint Augustine.

March 5, 1832.	*Monday.* Leaves Saint Augustine for Charleston aboard schooner *Agnes.* Forced into port at Savannah by storm. Continues to Charleston by mail coach.
March 15, 1832.	*Thursday.* Arrives in Charleston at home of Dr. Bachman. Awaits passage to Florida Keys.
April 19, 1832.	*Thursday.* Leaves Charleston aboard U.S. Revenue Cutter *Marion;* sails toward Florida peninsula.
April 24, 1832.	*Tuesday.* Sees Cape Florida light (Key Biscayne).
April 25, 1832.	*Wednesday.* Anchors at Indian Key.
April 26-29, 1832.	Visits Sandy Key, Cape Sable, and mangrove islands with Mr. Egan.
April 30, 1832.	*Monday.* Sails on *Marion* for Key West.
May 4, 1832.	*Friday.* Arrives at Key West; meets Dr. Benjamin Strobel.
May 10, 1832.	*Thursday.* Leaves for Dry Tortugas on *Marion.*
May 16, 1832.	*Wednesday.* Leaves Tortugas for return to Key West.
May 22, 1832.	*Tuesday.* Leaves Key West on board *Marion.*
May 28, 1832.	*Monday.* Anchored off Indian Key.
May 31, 1832.	*Thursday.* Leaves Indian Key on *Marion* en route to Charleston.

John James Audubon, 1785–1851

Audubon states in the *Ornithological Biography* that he "received life and light in the New World."[1] Various mysteries surrounding his origins puzzled scholars for many years. We know now that he was born in Aux Cayes, Santo Domingo, the illegitimate son of a prosperous, roving French sea captain named Jean Audubon and a French servant girl named Jeanne Rabine.

Captain Audubon met Jeanne Rabine on *Le Conquerant,* a ship on which they were both taking passage to Aux Cayes, Audubon to his plantation there, Jeanne as a chambermaid in the service of a distinguished French lawyer. Before the ship docked at Aux Cayes she was more than his friend, and after landing she became a guest at his plantation. There Catherine Bouffard, called "Sanitte," a lovely, graceful quadroon, was firmly situated as Audubon's housekeeper, mistress, and leading contender for his affections. The household included Audubon's and Sanitte's firstborn child, a little girl named Marie-Madeleine.

Jeanne soon became pregnant, and the future artist was born on his father's plantation in Aux Cayes on April 26, 1785. The infant was called Jean Rabine. After his natural mother died less than seven months later, he was cared for by Sanitte. Two years later Sanitte gave birth to Rose "Bonnitte," also fathered by Captain Audubon.

In 1790 when unrest among the blacks of Santo Domingo and rebellion against the whites and mestizos made living there increasingly hazardous for the French colonists, Captain Audubon left Aux Cayes for his home in Couëron, near Nantes, in France, never to return again. He made arrangements for his son and the boy's half-sister Rose to follow. After their arrival in France, the children were put into the custody of Anne Moynet Audubon, the captain's legal but childless wife. In time the couple legally adopted the children. The boy was baptized Jean Jacques Fougère Audubon on October 23, 1800. Thus the two little islanders were entered into French records bearing the Audubon name.

Madame Audubon, who was fourteen years her husband's senior, watched over little Jean, the image of his father, and Rose, a child of color, as if they were her own. Her affectionate care is repeatedly acknowledged in the journals written after her death by her stepson. Madame Audubon tried to keep secret the facts of young Audubon's birth. The boy showed an early interest in nature and a talent for sketching. The father, going his seafaring way, left orders that the children were to study music and mind their tutor, but Anne Moynet Audubon indulged the boy's whims.

The background and early period of Audubon's life will not be fully developed here, but interested readers may find the fascinating details, full of intrigue, in several excellent biographies.

Captain Audubon also had an estate near Valley Forge in Pennsylvania, and in 1803 when his son was eighteen, the father decided to send him to America both to keep him safe from conscription into the French army and to further erase the facts of his illegitimacy. A letter of introduction presented his son as John James Audubon, and he was so known thereafter. Upon landing in New York, young Audubon fell ill with yellow fever and was sent to New Jersey to be cared for by two Quaker women. On recuperation, he proceeded to his father's property, called Mill Grove, on the banks of the Perkiomen Creek near Schuylkill Falls. His newly-learned English was permanently influenced by the Quaker expressions of the kindly nurses.

At Mill Grove, François Dacosta, a Nantes acquaintance of Captain Audubon, was overseer. Dacosta was instructed to direct Audubon in the management of the property and to see that he studied English. But "Hunting, fishing, drawing, and music occupied my every moment" Audubon wrote of Mill Grove, "cares I knew not, and cared naught about them."[2]

Near Mill Grove an English gentleman, William Bakewell, lived with his family on Fatland Ford farm. Like any loyal Frenchman of that time, Audubon resisted meeting the Bakewells at first, but when he discovered that Bakewell had similar tastes for birding and hunting, he forgot his prejudices. He also discovered Mr. Bakewell's daughter. Recollecting his first visit to the Bakewell home, Audubon wrote "and there I sat, my gaze riveted, as it were, on the young girl before me, who half working, half talking, essayed to make the time pleasant to me. Oh! may God bless her! It was she . . . who afterward became my beloved wife."[3]

After meeting Lucy, Audubon spent most of his time near Mill Grove the following year, collecting nature specimens and drawing. He returned to France in 1805 to discuss with his father two burning questions that could not be successfully resolved by mail. One was Dacosta's management of Mill Grove; sharp disagreements over the control of a lead mine on the property were reason enough to bring these matters to his father's attention in person. Of more concern was the young man's desire to marry Lucy Bakewell, a step strongly opposed by Dacosta and a subject previously rejected by the elder Audubon in letters to his son.

In France, however, an even more pressing problem intervened. Napoleon Bonaparte was not content to be still, and all hearty Frenchmen, young and old, were subjects for conscription. It was decided in 1806 to send John back to Mill Grove where he would again be beyond the range of persistent French army recruiters. With him would go Ferdinand Rozier, the son of Claude François Rozier, a commercial judge at Nantes and family friend who had bought part interest in Mill Grove and its lead mine. The two young men signed a nine-year partnership agreement and were advised by their fathers to seek settlement with Dacosta, "a covetous wretch" whose grip on Mill Grove and the mine was highly undesirable. Furthermore, if these efforts failed, the young men were to stay in America and enter commerce elsewhere. The marriage of John to Lucy, they all agreed, would be postponed until these business matters in Pennsylvania were settled.

Disputes and unsuccessful negotiations with Dacosta led to a decision by the young Frenchmen to sell their own interests in Mill Grove. Neither was enchanted by the necessary routines of farming. They were ready to move on. Consequently, Mill Grove was sold to Dacosta with the exception of some 100 acres across the Perkiomen.

Having failed to prove to Lucy's father his stability in business at Mill Grove, in September Audubon took a job as an apprentice clerk in the New York counting house of Lucy's uncle, Benjamin Bakewell. Rozier found employment in Philadelphia. But both restless youths felt misplaced and were discontent. With their partnership wavering and Lucy's father doubting Audubon's ability to support a wife, Audubon and Rozier decided in August 1807 to head for the outpost region of Kentucky. They mortgaged their remaining acres at Mill Grove for $10,000 and departed for Louisville on the Ohio River, where they planned to use their funds to buy goods and set up a store.

Louisville in 1807 was a lively settlement of pioneer traders, the busiest river port between New Orleans and the East. Rozier was eager to make up for his earlier ill-spent experiences in America. The banks and the waterfalls of the wide Ohio lured Audubon day after day in search of wildlife. Their partnership was dealt another blow by the enactment of the Embargo Act, which cut off exports, in December of 1807. Nevertheless, the young merchants held on, and wedding plans began to crystalize at Fatland Ford.

John James Audubon and Lucy Green Bakewell were married April 5, 1808. They journeyed by flat-bottom boat from Pittsburgh, down the Ohio River to Louisville, the honeymoon voyage taking twelve days. "We lived," said Audubon, "two years at Louisville, where we enjoyed many of the best pleasures which this life can afford."[4] A son, Victor Gifford Audubon, who was later to greatly assist his father in the production of *The Birds of America,* was born at Louisville on June 12, 1809. While happiness reigned temporarily for the Audubons, the trading post suffered losses. In the spring of 1810, Audubon and Rozier moved their store to Henderson, Kentucky, farther down the Ohio, but the partnership was losing strength. Their last move, in December, was to Sainte Genevieve, a settlement on the Mississippi River, where the partnership was dissolved on April 6, 1811. Rozier concentrated his energies on trade and found wealth. Beset with frustrations, Audubon returned to Henderson, to Lucy and the infant Victor. Lucy, a woman of refinement and resourcefulness, her educational standard far above that of rural Kentucky, became a tutor.

In spite of previous failures involving conventional vocations, Audubon entered a partnership with Lucy's brother, Thomas Bakewell, in 1812, a New Orleans venture which failed the same year. Two happier circumstances followed. A second son, John Woodhouse Audubon, was born at Henderson on November 30, 1812, and in July of 1812 Audubon became an American citizen at Philadelphia. A second partnership with Bakewell involving a steam lumber and grist mill at Henderson failed two years later. Other misfortunes, meanwhile, gripped the Audubons. Two daughters, Lucy, born in 1815, and Rosa, born in 1819, died in 1817 and 1820, respectively. The mill was Audubon's last encounter with trade. In 1819 he was jailed for debt at Louisville and was released by declaring himself bankrupt.

"I paid all I could," he wrote, "and left Henderson poor and miserable . . . the only time in my life when the Wild Turkeys that so often crossed my path, and the thousands of lesser birds that enlivened the woods and the prairies, all looked like enemies, and I turned my eyes from them, as if I could have wished that they never existed."[5]

In 1820 Lucy stayed at Henderson with the children while her husband with the itching heel sought employment at Cincinnati. He became a taxidermist at the Western Museum, and Lucy and the boys were summoned to Cincinnati, where Lucy resumed teaching. Audubon's job, however, proved unsatisfactory, and a mix-up about his salary brought the family again to the point of financial strain. It is thought to have been here that Audubon began for the first time to seriously consider the possibility of publishing his drawings. To this end in the fall of 1820 he planned a journey through the South. At Natchez and New Orleans he lived hand to mouth, occasionally earning a few dollars at portraiture and teaching. Lucy, Victor, and John joined Audubon at New Orleans on December 8, 1821, where Lucy was soon engaged as a governess. She was encouraged to open a private school on a plantation in West Feliciana. Lucy remained at Beechwoods plantation for five years, assuming the support of her children, sure that her husband would find ultimate success in his mission.

In his travels through the South and in the Eastern states, in dire search for a steady course to follow, Audubon decided in 1824 to go to Philadelphia, then the mecca of scientific study, believing that his bird drawings were far superior to those of Alexander Wilson, the recognized ornithological authority whom he had met in Louisville. In Philadelphia, seeking a publisher for his drawings, he met the leading scientists and artists of the city. Among them were Robert and Rembrandt Peale, Charles Le Sueur, Thomas Sully, Richard Harlan, and Charles Lucien Bonaparte, a nephew of Napoleon Bonaparte, one of the first to befriend Audubon. Audubon often refers to Bonaparte in his writings as the Prince of Musignano, one of Bonaparte's titles. He introduced Audubon to scholars at the Philadelphia Academy of Natural Science. There Audubon's drawings were put on exhibition and received acclaim, and there a professional rivalry began with devotees of the Wilson school, especially George Ord, Wilson's staunch friend.

Audubon went on to New York, where he was elected to membership in the Lyceum of Natural History. His first writings were published in the *Annals* of that museum in 1824. While traveling in the East, the following months brought little gain. The next year, the American Woodsman returned to Louisiana and to his family. He taught music and art, saving for a trip abroad. He had firmly decided to take his drawings to Europe for publication, having failed to place them with an American publisher. "I had finally determined to break through all bonds, and follow my ornithological pursuits," Audubon wrote in 1823. "My best friends solemnly regarded me as a madman, . . . My wife determined that my genius should prevail, and that my final success as an ornithologist should be triumphant."[6]

Audubon was almost childishly devoted to Lucy, although he would leave her and their two small sons intermittently for months, even years. Lucy's patience was exceptional, and her positions as teacher and governess with well-to-do families, mostly in Louisiana, provided at times for the family's total subsistence.

Audubon took passage on the *Delos* and sailed from New Orleans April 26, 1826, to Liverpool, a voyage of sixty-five days. Two episodes, "A Long Calm at Sea" (p. 355) and "Still Becalmed" (p. 358) describe his experiences off the coast of Florida, and several plates for *The Birds of America* were started at this time. They include a bird now named for him, Audubon's Shearwater, which he called the Dusky Petrel in Plate CCLXXXXIX. In Liverpool Audubon was invited to show his drawings at the Royal Institution, a significant exhibition that lasted a month. He left Liverpool on September 10 to visit major cities in Scotland and England, ever hopeful that he could find a publisher. Attention came quickly at Edinburgh, where he made contact with William Lizars, an engraver and printer. "My God! I never saw anything like this before," Lizars is said to have exclaimed. He agreed at once to accept the work of engraving and coloring. "Mr. Audubon, the people here don't know who you are at all, but depend upon it, they *shall* know."[7]

On November 28, 1826, Lizars handed Audubon a first proof of the Wild Turkey Cock, which was soon followed by the Yellow-billed Cuckoo. Audubon became the talk of the city, gaining recognition that led to an exhibition at the Royal Institution of Edinburgh. The press gave flattering attention to the American Woodsman, whose unconventional appearance drew stares; with these attentions, Audubon's inherent French charm made many conquests. He was invited to hold honorary memberships in notable societies of science in Europe and America. On December 10 he wrote Lucy, "My situation in Edinburgh borders on the miraculous."[8]

But there were disappointments and setbacks to follow. The public reputation of Audubon grew and he gained subscribers to his work through tedious personal calls. Invitations from lords and ladies taxed his strength and took time away from soliciting subscribers; he needed funds to meet expenses with the engraver. He was alternately depressed and encouraged; he longed for Lucy, whom he addressed in letters as "My Beloved Friend"; he yearned for the mellow sound of the mockingbird.

Audubon headed toward London in the spring of 1827, adding more subscribers as he traveled. Shortly after arriving in London he had to look for another engraver because Lizars, whose colorers had struck, was forced to break his contract. Subscribers began to complain because delivery schedules were not kept. Audubon searched London for a suitable engraver. At the same time he was hard pressed for cash. "I painted all day, and sold my works during the dusky hours of the evening—never refusing the offer made me for the pictures carried fresh from the easel."[9] Low-spirited, yet confident that time would eventually resolve his problems, Audubon presented his drawing of the Prothonotary Warbler to another engraver, Robert Havell, at 79 Newman Street. The drawing had been partially engraved by Lizars. Their first encounter sealed a partnership that assured world recognition for Havell and especially for his son, Robert Havell, Jr., whose engravings are masterful, and a place in the Hall of Fame for John James Audubon.

An impressive figure, Audubon was almost six feet tall, with intense gray-blue eyes, and flowing, light-brown hair. He admired his own handsomeness and his aquiline profile. Obsessed and stimulated by his restless passions and his gregariousness, he boldly knocked on doors of royalty, presenting letters of introduction to persons of distinction whose influence and acceptance of his bird paintings could bring him closer to complete publication of his work. Consequently, his appearance varied, depending on the circumstances. In Scotland the American Woodsman attire, with leather leggings, boots, and jacket, seemed to fit his purpose. In a letter to Lucy from Europe, describing another costume, he said, "I have come to fine Dressing again—silk stockings and pumps, shave every morning and sometimes dress twice a day—My hairs are now so beautifully long and curly as ever and assure do as much for me as my Talent for Painting."[10]

Audubon's explosive temper often caused disagreements and confrontations with his associates and competitors. Among his acknowledged enemies, above all, was Alexander Wilson, ornithologist and bird painter. Wilson's editor and biographer, George Ord, was relentless in his charges against Audubon for plagiarism of Wilson's work. Charles Waterton of England condoned the opinions of the Philadelphia group and debated the credibility of Audubon's drawing of a rattlesnake in a mockingbird nest (Plate XXI, sketched in Louisiana in 1821 and published in 1827) and Audubon's article in the *Franklin Journal and American Mechanics' Magazine,* published in Philadelphia in 1828 and describing a rattlesnake climbing a tree. Immediate attacks on Audubon's veracity and whether or not rattlesnakes climbed trees ensued. Audubon was supported in print by a number of faithful friends, and much later he was proved to be accurate, but the derision about his portrayal of the reptile's open jaws with pointed fangs and its climbing abilities haunted Audubon for many years.

Audubon made a trip back to America in 1829, leaving the management of his work with John George Children, secretary of the Royal Society of London. He returned with Lucy in April 1830 and they settled in Edinburgh to begin work on the text of the *Ornithological Biography* with the help of William MacGillivray. The first volume, published in April 1831, was well received. The second volume of the large folio was under way.

"I have balanced my accounts with the *Birds of America,*" wrote Audubon on the eve of his departure from London in the summer of 1831. "*Forty thousand dollars!* have passed through my hands for the completion of the first volume. Who would believe that a lonely individual, who landed in England without a friend in the whole country, and with only sufficient pecuniary means to travel through it as a visitor, could have accomplished such a task as this publication?"[11]

The lonely man who, in 1826, had crossed the Atlantic on a seemingly preposterous mission returned as a victor. He had been elected to celebrated scientific societies in Europe. The highest honor given him was membership in the Royal Society of England in May 1830. A brief sojourn in London and Paris further enhanced Audubon's posture in Europe. He was introduced at a meeting of the French Royal Academy of Sciences by the eminent zoologist Baron Georges Cuvier, who proclaimed Audubon's bird portraits "the greatest monument ever erected by art to nature."[12]

Audubon now felt it was time to search for new birds to increase the folio and to campaign for subscribers in the United States. There were birds that had not yet been described, regions he longed to see. Plans were made before he left England to explore the Floridas, especially the eastern coast and the Florida Keys. He further considered an excursion through the Rocky Mountains to California.

On board the *Columbia* sailing to America with Audubon were his wife Lucy and Henry Ward, a young English taxidermist who had been engaged to preserve skins for the Florida expedition. They left London August 2, 1831, and arrived in New York after thirty-three days at sea. Audubon was anxious to move on to catch the bird migrations in the South.

At Philadelphia he hired George Lehman, a landscape painter of Swiss descent, to accompany him and Ward to Florida. Mrs. Audubon departed for Louisville where she would join her sons Victor and John and stay with her brother William and his family. Before leaving Philadelphia, Audubon also made arrangements with G. W. Featherstonhaugh, editor of *The Monthly American Journal of Geology and Natural Science,* to publish reports of his journey through the Floridas.

Audubon with his assistants proceeded to Washington, where he asked permission to travel on a government revenue cutter that made periodic visits to coastal outposts, including some on the fringe of the Florida wilderness. The request was promptly approved by Secretary of the Navy, Levi Woodbury, Lewis McLane, Secretary of the Treasury, and John James Abert of the Bureau of Topographical Engineers. The vessel was to sail from Charleston, but the departure date was some time away. Nevertheless, confident of their passage, the three men left Washington about October 15 and traveled by steamboat down the Chesapeake Bay and along the coast, with various stops, toward Charleston. According to a letter to Lucy, the last part of the trip was made by mail wagon.[13] He wrote Featherstonhaugh: "I cannot boast of the enjoyment I found; poor coaches, dragged through immense, deserted pine forests, miserable fare, and neither birds nor quadrupeds to be seen. We at length approached Charleston, and the view of that city from across the bay was hailed by our party with unfeigned delight. Charmed as we were, with having terminated our dreary journey, it did not occur to us to anticipate the extraordinary hospitality which awaited us there, and which led to a residence of a few of the happiest weeks I ever passed."[14]

The travelers had hardly settled at a Charleston inn when Audubon met the Reverend John Bachman, a Lutheran minister whose avocation coincided with Audubon's passion for the woodlands. Bachman opened his home to the party, and there they remained for a month, initiating a lifelong friendship between the quiet German-American theologian and the impetuous French-American. Bachman, an old friend of Alexander Wilson, took Audubon and his assistants to find specimens, introduced them to many hospitable Charlestonians, and generally made their long wait for the arrival of the schooner unexpectedly pleasant. While there, Audubon taught Bachman's sister-in-law Maria Martin to draw birds, insects, and plants. Many years later, Audubon and Bachman co-authored *The Viviparous Quadrupeds of North America,* and Audubon's sons married Bachman's daughters.

Audubon, Ward, and Lehman remained in Charleston with Bachman and his family until November 15, when they sailed for Saint Augustine. With them was Plato, a Newfoundland dog given to Audubon by Dr. Samuel Wilson, a Charleston hunting companion. Plato, evidently a white-spotted variety now called a Landseer, is often mentioned by Audubon during his early travels in East Florida.

Audubon's letters to Lucy, written with an iron pen, record his first impressions of Florida:[15]

JOHN JAMES AUDUBON, 1785-1851

St Augustine East Florida 23d Novr 1831

My Dearest Friend—

We arrived here on Sunday last in the morning after a passage of 5 days from Charleston on Board a Schooner called the Agnes, Cap*n* Sweazey—

The winds were contrary as so was the Cap*n* as poor a "shoat" as ever I have seen . . . at daylight we were in view of this famous City. The entrance of the Port here is shocking we spent the whole of Saturday and part of the night coming over the different Barrs not exceeding 4 miles *&c*—

Landed looked for Lodgings, ransacked the *four* Taverns that are here and at Last concluded to put up at a M*r* Fleshman for four and half Dollars per week each.—Hare, fish and venaison three times per day!—

St Augustine resembles some old French Village and is doubtless the poorest village I have seen in America—The Inhabitants principally poor Fishermen although excellent Fishers—The streets about 10 feet wide and deeply sanded—backed by some thousands of orange Trees loaded with fruit at 2 cents apiece—A Garrison of one Company—and an old Spanish Castle once the Pride of this Peninsula but now decaying fast.—it is built of *Shell Stone* or a concrete of shells which hardens by exposure to the Air and is curious to the Geologist.—*no back country* for after one leaves this would be a City no house is to be met with 30 miles—The whole Country sandy, Timber, Pine, Live oak and different species of Mirtles and Magnolias—Whilst our Schooner was at anchor we went on S*t* Anastasia's Island and collected some hundreds of shells—in some places we could have taken them up (Live ones) by the shovel full—Saw great number of Water Fowls, Pelicans, *&c* The weather was *then* very hot thermometer at 82, killed 2 large Snakes, Butterflies abundant—*&c* of course *some* flowers—Today the wind has been at Northwest and the glass has fallen down to 49 [29°]—have hunted a great deal but have shot only 2 birds to draw—one a beautiful Heron, the other a Sand piper. . . . I have been fretting myself with the Idea that Havell might be Dead . . . I will have to forego the receiving of letters for a long time as I find that no mail goes farther South than 30 miles—*Write here* untill to the contrary as I will make arrangements with the Commandant of the Garrison to forward wherever I may be by Indian Runners—. . .

I am told that *Tallahassee is a miserable place for Merchants* having no back Country, that all is sold at long credit *&c*—

. . . I wish thee to forward me *at New Orleans* to be kept for me some good socks as mine will be all worn out—the salt marshes through which I am forced to wade *every day* are the ruin of everything—

I have not shot but have seen a Hawk of great size entirely *new*—may perhaps kill him tomorrow—

. . . God bless thee my most and dearly beloved Wife and Friend—

Would to God that I had thee to comfort me this night.—do thou write often God forever bless thee—rememberances to William, his wife; and Dear Sons *&c*—Thine for ever

John J. Audubon

Nov 24*th* I have just returned from shooting up the North River so called here and have as much as will keep me very busy for 2 days nothing else new—

St. Augustine Florida Decr 5th 1831

My Dearest Friend—

At last I have a long letter from thee dated Oct*r* 21*st* Louisville and I dearly thank thee for it.—I am sorry to see the general tenure of its contents so very unpromising.—Not a word doth thou say of thy reception by William and his Wife the whole of which I have a particular desire to have to Judge how far constancy exists in relation's Friendship.—I have this day received a whole parcel of letters from Lord Stanley . . . Havell was going on *Well*! ! Do not despond my Lucy, depend upon it we must yet see better days and I think as I believe in God that *he* will grant me Life and health to enable me to finish my tremendous enterprise and grant us a happy Old Life.—I feel as young as ever and I now can undertake and bear as much hardship as I have ever done in my Life.—Industry and perseverance joined to a sound heart will carry me a great ways—indeed *nothing* but an *Accident* can destroy me in this Tedious Journey.—

. . . My name is now ranging high and our name will stand still higher should I live through my present travels therefore the name of our sons will be a passport through the World—I have now great Confidence in what I have undertaken and indeed feel so light hearted and willing to follow all my plans to the last that I only pray for your health and comfort untill I have the satisfaction of Joining you all again—Keep up a good heart my Lucy—be gay—be happy—collect all the Information in thy power to assist me in my future Publications—Urge our children to follow Honest men's conduct and to Interest them selves at all Leisure hours—I feel fully decided that we should all go to Europe together and to work as if an established PartnerShip for Life consisting of Husband Wife and Children—

. . . We have drawn 17 Diferent Species since our arrival in Florida but the Species are now exhausted and therefore I Will push off to Doc*r* Pochers and McCraigh's Plantation 46 Miles south of this along the coast in about 10 days—I expect innumerable difficulties afterwards between Indian River and Cape Florida as I am told we will have to walk along the Sea Shore beach for about 150 miles before we meet with an Inhabitant either white or red—but in this country we will not mind this much—My young men are both very willingly enclined and quite well therefore believe me we will proceed on if slowly regularly—I write to thee every Sunday punctually and will do so even in the Wilderness—waiting untill opportunities will offer to send my letters to some distant Post Office Thou wilt not hear from me so often as heretofore, but be assured that I will take all reasonable of my health and of that of my assistants—

. . . There is here a Mr *Hugh Williams* who has coasted this peninsula several times and once in an open skiff with his son when 14 years of age from whom I have derived a great deal of Information—Some Lakes says he exist in the Interior on which are Islands containing *Indian Tribes* who know nothing of the existance of *the Seminoles*—he assures me that Birds are most abundant and tame—that shells are superb and *Game* most plentiful . . .

S*t* Augustine is the poorest hole in the Creation—The living very poor and very high—was it not for the fishes in the Bay and a few thousand of oranges that grow immediately around the Village, the people must undoubtedly abandon it or starve for they are all too leazy to work, or if they work at such price as puts it out of the question to employ them. The Country around nothing but bare sand Hills—hot one day cold another *&c &c*

A botanist arrived to day who Inquired for me at table in my presence—a man of most comely appearance but one who unfortunately is possesed of Pulmonic Constitution so hoarse and so thin that I doubt if he will surpass this Winter.—yet he speaks of visiting the *Interior*—God—I will visit it and then will be able to say something on the Subject—

Now my Dearest Friend my Dearly beloved Wife once more *fare thee* well—give my kindest rememberances to Wam and to his Wife and to thy Brother Thomas when thou seest him—did thou see him at Cincinnati—I am glad to hear how your evenings are spent would to God I could Join you all every night and resume my Labours every morning. . . .—I have written to thee before that we have found here a new Species of Vulture—God bless thee and our Dear Sons—and may I have the good fortune to meet you all again in good health on my return—Again and again thine for ever most devotedly attached Friend and husband—

John J. Audubon

Also received my large trunk *&c.*

This is the *7th* and merely have to say again God bless Thee.

Thy Thine Friend,

J.J.A.[16]

In a report dated December 7, 1831, to G. W. Featherstonhaugh, publisher-geologist, Audubon wrote:[17]

St. Augustine, whatever it may have been, is far from being a flourishing place now. It lies at the bottom of a bay, extremely difficult of access, even for vessels of light draft, which seldom reach the "city" in less than a day. I cannot say much for the market, nor the circumjacent country. Oranges and plenty of good fish seem to contribute the wealth of the place. Sands, poor pine forests, and impenetrable thickets of cactus and palmettos form the undergrowth. Birds are rare, and very shy; and with all our exertions, we have not collected one hundred skins in a fortnight that we have been here. I have received many kind attentions, and numerous invitations to visit plantations, on our way to the south, where I shall direct my steps in a few days. I have drawn seventeen species, among which one *mongrel vulture,* which I think will prove new. You will see it, I hope, very soon.

I will give you a sketch of our manner of passing the time. We are up before day, and our toilette is soon made. If the day is to be spent at drawing, Lehman and I take a walk, and Ward, his gun, dog, and basket, returning when hungry or fatigued, or both. We draw uninterruptedly till dusk, after which, another walk, then write up journals, and retire to rest early. When we have nothing on hand to draw, the guns are cleaned over night, a basket of bread and cheese, a bottle with old whiskey, and some water, is prepared. We get into a boat, and after an hour of hard rowing, we find ourselves in the middle of most extensive marshes, as far as the eye can reach. The boat is anchored, and we go wading through mud and water, amid myriads of sand-flies and mosquitoes, shooting here and there a bird, or squatting down on our hams for half an hour, to observe the ways of the beautiful beings we are in pursuit of. This is the way in which we spend the day. At the approach of evening, the cranes, herons, pelicans, curlews, and the trains of blackbirds are passing high over our heads, to their roosting places; then we also return to ours. If some species are to draw the next day, and the weather is warm, they are *outlined* that same evening, to save them from incipient putridity. I have ascertained that *feathers* lose their brilliancy almost as rapidly as flesh or skin itself, and am of opinion that a bird alive is 75 per cent more rich in colours than twenty-four hours after its death; we therefore skin those first which have been first killed, and the same evening. All this, added to our other avocations, brings us into the night pretty well fatigued. Such, my dear friend, is the life of an active naturalist; and such, in my opinion, it ought to be. It is nonsense ever to hope to see in the closet what is only to be perceived—as far as the laws, arrangements and beauties of ornithological nature is concerned,—by that devotion of time, opportunities, and action, to which I have consecrated my life, not without hope that science may benefit by my labours.

As to geology, my dear Friend, you know as well as myself, that I am not in the country for that. The instructions you gave me are very valuable, and I shall be vigilant. The aspect of the country will soon begin to change, and as I proceed, I will write to you about all we see and do. . . . Do not be afraid of my safety; I take a reasonable care of my health and life. I know how to guard against real difficulties, and I have no time to attend to that worst of all kinds of difficulties, —imaginary ones. Circumstances never within my control, threw me upon my own resources, at a very early period of my life. I have grown up in the school of adversity, and am not an unprofitable scholar there, having learnt to be satisfied with providing for my family and myself by my own exertions. The life I lead is my vocation, full of smooth and rough paths, like every vocation which men variously try. My physical constitution has always been good, and the fine flow of spirits I have, has often greatly assisted me in some of the most trying passages of my life. I know I am engaged in an arduous undertaking; but if I live to complete it, I will offer to my country a beautiful monument of the varied splendour of American nature, and of my devotion to American ornithology.

John James Audubon.

Further correspondence to Lucy Audubon overflowed with complaints. Rainy weather and the scarcity of birds at Saint Augustine had evoked multiple anxieties. Feeling "wretched when one hour without work," there was time to consider old wounds and comment on family affairs. Among them was son John's misbehavior. He was not getting along well, Lucy had said, because of the many children and confusion in the household, where her discontentment too was rising. Audubon suggested putting him on a "good Steam Boat under a good Commander."

In the letter to Lucy dated December 8 he said, "indeed I much fear that no portion of this Peninsula is possessed of the rich Lands and advantages represented to exist in it—Time will however show to me and I will not suffer an opportunity [to] escape without acquainting you all with my observations."[18]

The revival of the old and lingering rattlesnake controversy also claimed the naturalist's attention. From Saint Augustine on December 8 he wrote Lucy of his latest verification to disprove the allegation:[19]

I find the News Papers very busy about me and discover with great Satisfaction that the Current of Opinion is greatly changed in my favor by all the great attention paid to me and to my Party wherever we have been—I hope it will continue; this I well can assure thee of that nothing on my part will tend to diminish the Impression now existing.—The Scriblers about Rattlesnake *Stories* will now have to hang their ears and shut their invidious mouths—hast thou read the letter of Colo*l* J. J.

> Abert to Harlan and published in F.'s journal? I have a more extraordinary account in store representing these reptiles.—One was found in this Place, Twisted around the top of a mahogany bed Post in the chamber of a most Venerable Lady, and I have a certificate well attested of that fact. . . .
>
> . . . Lehman is at my Elbow finishing a Drawing of a Gull with a beautiful group of Racoon Oysters.—Henry is packing shells in papers *&c* So that rain or no rain we make out to be employed. The thermommeter was at 78 yesterday the wind at South.—The musquitoes shocking as well as the sand flies.—this morning the wind is at Northwest pouring rain and the thermometer at 60.
>
> Our room gives sight to the entrance to the harbour and I can see the Brown Pelicans by hundreds amid clouds of Gulls *&c* but the Rascals are so wary and so shy that there is no coming near them—further South where no gunners are I am told they are as aboundant and quite Gentle.—
>
> . . . I write my observations on the Birds every night and I hope will find but little dificulty when I write their Biography.—I find however that to observe the manners of the Water Fowls is much dificult to do than that of the Land Birds.

Most notable of the sketches made in this area and chosen for reproduction for *The Birds of America* are the following: Plate CLXI, the Caracara, which Audubon started painting right after it was shot on November 27 in Saint Augustine; Plate CLXIII, the Yellow Red-poll (Palm) Warbler, shown perched on a bough of the wild orange tree; Plate CCIX, Wilson's Plover, done in January with the birds in breeding plumage; Plate CCLXXVIII, Schinz's Sandpiper, with sand dunes and ocean background; and Plate CCXCI, the Herring Gull, with a view of the entrance to Saint Augustine harbor. The young gull in the foreground is, according to Edward Dwight, the only bird figure in *The Birds of America* definitely drawn by Lehman.

Castillo de San Marcos is featured prominently in Plate CCLXIX, the Greenshank, with a sweeping view of Saint Augustine in the distance. Audubon described seeing the Greenshank later at Sandy Key, though it is a European species never recorded before or since in North America. It is thought that Audubon probably mistook a Greater Yellowlegs for the Greenshank.

Florida at this point had indeed not measured up to the flowery sayings of the naturalist William Bartram, and Audubon and his companions were still months away from the ends they sought.

Lucy and Featherstonhaugh were concerned about Audubon's ventures into the Florida wilds. Their fears were well grounded on reports of Indian disturbances and wreckers who roved the southern reefs. President Andrew Jackson had signed the Indian removal act on May 28, 1830. The order directed the Seminoles to move from the Florida Territory to regions west of the Mississippi. Indian removal had become a national issue in 1829 when Jackson became president. His impatience with the Indians was well known. After his bloody victory over the Creeks in 1814 at Horseshoe Bend on the Tallapoosa River in Alabama, there was no doubt of his stern position. Following the bitter campaign and Chief Weatherford's surrender, the Creek nation crumbled. Its remnants were captured or sold in slavery while other stragglers joined neighboring camps. Florida Seminoles became a known force of resistance. They came from a branch of Georgia Creeks, Oconee tribe, who migrated south from the farmlands and joined other refugees from the north, including the Yamasees. From this melding of migrant tribes, a nucleus was formed about 1750 that became the high-spirited and recalcitrant Seminole Nation.

By the nineteenth century in East Florida, colonization was still limited primarily to the coastal areas and to river routes. A stagecoach passageway was cleared during the English period (1763-1783) from Saint Augustine to the Saint Marys River, immediately north of the oldest city. The leading thoroughfare was King's Road, a passageway from King's Ferry on the Saint Marys to New Smyrna. A trail cut out during the Spanish period led from Saint Augustine to Saint Marks on the Gulf of Mexico. A similar road linking Indian trails ran from Tallahassee to Saint Marks. Along the banks of Halifax River, plantation life sprawled from Saint Augustine to New Smyrna. In East Florida in 1831 there were sixteen plantations of sizable holdings, the work of eager settlers. Elevated log roads led through hammocks and swamps from their plantations to the King's Road. Toward the spring country, westward in north central Florida, Indian trails formed a subtle network of communication between tribal villages, threading through abundant hunting grounds. The white man had little knowledge of the wilderness beyond these limits.

After about three weeks of hunting and drawing in the neighborhood of Saint Augustine, Audubon, Ward, and Lehman accepted an invitation to visit General Hernandez's plantation, thirty miles to the south. They stayed ten days, although the host and the naturalist did not ever reach a warm relationship. The dignified Spanish-American general regarded Audubon as a spectacle of the backwoods, a man of unwarranted and unreasonable vocation. The two men could not reach a mutual ground of communication, so each went his own way, Hernandez ruling his rich cane fields while Audubon roamed the woods. Hernandez did not subscribe to *The Birds of America.*

On Christmas morning, 1831, Audubon, bidding a cool farewell to the general, hiked fifteen miles to the sugar plantation owned by John J. Bulow. The Indians were outwardly friendly to this prosperous settler. Indians supplied Bulow with fresh meat—venison and wild turkey. From the Bulow plantation large quantities of sugarcane, indigo, cotton, and rice were floated on the Matanzas River to Saint Augustine for shipment to northern and foreign ports. Bulow, a young man, frequently took his guests on trips in his sailboat as far down the coast as Jupiter Inlet. He traveled luxuriously, with cooks, tents, servants, and a crew to mind the mast. At Bulow plantation, three hundred slaves brought from Charleston erected the settlement buildings from coquina rock, a resilient formation of tiny seashells found from one to thirty feet in substratum soil. There was ample timber for construction. Slaves turned the soil, harvested the crops, ran the mill, and boiled cane juice, yearly increasing the stature of Bulow Ville. Unlike his visit with Hernandez, Audubon spoke warmly of his new host: "During the whole long stay with Mr. Bulow, there was no abatement of his kindness, or his unremitted efforts to make me comfortable, and to promote my researches. I shall ever feel grateful to one of the most deserving and generous of men."[20]

A second report to Featherstonhaugh was written from Bulow Ville on December 31, 1831. After explaining his being at the home of the hospitable Bulow, who had suggested that they proceed down the Halifax River in search of new or valuable birds, he continued: [21]

> Accordingly, the boats, six hands, and "*three white men,*" with some provisions, put off with a fair wind, and a pure sky. . . . We meandered down a creek for about eleven miles—the water torpid yet clear—the shore lined with thousands of acres covered by fall grapes, marshes, and high palm trees, rendering the shore quite novel to my anxious eye. Some birds were shot, and secured so as to be brought back, in order to undergo the *skinning operation.* Before long we entered the Halifax

river, an inland arm of the sea, measuring in breadth from a quarter to nearly a mile. . . . The fact is, that I was anxious to kill some 25 brown Pelicans . . . to enable me to make a new drawing of an adult male bird, and to procure the dresses of others. I proceeded along a narrow, shallow bay, where the fish were truly abundant. Would you believe it, if I was to say, that the fish nearly obstructed our head-way? Believe it, or not, so it was; the waters were filled with them, large and small. I shot some rare birds, and putting along the shore, passed a point, when lo, I came in sight of several pelicans, perched on the branches of the mangrove trees, seated in comfortable harmony, as near each other as the strength of the boughs would allow. I ordered to back water gently; the hands backed water. I waded to the shore under cover of the rushes along it, saw the pelecans fast asleep, examined their countenances and deportment well and leisurely, and after all, levelled, fired my piece, and dropped two of the finest specimens I ever saw. I really believe I would have shot one hundred of these reverend sirs, had not a mistake taken place in the reloading of my gun. A mistake, however, did take place, and to my utmost disappointment, I saw each pelecan, young and old, leave his perch, and take to wing, soaring off, well pleased, I dare say, at making so good an escape from so dangerous a foe. . . .

[Later] preparations were accordingly made, and we left the schooner, with the tide and wind in our teeth, and with the prospect of a severe, cold night. Our hands pulled well, and our bark was light as our hearts. All went on merrily until dark night came on. The wind freshening, the cold augmenting, the provisions diminishing, the waters lowering, all—all depreciating except our enterprising dispositions. We found ourselves fast in the mud about 300 yards from a marshy shore, without the least hope of being to raise a fire, for no trees except palm trees were near and the *grand diable* himself could not burn one of them. Our minds were soon made up to do—what? Why, to roll ourselves in our cloaks, and lay down, the best way we could at the bottom of our light and beautiful barque. Good God, what a night! To sleep was impossible; the cold increased with the breeze, and every moment seemed an hour, from the time we stretched ourselves down until the first glimpse of the morn; but the morn came, clear as ever morn was, and the north-easter as cold as ever wind blew in this latitude. All hands half dead, and masters as nearly exhausted as the hands—stiffened with cold, light-clothed, and but slight hope of our nearing any shore; our only resort was, to leap into the mire, waist-deep, and to push the barque to a point, some five hundred or six hundred yards, where a few scrubby trees seemed to have grown to save our lives on this occasion. "Push boys, push! Push for your lives," cry the generous Bulow, and the poor Audubon.—"All hands push!" Aye and well might we push: the mire was up to our breasts, our limbs becoming stiffened and at every step we took. Our progress was as slowly performed as if we had been clogged with heavy chains. It took us two and a half hours to reach the point, where the few trees of which I have spoken were; but, thank God, we did get there.

We landed . . . and well it was that we did; for on reaching the margin of the marsh, two of the negroes fell down in the marsh, as senseless as torpidity ever rendered an alligator, or a snake; and had we, *the white men,* not been there, they certainly would have died. We had carried them into the little grove, to which, I believe, all of us owe our lives. I struck a fire in a crack; and, in five minutes, I saw, with indescribable pleasure, the bright, warming blaze in a log pile in the center of our shivering party. We wrapped the negroes in their blankets—boiled some water, and soon had some tea—made them swallow it, and with care revived them into animation. May God preserve you from ever being in the condition of our party at this juncture; scarcely a man able to stand, and the cold wind blowing as keenly as ever. Our men, however, gradually revived—the trees, one after another, fell under the hatchet, and increased our fire—and in two hours I had the pleasure of seeing cheerful faces again. . . . [We were] confined in a large salt marsh, with rushes head high, and miry; no provisions left, and fifteen miles from the house of their host.

Not a minute was to be lost, for I foresaw that the next night would prove much colder still. The boat was manned once more, and off through the mud we moved, to double the point, and enter the creek, of which I have spoken, with the hope that in it we should find water enough to float her. It did happen so, thank God! As we once more saw our barque afloat, our spirits rose,—and rose to such a pitch that we in fun set fire to the whole marsh: crack, crack, crack! went the reeds, with a rapid blaze. We saw the marsh rabbits, scampering from the fire by the thousands, as we pulled our oars. . . .

[Later, after abandoning the boat again, they walked] through sand that sent our feet back six inches at every step of the two feet that we made. Well, through this sand we all *waded,* for many a long mile, picking up here and there a shell that is nowhere else to be found, until we reached the landing place of J. J. Bulow. Now, my heart, cheer up once more, for the sake of my most kind host . . . I assure you, I was glad to see him nearing his own comfortable roof; and as we saw the large house opening to view, across his immense plantation, I anticipated a good dinner with as much pleasure as I ever experienced.

All hands returned alive; refreshments and good care have made us all well again, unless it be the stiffness occasioned in my left leg, by nearly six weeks of wading through swamps and salt marshes, or scrambling through the vilest thickets of scrubby live oaks and palmitoes that appear to have been created for no other purpose but to punish us for our sins. . . .

The land, if land it can be called, is generally so very sandy that nothing can be raised upon it. The swamps are the only spots that afford a fair chance for cultivation; the swamps, then, are positively the only places where plantations are to be found. These plantations are even few in number; along the east coast from St. Augustine to Cape Canaveral, there are about a dozen. These, with the exception of two or three, are yet young plantations. General Hernandez's, J. J. Bulow's, and Mr. Durham's are the strongest, and perhaps the best. Sugar cane will prosper, and doubtless do well; but the labour necessary to produce a good crop, is great! great!! great!!! Between the swamps of which I now speak, and which are found along the margin laying west of the sea inlet, that divides *the main land* from the Atlantic, to the river St. John of the interior of the peninsula, nothing exists but barren pine lands and poor timber, and immense savannas, mostly overflowed, and all unfit for cultivation. That growth, which in any other country is called underwood, scarcely exists; the land being covered with low palmitoes, or very low, thickly branched dwarf oaks, almost impenetrable to man. The climate is of a most unsettled nature, at least at this season. The thermometer has made leaps from 30 to 89 degrees in 24 hours, cold, warm, sandy, muddy, watery,—all of these varieties may be seen in one day's travelling. . . . Game and fish, it is true, are abundant; but the body of valuable tillable land is too small to enable the peninsula ever to become a rich state. . . .

Following the Halifax River trip to Live Oak Landing, along with an engineer from Bulow Plantation, Audubon rode an Indian pony to Spring Garden, the plantation of Colonel Orlando Rees. During this visit of two days, he viewed the "curious Spring" and, in the company of Colonel Rees, he went in a small boat from Spring Garden Creek through lakes Woodruff and Dexter to the Saint Johns River. In the Spring Garden episode (p. 309) Audubon wrote that "the group of islands seemed to me like a rich bouquet formed by nature to afford consolation to the weary traveller," but in writing to Featherstonhaugh, Audubon describes the island named for him somewhat differently:[22]

We landed on a small island of a few acres, covered with a grove of sour orange trees, intermixed with not a few live oaks. The oranges were in great profusion on the trees—everything about us was calm and beautiful and motionless, as if it had just come from the hand of the Creator. It would have been a perfect Paradise for a poet, but I was not fit to be in Paradise; the loss of my ibis made me as sour as the oranges that hung about me. I felt unquiet, too, in this singular scene, as if I were almost upon the verge of creation, where realities were tapering off into nothing. The general wildness the eternal labyrinths of waters and marshes, interlocked, and apparently never ending; the whole surrounded by interminable swamps—all these things had a tendency to depress my spirits, notwithstanding some beautiful flowers, rich looking fruits, a pure sky, and ample sheets of water at my feet. Here I am in the Floridas, thought I, a country that received its name from the odours wafted from the orange groves, to the boats of the first discoverers, and which from my childhood I have consecrated in my imagination as the garden of the United States. A garden, where all that is not mud, mud, mud, is sand, sand, sand; where the fruit is so sour that it is not eatable, and where in place of singing birds and golden fishes, you have a species of ibis that you cannot get when you have shot it, and alligators, snakes, and scorpions.

Mr. Bartram was the first to call this a garden, but he is to be forgiven; he was an enthusiastic botanist, and rare plants, in the eyes of such a man, convert a wilderness at once into a garden.

When we had eaten our humble repast at the sweet little Orange Grove Island, we left it "alone with its glory," but not without a name. It was determined, nolens volens, that it should be called Audubon's Island, on the St. John's river. Lat. 29° 42'.

From Spring Garden, Audubon returned to Bulow Ville to meet Lehman and Ward. The ten-day visit to Bulow Ville, pleasant as it was for the most part, fell short of expectations, although Audubon reported to Lucy that during his stay in East Florida he had collected 550 skins, two boxes of shells, some "curious seeds," and had twenty-nine drawings.[23]

Awaiting passage to the southern peninsula had become progressively frustrating, but the restless bird painter had no choice. The government schooner was not in sight. To pass the time Audubon wrote long letters to Lucy telling her of his anxieties; he also kept up the usual heavy correspondence with associates in England. From Bulow Ville on January 4, 1832, he penned some lighter impressions of the plantation to Lucy, indicating temporary resignation to his plight:[24]

> . . . I see by all the papers that the Winter has been early and severe to the Eastward—here we have had a few cold nights but nothing which can be called Winter—Indeed the trees are all green—There are Butterflies to be seen each fine day and some Flowers in the Swamps.—The Alligators come out of their holes when the sun shines for a few hours &c—Snakes are brought to us very often and are said to be most aboundant in the Summer—Harlan says that my friend Ord has returned to Philadelphia and is as silent as the tomb about me.—and well he may be!—
>
> The woods here are filled with the *Casava* Root [Coontie] which

makes the finest food for the Indians and the best for the Whites—I have some of the seeds of it and of splendid Lilly which we found growing 6 feet high in the marshes . . . through [which] I have to scramble and wade every day—I doubt if ever a man has undergone more fatigues than I now undergo and if I do not succeed I am sure it will not be for want of exertion.

I was handed the New York Papers which give very disagreable accounts of the state of affairs in that country—The Riots are certainly getting to a frightful pitch and I fear a Revolution there unless the Reform Bill is passed—Bristol it seems has been terriby burnt and some life lost.—do my Sweet Wife try to let me know about Havell as often possible.

A "Waggon and 6 Mules with Two Servants" transported the travelers with the dog Plato to Saint Augustine on January 14, 1832. The forty-mile journey took one day. Back in Saint Augustine, brief good fortune was soon to appear. A letter from Louis McLane, secretary of the treasury, was waiting for them. In it were instructions to Lieutenant William Piercy, commander of the revenue cutter *Spark,* to take the three naturalists to Jacksonville where they would enter the Saint Johns River. Seizing this opportunity to reach the Florida interior, Audubon wrote Lucy January 16, 1832, of the outcome:[25]

. . . I presented myself to him in Company with Doc*r* Simmons and Lieut*t* Smith of the Army and was received in a *blunt Sailor like manner* and assured that it would give him great pleasure to Convey me and party—he ordered a bottle of Madeira which was drank by us &c I afterwards Invited him to come and Spend the evening with me—I also asked about a dozen Gentlemen with whom I am acquainted here—We spent our time agreably and *Soberly* after which My rough Lieut*t* took me by both hands and reassured me that he would do *all in his power* to promote my Wishes—

This now appearing I have determined to go with him first up the S*t* John's River as far as Navigation will permit which in all probability will take 4 or 5 Weeks—after which we return here for a few days, then go to Charleston for 8 or 10 days for a new set of Sails and proceed back to the Floridas coasting it and Making inland excursions at all the places which may be likely to promote my Views Joined to the Service of the United States proceeding as far as Cape Sable after which I will proceed to Mobile and New Orleans still anxious to reach that City on or about the 1*t* of June next.— The Lieut*t* Pearcy has Two officers under him and I have Two assistants and he proposed that We Should all mess together and divide the expenses which I think quite fair and have

> promised to do.—These are my present Plans and if the Commandant and I agree I will Stick to the Schooner *Spark* untill I have drawn many a fine Bird—Should he prove unkind or Two rough I will leave him at Charleston and then take the *Revenue Cutter* of that Station to Convey us to Key West.

Other statements in this letter were equally as bright. The South Carolina legislature had subscribed to *The Birds of America;* and he told Lucy that

> . . . on the Head waters of the S*t* John by Land from the Alifax [Halifax] River across the wildest desolate tract of Pine Barrens, Swamp and Lakes that I ever saw . . . [I] had an island named for me—a Compleat mass of orange Trees and Live Oaks . . . I have found Three Species of Heaths—one New Ibis and Some fresh Water Shells. . . .
>
> I hope I will possess as much information respecting the Floridas as they now are as any man living and will try to render this information of advantage to us—
>
> I expect that Thou would find Kentucky rather rough after returning from Europe but think of me when I say that Kentucky nay the worst of Kentucky is a Paradise compared with this *Garden of the United States*—
>
> What will my Philadelphia Friends say or think when they read that Audubon is on board of the U.S. Schooner of War the Spark going around the Floridas after *Birds*? I assure thee my Sweet Girl I begain to be proud of myself when I see that my Industry, perseverance and honesty has thus brought me So high from So Low as I was in 1820 when I could not even procure through my Relations and former Partners the Situation of a Clerk on Board an Ohio Steamer.—now they Prize me—nay wish me well—very good I wish them the same and may God grant them peace and plenty—
>
> I wrote to thee to invite thee to meet me at New Orleans about the first of June—I think it would do thee good and the expense would not be much . . .
>
> . . . I will now put this aside as I am obliged to Dress to receive Some Ladies who come boring me by asking to see my Drawings.—it must be done for Politeness sake and to be polite is very necessary and sometimes of great service . . .
>
> . . . I fear that in a Month or six weeks I will have great difficulties in hearing from Thee—Meantime let me engage thee to care of Thy Dear Sweet Self for my own Sake . . . I will see that the movements of *the Spark* or any Vessel on board of which I may remove the names of Which I will send thee will be announced in the News Papers at Diferent points of the Union—nothing less than the total Loss of the Vessel in

great distance from the shore can Injure me for I can Swim well and far Thou Knowest and my heart and Cause are equally good with my bodily Strength. . . .

Thou wilt be surprised to read that I have *abandoned Snuff for ever*! And So has Lehman—I came to that determination on the 1*t* of this Month—I am So tanned and burnt that thou might easily take me for an Indian—My beard has grown unshorn these 5 Weeks.

All aspects of the Saint Johns River trip seemed doomed and dreary. Audubon was out of communication with Lucy and news from England. Each new direction in his search for birds held promise, but none materialized to his satisfaction. Disappointed and depressed, Audubon wrote to Lucy:[26]

St. Augustine, Feb'y 1st. 1832

. . . We started from this dull place last Wednesday at 12 o'clock with a beautiful prospect—the wind was fair—our Commander *Jolly* and it was expected ere evening's dusk came on we would be moored within the barr at the Entrance of the S*t* John's River—at 4 o'clock the wind hauled round to the Northwest—the sky became suddenly clouded, the breese sprung into a Gale and by 8 o'clock . . . it blew a compleat hurricaine—Thy poor Friend was dreadfully sea sick—his assistants not much better off—Our Gallant Commander had everything arranged to insure the safety of the Vessel and of our selves—he gave me his own Birth and waited upon me as a Brother would but *he* could not soften the fury of the Gale—It continued to blow tremendously—our light bark danced over the Billows as if quite at her ease until the return of Day—The breese moderated a little but was still so strong and we had gone so far *back* to the South and Eastward that it was thought prudent to return to S*t* Augustine; luckily we did so for in the course of the next night the Gale Increased and the Cold became so intense that everything like a fluid froze on board our *Craft*—Another Vessel that had left at the same time with us for Charleston, returned and reached Port one hour before us.—

Thus my Initiation to U.S. Schooner Spark has been a severe one—I have been much gratified to see how well everything is managed on Board of a U.S. Vessel of War—the perfect order, silence and promptitude with which every order is obeyed and fullfilled is quite new to me and Impresses the mind with something far above anything I ever saw on board of any vessel in which I have been—the fact is that I am delighted with Lieut Piercy who in fact is a *thorough Goeer* and a brave fellow—I have written to Government to try to have for him Leave to go where ever he may think fit and proper during this spring and I sincerely hope that our Government will be pleased to afford us the means of exploring *the within* as well as *the without* of the Floridas.—

> *Should* this be granted to us depend upon it we will gather something more than *Shells.*—
>
> Do not my Dearest Love be afraid of my being in the South this Spring. I will take all the care I can of myself and will reach New Orleans by the first of June if possible. . . . I am much pleased at being relieved respecting Havell, and am glad that thou dost keep *an open* correspondence with him. . . .
>
> I write this Laconically because I have reasons for so doing as long as I am at S*t* Augustine; a place which I assure thee is far from being *generally* pleasant.—
>
> . . . I have been extremely mortified that *not one Drawing* have we made since one whole month detained by winds &c and the scarcity of Specimens—The wind is fair this afternoon and I hope to sail tomorrow morning for the S*t* John.

It was February 5 before the *Spark* embarked again from Saint Augustine to enter the Saint Johns River. Four days later Audubon told Lucy of his progress, while lamenting the fact that he had been in "compleat Idleness since the 25*th* of Dec*r*." He was not, he said, "Born for a *Sea Man* any more than thou for the wife of one." Desperate as he was to find something to draw, he had had "two frolics at Shooting White headed Eagles and killed 5 in 24 hours which is more than most Sportsmen can boast of."

"The weather," he said, "was so fair and the sea so gentle in her motions that I felt no indisposition whatever.—rather before day Cap*n* Pearcy ordered the Firing of our *Great Gun* to Inform the Pilot of our arrival—the report sounded far over the flat shores of the Floridas—Sometime elapsed, no Pilot was there in sight—the breeze freshened and as on this coast not a moment must be lost to ensure the entrance of an harbor a second Gun was fired—We with pleasure saw the return of our Signal at the Light house—; and shortly after, the Light Craft of the Piloter was in view bouncing over the resisted current of the River by the Ocean and approaching us a pace—I assure thee I was glad of it . . .

"We have ascended thus far gradually when ever the *Tide* and Winds have been fair and we intend . . . going as far up this Dingy looking River as the draft of the Spark will allow (this is nearly 6 feet) and which I hope will prove to be about 200 Miles and where I further hope that I may find something to Draw . . .

"I feel quite comfortable and as Happy as possible when traveling without thy Dear Self at my side."[27]

JOHN JAMES AUDUBON, 1785-1851

U. S. Schooner Spark 100 *Miles up the St. John's River, bound upwards—Feb.y* 17—1832

My Beloved Wife—

A dreadful accident gives me an opportunity of writing a few Lines to thee, and I embrace it with as much pleasure as I have felt *sickened* at the occurence—through which the *chance* of sending this to S*t* Augustine does take place.—One of our Sailors accidently *shot* himself through the Hand and forehead, and our Cap*n* is going to convey him at day break tomorrow to S*t* Augustine—

. . . the stink of the River Water I fear has caused one half of our Crew to be sick—we will probably remain at our present anchorage for 3 or 4 days more after which will proceed up to Lake George and I hope somewhat further . . . Scarcely a Bird to be seen and these of the most common sort—I look to the leaving of it as an Happy event—

. . . God only knows if this will ever reach *thee*, but I write it in hopes it may do so—and pray that God may ever bless thee and our Dear Sons.—I am now truly speaking in a *wild* and *dreary* and desolate part of the World—No one in the Eastern States has any *true* Idea of this Peninsula—My *account* of what I have or shall see of the Floridas will be far, very far from corroborating of the *flowery sayings* of M*r* Barton [Bartram] the Botanist.—

We are surrounded by thousands of Alligators and I dare not suffer my beautiful and faithful and good Newfoundland Dog *Plato* to go in the River although I have seen him leaped over board and give chase to Porpoises—

Nothing but sand Barrens are about and around us—When now and then an *Impenetrable* swamp is in sight it is hailed with the greatest pleasure for in them only Game or birds of any sort can be procured.—

. . . We are now living *not "on the fat of the Land"* for fat there is none, but the poorest of "Poor Jobs" oppossums—young alligators *&c &c*—Henry caught 5 young alligators at one grasp the other morning, and we have 25 or 30 alive on Board.—

Write to *Harlan* and let him know where I am . . . Again and again my Dearest beloved God bless thee—

Thine for ever
John J. Audubon[28]

Contrary to these impressions written to Lucy, the episode "St. John's River in Florida" (p. 314) expressed a different point of view. In the following letters to Levi Woodbury, Secretary of the Navy, Lieutenant Piercy describes his version of the river trip:[29]

United States Sch*r* Spark
St. Augustine 18*th* Jany, 1832

Sir

I have the honour to report that in my last communication I omitted reporting the loss of an Anchor, it Broke in two when let on a fine sandy bottom, and in light weather, it was new and made in the Navy Yard at Washington, but like other iron work put on board the Spark, from that Navy Yard, it proved Brittle and unserviceable—

Enclosed I have the honour to forward the letter of acceptance from Acting Mid*n* Mathias Marine, together with one addressed to me by Mid*n* John C. Harker If the Department has made no arrangements to relieve M*n* Harker, I would like much to have him continued with me untill next Fall, as he has been, and will continue to be of much service to me, particularly, in my exploring expeditions.

J. J. Audubon Esq*r* accompanies me up the St John. It affords me much pleasure to be enabled to aid his scientific researches without its interfering with my duty.

I am still detained here for want of a wind to get to Sea.

I have the honour to be

Very respectfully
Sir
Your obedient Serv*t*
W*m* P. Piercy
Lieut. Com'd'g

The Hon*ble*
Levi Woodbury
Secty of the Navy
Washington City

U. S. Schooner Spark
S*t* Augustine - 8*th* March 1832.

Sir

I have the honour to report my return, from the S*t* Johns, and acknowledge the receipt of your order, of the 25*th*, of January, which shall be obeyed, as soon as the weather will justify my going to sea, after patching and banding my sails.—I proceeded as far up the S*t* Johns River, with the Spark, as you will find marked, on the Chart which I have the honour to enclose, and then (in consequence of the narrow and intricate passage) I took my boat and pulled up within 5 or 6 miles of Lake George, when I returned, as I found it a useless expense, of time, and labour, the Land on both sides of the River (alternately) consisting of Pine Barrens and endless Swamps. The banks, where the Barrens exist, are from 5 to 15 feet in height, and are formed of a concretion, of what is usually termed, snail shells, with no Live Oak. There are however a few scattering swamp & water Oak trees, on the edges of the River, in fact there is no Live Oak timber, on the S*t* Johns that is of sufficient Growth for naval purposes, except a few scattering Trees on lands owned by individuals and engaged by Mess*rs* Palmer and Terrie to complete their contract, with the Government.—The following accident, occuring on board, gave me an opportunity of seeing more of the country, than I otherwise should.—The morning after I anchored at Buenavista, I went on shore to examine the country,—after landing, I sent on board for my gun as the weather was quite warm and a probability existed of my falling in with some Rattle Snakes (a large one having been killed the day before) at the same time cautioning the man, I sent, to be careful as the Gun was loaded; in handing it in the Boat by carelessness combined with accident it went off, the load (fortunately a small one) passing through his hand. I immediately went on board, and with great difficulty stopped the bleeding; after which upon mature deliberation I determined to send him to S*t* Augustine, that he might have the advantage of surgical aid. Upon further reflection, I deemed it necessary to accompany him myself, as I was apprehensive the wound might (from motion) bleed afresh, and neither of my officers would know how to stop it.—I was able to procure but one Horse, and a small Cart, to convey the man in, and the next morning I started on foot (taking another of my crew to lead the Horse) to perform a journey of 40 miles through a wilderness; my only road an old Indian trail;—we arrived at S*t* Augustine at 1/2 past 11 o'clock that night, much fatigued, and drenched to the skin, by the rain that fell in torrents, after night fall; the next morning I placed the man in the Army Hospital and after a rest of two days I returned by way of Picolatta, almost broken down. The man, however, I am happy to say, is nearly well and has sustained no material injury, at least so says the Surgeon.

The country between Beanavista, Picolatta, and S*t* Augustine is miserably poor, in fact it is nothing but sand with indifferent Pines, Palmetos, and a few Cypress Swamps. The trees of which are quite small and consequently useless.

The Lands on the margin of the S*t* Johns as high as Bounavista are of a very light, but often rich soil and are principally cultivated for the growth of Sugar, with numerous Groves of Orange trees, of superior quality. But the Planters have adopted and (with few exceptions) continued to pursue a most ruinous system; they clear as much land as their force can work, and without aiding or strengthening the soil, they continue to plant it for 2 or 3 & sometimes 4 years, by this time it can yield no more, it is then deserted and another spot is cleared & cultivated in the same manner, as the Planters say, it is less expensive, to clear one year, than to manure 3 or 4.—Some samples of Sugar was shewn me of last Years crop, I think it was of as superior a quality as any I ever saw.

Col*n* Reese who has a large plantation at Spring Garden 16 or 20 miles above Lake George has (I am informed) a quantity of large Live Oak, but will not sell at present.

Mid*sm* Sully, Minory & Marine have joined me.

I have the honour to be, very Respectfully

Sir,

Your obedient Servant,

W*m* P. Piercy Lt Com'd'g

Hon Levi Woodbury
Sec. of the Navy
Washington City

The logbook of the USS *Spark* outlines the trip succinctly. On February 6 or 7 the *Spark* started up the Saint Johns River; on February 15 "Wm Purley ordinary seaman was badly wounded in the hand by a gun going off accidentally"; the next day Captain Piercy and the wounded seaman left the *Spark* to go to Saint Augustine, returning on February 22 and continuing up the river. On February 23 the *Spark* started back down the Saint Johns, arriving at Saint Augustine on March 6. The logbook contains no reference at all to Audubon.[30]

Audubon, meanwhile, had left the *Spark* after the shooting incident, hiring a boat to take him from Buena Vista (Palatka) to an Indian trail at Picolata landing, then continuing on foot during a storm as described in the Saint Johns River episode.

In Saint Augustine for the last time, the frustrated man of the woods still wanted most of all to see the water birds of South Florida. To pass the time, he hunted for about two weeks with the "Live-oakers," a colorful breed of men who came seasonally to the bend of the river near Green Cove Springs to cut and ship timber for northern markets. Two episodes, "The Live-oakers" (p. 319) and "The Lost One" (p. 323) are based on these experiences.

Of the twenty or more references in the *Ornithological Biography* to birds Audubon hunted, described, or sketched in East Florida, four are of particular interest. The American Coot in Plate CCXXXIX was procured at General Hernandez's plantation. The background of a freshwater pond, cattails, and sabal palms, painted by Lehman, is typical of the region. Plate CCXXX, the Sanderling, shows two bird figures on a sand beach, which Audubon identifies as having been painted in December 1831. The scene, by Lehman, is inland, possibly a cove along the banks of the Saint Johns. A male sanderling appeared much later in *The Birds of America* (Plate CCLXXXV), because of an oversight, Audubon explained. The specimen of Glossy Ibis in Plate CCCLXXXVII, "a male bird in superb plumage," though painted later, was procured when Audubon visited the woodcutters on the Saint Johns. The Lehman background includes a woodcutter's cabin on the bluffs of the river. Audubon's narrative of "The Lost One" is an accurate reflection of the woodlands near the Saint Johns and along the banks of the river. Finally, according to Edward Dwight, Audubon and Lehman collaborated on the painting for the Orange-crowned Warbler, Plate CLXXVIII. The delicate bough on which two birds are perched is from the sparkleberry tree.

The weary travelers left Saint Augustine for Charleston on March 5, 1832, aboard the schooner *Agnes,* convinced that chances were more favorable for sailing from there to south Florida than from the "wretched" Spanish village. As they sailed from shore, the *Spark* overtook their vessel in the harbor. The sight of Lieutenant Piercy rekindled the resentment that Audubon felt for him because of the delays brought on by the accidental gunshot, his not getting to enter Lake George, and the harrowing walk back to Saint Augustine through the storm. However,

> the Commandant came on board of us, presented me with a most Superb pair of Swans and said *he hoped* I would not say to any one the reasons why I had left his Vessel.—The man may have a good heart, but if his head like an empty box contains not brains enough to enable him to be a *worthy Gentleman*—the man and the head may go a'drift for me.[31]

The swans were not the ones used as models for Plate CCCCXI, but the three yellow water lilies in the foreground were the source of considerable discussion. The actual existence of the lilies was questioned for thirty-nine years, after which a Florida traveler rediscovered the lily and reported her findings to botanist Samuel Lockwood. His acknowledgment that Audubon had discovered the lilies appeared in *Popular Science Monthly* in 1877:

> Beholding it with his own eyes, the great painter put it in one of his own glorious bird-pictures and, having given the portrait of his floral beauty, he named it *Namphaea lutea,* or in plain English, the yellow water lily. But this pretty flower had never been seen by the botanists, and so, forsooth, the thing was absolutely ignored—treated as a pretty fable, a bit of art extravagance. . . . Last summer, in Florida, Mrs. Mary Treat rediscovered the long-lost flower of Audubon. Professor Asa Gray duly acknowledged it as the long ignored *Namphaea lutia* . . . Were it scientifically orthodox to rechristen the rediscovered flower we would have its history crystalized in a new scientific name—*Nymphaea Audubonii.* Which, after so long incredulity, would be doing the bonny thing; and thus the yellow water lily would dot, with golden memories of the gentle enthusiast, the waters of the rivers of time.[32]

The effect of the finished plate puzzled Audubon, also, for some time. He later wrote to Dr. Bachman from London, April 14, 1838, asking "Has Leitner published the New Plants he discovered in the Floridas? I ask this latter question because on the 83 number of my work, Plate 411, I have represented a New Nymphea, which [if] unpublished by him, I would like in my letter press to name after Docr Leitner's name, *Nymphea Leitneria!*"[33] Dr. Edward Leitner, a German physician living in Charleston, made expeditions to Florida as a botanist in 1836 and 1838. He had described the same water lily as *Nymphaea flava.* Leitner was shot and scalped by the Indians at Jupiter Creek in 1838.

Delays continued to plague the travelers. The *Agnes* was forced into the Savannah harbor by a storm. Audubon stayed at the City Hotel where his "beard and a pair of Mustacios" attracted much attention. That night and the next morning before leaving Savannah on the mail coach for Charleston, Audubon visited William Gaston, a wealthy merchant, who subscribed to *The Birds of America.* "My Drawings were put in battle array *on the floor of the House* and in about one hour I had 2 more names and 400$ more in my Pocket," he wrote to Lucy on March 13. "I have been forced to perform a counter march but it has proved like some performed by Greater Generals than myself a most Honourable and profitable retreat." [34]

In Charleston, Bachman was again host to the Florida-bound travelers. They stayed a month. Again they hunted specimens and sought subscribers, and Audubon taught Bachman how to dip snuff. Meanwhile, Lucy was complying as best she could with her husband's wishes. The following letter is one of many she wrote to expedite their business affairs overseas while her husband was "proceeding on if slowly regularly" in Florida.[35]

> *To* Robt Havell Esq.
> 77 Oxford Street, London
>
> *Louisville March* 22, 1832
>
> Your favour of Jany 31. has this moment been handed to me your letter and the three papers spoken of as being sent the 10*th* I have not heard of nor the box containing the bonnet &c—for which accept my sincere thanks, and now to refer to your letter I am very sorry any expressions of mine should have offended you, that was not our intention, but whatever remarks I made were in consequence of the facts which I stated to you respecting the plates and work, and from authority of my husband repeated in his letter since we parted, to give you

notice of any errors that you who are always at the work can not see so clearly as those who only occassionally look it over, and I assure you Mr Audubon will thank me for pointing out to you those things which I have and on which his success and reputation so much depend. . . . Mr A was on the 17 february in the centre of Florida on the St. Johns river in the United States Schooner Spark Captain Percy—suffering from deprivation of every sort—He tells me in every letter to write to you and state how things are. . . .

Yours
L. Audubon

Several interesting letters reveal how Audubon's ultimate transportation to the Keys was arranged. In the records of the National Archives, along with the logbook of the cutter (see Appendix) is a letter from J. R. Pringle, Director of the Port of Charleston, to Lieutenant Robert Day, acting commander of the *Marion,* dated March 24, 1832, as follows:

> Orders: to proceed to Port of Key West, observing during the cruise the Printed Instructions from the Treasury Department.
>
> Immediately on your arrival at Key West you will report to the Collector of Customs and attend to his orders when in the waters contiguous to that district. On the termination of the cruise, which may be from 20th to 25th of May next, you will leave that port of Key West on your return to this port with the like attention to the printed instructions as you are required on your cruise to Key West."

Another letter is from W. A. Whitehead, Collector of Customs, Key West, to Lieutenant Day on April 1, 1832: "Some alterations having been made to the Tortugas Light House rendering it advisable that an examination should be made of this utility and the general condition of the light at present, you will therefore get the Cutter now under your command, as soon as practicable, under way for the Tortugas and make the necessary inquiries."

It almost appears that the Treasury Department was attempting to keep secret the fact that it was providing free transportation for the naturalist, since they sent printed instructions to the commander of the ship and followed up with letters to make it evident that the trip was clearly and properly authorized. While the trip from Indian Key to Key West normally took about a day and a half, the log indicates a leisurely journey, giving Audubon time to explore Cape Sable and Sandy Key both going and returning.[36]

On April 15 Audubon wrote his last long letter from Charleston to Lucy. Thereafter his attentions were placed on the "objects that allured" him—the Florida Keys and the water birds.[37]

> I have waited with great impatience for a U.S. Vessel to convey me and my *Lads* to the confines of our Southern Coast and now this opportunity offers itself—The U.S. Schooner *Marion* came in 2 days ago—I called on the Commander Lieut*t* Day and found him *a Gentleman*—he sent me to the Collector of this Port, M*r* James R. Pringle, under whose immediate command the *Marion* is—I was glad to find that I was already acquainted with him . . . —The Collector asked me where and when I wish to go—I told him *to the Keys* of the Florida and could be ready in a few days—he immediately sent an order to the Captain to make ready for Sea on Wednesday next and assured me that *every* facility would be given me to serve my views and Science. . . . Thus my Lucy I will once more put to sea on board a man of War and again visit that poor Country the Floridas! !

The *Marion,* a United States revenue cutter, was a keel boat designed for shoal water stations and movability. Built at Baltimore in 1825, the *Marion* was sixty feet long, twenty-two feet four inches wide at extreme beam, with a seven foot deep hold. She carried "77 64/98 tons burthen." She was armed with two long four-pounders and four eighteen-pounders, and with her deep bulwarks and large rigs she was capable of better than standard speed.[38]

Audubon, Ward, and Lehman, along with the dog Plato, left Charleston April 19, 1832 aboard the *Marion.* Plato might have been more willing to resume his former life-style in South Carolina. He had been mercilessly pecked in the nose while retrieving birds from the Saint Johns and had led Audubon to safety through the woods on an Indian trail in a thunderstorm. Toward the end of his first four months with the Audubon party in the area of Saint Augustine he could barely stand erect because of the pain of wounds from razor-sharp raccoon oysters.

The party arrived at Indian Key on April 25. The *Marion* remained at anchor at Indian Key for seven days. There was little time now for Audubon to write letters to Lucy or to fret about previous or future hardships. The great bird painter had finally found what he was looking for, and now his journals burst with flowery sayings: "The birds which we saw were almost all new to us; their lovely forms appeared to be arrayed in more brilliant apparel than I had ever before seen, and as they gambolled in happy playfulness among the bushes, or glided over the light green waters, we longed to form a more intimate acquaintance with them."[39]

In the Florida Keys, mangrove islets rise from the shallows and along the shores. Gnarled roots and bushy foliage extend a few feet above the water, presenting a wide vista of emerald Atlantic waters on the ocean side and everchanging shades of blue, green, and gold aquatic ribbons in the Gulf of Mexico. Here the land is not "all sand," as Audubon assessed the terrain of East Florida, but the sky is visually all sky, enlarging its proportion to the horizon by the absence of tall trees.

Audubon does not mention by name his Indian Key host, Jacob Housman, a wrecker king, yet his visit came during Housman's most prosperous years. Lieutenant Day, whose business it was to be acquainted with such coastal affairs, was certainly aware that Indian Key was a wrecker port and that Housman played the wreckers' game according to his own rules, not according to the courts in Key West where salvage fees were established by law. In spite of Housman's turbulent way of life, he was known to be a generous man to his employees and to his wife, Elizabeth Ann. Audubon received the full benefits of Housman's hospitality, but of more concern to the naturalist than Housman's occupation was his admiration for Mr. Egan, an alert guide whose knowledge of the channels led them to "regions seldom visited by men." This same knowledge also qualified Mr. Egan to be a first-rate wrecker, of course.

Audubon's heart "swelled with uncontrollable delight" at reaching Indian Key. In the episodes "Florida Keys I" (p. 327) and "Florida Keys II" (p. 332) he describes some of his adventures exploring the nearby keys as well as Sandy Key and Cape Sable in the Everglades.

Dwight credits at least five plates in *The Birds of America* to this April period of Audubon's travels: Plate CLXX, the Pipery Flycatcher or Gray Kingbird; Plate CLXXVII, the White-crowned Pigeon; Plate CCLX, the Roseate Tern; Plate CCLII, the Double-crested Cormorant; and Plate CCLVI, the Reddish Egret.

The cormorant, a subspecies that Audubon discovered, was drawn at Indian Key on his forty-seventh birthday, April 26, 1832. The Roseate Tern was drawn two days later. Audubon apparently drew the backgrounds for the cormorant and the egret, with Lehman supplying the foliage used on the Kingbird and White-crowned Pigeon plates, probably later in Key West.

In visiting other islands in the vicinity of Indian Key both going to

Pirate's Well, lithograph by George Lehman

and returning from Key West in May 1831, Audubon made other drawings for *The Birds of America,* including those for Plate CLXII, the Zenaida Dove, with Lehman's pond apple branch; Plate CCXVII, the Louisiana Heron; one figure (on the left) for Plate CCXXXVIII, the Great Marbled Godwit; Plate CCLI, the Brown Pelican, perched on a mangrove branch drawn by Lehman; Plate CCLXXI, the "Frigate Pelican" or Magnificent Frigatebird; and Plate CCLXXIII, the Cayenne (Royal) Tern, with Audubon's Keys background.

In the Zenaida Dove history Audubon related a conversation with a former pirate and mentions certain wells dug in the Keys. Lehman did a separate and dramatic drawing of such a well (see above).

On April 30, 1832, the *Marion* set sail from Indian Key toward

Key West. On board with the Audubon party was the pilot Egan, who had become an indispensable companion. They anchored overnight at Key Vacas Harbor, and anchored the next day at the Key of Honda (Bahia Honda). On May 4 they checked a beacon near Looe Key, reaching Key West that evening.

Key West, the most tropical city in North America, rises from a shimmering sea on a coral island approximately four miles long and two miles wide, 100 miles from the Florida mainland. In 1832 this southernmost point of the Florida Keys was a mecca for adventurers, a hearty lot comprising British colonists from the Bahamas, Cubans, Spaniards, and assorted seekers of fortune. Among them were a few educated men from Virginia, New England, and the West Indies. The settlement of about 500 people subsisted primarily on proceeds from the salvage of ships that went aground on the reef. Many of the early inhabitants, some of whom were rescued from wrecked ships, continue to be honored by street markers and locations named for them, such as Whitehead, Greene, Simonton, and Mallory.

Key West's natural deep-water harbor has been on record for three centuries. Indian canoes, sailing vessels of many nations, pirate craft, and United States Navy and Coast Guard ships have entered Old Nor'west Channel.

Dr. Benjamin Strobel, resident only three years but already town physician, surgeon of the newly established army post, editor-publisher of the *Key West Gazette,* and town councilman, met Audubon at the dock. Their introduction had been arranged by their mutual friend Dr. Bachman of Charleston. Strobel, an amateur collector, was a former Charlestonian, and he was sending back to Bachman specimens of shells, bird skins, and tropical plants.

Audubon and Strobel were frequent companions during the naturalist's seventeen-day visit at Key West and its nearby islands. They hunted and went to a turtle crawl together, and Strobel procured the bough of the Geiger tree that provided the background for the White-crowned Pigeon plate. Strobel was particularly interested in wreckers and wrecking, and doubtless related to Audubon firsthand experiences he had had with them. Strobel sang the "Wrecker's Song" for Audubon (see p. 342), apparently to the tune of "The Garden Gate," a Scotch air dating from 1809.[40] Much of the information incorporated in Audubon's episodes "The Wreckers of Florida" (p. 337), "Death of a Pirate" (p. 343), and "The Turtlers" (p. 348) was obtained through Strobel, another keen and intelligent observer.

Since he was constantly absorbed in the pursuit of birds in and near Key West, Audubon's daily ledger was apparently reduced to shorter notations than usual, enough, however, to recreate vivid impressions for the bird histories that would be written for the *Ornithological Biography.* Strobel's reports of their association made a worthy contribution to this period of Audubon's Florida travels. His eye-witness announcements of the naturalist's arduous employment at Key West and the Dry Tortugas were published in the *Key West Gazette.* Upon Strobel's return to Charleston in 1833, portions of his unfinished book, "Sketches of Florida," appeared in two Charleston newspapers, reaffirming his affinity with the great bird painter and his work.

Charleston Mercury June 28,1833:

> In the months of March and April, 1832, he [Audubon] visited the Florida Reef, and touched and remained three or four weeks, off and on, at Key West, where I had a good opportunity of becoming acquainted with him. By a friend (from whom he bore a letter of introduction) I had been apprised of his expected arrival in the Revenue Cutter Marion, Capt. Day. It being intimated that he was coming ashore in one of the boats, I walked down about sun set with a number of persons to see him land. On his landing, I was introduced to him by

Key West, 1838

Capt. Day. He immediately took me aside, informed me that he had letters for me from my friend Mr. B. and that he was anxious to have some conversation with me. I invited him to my house, where we sat down; Mr. Audubon at once proceeded to business, making a number of enquiries respecting birds and other objects of his pursuit. After a long conversation, we parted for the night. I saw him again the following day, and almost every day when he came ashore during his stay. Mr. Audubon is a very extraordinary man. An acquaintance of half an hour enabled me to enter at once into his character and feelings. Divested of every thing like pedantry, he is frank, free and amiable in his dispositions, and affable and polite in manners. His engaging manner and mild deportment, united to a perfect possession of what the French term "Savior [sic] faire," enables him to accomplish many things, which to another person would be unattainable; every one appears to enlist at once in his service, and to be disposed to promote his views. In addition to the possession of these qualities, Mr. Audubon is the most enthusiastic and indefatigable man I ever knew. It is impossible to associate with him without catching some portion of his spirit; he is surrounded with an atmosphere which infects all who come within it, with a mania for bird-killing, and bird stuffing. For my own part, I must confess that I have become an incurable victim to the disease.

When we examine Mr. Audubon's celebrated drawings and plates, we can not but yield him our warmest approbation and applause; but how few of us can estimate the danger and toil which they have cost him, or through what "untried scenes and changes" he has passed in procuring his specimens. In our admiration of the Artist we are too apt to forget the labor and privations of the man. In order to give some faint idea of Mr. Audubon's exertions, I will briefly relate the occurrences of one day's excursion, on which I accompanied him. At half past two o'clock, A.M. our party assembled at a given place, we were provided with two good boats, a number of hands and all the necessary apparatus. At three o'clock we started, and steered for 2 or 3 small Mangrove Keys lying to the Northward of Key West; we made a circuit around them, but saw nothing worthy of note. Previous to our getting clear of these Keys, we got ashore upon a long bank making out from one of them, which rendered it necessary for all hands to get overboard, Mr. Audubon being among the foremost. We hauled the boat over the bank, and bore away for a narrow opening between Key West and Stock Island, through which we proposed passing. There we again got into shoal water, and were again compelled to get overboard. Our boats were hauled over a flat nearly a mile in length before we could get them afloat.—Having passed through the cut, we landed on a long sandbank on the Eastern extremity of Key West. An hour or more was spent here in collecting shells; after which, we footed it around to Key West while the boats were rowed along the beach by the hands. Not a pond, lake or bog, did we leave unexplored, often did we wade through mud up to our knees, and as often were we obliged to scramble over the roots of the Mangrove trees which happened in our course. About 8 o'clock, the sun came out intensely hot; we occasionally penetrated the woods to escape his scorching beams, and as often were driven from the woods by myriads of Musquetoes and Sandflies. One of our party gave out about this time and took to a boat. Most gladly would I have followed his lead, but was deterred by pride. Onward we went, baking and broiling, and what was more discouraging still, we could discover not a single bird worthy of note. Mr. Audubon went on neither dispirited by heat, fatigue, nor bad luck, whilst we began to lag, and occasionally would dodge under some tree, to catch a breath, or sit down to blow. We toiled along in this way for several miles, and finally reached the Light House, tolerably well broken down. I gladly accepted of the use of a horse, whilst the rest of the party returned to town in a boat. I arrived at home about 11 o'clock, A.M. having made the circuit of Key West. I went to bed immediately and slept soundly for several hours, when I got up and took some refreshment, pretty well satisfied with the jaunt, and no ways ambitious of repeating it. To Mr. Audubon this was an every day affair; he rose every morning at 3 o'clock and went out in a boat, and cruized in search of birds, etc. until 12 or 1 o'clock, at which time he usually returned to dinner. During these expeditions he took no refreshments but biscuit and molasses and water, proving by his example that ardent spirits are never necessary to health even under the greatest exposure and fatigue. Before and after dinner, as soon as he returned from the morning jaunt, Mr. Audubon employed himself in drawing such birds as he might have procured during the morning, and in the evening he was on the hunt again. Thus has Mr. Audubon been employed day after day, for weeks and months on the Florida Reef, exploring Mangrove Keys, swamps and other places, into which I question much, if any animal two legged or four legged, had ever before penetrated, unless it was the Pelican or Cormorant.

Not soon will the recollection of this surprising man pass from my memory, and often as I call him to mind will I admire his unquenchable ardor in the pursuit of science, and his amiable deportment as a gentleman; nay more, the recollection will always be associated with a warm sensation of gratitude, for his kindness and friendship to one, from whom he had reason to expect but little in return.

The Key West Gazette, May 5, 1832.

. . . We are informed that he [Audubon] has been very successful in procuring Birds, along the Reef, and on the Florida Keys. We understand that the use of United States' vessels have been generously tendered to this gentleman. We cannot sufficiently express our pleasure and approbation at this liberal course without adding anything to the expense of government. It offers great facilities to scientific men in the pursuit of their labors.

The Key West Gazette, May 9, 1832.

> Mr. Audubon, we understand, is highly gratified with his trip to the Florida Keys, having already discovered five new species of Birds. . . . He has also procured a number of specimens of Birds, already described, and several new plants. He left here in the Cutter Marion on Tuesday for Tortugas, from whence he will probably return in 4 or 5 days.

At the Tortugas, Audubon was invited aboard a wrecker's ship where, in a short time, they were all "extremely social and merry." The wreckers offered their services in procuring specimens of birds, eggs, turtles, and sea shells, and shared their knowledge of the habits of wildlife in the Tortugas.

Three future plates for *The Birds of America* were drawn there: on May 10 the Sooty Tern (Plate CCXXXV), on May 11 the Noddy Tern (Plate CCLXXV), and on May 14 the Brown Booby (Plate CCVII). Audubon did not see the White-tailed Tropic-bird during this visit, but was later sent specimens from the Tortugas by Lieutenant Day which were used for Plate CCLXII.

The *Marion* returned to Key West from the Tortugas on May 16 and remained there at anchor for six more days. During his Key West visit Audubon portrayed more birds for *The Birds of America.* Plate CLXVII shows two Key West Quail-Doves with a background by Lehman of a graceful railroad vine with large purple flowers and a white flowering rubber vine. Audubon wrote in the *Ornithological Biography* "I have taken it upon myself to name this species the Key West Pigeon, and offer it as a tribute to the generous inhabitants of that island, who favoured me with their friendship." Plate CLXIX, the Mangrove Cuckoo, was a species new to Audubon; the bird is shown on a branch of a seven-year apple drawn by Lehman. Plate CLXXII, the Blue-headed Quail-Dove, like the Greenshank plate, portrays a species not seen in the Keys since Audubon drew these on this visit. A similar case is that of the Black-throated Mango, Plate CLXXXIV; the male specimens of these Mango Hummingbirds were sent to Audubon after his departure by Strobel, who found them in Key West although they are a South American species.

On May 22, 1832, the *Marion* sailed from Key West. In respectful tribute to the explorer-artist, and to further publicize his high opinion of him, Dr. Strobel published the following editorial:

The Key West Gazette, May 23rd, 1832.

> Mr. Audubon.—This Gentleman left here in the Revenue Cutter Marion, on Monday last for Charleston, calculating to touch on his way at the Florida Keys, and probably the main land. It affords us great pleasure to state, that this expedition has given him much satisfaction and added largely to his collection of specimens, &c. Mr. Audubon is a most extraordinary man;—possessed of an ardent and enthusiastic mind and entirely devoted to his pursuits, danger cannot daunt, and difficulties vanish before him. During his stay here, his hour of rising was three o'clock in the morning; from that time until noon, and sometimes even until night, he was engaged in hunting among the Mangrove Keys—despite of heat, sand-flies and musquitoes. On his return from these expeditions, his time was principally employed in making sketches of such plants and birds as he may have procured: This was not an extraordinary effort for a day—it was continued for weeks; in short, it appeared to constitute his chief aim, as it is his happiness. Mr. Audubon has adopted a most excellent plan of connecting with his drawing of birds, such plants as may be found in the neighborhood where they are taken. We hesitate not in giving it as our opinion, that his work on Ornithology, when completed, will be the most splendid production of its kind ever published; and we trust that it will be duly estimated and patronized. The private character of Mr. Audubon corresponds with the nature of his mind and pursuits—he is frank, free, and generous, always willing to impart information, and to render himself agreeable. The favorable impressions which he has produced upon our minds will not soon be effaced.

Audubon was not unmindful of the friendship that he had found in Dr. Strobel. In Volume Two of his *Ornithological Biography,* numerous kindly references are made to "my friend Strobel."

Audubon's quest for water birds in Florida was not yet ended. After the *Marion* left Key West, Lieutenant Day stopped at Indian Key, where the party again engaged the services of Mr. Thruston's "beautiful barge" and went back to Cape Sable and Sandy Key. Dwight says that the drawing for Plate CCLXXIX, the Sandwich Tern, was made on the same day Audubon first saw it, May 26, 1832.

The Great White Heron, perhaps Audubon's prize find of the trip, carries Audubon's name as its discoverer: *Ardea occidentalis* Audubon. The drawing for the Great White Heron plate is said also to have been made on May 26; the detailed background painting of Key West by Lehman for Plate CCLXXXI was done separately.

The *Marion* sailed away from Indian Key on May 31, 1832,

headed for Savannah and Charleston. The long-awaited journey to Florida had provided valuable additions to *The Birds of America.* In the Introduction to Volume III of the *Ornithological Biography,* which contains many of the water birds, Audubon seems to sum up his impressions:[41]

> The difficulties which are to be encountered in studying the habits of our Water Birds are great. He who follows the feathered inhabitants of the forests and plains, however rough or tangled the paths may be, seldom fails to obtain the objects of his pursuit, provided he be possessed of due enthusiasm and perseverance. The Land Bird flits from bush to bush, runs before you, and seldom extends its flight beyond the range of your vision. It is very different with the Water Bird, which sweeps afar over the wide ocean, hovers above the surges, or betakes itself for refuge to the inaccessible rocks on the shore. There, on the smooth sea-beach, you see the lively and active Sandpiper; on that rugged promontory the Dusky Cormorant; under the dark shade of yon cypress the Ibis and Heron; above you in the still air floats the Pelican or the Swan; while far over the angry billows scour the Fulmar and the Frigate bird. If you endeavour to approach these birds in their haunts, they betake themselves to flight, and speed to places where they are secure from your intrusion.
>
> But the scarcer the fruit, the more prized it is; and seldom have I experienced greater pleasures than when on the Florida Keys, under a burning sun, after pushing my bark for miles over a soapy flat, I have striven all day long, tormented by myriads of insects, to procure a heron new to me, and have at length succeeded in my efforts. And then how amply are the labours of the naturalist compensated, when, after observing the wildest and most distrustful birds, in their remote and almost inaccessible breeding places, he returns from his journeys, and relates his adventures to an interested and friendly audience.

Audubon had hoped to continue his quest for birds in Florida in 1833 with his son John, but pressures concerning production of *The Birds of America* in England, publication of the *Ornithological Biography,* and the imminence of war between the United States and the Seminole nation prevented his return. The second volume of the *Ornithological Biography* was published in 1834, the third in 1835, the fourth in 1838, and the final volume in 1839. *The Birds of America* folios were completed in 1838.

After leaving Florida, Audubon followed bird migrations to some of the eastern states and to Labrador. While his work continued in production, Audubon's last years were spent near New York City at

ORNITHOLOGICAL BIOGRAPHY,

OR AN ACCOUNT OF THE HABITS OF THE

BIRDS OF THE UNITED STATES OF AMERICA;

ACCOMPANIED BY DESCRIPTIONS OF THE OBJECTS REPRESENTED IN THE WORK ENTITLED

THE BIRDS OF AMERICA,

AND INTERSPERSED WITH DELINEATIONS OF AMERICAN SCENERY AND MANNERS.

BY JOHN JAMES AUDUBON, F.R.S.S.L. & E.

FELLOW OF THE LINNEAN AND ZOOLOGICAL SOCIETIES OF LONDON; MEMBER OF THE LYCEUM OF NEW YORK, OF THE NATURAL HISTORY SOCIETY OF PARIS, THE WERNERIAN NATURAL HISTORY SOCIETY OF EDINBURGH; HONORARY MEMBER OF THE SOCIETY OF NATURAL HISTORY OF MANCHESTER, AND OF THE SCOTTISH ACADEMY OF PAINTING, SCULPTURE, AND ARCHITECTURE; MEMBER OF THE AMERICAN PHILOSOPHICAL SOCIETY, OF THE ACADEMY OF NATURAL SCIENCES AT PHILADELPHIA, OF THE NATURAL HISTORY SOCIETIES OF BOSTON, OF CHARLESTON IN SOUTH CAROLINA, &c. &c.

VOL. II.

EDINBURGH:

ADAM & CHARLES BLACK, EDINBURGH;

LONGMAN, REES, BROWN, GREEN, & LONGMAN, LONDON; R. HAVELL, ENGRAVER, 77. OXFORD STREET, LONDON; THOMAS SOWLER, MANCHESTER; MRS ROBINSON, LEEDS; ALEXANDER HILL, EDINBURGH; BEILBY, KNOTT & BEILBY, BIRMINGHAM; E. CHARNLEY, NEWCASTLE-UPON-TYNE; AND GEORGE SMITH, LIVERPOOL.

MDCCCXXXIV.

a woodland estate purchased in 1842, which he called Minnie's Land. His sons lived nearby. The present location of Minnie's Land is a short distance from Harlem, at Riverside Drive and 159th Street. The area, in Audubon's time called Carmensville, was later known as Washington Heights.

At Minnie's Land, Audubon enthusiastically formulated plans with his son John and Dr. Bachman of Charleston to publish *The Viviparous Quadrupeds of North America.* Audubon drew seventy-six of the original figures in the publication, which was issued in thirty parts of five plates each between 1845 and 1849. The remaining seventy-four plates were reproduced from paintings made by John Woodhouse Audubon. Audubon's son Victor painted the backgrounds. Six editions were released by American publishers, the last two after the elder Audubon's death.

In order to collect material on the quadrupeds, and always interested in finding more material on birds, the great bird painter made his final expedition in 1843. The Missouri expedition to Fort Union lasted eight months. He was fifty-eight years old, not an old man and quite able to walk thirty-five miles a day in the West. But exposure to weather and the hardships of the long journey slowed down his pace thereafter. Three years after his return to New York, Audubon's eyesight failed, although he never became totally blind.

Audubon's noble mind and body seemed to wither when he could no longer see a drawing board or manipulate his skillful hands. On the banks of the Hudson River he would wander, accompanied by a servant, his snowy white hair falling on his drooping shoulders. On January 27, 1851, the American Woodsman died peacefully at Minnie's Land. He was buried in the Trinity Church Cemetery at 155 Street and Broadway in New York City. The ashes of his beloved Lucy were laid at his side in 1874.

Title page, Ornithological Biography

Retracing Audubon's Florida Travels

While compiling these materials on Audubon's Florida travels of 1831-1832, I became fascinated with the idea of retracing his explorations through the state and describing how the sites he visited appear today. Many are readily accessible; others were not difficult to find with the help of Audubon's journals and other references as guides.

With the help of modern conveyances, I followed Audubon's treks, from Saint Augustine to Ponce de Leon Springs and the Saint Johns River, to Indian Key, to Cape Sable, to Sandy Key, and to Key West and the Dry Tortugas. With the exception of Saint Augustine, De Leon Springs, and Key West, I was surprised and pleased to find the other locations relatively unchanged and still sparsely populated because of their general inaccessibility. In the more populated areas, history-conscious citizens have done much to preserve and reconstruct reminders of the past.

My first trip in search of Audubon's trail began in Saint Augustine, a city of approximately 12,500 present-day inhabitants. In the center of town, the ancient Plaza de la Constitución once served as a military parade ground and park. Around the plaza, in the customary colonial plan, a church, a house for the governor, and small public buildings were built. Ships unloaded cargo at the edge of the plaza in early days. On Matanzas Bay, the elaborate quadrangle-shaped fortress Castillo de San Marcos, now a National Monument, remains intact. The oldest standing fort in the United States, it was 84 years under construction—from 1672 until 1756. Its outer walls, 16 feet thick at the base, are built of coquina, a rocklike formation of shells

A narrow Saint Augustine street

and porous limestone quarried at Anastasia Island across the bay. From Anastasia the coastal highway leads to Saint Augustine Beach; both are now residential districts. As a further protection from invaders, the Spaniards built a wall of coquina on the northern boundary of the settlement; the old city gates with sentry boxes at St. George and Orange streets are the surviving vestige of the wall that once stretched across the narrow peninsula.

South of the plaza two-story wood and coquina homes, built during Spanish occupation, line narrow streets. Living rooms are on the second floor with balconies overlooking walled gardens of subtropical vines, flowers, and trees. First floor bedrooms are well shaded and cooled by the natural flow of air vented from the narrow streets.

Time has not diminished the Old World atmosphere and particular charm of long-ago Saint Augustine. The narrow balconied streets, the mighty fort, the wild orange trees have weathered many a siege and storm. From the Plaza the mind's eye can focus on the waterfront location of Mr. Fleshman's tavern where Audubon and his companions were boarders. Saint Augustine's boundaries by land and by water have not changed their course since Juan Ponce de León sighted this shore in 1513 or since Don Pedro Menéndez de Avilés landed to a roll of drums in 1565 bearing the colors of Castile and Aragon.

Much of the fascinating history of Saint Augustine can be learned from visiting the scenic and historic sites, museums, and other buildings of this oldest permanent white settlement in the United States.

Audubon's trail to plantation sites south of Saint Augustine was the next course to explore. Like Audubon, I was fortunate in having congenial companions. Our goal was to trace Audubon's route from Bulow Plantation to that "certain spring," as he describes it in the episode "Spring Garden" (p. 311), "near the sources of the St Johns River, so impregnated with sulphur that it emits an odor which to me was highly nauseous."

I had questioned several naturalists about the smelly spring. They all agreed that Florida springs do not smell like bilge water. On the other hand, springs are known to move, even disappear, in dry seasons. As the water table rises with seasonal rains, they may reappear in new locations.

The spring to which Audubon referred is Ponce de Leon Springs, wide and deep, in central Florida near De Land. Its waters rush and boil on the surface from the force of several springs below. I wanted to see it for myself.

On a bright morning in July we left Saint Augustine in two vehicles. F. Xavier Pellicer, local banker and historian, had made the arrangements for our journey and had carefully plotted the route. His wife Catharine, Ray Vinten of the National Park Service, his wife Rose, and my husband Lucien shared in the adventure. Xavier led the way in his jeep. I bounced along with him on the front seat. Catharine followed close behind us with the others, driving the Pellicer family sedan.

Nineteen miles south of the city on U.S. 1, we turned left toward the ocean and followed a blacktop road for a short distance to the old King's Road, parallel to the ocean. The passage narrowed to a sandy lane. Sand pines almost touched above us. Saw palmetto grows at the road's edge, intermingled with lantana bushes, wild grape, and morning-glory vines. Slash pines, sabal palms, and sparkleberry trees spring up between dense stands of scrub oaks.

As we approached Tomoka River Hammock the vista widened. Along the road, low-growing palmetto stretches toward fertile hammock land and scattered farm plots. Rising high above the scrub are stands of dark green gordonia trees. Their spectacular white flowers in full bloom resemble the magnolia in texture and color. But flowers of the gordonia tree hang like ornaments from long pendicles on the ends of thick branches.

The scene so far, according to Audubon's journals, was much as he saw it in 1831, when he walked south from Saint Augustine to General Joseph M. Hernandez's plantation and on to Bulow Ville. The most traveled roadway at that time, King's Road, was built during the English period from Saint Marys River to New Smyrna, forming the western boundary to these and other plantations of East Florida. Remnants of King's Road are now difficult to trace.

There was a decided change of pace as we left the solemnity of the woods. A short jog in the road from the woods put us back in heavy traffic on State Highway 11. But in a few minutes we again reentered the woodlands and drove slowly down a mile-long hammock road to the site of Bulow Plantation, now Bulow Ruins State Park, near Flagler Beach on U.S. A1A.

I was immediately envious of John James Audubon, who had

Road leading to Bulow Plantation

visited this place in its magnificent days, when Bulow's mansion in the Florida wilderness was a place of gracious living. There is nothing left of it but the coquina foundations, a few arches, and chimneys. South of the lush hammock lawn, there are three boat slips at Bulow Creek, a thin stream that winds east to the Halifax River. Beyond the creek an extensive field of saw grass bends in the wind, and clumps of cabbage palms rise in the distance. The dashing young John J. Bulow, Audubon's bachelor host, left evidence at the docks of a luxury befitting his life-style. He lined the boat slips with imported wine bottles to prevent erosion, but most of them have been removed by souvenir collectors. It was from this anchorage on Bulow Creek that Audubon, Ward, Lehman, and the planter Bulow "put off with fair wind and pure sky" toward the Halifax River. Their overnight expedition, described in a long letter, was to provide material for one of Audubon's most spirited narratives of East Florida (pp. 22-25).

Half a mile away are coquina ruins of Bulow's massive sugar mill.

Close by are several wells and a spring house, well-preserved, surrounded by hammock growth typical of the region—hardwood trees, palms, palmettos, and ancient oak trees. It takes little effort to visualize the ever-curious, never-shy Audubon inquiring of all things new to him, walking and riding horseback over most of the acres of Bulow Ville, in company with his cheerful host. Audubon may not have known of the destruction that took place there after his visit. Major Benjamin Putnum made the plantation his headquarters in the early days of the Seminole War. John J. Bulow disagreed with the edict to send the Indians west of the Mississippi. He fired a small cannon (a four-pounder) at Putnum and his troops, in resistance to their occupation. Putnum held Bulow as a prisoner and kept him under guard in the house. After many unsuccessful skirmishes with the Indians, settlers in the Halifax region were ordered to evacuate to Saint Augustine. The famed estate was looted by the Seminoles and burned to the ground in 1836. The debonair twenty-six-year-old planter, still a bachelor, returned to Paris, where he died that same year.

Bulow Creek

Under the great oak trees at Bulow Ville stands a small concrete building, the park headquarters, where Pellicer had arranged for us to meet the late Dewey Moody, a surveyor from Bunnell, and his assistant, Tommy Durance. Both men had read Audubon's episode "Spring Garden," and were ready to describe our route from Bulow Ville to the "curious spring." Moody was highly qualified to interpret our charts, as he had laid section lines in East Florida for more than thirty years.

Durance was on vacation, busy digging a new well at his place on nearby Haw Creek, but agreed to be our guide in the backcountry where he had gained his knowledge of the woods and streams first from cow hunting when he was a little boy and later from seasonal game hunting and fishing.

Mr. Moody spread a section map on a table inside the park headquarters. He pointed to Indian trails recorded in East Florida by government surveyors Henry Washington and A. M. Randolph, be-

Ruins of Bulow Plantation sugar mill

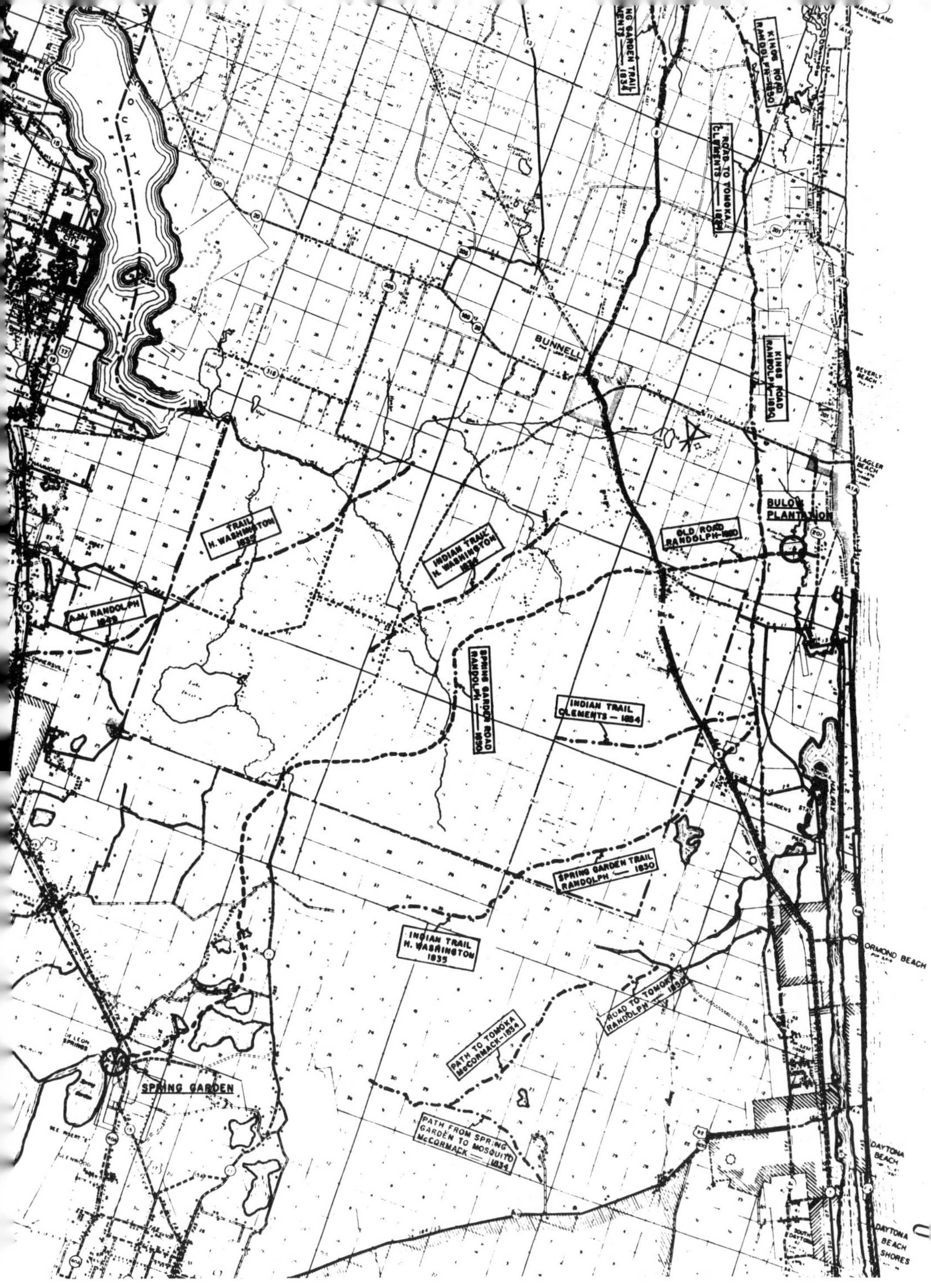

Portion of Dewey Moody's section map

tween the years 1834 and 1850. His steady hand moved westward from Bulow Ville.

"You see," he began, "Indians always took the high ground to avoid the water. It's tiresome to horses and makes their feet and legs tender. Mr. Audubon's guide, the engineer, knew the country or else he wouldn't have been choosey to take him through the swamps. That was dangerous country."

Our briefing was explicit, and quite definitely fit Audubon's journal. We were later to cross King's Road and look out for some tall grass and muck beds covered with saw grass. From there, we were to turn west to a place now called Korona, then take a shortcut to Dupont.

"From there," continued Mr. Moody, "you're on a direction toward Haw Creek. From the north end of the saw grass to Haw Creek you'll go through heavy pine timber for a distance, then break out in the open woods.

"Now following along on the northwesterly side of Dupont Graded [a dirt road] is higher ground and a few ponds. You'll notice the water getting deeper, a half or quarter mile west of Sweetwater Branch, a sand-bottom shallow the Indians used for watering their horses. Mr. Audubon called Sweetwater one of the heads of Haw Creek. He's right. It runs into Big Haw Creek.

"On the west side of Sweetwater the land jumps up quicker and is fairly out of water 'til you get to Middle Haw Creek. Water gets deeper there. The crossing Mr. Audubon made at Middle Haw was close to the existing bridge there now. It has a sand bottom and's not boggy. Moving southwesterly you'll soon cross Little Haw Creek. A bridge is built over the crossing the Indians used.

"From there the land starts to rise, and on these high hills you'll find large oak trees, salamanders, and gopher burrows. They and the turtles make horseback traveling uneasy, just like Mr. Audubon said. From there on in, you'll pass some lakes here and there until you get to Spring Garden at De Leon Springs. Mr. Audubon crossed Haw Creek three times and so will you."

This time Tommy Durance and I led the caravan in his Volkswagen. We took one short cut to Korona and another to Dupont Graded, which led to Highway 11. The Indian trail, he said, was in the woods, about half a mile from the highway. We could walk or go in the jeep. It would take longer to walk, so we jostled through the woodlands and over gopher holes, riding in the jeep and the Volkswagen, blazing a trail in the direction of our destination. After a while, we saw a lane through the trees that was without a doubt the ancient trail. Our maps verified the fact, and Tommy said it is still used by people who live in the backcountry.

It was close to two o'clock that afternoon when we crossed Sweetwater. Middle Haw and Little Haw are clear, meandering streams; the land does "jump up quicker." As we crossed the tiny bridge at Little Haw Creek, there was even a fat, sleeping alligator sprawled against the bank, its nose tipping the surface of the water.

Back on the highway, just before we reached our destination, the lake district was clearly discernible. Through large oaks and heavy timber we could see swatches of water—larger lakes—as we sped along toward Spring Garden.

A few minutes from the city limits of De Land, our company of weekend travelers stopped at the garden entrance of De Leon Springs, paid the fee, and followed markers to a parking area. Big trees with Spanish moss shade the pathway. A bald cypress spreads its branches high above the tops of all other trees. Named Old Methuselah, it is estimated to be over 2,700 years old. Oak trees, heavy with age, stand there, with their top branches out of sight. One of them is called Hangman's Oak. Perhaps Audubon heard tales of the Spaniards, British soldiers, and Indians who perished by the loop, hanging from its mighty limbs. Finally, past a clearing, through the trees, I stood at the water's edge and looked upon the boiling spring, once a part of Spring Garden plantation, owned by Colonel Orlando Rees, who was Audubon's host at Spring Garden in January of 1832.

The Indians and soldiers are said to have taken their wounded and dying to this spring to be restored. They called it the Spring of Healing Waters. I wanted to dive in and see for myself the deposits of shells and matter that rise from the forceful depths as Audubon had seen them. I wanted the spring to smell like bilge water, but it didn't. Disheartened by the commercial trade that hums in every direction at De Leon Springs, I took off my shoes and sat down on the concrete apron that circles the spring, dangling my feet in the magic water.

There was one more question to settle. On our return trip toward Big Haw Creek, where Tommy lived and where he would leave our party, it occurred to me to ask him how his new well was coming along. His answer was not direct, but answered a larger question. "That old one," he said, "turned so, I had to hold my breath every morning to wash my face. It smelled like rotten eggs."

Bilge water. Rotten eggs. The answer was clear. Sulphur too has a similar odor.

Then, as if surprised, Tommy stared at the trail behind us. He smiled, and gently kicked at the trunk of a hawthorn bush. "You know," he said, "since we made this trip like Mr. Audubon, I do believe he came right through my backyard."

The circumstances and pleasures of our journey from Bulow Ville to Spring Garden sparked additional enthusiasm for following Audubon's travels through Florida. Each trip differed in context, in companions, and in unexpected side adventures, but our preparations followed a similar course. We would all read Audubon's journal pertaining to the location we were to visit, and in each instance my companions contributed immeasurably to the venture.

On a separate occasion, my husband and I made a side trip to the Hernandez plantation site. Now known as Washington Oaks Gardens State Park, it can be reached from U.S. A1A approximately thirty miles south of Saint Augustine.

General Joseph M. Hernandez was born in Saint Augustine in 1792. He served in a number of important positions in the Territory of East Florida and was its first delegate to the United States Congress. At the time of Audubon's visit Hernandez had developed a rich sugar plantation at this site. Later it became an orange grove, and in this century, extensive gardens and plantings were added. It is a restful and quiet area with benches conveniently placed near the spectacular beds of flowering plants. Adjacent to the river's edge, huge old trees indicate the site of the original plantation home of General Hernandez.

The Saint Johns flows through the city of Jacksonville in the shape of a rollercoaster. At the mouth of the river, on the north bank, high sand dunes, powdery, white, and windblown into rolling heaps of shifting sand, line the river entrance at Surfers Point on Fort George Island.

The south bank is conspicuously occupied by the United States Naval Station at Mayport, the home base of the Seventh Fleet. As the

Site of Hernandez Plantation

Saint Johns bends, the old lighthouse Audubon saw from the schooner *Spark* stands on the south bank, one block from the intersection of Ocean and Broad streets in Mayport.

A view of the river entrance from the Atlantic, and the lighthouse, as Audubon saw it in 1832, is best seen from across the river at the dunes on Fort George Island. Aircraft carriers line both sides of the high bluffs at Mayport and obstruct the view. Fort George ferry crosses the Saint Johns a short distance from the lighthouse. Near the ferry, fleets of shrimp boats tie up at the docks. At this point, the river weaves west. It rises, dips, and rises again at Fort Caroline and Saint Johns Bluffs on the south bank, about six miles from the mouth of the river. On this site were the original river settlements. In 1830, according to the census, there were 1,970 people in Duval County, but less than three hundred of them dwelled in Jacksonville.

From Saint Johns Bluffs, the river has hardly begun its course through the city. Broward and Trout rivers meet the Saint Johns and form a wide confluence before turning sharply south, then west to the narrowest point, a mile wide, known as the Cowford, an ancient cow crossing, near Liberty Street and the Main Street bridge. The Duval County Courthouse, the City Hall, and Jacksonville's lively business center are in this area, from which the river turns south on a wide and meandering course toward Lake George. South of the city, the Saint Johns is more than two miles wide. Residences have the appearance of well-appointed estates, and, farther south, boat-builders and dry docks flank the west bank and coves of the Ortega River.

In 1832, the twisting and turning of the Saint Johns, from the mouth of the river, would have been a lonely and fascinating trip in a sailing ship. Unbroken forests lined the river and Saint Johns Bluffs emerged as the only change in the scenery.

On a balmy February morning, Cindy Purcell, a Jacksonville yacht broker, Jeff Willard, a restoration artist and naturalist, and I boarded Cindy's sleek Silverline craft at Huckins Docks on the Ortega River. Our prospective journey from Jacksonville up the river to Lake George had been planned the night before at Jeff's spectacular, early nineteen-hundreds, shingled house on the ocean at Atlantic Beach. Cindy said there would not be much to see, for the river, past Racy Point, is wide, some fifty miles south, then twists like a charging snake toward Palatka and beyond. Later it elbow-turns into narrow passageways and small lakes until it reaches Little Saint George. The final approach to Lake George at Drayton's Island, she said, would be several days away by boat.

Cindy was born on the river at Orange Park. With childhood friends at Orange Park, Cindy caught baby turtles in the river tributaries and anticipated the seasonal changing of the leaves to orange, red, and gold. When she was ten years old, she swam across the Saint Johns from Orange Park to Manderin on the east bank, her father following her in a skiff. From shore to shore, the river is a mile and a half wide. He had told her she could have a boat of her own when she passed this test. She salvaged a Sailfish, put it in shape, and learned to sail, feeling the wind and knowing its directions by ear.

I watched the ease with which Cindy steered her boat into the mainstream of the Saint Johns that February morning. She scanned the shores, markers, and the river traffic, her long blond ponytail flying almost in line with our wake.

My geodetic maps of the river were of no value to Cindy, but of great interest to me. Audubon had not mentioned landmarks on the Saint Johns, and I wondered why. It was apparent that he couldn't see the banks from the schooner *Spark*. I felt a similar detachment. Both sides of the river south of Jacksonville appear as indistinguishable lines of thick forests, the river being more than three miles wide.

The Saint Johns is generally wide and shallow, except for the narrows approaching Lake George. The headwaters rise from springs south of Lake George, and the river flows north. The springs are diaphanous, but tannic acid darkens the Saint Johns, so the river water is the color of coffee.

There are landings known to have been used regularly by the Indians and early settlers on the Saint Johns. Manderin Point is one of these. Our first stop was farther up the river, past Green Cove Springs at Six-mile Creek, near Pacetti Point.

As we veered toward the east bank, leading to a gas dock, Cindy lowered our speed. She propped her feet on a pillow beside the instrument panel, and leaned back in her seat as if refreshing her memories to the meaning of spring. From the middle of the river the tall, faceless forests became a panorama of nature's colors. The flora, endemic to the area, grows trunk to trunk. Water oaks are lacy and broad. Some of them lean from the edge of the forest and reflect in the water. Cypress, pines, and cabbage palms stand straight and tall, in contrasting shades of green. Outstanding in the forests were white and red blooms of wild dogwood and redbud trees, a definite announcement of spring. In this conglomerate mass of woodlands, the bare, spiney branches of hickory trees retained their spread of last year's growth; they would be the last to bud.

At certain unknown places along the river the *Spark* anchored and Audubon entered these "impenetrable forests." He mentions wild orange trees, which indicates he visited homes of the settlers, perhaps at Hibernia Point, where there are sizable old homesites. The logging camps, where Audubon was "guided by some friendly live-oakers," ceased to operate long ago. Vast stands of oak and cypress trees grow inland, near tributaries of the Saint Johns that were once used to float logs to the river.

The *Spark*, according to Audubon, was a hundred miles up the river near the entrance to Lake George when the captain ordered soundings and a sailor was accidentally shot in the foot, delaying the *Spark's* journey. Audubon left the *Spark* and hired a boat to take him and one of his assistants down the river to a landing used by the Seminoles, eighteen miles from Saint Augustine. The shortcut, he said, was forty miles from their point of departure. They left early in the morning and reached the landing, apparently Picolata, about four in the afternoon.

Barges, pleasureboats, and sports fishermen stir the waters of the Saint Johns. A few cormorants and fish hawks perch on water markers, and coots feed among the hyacinths. The Saint Johns is a serviceable river, and desirable as a place to live. Expensive homesites for permanent residents and vacation homes border its shores.

Periodic spraying from helicopters, to control the rampant growth of hyacinths, kills vegetation and marine life. The "thousands of snowy pelicans, numberless herons, and extremely abundant alligators" Audubon mentions are seldom encountered, except in their remote habitats. There still are, Cindy said, thousands of coots and brown ducks in Lake George, which is eleven miles long and six miles wide. They still fly in great flocks, an estimated twenty to thirty thousand.

A few miles south of Racy Point, toward Lake George, the river makes its last, wide hairpin turn to Palatka, and the narrows begin. There are homes, piers, and lodges on both sides of the Saint Johns, and the river becomes a peaceful stream, similar to a quiet canal. Boats are required to cruise at minimum speeds.

Like Audubon, we didn't get to Lake George. But our day-long cruise up the Saint Johns had served its purpose well. Cindy turned the boat around. We cruised downstream, and reached Jacksonville at sunset.

"Audubon's Isle," west of De Leon Springs, is unknown by that name today. Audubon's episode "Spring Garden," however, clearly describes its location. There is a discrepancy in his account of the lakes he passed through before arriving at the island Colonel Rees named for him. From Spring Garden Creek, the first lake is Woodruff, then follows Lake Dexter. Audubon wrote that Woodruff, rather than Dexter, empties into the Saint Johns River. With this in mind, the search for Audubon's Isle did not appear to be difficult. The difficulty came in trying to get a boat to take me through the three small lakes.

I decided to reverse Audubon's course and enter the Saint Johns from Astor, Florida. Astor is not listed as one of Florida's singular attractions. But to the river people who live there, maybe ten families in all, and to people who go there to fish the lakes and enjoy scenes of Florida as it looked a hundred years ago, Astor is far, far removed from urban cares. The only remaining bridgetender's house in Florida that has land traffic passing under its portico is at Astor, on the Saint Johns.

At a landing near the bridge, I looked for a fisherman, hopefully an old-timer, to take me through the lakes to Spring Garden Creek. The old-timers, I was told, were " 'bout gone." A fisherman named Bob Folks who lives in a tent five miles up the river might be able to go the next morning, I was told, but he was out catching catfish and wouldn't come until dark to the landing, where he sometimes ate his supper.

Jim Lucas, proprietor of the landing operation, was quick to understand my quest. We checked his regional map tacked to the door of his store. His knowledge of the area qualified him to be a young old-timer, for he had grown up on the river and was familiar with every land and river mark, even with their old-time names. As we pondered the situation, Lucas was interrupted, off and on, by fishermen who needed adjustments to their motors or a supply of bait. We resumed our discussion, looking at the map, and soon agreed that Audubon's Isle, although unknown by that name in the district, could possibly be located at the east end of Lake Dexter, near Tick Island Creek, also known as Bird Run. Several islands meeting the description were there, he said at first, but on second thought, decided all of them were marshy and hardly good places to spread a cloth and have a picnic. The other possibility, he said, was at a point where the river turns east into Lake Dexter at a place called Idlewilde Point. We decided to wait for Bob Folks who might take me there.

Lucas was tinkering with a motor, about five o'clock, and I was sitting by the troughs of live bait, drinking orange pop, when a green skiff flashed past the dock. It was Bob Folks. Lucas yelled for him to stop. Folks came ashore, and he agreed to be my guide on the following day.

I spent a restful night in a cabin on the river. Early the next morning, a lone American Egret stood outside my door and took flight toward the landing as if showing me the way. Bob Folks was waiting at the dock, and we started up the Saint Johns in search of Audubon's Isle.

The Saint Johns, south of Lake George, is narrow and deep. Bob Folks calls it "deep and black." He fishes for "big cats" (twenty to forty pounds) and sells them at the Astor fish market, where fish are shipped to commercial packers. He hadn't heard of *The Birds of America,* or of Audubon, but he was obviously intrigued with the idea of finding the island, and kept a constant check of our route up the river on my geodetic chart. The little green skiff was swift, and it was easily manipulated through the sharp turns and inlets. We were soon across Lake Dexter and past the islands clustered at the east end of the lake. I was disappointed that these little islands had no semblance to the one we were looking for. Bird Island, said Folks, is covered with egrets at night. Coots flew in front of the skiff, some of them landing on clumps of hyacinths. Hyacinths are cleared from these lakes several times a year, and are known to reach such heights as to block the view of boaters. Tick Island Creek is about a hundred feet wide. It curves along the north bank of Tick Island, a federal wildlife sanctuary, surrounded by marshes and swamps. A chorus of bird calls came from the island. Egrets, anhingas, ospreys, great blue herons, and green herons appeared along the way. We crossed Lake Woodruff into Spring Garden Run and Spring Garden Creek. I had followed Audubon's trail through the lakes in reverse. His descriptions of them are still amazingly accurate.

On our return to Astor, we planned to stop at Bob Folks's camp at Idlewilde Point to compare a group of islands just past the inlet to Stagger Mud Lake with the marshy ones we had discounted in Lake Dexter.

"You might say these are near where Dexter empties into the Saint Johns, even though they're just around the bend from where I live on the river," Bob said.

There are no houses on the river or through the lakes from Astor to Spring Garden Creek. Marshlands are level with the water. "There are two exceptions," said Folks. "There's a shell mound out of the water on Tick Creek. The only other shell mound, lots higher, is where I stay at Idlewilde Point. This is fine country. Nobody here. Forty square miles to myself."

At the west end of Lake Dexter, we entered the inlet to Stagger Mud Lake. Here the islands are large enough to spread a cloth and have a picnic. Hardwood trees grow in the center of them, and any one of them meets the description of Audubon's Isle. It was possible, we decided, that he came here, although the location is out of the mainstream of the river. I asked Bob Folks if there were wild orange trees in the area. He replied, "Not here, but there's wild orange trees at my camp."

He turned the skiff around and we landed at Idlewilde Point, a few yards away. We stepped out on high, dry land, amid the scent of wild orange trees, "the luxuriance and freshness of which were . . . pleasing to the sight." Idlewilde Point, says Folks, is indeed an island. When the water table falls, the high ground is separated from the swamp beyond the trees.

We spread our cloth under the wild orange and live oak trees and enjoyed our meal of cheese and wine, feeling sure our quest for Audubon's Isle had been successful.

Spring Garden

Southwest shore of Indian Key

Indian Key is an uninhabited island, eleven acres in size, a short distance by skiff from the Overseas Highway, near Upper Matecumbe on the Florida Keys. To a casual viewer, it appears insignificant among the many offshore islands in the vast stretch of verdant rises from the Atlantic and the Gulf of Mexico along U.S. 1. An immediate distinction appears, however, in what seem to be hundreds of radar antennae pointing toward the sky, high above the vegetation. These rodlike prongs are deceiving to the eye, for they are, in fact live projectiles from sisal plants. *Agave sisalana* is a variety of sisal brought to Indian Key by Dr. Henry Perrine, noted botanist and former U.S. Consul to Campeche, Mexico, in the late 1830s.

With the exception of a short stretch of sand on the curving southwest shore, the island, beneath thin subterranean soil, is formed of coral and has thereby retained its basic shape through centuries of winds and tides. It has not been occupied by permanent residents since 1840 when Dr. Perrine and six other residents were massacred by angry and drunken Indians who came there in a predawn raid to retaliate against their foe, Jacob Housman. Housman, an infamous wrecker, escaped the Indian attack. He had wrested the key from squatters and built a large wrecker kingdom for himself between 1825 and 1840. During that time on Indian Key there were rows of houses, stores, a large warehouse, a central square with grass, trees, and flowers, and the Tropical Hotel with a bar, billiard hall, and bowling alley. The settlement was more than a raw arrangement of makeshift dwellings. It has been called South Florida's first real estate development. Jacob Housman even persuaded the state legislature to make it the seat of a new county. He named it Dade, after Major Francis Dade, who was ambushed with over 100 men at the beginning of the Seminole War in December, 1835.

It is doubtful if Audubon ever heard of Housman's eventual fate. After the massacre, he lived for nine months in Key West, finishing his days as a crewman on a wrecking ship, under the jurisdiction of his former foes. On May 1, 1841, Housman lost his footing and fell between two ships tossing side by side in a high sea. His body was crushed between the vessels.

The coral rock foundations of Housman's little kingdom are haunting reminders of the island's charm and appearance in the 1830s when Audubon visited there. A miniature reconstruction of

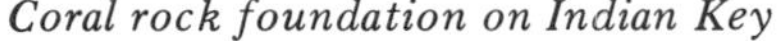

Coral rock foundation on Indian Key

the island and its buildings may be seen in the Key West Historical Museum.

In 1972, Indian Key was purchased from private owners by the state of Florida for $240,000. The price includes title to 95.34 submerged acres surrounding the island. Because of the cultural history of Indian Key, the Florida Division of Recreation and Parks is considering restoration of the historic structures. The solid foundations, with exquisite marine fossils, are well preserved in the original locations. The island is not presently open to the public but will be made available when appropriate visitor arrangements have been completed.

Captain Ralph Miele, ranger-pilot of the Everglades National Park, arranged an overnight trip to Cape Sable, another to Sandy Key, and a three-day trip to the Dry Tortugas for me and my companions. Cape Sable is the southernmost part of the American mainland, a desolate section of the Everglades, rimmed by the wide-stretching, white beaches of Florida Bay. Sea turtles are known to lay eggs there in the sand during the summer months. Audubon observed sea turtles at Cape Sable, Key West, and the Dry Tortugas. He was immensely attracted to the habits and manner in which sea turtles

Beach at East Cape Sable

lay eggs. At the Tortugas Audubon reported witnessing this spectacle in the moonlight (p. 349).

Ranger Miele told me that there were no turtle tracks presently at the Dry Tortugas, although Audubon reported they had been there in great numbers. Key West, now densely populated, sells turtle meat brought from Nicaragua via Georgetown, Grand Cayman, so Key West was out as a likely place to go turtle-watching. But Miele had seen a few tracks from the air at Cape Sable, and we agreed to go as soon as possible.

There were four of us in the skiff. We left the park ranger station at Flamingo at dusk, skimming over emerald water around the lower, or East, Cape toward the sand beaches sixteen miles away. We were to spend the night in an abandoned shack on Middle Cape, where Miele said sea turtles were sure to crawl. The shack, he said, would be the only available shelter and the sole trace of civilization. Swarms of humming, black mosquitoes attacked us at the wooden dock. We knew a wind would bring them from the Everglades, but not in such abundance. Our three layers of clothing gave little protection from them, and a repellent for our hands and faces didn't seem to work at all. We built a buttonwood fire in the shack on the sand floor and awaited the moonrise. In a little while we sat comfortably in the light of the fire. The pleasant hickory odor of smoldering buttonwood mingled with the comforting smell of coffee. Mosquitoes, we discovered, are not fond of smoke.

Just before midnight the moon came up. On the beach, as we walked toward East Cape, an occasional breeze brought periodic relief from the mosquitoes. Pesky as they were, there was no use turning back. We fell behind the ranger after a while, our steps in the loose white sand dwindling to a slower gait until his light signaled us to hurry on.

Fresh tracks more than three feet wide came from the sea. A large sea turtle had crawled through the sand up to the line of low scrub grass that grows on the cape, beyond the beach. She had dug a round nest, a perfect cylinder about twelve inches deep and six inches wide. It was evident that we were late. Eggshells covered the ground.

Beyond our lights something moved in the grass. A raccoon lunged into the nest. Undaunted by our presence or our voices, he ate each egg as it dropped from the turtle. Miele held his light on the scene. None of us had ever before witnessed such an audacious theft.

Raccoon devouring newly laid turtle eggs.

Close-up of eggs being deposited.

The turtle continued to lay, unaware of the devastation taking place behind her. She sighed repeatedly, contracting her flippers, continuing the procedure. At the end of the laying, she used her back flippers to cover the cache of eggs that should have been there. We tried to pick her up, hoping to judge her weight, but she was too heavy to manage.

The raccoon waited until the turtle crawled slightly away from the smooth surface she had instinctively pressed to disguise the nest. On his haunches in anticipation of her move, he scratched to the bottom, throwing sand on her back. He found two more eggs, then scampered into the darkness. There were other nests, on East Cape and along the crescent beach to Northwest Cape. Only one of them, found just before dawn, was undisturbed.

A few weeks later, we again left Flamingo, this time headed for Sandy Key in Florida Bay, about eight miles southwest of Flamingo. It was April, the same month in which Audubon saw the thin little island in 1832.

From Flamingo we passed Murray Key and the Oyster Keys, a line of mangrove islets not far from the mainland. The tip of East Cape Sable rose in the distance. In a short time Ranger Miele sighted the tree line of Sandy Key, but our approach to it was some maneuvering away. At Sandy Key Basin we followed a channel due west three miles, around a soft mudbank, before turning east on course.

Miele made three attempts to reach the shore. Each sweep in that direction left a propeller trail in the mudbank. Our plan was to go ashore at high tide when the water level would be three feet deep. The Sandy Key flats are known to be hazardous for boatmen who are not aware of these extreme shallows.

We finally anchored, a city block from shore in a chilling rain, and carried our supplies through waist-deep water to the beach. Firewood was not hard to find. Dried limbs of buttonwood trees killed by Hurricane Donna in 1960 were within easy reach, for Sandy Key had been near the eye of the storm.

I hoped to be as "amazed at the appearance of things around me" as was John James Audubon. "Sandy Isle," he said, "is remarkable as a breeding-place for various species of water and land birds. It is about a mile in length, not more than a hundred yards broad, and in form resembles a horse-shoe, the inner curve of which looks toward Cape Sable in Florida Bay, from which it is six miles distant" (p. 235).

The same species of birds still nest there—great white, great blue, and Louisiana herons. The amazing appearance is due not altogether to the birds, I later discovered, but to the tide, as Audubon also noted.

On a subtropical island, away from human habitation, the arrival of evening swiftly settles anxieties of the day. Food tastes better, stars are brighter, friends are more companionable than usual; the world, for a little while, seems peaceful.

A safeguard for the boat, prepared by the ranger, paid off. At low tide we would be asleep, he said, and there was a possibility that the boat would sink deep in the sand flats, making our departure difficult the next day. If this should happen, we would probably have to wait for high tide to float the boat. But he would be awakened when the tide went out so we could move the boat to deeper water. Miele waded to the boat and tied a long rope to the bow, pulled the rope across the beach to the tent, and carefully measured the tautness of the line from the boat to his sleeping bag. He tied the end of the rope to a round canvas life preserver, and then firmly strapped the life preserver around his ankle. He was awakened before morning by a tug on the life preserver, signifying the boat was moving. He came out of the tent on his knees to judge the situation. The boat was listing portside, the propeller sinking fast in the sandy marl. But there was time to right the vessel and push it to deeper water.

Our experience was similar to Audubon's in 1832. He wrote, "When we laid ourselves down in the sand to sleep, the waters almost bathed our feet; when we opened our eyes in the morning, they were at an immense distance. Our boat lay on her side, looking not unlike a whale reposing on a mud bank" (p. 333).

The next morning I arose from my sleeping bag before dawn, restless to see the day. "I left you abruptly, perhaps uncivilly, reader, at the dawn of day," wrote Audubon, startled by what he saw. I, too, was startled by what I saw and heard. The sky was teeming with birds in flight to their feeding grounds. I could barely see their forms in the pale light, but loud flappings of wings and sharp calls gave the feeling of a thick, billowy blanket held in suspension between the sand and the clouds.

I was increasingly amazed at the appearance of things about me. On the east side of the island, no more than sixty yards away, birds in myriads were probing exposed feeding grounds. The expansive mud flats looked fifteen miles wide; a startling transition had taken place.

The island is no longer shaped like a horseshoe, but more like a punchbowl ladle, the handle pointing toward Flamingo. Hurricane Donna obliterated the eastern side of the horseshoe but left the thick stand of gumbo-limbo, buttonwood, and black mangrove trees, cabbage palms, cactus, and vines. This impenetrable sanctuary in the bowl is where Audubon and his men gathered eggs for their breakfast. The number of birds they shot "looked not unlike a small haycock" (p. 334).

Mud flats

I have returned to Sandy Island three times, for surely it is one of the most unique islands in Florida waters.

The Dry Tortugas are seven islands located fifty miles west of the Marquesas Keys in the Gulf of Mexico, sixty-eight miles west of Key West. The Tortugas and the surrounding shoals and waters are included in the Fort Jefferson National Monument.

Audubon sailed on the *Marion* to these lonely islands especially to see the sooty terns that fly there yearly to nest and raise their young before returning to South America and the Yucatán peninsula. This phenomenon has been witnessed for centuries and remains an astonishing feat of avian migration.

Passage to the Dry Tortugas should be confirmed before one goes to Key West, the closest point of departure. Charter seaplane service may not be available, and charterboats are subject to storm warnings. My first four attempts to see the Tortugas were unsuccessful; one of these was a bold plea to the captain of a shrimp boat making weekly sweeps of shrimp beds in close proximity to the islands. My trip was finally arranged by the late Commissioner Ralph Jordan of Homestead. He had business to transact at Fort Jefferson for the National Park Service and had space for one passenger, although "civilians," he said, would not ordinarily be permitted to fly in the government plane.

We boarded the department's amphibious plane at Homestead Airport. I fastened my seat belt and looked at the tiny engine mounted amidship. It looked like a freezing unit in an old-fashioned refrigerator. I wasn't sure I wanted to go after all, but Miele, who was the pilot and a former Navy flier, soon won my confidence.

We took off. The sites below were all new to me. We followed a portion of Shark River and looked down on a ridge of limestone rock that geologists are studying, Miele said, as a possible ancient water and land line. Scanning the view below, I saw a string of shrimp boats pointed to the open sea from the mainland. Shadows of light at the top of the reef gradually darkened in deeper water surrounding the great Florida reef that extends westward to the Tortugas, "the coral reef that every where stretches along the shore like a great wall, reared by an army of giants," as Audubon described it at Indian Key (p. 327).

Over the open sea the water is deep blue; whitecaps dance on the surface. Then, as if an unyielding mirage, Fort Jefferson looms in the distance at Garden Key like a monstrous red-brick castle. Magnificent frigatebirds float in a circular flight pattern high over the southeast wing of the fort, riding air thermals that constantly rise from that end of the island.

Letting down, we flew over East Key and Middle Key; I spotted Hospital Key off the right wing. Lowering gently toward a strip of water that divides Garden Key from Bush and Long Keys, thousands of terns and noddies swarmed high in the air and on the sand. Out the windows each little key zoomed closer. A big nurse shark treaded its fins on the rim of East Key in the shallows. And brilliant swirls of color in shades of blue, gold, and green reflected streaks of light from the reefs and shallows to the surface of the water.

I braced myself for a water landing, expecting the plane to be flooded. The landing was smooth, as pilot Miele had assured us it would be. Casting a small wake, he taxied toward the sand beach at Garden Key.

Wheels down, the plane rolled on dry land to within a few yards of the fort entrance. We crossed the moat bridge, walked around the island, and surveyed the huge hexagon-shaped building that covers most of the island's sixteen acres. Somebody said the ghost of Dr. Samuel Mudd walks down the long corridors after midnight. The Maryland physician was a prisoner at the Dry Tortugas from 1865 to 1869, the result of his alleged crime of setting the leg of John Wilkes Booth, the man who shot Abraham Lincoln at the Ford Theatre. Audubon was spared this intrigue, as construction of the fort did not begin until 1846.

I stood on top of the fort, at a height of fifty feet, and looked down on the moat. A school of parrot fish thrashed the water and streaked toward the moat bridge, where a little boy sat, gleefully dropping bread crumbs. From this altitude, the Dry Tortugas, I thought, were almost as Audubon had described them. The lighthouse that he saw from the *Delos* sailing through the Florida Straits in 1826 was built in 1825 on Garden Key. It was reduced to a harbor light in 1856, when a larger lighthouse was erected on Loggerhead Key, about three miles away. The nest of coral keys covers a

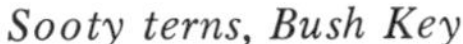

Sooty terns, Bush Key

View from Fort Jefferson

Aerial view of Fort Jefferson

ten-mile span of kinetoscopic colors, the dramatic end of the Florida reefs.

Miele led us down a narrow, circular staircase. I was dizzy when we got to the bottom of the fort, and walked out onto the parade ground, a monstrously large inner courtyard.

That afternoon we dropped anchor at the east end of Loggerhead, pulling the boat a few yards to the beach over flats covered with razor-sharp shells in water up to our knees. I thought of Audubon's complaint, that near some "distant isle" in the Florida Keys he and his companions pushed two boats "for upward of nine miles, over the flats" (p. 336).

Loggerhead Key is long and thin, covered in the middle with a thick stand of Australian pines, sea grape, and gumbo-limbo trees. Walking along the beach toward the lighthouse, we turned inland for awhile to a path through the middle of the trees. Pine needles cover the path, flanked on both sides with cactus plants and other subtropical vegetation. Most of the way, beaches are visible on both

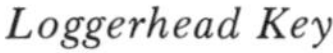

Loggerhead Key

sides. The shape of the island has not noticeably changed since Audubon was there; its area is still approximately thirty acres. On the north shore a strange formation of coquina rock has withstood many a tide and storm. Geologists have questioned its origin, for coquina rock is indigenous only to northeast Florida. Walking back along the Gulf beach at Loggerhead toward the boat, we found shells more brilliant than I have ever seen.

Very late in the afternoon we took up the anchor and started back to Garden Key. Then a wonderful thing happened, a sunset as complete as if John James Audubon's "blaze of refulgent glory" had been written that day (see p. 348).

That night I slept in the barracks near Dr. Mudd's cell, falling asleep to an unusual mixture of sounds—a piercing chorus of terns, a wooden storm shutter tapping somewhere down the long dark corridor, and the ever-soothing waves lapping systematically against the fort wall.

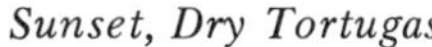

Sunset, Dry Tortugas

Shrimp boats, Key West

In present-day Key West the old section of the city, on the south end of the island, is still the principal center of interest. Duval Street is the main thoroughfare, a business street that runs the width of the island from the Atlantic Ocean to Front Street on the Gulf of Mexico.

Life is unhurried at Key West. Traffic moves slowly, and walking is commonplace. Native Key Westers may speak Spanish or English. Their expressions are uniquely their own, often flavored with the salty language of their forefathers who were principally seagoing men. The social attitude of long-time citizens is unusually self-containing, for Key West was isolated for centuries. A person born off "The Rock," although he has lived a long life there, is called a stranger, and a large percentage of the population claims to have never left the island.

On the Gulf end of Key West, townspeople and tourists gather on the wharf at dusk to watch the sunset. Fishermen pull up their motorboats, returning from the flats and reefs. Cruisers bring in sailfish, bonito, marlin, dolphin, and other deepwater fish from the waters farther out and from the Gulf Stream, seven miles off shore. At the north end of Front Street, on Key West Bight, shrimp boats attract a curious audience: the bulky hulls and stalwart crews are

Rooftop view, Key West

reminiscent of Spanish galleons, ships of mystery and adventure. On the edge of the cove are turtle crawls, fish markets, and the ice plant. Old Key West stems from this area and from Mallory Square, paved with ballast stones. The small native dwellings and two-story balconied houses are made of wood. They may be compared in architectural style to colonial New England and colonial houses of the Bahamas. Built close together, weathered by the salt air, they have resisted many winds and storms. Before water was piped to Key West from the mainland in 1942, rain water from the sloping roofs drained into cisterns, some of which are still in use. On a number of the roofs you will notice cupolas, which served as look-out posts, or widow's walks, used in the 1830s to sight wrecks on the reefs. Throughout the quaint streets, lanes, and dead-end alleys, tropical plants, vines, and trees are in bloom throughout the year.

From a depot at Front Street, near the old aquarium, tourist trams circle the island all day, seven days a week. The drivers' commentaries are filled with tales of the past and the present, as visitors roll by the Navy Base, Hemingway House, the southernmost house on the Atlantic, the Martello Towers, and the airport. The tram makes a turn on the north side of Key West, where the Overseas Highway meets Roosevelt Boulevard, near Stock Island. Roosevelt becomes a picturesque *malecón* on the Gulf before returning to Front Street. Small shops, bars, coffee houses, and ice cream parlors abound in Key West, along with native crafts and art galleries. Many of the private homes and gardens are open to the public during Old Island Days each year from February 15 to March 15.

Restoration of Old Key West was begun in the late 1950s by a handful of citizens who did not want demolition crews to knock down historic buildings to make room for parking lots. The most ambitious residential restoration, which brought national acclaim and sparked the restoration movement in Key West, was that of the Geiger house, now Audubon House, located on the corner of Greene and Whitehead Streets.

The property was bought by Mitchell Wolfson of Miami, who was born in Key West. The house and gardens, at that time in pitiful condition, were restored by Mr. Wolfson and his wife Frances, also a native Floridian. Refurnished with antiques of the 1820s and 1830s, the rarest objects on display are the complete, original *Birds of America* Double Elephant Folios of Audubon, acquired for the house after a worldwide search by the Wolfsons. The Audubon House is maintained by the Mitchell Wolfson Family Foundation.

In 1832 John James Audubon was the guest of the jovial Captain John H. Geiger, a retired pilot and wrecker. Geiger built the house

Audubon House, Key West

in 1830 and was known to be a sociable host. Audubon's white-crowned pigeon, Plate CLXXVII, was sketched on a bough of the Geiger tree (*Cordia sebestena*). Geiger trees still grow profusely in Key West. The twisted trunk, dark green leaves, and clusters of reddish flowers make the Geiger tree a valued ornamental.

Key West, a hundred miles from the mainland, is reached by the highway that literally goes to sea. In Old Key West, the rollicking tales of yore come to life, and visitors who sense these ancient flavors are reluctant to leave it.

PART TWO

BY JOHN JAMES AUDUBON

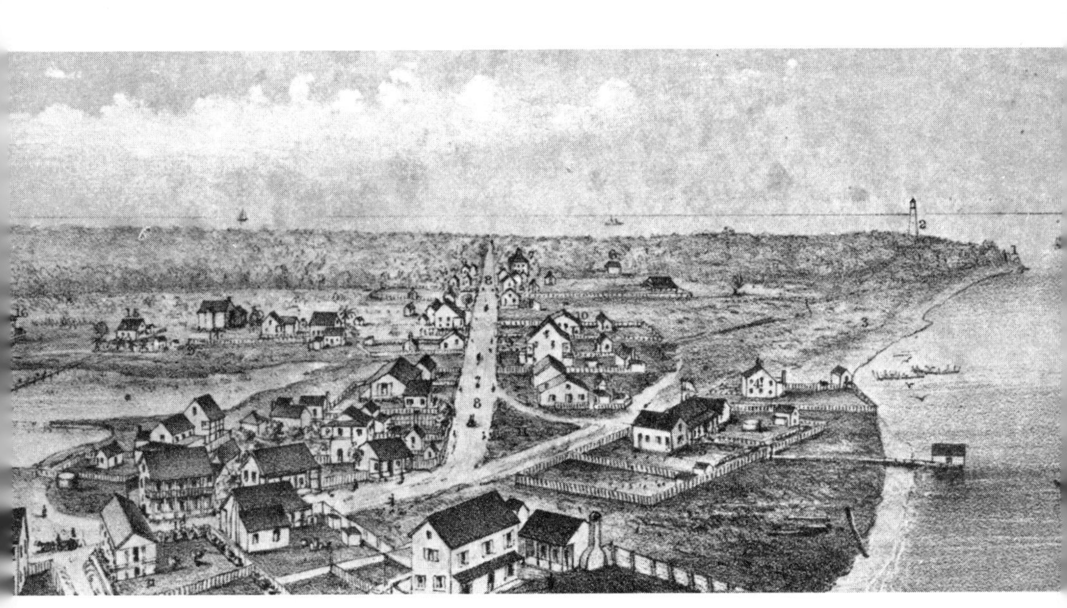

Plate CCLXXIII. *Cayenne Tern*

Ornithological Biographies

THE CAYENNE TERN

Sterna cayana, Lath. [Royal Tern, *Thalasseus maximus*]
Plate CCLXXIII. Male. [Caspian Tern, *Hydroprogne caspia*]

On reaching the entrance of the little port of St. Augustine in East Florida, I observed more Cayenne Terns together than I had ever before seen. I had afterwards good opportunities of watching them both during that season and the following, about the Keys. Their shyness surprised me not a little, especially as they are very seldom molested, and it was such that I could study their habits only with the aid of a good glass. I found them at first in great flocks, composed of several hundred individuals, along with Razor-billed Shearwaters, which also congregated there in great numbers. During low water, both species resorted to a large flat sand-bar in the middle of the channel, where they reposed until the return of the tide, sitting close together, in an easy posture, with their heads facing the breeze. They kept separate, however, placing themselves in parallel lines twenty or thirty paces asunder, and either lay flat on the sand, or stood up and plumed themselves. My attempts to procure some of them were always futile, for they flew off when I was yet several hundred yards distant, and moved directly towards the sea. It was pleasing to see the whole of these birds take to wing at the same moment, the jetty hue of the Shearwaters contrasting with the pale blue of the Terns, and the brilliantly-coloured bills of both species, their different modes of flight, and their various evolutions presenting a most agreeable sight. The Terns on these occasions constantly emitted their harsh loud cries, while the Shearwaters moved in perfect silence. After spending several days in unsuccessful endeavours to approach them, I employed several boats, which advanced towards the sands at several points, and we shot as many as we wished, for as the flocks passed over any of the boats, several individuals were brought down at once, on which the rest would assail the gunners, as if determined to rescue their brethren, and thus afford subjects for them on which to exercise their skill. We found it necessary to use large shot, the Cayenne Tern being a strong and tough bird, the largest of the genus met with on our Atlantic coasts. When wounded, however slightly, they disgorged in the manner of Vultures; and when brought to the water disabled, they at once endeavoured to make off from the shores, swimming with buoyancy and grace, though without making much progress. When seized they at once erected their beautiful crest, threw up the contents of their stomach, uttered loud cries, and bit severely. One that was merely touched in the wing, and brought ashore, through a high surf, by my Newfoundland dog, stuck fast to his nose until forced to relinquish its hold by having its throat squeezed, after which it disgorged seven partially digested fishes.

Although the Cayenne Tern often searches for food over the sea, and at times several miles from the shore, it gives a decided preference to the large inlets running parallel to the coast of the Floridas, within the high sandy embankments, as well as the rivers in the interior of the peninsula. They alight on the banks of racoon oysters, so abundant in the inlets, and are seen in company with the Semipalmated Snipe and the American Oystercatcher, searching for food like these birds, and devouring crabs and such fishes as are confined in small shallow pools. These they catch with considerable agility, in a manner not employed by any of our other Terns. While on the St. John's River, I saw them alight on stakes, in the manner of the Marsh Tern and the Noddy; and as I ascended that stream, I often saw them, at the distance of seventy miles from the sea, perched in the middle of the river, on the same sticks as the Florida Cormorants, and found them more easily approached in the dusk than during broad daylight. Until then I had supposed this species to be entirely oceanic, and averse from mingling with any other.

The flight of the Cayenne Tern is strong and well sustained, although less lively or graceful than that of the smaller species, excepting on particular occasions. They usually incline their bill downwards, as they search for their prey, like the other Terns, but keep at a much greater height, and plunge towards the waters with the speed of an arrow, to seize on small fishes, of which they appear to capture a great number, especially of the "mullets," which we saw moving about in shoals, composed of individuals of different sizes. When travelling, these birds generally proceed in lines; and it requires the power of a strong gale to force them back, or even to impede their progress, for they beat to windward with remarkable vigour, rising, falling, and tacking to right and left, so as to seize every possible opportunity of making their way. In calm and pleasant weather, they pass at a great height, with strong unremitted flappings, uttering at intervals their cries, which so nearly resemble the shrieking notes of our little Parrakeet, that I have often for a moment thought I heard the latter, when in fact it was only the Tern. At times their cries resemble the syllables *kwee-reek,* repeated several times in succession, and so loudly as to be heard at the distance of half a mile or more, especially when they have been disturbed at their breeding places, on which occasion they manifest all the characteristic violence of their tribe, although they are much more guarded than any other species with which I am acquainted, and generally keep at a considerable distance from their unwelcome visitors.

On the 11th May 1832, I found the Cayenne Terns breeding on one of the Tortugas. There they had dropped their eggs on the bare sand, a few yards above high-water mark, and none of the birds paid much attention to them during the heat of the day. You may judge of my surprise when, on meeting with this Tern breeding on the coast of Labrador, on the 18th of June 1833, I found it sitting on two eggs deposited in a nest neatly formed of moss and placed on the rocks, and this on a small island, in a bay more than twelve miles from our harbour, which itself was at some distance from the open Gulf. On another equally sequestered islet, some were found amidst a number of nests of our Common Gull; and, during my stay in that country, I observed that this Tern rarely went to the vicinity of the outer coast, for the purpose of procuring food, probably because there was an extreme abundance of small fishes of several kinds in every creek or bay. Until that period I was not aware that any Tern could master the *Lestris Pomarinum* [Pomarine Jaeger], to which, however, I there saw the Cayenne Tern give chase, driving it away from the islands on which it had its eggs. On such occasions, I observed that the Tern's power of flight greatly exceeded that of the Jager; but the appearance of the Great Black-backed Gull never failed to fill it with dismay, for although of quicker flight, none of the Terns dared to encounter that bird, any more than they would venture to attack the Frigate Pelican in the Floridas.

The Cayenne Tern usually lays two eggs; in a few instances I found only one, and I concluded that no more had been laid, as it contained a chick, which would not have been there had the Great Gull ever visited the nest. The eggs measure two inches and six-eighths in length, by one inch and six and a half eighths in breadth, and are rather sharp at the smaller end. They have a pale yellowish ground colour, irregularly spotted with dark umber and faint purplish marks, dispersed all over but not close. The eggs, like those of the other species, afford good eating.

I never saw the young of this bird while small, and cannot speak of the changes which they undergo from their first state until autumn. Then, however, they greatly resemble the young of the Sandwich Tern, their colour being on the upper parts of a dark greyish-brown, transversely marked with umber, and on the lower dull white. While in this plumage, they keep by themselves, in flocks of fifty or more individuals, and remain separated from the old birds until spring, when they have acquired the full beauty of their plumage, although they appear rather inferior in size.

My surprise at finding this species breeding in Labrador was increased by the circumstance of its being of rare occurrence at any season along the coasts of our Middle and Eastern Districts. Nor does it become abundant until you reach the shores of North Carolina; beyond which it increases the farther south you proceed. It winters in the Floridas, and along the shores of the Mexican Gulf; but I never saw it far up the Mississippi. While on the coast of Newfoundland, on the 14th of August, I saw several individuals on their way southward, flying very high, and keeping up their remarkable cries.

The flesh of every species of Tern is oily, like that of the Gulls and Jagers, and the smallest hole made by shot affords an exit to the grease, which is apt to destroy the beauty of their elastic plumage, so that it is very difficult to preserve them, both on account of this circumstance, and of the quantity of oil that flows from their bill. In no species have I found this to be more remarkably the case than in the Cayenne Tern.

The figure of the Crab [Spider Crab] in the plate was introduced on account of its singularly bright red colour, which, when the animal is boiled, changes to pale yellow. It is rather common along the rocky shores of some of the Florida Keys, and is excellent eating.

[From *Ornithological Biography,* Vol. III, pp. 505-508, 509.]

THE CARACARA EAGLE

Polyborus vulgaris, Vieill.
Plate CLXI. Adult.

[Caracara, *Caracara cheriway,*
ssp *C. Cheriway audubonii* (Cassin)]

I was not aware of the existence of the Caracara or Brazilian Eagle in the United States, until my visit to the Floridas in the winter of 1831. On the 24th November of that year, in the course of an excursion near the town of St. Augustine, I observed a bird flying at a great elevation, and almost over my head. Convinced that it was unknown to me, and bent on obtaining it, I followed it nearly a mile, when I saw it sail towards the earth, making for a place where a group of Vultures were engaged in devouring a dead horse. Walking up to the horse, I observed the new bird alighted on it, and helping itself freely to the savoury meat beneath its feet; but it evinced a degree of shyness far greater than that of its associates, the Turkey Buzzards and Carrion Crows. I moved circuitously, until I came to a deep ditch, along which I crawled, and went as near to the bird as I possibly could; but finding the distance much too great for a sure shot, I got up suddenly, when the whole of the birds took to flight. The eagle, as if desirous of forming acquaintance with me, took a round and passed over me. I shot, but to my great mortification missed it. However it alighted a few hundred yards off, in an open savanna, on which I laid myself flat on the ground, and crawled towards it, pushing my gun before me, amid burs and mud-holes, until I reached the distance of about seventy-five yards from it, when I stopped to observe its attitudes. The bird did not notice me; he stood on a lump of flesh, tearing it to pieces, in the manner of a Vulture, until he had nearly swallowed the whole. Being now less occupied, he spied me, erected the feathers of his neck, and, starting up, flew away, carrying the remainder of his prey *in his talons.* I shot a second time, and probably touched him; for he dropped his burden, and made off in a direct course across the St. Sebastian River, with alternate sailings and flappings, somewhat in the manner of a Vulture, but more gracefully. He never uttered a cry, and I followed him wistfully with my eyes until he was quite out of sight.

The following day the bird returned, and was again among the Vultures, but at some distance from the carcass, the birds having been kept off by the dogs. I approached by the ditch, saw it very well, and watched its movements, until it arose, when once more I shot, but without effect. It sailed off in large circles, gliding in a very elegant manner, and now and then diving downwards and rising again.

Two days elapsed before it returned. Being apprised by a friend of this desired event, instead of going after it myself, I dispatched my assistant, who returned with it in little more than half an hour. I immediately began my drawing of it. The weather was sultry, the thermometer being at 89°; and, to my surprise, the vivid tints of the plumage were fading much faster than I had ever seen them in like circumstances, insomuch that Dr. Bell of Dublin, who saw it when fresh, and also when I was finishing the drawing twenty-four hours after, said he could scarcely believe it to be the same bird. How often have I thought of the changes which I have seen effected in the colours of the bill, legs, eyes, and even the plumage of birds, when looking on imitations which I was aware were taken from stuffed specimens, and which I well knew could not be accurate! The *skin,* when the bird was quite recent, was of a bright yellow. The bird was extremely lousy. Its stomach contained the remains of a bullfrog, numerous hard-shelled worms, and a quantity of horse and deer-hair. The skin was saved with great difficulty, and its plumage had entirely lost its original lightness of colouring. The deep red of the fleshy parts of the head had assumed a purplish livid hue, and the spoil scarcely resembled the coat of the living Eagle.

I made a double drawing of this individual, for the purpose of shewing all its feathers, which I hope will be found to be accurately represented.

Since the period when I obtained the specimen above mentioned, I have seen several others, in which no remarkable differences were

Plate CLXI. *Brasilian Caracara Eagle*

observed between the sexes, or in the general colouring. My friend Dr. Benjamin Strobel, of Charleston, South Carolina, who has resided on the west coast of Florida, procured several individuals for the Reverend John Bachman, and informed me that the species undoubtedly breeds in that part of the country, but I have never seen its nest. It has never been seen on any of the Keys along the eastern coast of that peninsula; and I am not aware that it has been observed any where to the eastward of the Capes of Florida.

The most remarkable difference with respect to habits, between these birds and the American Vultures, is the power which they possess of carrying their prey in their talons. They often walk about, and in the water, in search of food, and now and then will seize on a frog or a very young alligator with their claws, and drag it to the shore. Like the Vultures, they frequently spread their wings towards the sun, or in the breeze, and their mode of walking also resembles that of the Turkey Buzzard.

[From *Ornithological Biography,* Vol. II, pp. 350-352.]

THE YELLOW RED-POLL WARBLER

Sylvia petechia, Lath. [Palm Warbler, *Dendroica palmarum*]
Plate CLXIII. Adult and Young.

The Yellow Red-Poll Warbler, of which an old bird in summer and a young one fully fledged are represented in the plate, being abundant in East Florida, and especially in the neighbourhood of St. Augustine, the most prosperous town on the eastern coast of that peninsula, I hope you will not think it irrelevant to say a few words respecting that place, to whose inhabitants I am indebted for many acts of kindness.

To reach St. Augustine, the navigator has first to pass over a difficult sand-bar, which frequently changes its position; he then, however, finds a deep channel leading to a safe and commodious harbour. The appearance of the town is rather romantic, especially when the Spanish Fort, which is quite a monument of ancient archi-

Plate CLXIII. *Palm Warbler*

tecture, opens to the view. The place itself is quite Spanish, the streets narrow, the church not very remarkable, and the market-place the resort of numerous idlers, whether resident or from other parts. It is supplied with, I believe, the best fish in America, the "sheep-head" and "mullet" being the finest I have ever seen; and its immediate neighbourhood produces as good oranges as can any where be found. The country around is certainly poor, and although in an almost tropical climate, is by no means productive. When the United States purchased the peninsula from the Spanish Government, the representations given of it by Mr. Bartram and other poetical writers, were soon found greatly to exceed the reality. For this reason, many of the individuals who flocked to it, returned home or made their way towards other regions with a heavy heart; yet the climate during the winter months is the most delightful that could be imagined.

In the plate you will find a branch of the wild orange, with its flowers. I have already spoken of the tree at p. 260 [see below], to which I refer you. Whatever its original country may be *supposed* to be, the plant is to all appearance indigenous in many parts of Florida, not merely in the neighbourhood of plantations, but in the wildest portions of that wild country.

[From *Ornithological Biography*, Vol. II, p. 360.]

The Wild Orange Tree

Nothing can be more gladdening to the traveller, when passing through the uninhabited woods of East Florida, than the wild orange groves which he sometimes meets with. As I approached them, the rich perfume of the blossoms, the golden hue of the fruits, that hung on every twig, and lay scattered on the ground, and the deep green of the glossy leaves, never failed to produce the most pleasing effect on my mind. Not a branch has suffered from the pruning knife, and the graceful form of the trees retains the elegance it received from nature. Raising their tops into the open air, they allow the uppermost blossoms and fruits to receive the unbroken rays of the sun, which one might be tempted to think are conveyed from flower to flower, and from fruit to fruit, so rich and balmy are all. The pulp of these fruits quenches your thirst at once, and the very air you breathe in such a place refreshes and reinvigorates you. I have passed through groves of these orange trees fully a mile in extent. Their occurrence is a sure indication of good land, which in the south-eastern portion of that country is rather scarce. The Seminole Indians and poorer Squatters feed their horses on oranges, which these animals seem to eat with much relish. The immediate vicinity of a wild orange grove is of some importance to the planters, who have the fruits collected and squeezed in a horse mill. The juice is barrelled and sent to different markets, being in request as an ingredient in cooling drinks. The straight young shoots are cut and shipped in bundles, to be used as walking sticks.

[From *Ornithological Biography,* Vol. II, p. 260.]

THE AMERICAN COOT

Fulica americana, Gmel.
Plate CCXXXIX. Male.

[American Coot, *Fulica americana*]

From November until the middle of April, the Coots are extremely numerous in the southern parts of the Floridas, and the lower portions of Louisiana. At that season they are seen in flocks of several hundreds, following their avocations on all the secluded bayous, grassy lakes, and inlets, which are so plentiful in those countries; but after the period above mentioned none remain, and therefore it is certain none can breed there, although such is asserted by Mr. Bartram, who no doubt mistook the Common Gallinule for the Coot, that bird breeding in those places in considerable numbers. During the month of September, the Coot is also abundant on all the western waters, and its appearance in those districts being so much earlier than in the Floridas, is a sure indication of the inland course of its migrations. On the sea coast, in fact, it is comparatively rare.

Although the curious form of their feet, and the situation of their legs, might induce one to suppose these birds incapable of moving on land with ease, experience proves the contrary, for they not only walk with freedom, but can run with great speed when necessary.

Plate CCXXXIX. *American Coot*

They are accustomed to leave the water too, and resort to open lands on the margins of streams and lakes, for the purpose of feeding, both in the morning and in the evening. While ascending the Mississippi, being about fifty miles above New Orleans, on the 21st of March 1822, the weather cloudy, I had the pleasure of seeing about six or seven hundreds of these birds feeding on the grass of a savannah bordering the river. I took them while at some distance, for a great flock of Guinea Fowls. Their movements were brisk, they often struck at each other in the manner of the domestic fowl, and ran with surprising celerity. As I approached nearer, I plainly saw them nibble the tender grass, in the same manner as poultry; and having found a place of concealment behind a rise of the ground, I laid myself flat, and observed their motions at leisure; but during twenty minutes spent in that situation, I did not hear a single note from the flock. I fired among them, and killed five, on which the rest, after running a few steps, all rose and flew off with speed towards the river, mounted high in the air, came curving over me, their legs hanging behind, their wings producing a constant whir, and at length alighted on a narrow channel between the shore, where I was, and a small island. Following them with caution, I got sufficiently near to some of them to be able to see them leap from the water to seize the young leaves of the willows that overhung the shores. While swimming, they moved with ease, although not with much speed, and used a constantly repeated movement of the head and neck, corresponding with that of the feet. Now, twenty or thirty of them would close their ranks, and swim up the stream in a lengthened body, when they would disperse, and pick up the floating substances, not one of them diving all the time. On firing at a large group of them that had approached me, they started off in various directions, patting the water with their feet, and rushing with extended wings, for thirty or forty yards, but without actually flying. After this, they made towards the brushy shores, and disappeared for about a quarter of an hour. The rest of the birds, which were a few hundred yards off, scarcely took notice of the report of the gun; and before I left the place, they had returned to the shore, and walked into another savannah, where they probably remained until night. The next morning not a single Coot could I find while looking for them, for several miles along the river, and I concluded that they had left the place, and continued their migratory journey northward, this being about the beginning of the time of their general departure.

Whilst at General Hernandez's, in East Florida, I found the Coot abundant in every ditch, bayou, or pond. This was in December 1831, and in the next month I saw great flocks of them near the plantation of my friend John Bullow, Esq. Whilst on a visit to Spring Garden springs, at the head of the St. John's River, I observed them to be equally abundant along the grassy margins of the lagoons and lakes. On my return from the upper parts of that river to St. Augustine, on the 28th February, I saw large flocks of them already moving northward. They had suddenly become shy, and would rise before our boat, at a distance of a hundred yards or so, with apparently scarcely any difficulty, and fly in loose flocks at a considerable height, half a mile or more at a time, and without uttering a note. Indeed, the only sound I ever heard these birds utter, is a rough guttural note, somewhat resembling *cruck, cruck,* which they use when alarmed, or when chasing each other on the water in anger. I am doubtful whether our Coot cackles and cries by night and by day, as has been reported; on the other hand, I am pretty well assured that Gallinules and Rails of different species have been confounded with the Coot in this respect.

I never saw this species dive for food, and the only fish that I ever found in the many that I have opened, was very small minnows or fry, which I think they catch along the shallow edges of the water. Indeed, unless when wounded, our Coot feels great reluctance at immersing its body in the water; at all events, it has not the quickness of any of the diving birds, and rarely escapes the shot of a common flint gun while attempting to get away. When wounded it dives to some distance, but as soon as it reaches the grass or reeds, it contents itself with lying flat on the water, and thus swimming to the nearest shore, on reaching which it at once runs off and hides in the first convenient place. When undisturbed, it feeds both by day and by night, and as often on land as on the water. Its food consists of seeds, grasses, small fishes, worms, snails, and insects, and along with these it introduces into its stomach a good quantity of rather coarse sand.

The principal breeding places of this species are yet unknown to me. At Charleston it was supposed that it breeds in the neighbourhood of that city; but my friend Bachman while searching for their nests at the proper season, saw that the Common Gallinule was in fact the bird that had been taken for the Coot. My learned friend Nuttall mentions that a pair had bred in Fresh Pond near Boston, and that he there saw parents and young. Some travelling lumberers assured me that the Coot breeds in numbers in the lakes lying between Mars Hill in Maine and the St. Lawrence River; but I can find no authentic accounts of its nest having been found in any part of the United States, although some probably breed on the borders of our northern lakes.

In Louisiana, this species is named *Poule d'Eau,* which is also applied to *Rallus crepitans.* In all other parts of the Union, it is known by the names of Mud Hen and Coot. The appellation of "Flusterers" given to it by Mr. Lawson in his History of South Carolina, never came to my ear, during my visits to that State.

These birds are frequently caught in the nets placed across the bayous of the lakes in the neighbourhood of New Orleans, for the purpose of catching Blue-winged Teals and other Ducks. They come against them while flying, but if the hunter is not extremely quick they make their escape by nimbly scrambling up, using their bill and feet until they reach the outer part of the net, when they drop into the water like so many terapins. At times they congregate in vast numbers, and swim so closely that a hunter in my employ, while on

Lake Barataria, killed eighty at a single shot. They are extremely abundant in the New Orleans' markets during the latter part of autumn and in winter, when the negroes and the poorer classes purchase them to make "gombo." In preparing them for cooking, they skin them like rabbits instead of plucking them.

Both old and young birds differ considerably in size and weight. The male, from which I drew the figure in the plate, was procured at General Hernandez's, in East Florida, and was among the best of about thirty shot on one of my excursions there.

[From *Ornithological Biography,* Vol. III, pp. 291-294.]

SCHINZ'S SANDPIPER

Tringa Schinzii, Brehm.
Plate CCLXXVIII. Male and Female.

[White-rumped Sandpiper, *Erolia fuscicollis*]

Although I have met with this species at different times in Kentucky, and along our extensive shores, from the Floridas to Maine, as well as

Plate CCLXXVIII. *Schinz's Sandpiper*

on the coast of Labrador, I never found it breeding. Indeed, I have not met with it in the United States excepting in the latter part of autumn and in winter. Those procured in Labrador were shot in the beginning of August, and were all young birds, apparently about to take their departure. My drawing of the two individuals represented in the plate was made at St. Augustine in East Florida, where I procured them on the 2d December 1831. I have always found these birds gentle and less shy than any other species of the genus. They fly at a considerable height with rapidity, deviating alternately to either side, and plunge toward the ground in a manner somewhat resembling that of the Solitary Sandpiper. When accidentally surprised, they start with a repeated *weet,* less sonorous than that of the bird just mentioned. They search for food along the margins of pools, creeks and rivers, or by the edges of sand-bars, and mix with other species.

[From *Ornithological Biography,* Vol. III, p. 529.]

THE HERRING GULL

Larus argentatus, Brunn. [Herring Gull, *Larus argentatus*]
Plate CCXCI. Male.

The Herring Gull has a greater range of migration along our coast and in the interior than any other American species. I have found it on our great lakes, and on the Ohio, Missouri and Mississippi, down to the Gulf of Mexico, during the autumnal months, and in winter along the shores of the latter, and all our eastern coasts. It may be said to be resident in the United States, as it breeds from off Boston to Eastport in Maine; but the greater number go farther north. We found the nests of some on the bare rocks of the Seal Islands off Labrador, but not on the coast itself. They were composed of dry plants and moss brought from the mainland. The birds kept by themselves, and appeared to be completely mastered by the Great Black-backed Gulls. On our return we saw old and young on the northern

Plate CCXCI. *Herring Gull*

coast of Newfoundland, and on the different bays over which we passed.

I have represented an adult male, but not one of the largest, and a young bird shot in winter, which I have placed on a bunch of Racoon oysters, where it was standing when shot.

[From *Ornithological Biography,* Vol. III, pp. 592-593.]

RUDDY DUCK

Fuligula rubida, Bonap.
Plate CCCXLIII. Male, Female, and Young.

[Ruddy Duck,
Oxyura jamaicensis]

Look at this plate, Reader, and tell me whether you ever saw a greater difference between young and old, or between male and female, than is apparent here. You see a fine old male in the livery of the breeding season, put on as it were expressly for the purpose of pleasing the female for a while. The female has never been figured before; nor, I believe, has any representation been given of the young

Plate CCCXLIII. *Ruddy Duck*

in the autumnal plumage. Besides these, you have here the young male at the approach of spring.

The Ruddy Duck is by no means a rare species in the United States; indeed I consider it quite abundant, especially during the winter months, in the Peninsula of Florida, where I have shot upwards of forty in one morning. In our Eastern Districts they make their appearance early in September, and are then plentiful from Eastport to Boston, in the markets of which, as well as of New York, I have seen them. On the Ohio and Mississippi they arrive about the same period; and I have no doubt that they will be found breeding in all our Western Territories, as soon as attention is paid to such matters as the searching for nests with the view of promoting science, or of domesticating birds which might prove advantageous to the husbandman. . . .

The flight of the Ruddy Duck is rapid, with a whirring sound, occasioned by the concave form of the wings and their somewhat broad ends, the whistling sound produced by other species having more pointed and stiffer quills, not being heard in this, or only in a very slight degree. They rise from the water with considerable difficulty, being obliged to assist themselves with their broad webbed feet, and to run as it were on the surface for several yards, always against the breeze, when it blows smartly. The strength of the muscles of their feet enables them to spring from the ground at once. When they are fairly on wing, they fly in the same manner as most of our travelling ducks, sustain themselves with ease, and are apt to remove to great distances. They alight on the water more heavily than most others that are not equally flattened and short in the body; but they move on that element with ease and grace, swimming deeply immersed, and procuring their food altogether by diving, at which they are extremely expert. They are generally disposed to keep under the lee of shores on all occasions. When swimming without suspicion of danger, they carry the tail elevated almost perpendicularly, and float lightly on the water; but as soon as they are alarmed, they immediately sink deeper, in the manner of the Anhinga, Grebes, and Cormorants, sometimes going out of sight without leaving a ripple on the water. On small ponds they often dive and conceal themselves among the grass along the shore, rather than attempt to escape by flying, to accomplish which with certainty they would require a large open space. I saw this very often when on the plantation of General Hernandez in East Florida. If wounded, they dived and hid in the grass; but, as the ponds there were shallow, and had the bottom rather firm, I often waded out and pursued them. Then it was that I saw the curious manner in which they used their tail when swimming, employing it now as a rudder, and again with a vertical motion; the wings being also slightly opened, and brought into action as well as the feet. They are by no means shy, for I have often waded toward them with my gun until very near them, when I cared not about shooting them, but was on the look-out for a new Rail or Gallinule, along the margin of the ponds. They are often seen in company with Teals, Scaup Ducks, Gadwalls, Shovellers, and Mallards, with all of which they seem to agree.

My opinion that the males of this species lose the brightness of their spring dress before they return to us in autumn, is founded on the occurrence of multitudes of males at that season destitute of the garb in question, and my examination of many for the purpose of determining their sex and ascertaining that they were old birds. In February 1832, I saw immense flocks of Ruddy Ducks about an hundred miles up the St. John's in Florida. They would start from the water, as our schooner advanced under sail, patting it with their feet, so as to make a curious and rather loud noise, somewhat resembling the fall of hailstones on the shingles. Their notes are uttered in a rather low tone and very closely resemble those of the female Mallard. They afford good eating when fat and young, and especially when they have been feeding for some weeks on fresh waters, where their food generally consists of the roots and blades of such grasses as spring from the bottom of rivers and ponds, as well as of the seeds of many gramineae. When on salt marshes, they eat small univalve shells, fiddlers, and young crabs, and on the sea-coast, they devour fry of various sorts. Along with their food, they swallow great quantities of sand or gravel.

At St. Augustine, in Florida, I shot a young bird of this species immediately under the walls of the fort. Although wounded severely and with one of its legs broken close to the body, it dived at once. My Newfoundland dog leaped into the water, and on reaching the spot where the bird had disappeared, dived also, and in a few moments came up with the poor thing in his mouth. When the dog approached I observed that the duck had seized his nose with its bill; and when I laid hold of it, it tried to bite me also. I have found this species hard to kill, and when wounded very tenacious of life, swimming and diving at times to the last gasp.

In the Fauna Boreali-Americana, the tail of the Ruddy Duck is said to be composed of sixteen feathers, and in Nuttall's Manual of twenty; but the number is eighteen.

[From *Ornithological Biography,* Vol. IV, pp. 326-328.]

THE BROWN PELICAN

Pelecanus fuscus, Linn.
Plate CCLI. Male.

[Brown Pelican,
Pelecanus occidentalis]

The Brown Pelican, which is one of the most interesting of our American birds, is a constant resident in the Floridas, where it resorts to the Keys and the salt-water inlets, but never enters fresh-water streams, as the White Pelican is wont to do. It is rarely seen farther eastward than Cape Hatteras, but is found to the south far beyond the limits of the United States. Within the recollection of persons still living, its numbers have been considerably reduced, so much indeed that in the inner Bay of Charleston, where twenty or thirty years ago it was quite abundant, very few individuals are now seen, and these chiefly during a continuance of tempestuous weather. There is a naked bar, a few miles distant from the main land, between Charleston and the mouth of the Santee, on which my friend John Bachman some years ago saw a great number of these birds, of which he procured several; but at the present day, few are known to breed farther east than the salt-water inlets running parallel to the coast of Florida, forty or fifty miles south of St. Augustine, where I for the first time met with this Pelican in considerable numbers.

My friend John Bullow, Esq. took me in his barge to visit the Halifax, which is a large inlet, and on which we soon reached an island where the Brown Pelicans had bred for a number of years, but where, to my great disappointment, none were then to be seen. The next morning, being ten or twelve miles farther down the stream, we entered another inlet, where I saw several dozens of these birds perched on the mangroves, and apparently sound asleep. I shot at them from a very short distance, and with my first barrel brought two to the water, but although many of them still remained looking at us, I could not send the contents of my second barrel to them, as the shot had unluckily been introduced into it before the powder. They all flew off one after another, and still worse, as the servants approached those which had fallen upon the water, they also flew away.

On arriving at the Keys of Florida, on board the Marion Revenue Cutter, I found the Pelicans pretty numerous. They became more abundant the farther south we proceeded, and I procured specimens at different places, but nowhere so many as at Key West. There you would see them flying within pistol-shot of the wharfs, the boys frequently trying to knock them down with stones, although I believe they rarely succeed in their efforts. The Marion lay at anchor several days at a short distance from this island, and close to another. Scarcely an hour of daylight passed without our having Pelicans around us, all engaged at their ordinary occupations, some fishing, some slumbering as it were on the bosom of the ocean, or on the branches of the mangroves. This place and all around for about forty miles, seemed to be favourite resorts of these birds; and as I had excellent opportunities of observing their habits, I consider myself qualified to present you with some account of them.

The flight of the Brown Pelican, though to appearance heavy, is remarkably well sustained, that bird being able not only to remain many hours at a time on wing, but also to mount to a great height in the air to perform its beautiful evolutions. Their ordinary manner of proceeding, either when single or in flocks, is by easy flappings and sailings alternating at distances of from twenty to thirty yards, when they glide along with great speed. They move in an undulated line, passing at one time high, at another low, over the water or land, for they do not deviate from their course on coming upon a key or a point of land. When the waves run high, you may see them "troughing," as the sailors say, or directing their course along the hollows. While on wing they draw in their head between their shoulders, stretch out their broad webbed feet to their whole extent, and proceed in perfect silence.

When the weather is calm, and a flood of light and heat is poured down upon nature by the genial sun, they are often, especially during

Plate CCLI. *Brown Pelican*

the love season, seen rising in broad circles, flock after flock, until they attain a height of perhaps a mile, when they gracefully glide on constantly expanded wings, and course round each other, for an hour or more at a time, after which, in curious zigzags, and with remarkable velocity, they descend towards their beloved element, and settle on the water, on large sand-bars or on mangroves. It is interesting beyond description to observe flocks of Brown Pelicans thus going through their aerial evolutions.

Now, Reader, look at those birds standing on their strong column-like legs, on that burning sand-bar. How dexterously do they wield that great bill of theirs, as they trim their plumage! Now along each broad quill it passes, drawing it out and displaying its elasticity; and now with necks stretched to their full length, and heads elevated, they direct its point in search of the insects that are concealed along their necks and breasts. Now they droop their wings for a while, or stretch them alternately to their full extent; some slowly lie down on the sand, others remain standing, quietly draw their head over their broad shoulders, raise one of their feet, and placing their bill on their back, compose themselves to rest. There let them repose in peace. Had they alighted on the waters, you might have seen them, like a fleet at anchor, riding on the ever-rolling billows as unconcernedly as if on shore. Had they perched on yon mangroves, they would have laid themselves flat on the branches, or spread their wings to the sun or the breeze, as Vultures are wont to do.

But see, the tide is advancing; the billows chase each other towards the shores; the mullets joyful and keen leap along the surface, as they fill the bays with their multitudes. The slumbers of the Pelicans are over; the drowsy birds shake their heads, stretch upon their mandibles and pouch by way of yawning, expand their ample wings, and simultaneously soar away. Look at them as they fly over the bay; listen to the sound of the splash they make as they drive their open bills, like a pocknet, into the sea, to scoop up their prey; mark how they follow that shoal of porpoises, and snatch up the frightened fishes that strive to escape from them. Down they go, again and again. What voracious creatures they are!

The Brown Pelicans are as well aware of the time of each return of the tide, as the most watchful pilots. Though but a short time before they have been sound asleep, yet without bell or other warning, they suddenly open their eyelids, and all leave their roosts, the instant when the waters, which have themselves reposed for a while, resume their motion. The Pelicans possess a knowledge beyond this, and in a degree much surpassing that of man with reference to the same subject: they can judge with certainty of the changes of weather. Should you see them fishing all together, in retired bays, be assured, that a storm will burst forth that day; but if they pursue their finny prey far out at sea, the weather will be fine, and you also may launch your bark and go to the fishing. Indeed, most sea-birds possess the same kind of knowledge, as I have assured myself by repeated observation, in a degree corresponding to their necessities; and the best of all prognosticators of the weather, are the Wild Goose, the Gannet, the Lestris, and the Pelican.

This species procures its food on wing, and in a manner quite different from that of the White Pelican. A flock will leave their resting place, proceed over the waters in search of fish, and when a shoal is perceived, separate at once, when each, from an elevation of from fifteen to twenty-five feet, plunges in an oblique and somewhat winding direction, spreading to the full stretch its lower mandible and pouch, as it reaches the water, and suddenly scoops up the object of its pursuit, immersing the head and neck, and sometimes the body, for an instant. It immediately swallows its prey, rises on wing, dashes on another fish, seizes and devours it, and thus continues, sometimes plunging eight or ten times in a few minutes, and always with unerring aim. When gorged, it rests on the water for a while, but if it has a brood, or a mate sitting on her eggs, it flies off at once towards them, no matter how heavily laden it may be. The generally received idea that Pelicans keep fish or water in their pouch, to convey them to their young, is quite erroneous. The water which enters the pouch when it is immersed, is immediately forced out between the partially closed mandibles, and the fish, unless larger than those on which they usually feed, is instantly swallowed, to be afterwards disgorged for the benefit of the young, either partially macerated, or whole, according to the age and size of the latter. Of all this I have satisfied myself, when within less than twenty yards of the birds as they were fishing; and I never saw them fly without the pouch being closely contracted towards the lower mandible. Indeed, although I now much regret that I did not make the experiment when I had the means of doing so, I doubt very much if a Pelican could fly at all with its burden so much out of trim, as a sailor would say.

They at times follow the porpoise, when that animal is in pursuit of prey, and as the fishes rise from the deep water towards the surface, come in cunningly for their share, falling upon the frightened shoal, and seizing one or more, which they instantly gobble up. But one of the most curious traits of the Pelican is, that it acts unwittingly as a sort of purveyor to the Gulls just as the Porpoise acts toward itself. The black-headed Gull of Wilson, which is abundant along the coast of the Floridas in spring and summer, watches the motions of the Pelicans. The latter having plunged after a shoal of small fishes, of which it has caught a number at a time, in letting off the water from amongst them, sometimes allows a few to escape; but the Gull at that instant alights on the bill of the Pelican, or on its head, and seizes the fry at the moment they were perhaps congratulating themselves on their escape. This every body on board the Marion observed as well as myself, while that vessel was at anchor in the beautiful harbour of Key West, so that it is not again necessary for me to lay before you a certificate with numerous signatures. To me such sights were always highly interesting, and I doubt if in the course of my endeavours to amuse you, I ever felt greater pleasure than I do at this moment, when, with my journal at my side, and the Gulls and Pelicans in my mind's eye as distinctly as I could wish, I ponder on the faculties which Nature has bestowed on animals which we merely consider as possessed of instinct. How little do we yet know of the operations of the Divine Power! On the occasions just mentioned, the Pelicans did not manifest the least anger towards the Gulls. It is said that the Frigate Pelican or Man-of-war Bird, forces the Brown Pelican to disgorge its food, but of this I never saw an instance; nor do I believe it to be the case, considering the great strength and powerful bill of the Pelican compared with those of the other bird. Indeed, if I had been told that when the Frigate Bird assails the Pelican, the latter opens its large pouch and swallows it entire, I might as soon have believed the one story as the other. But of this more anon, when we come to the habits of the bird in question.

On the ground this species is by no means so active, for it walks heavily, and when running, which it now and then does while in play, or during courtship, it looks extremely awkward, as it then stretches out its neck, partially extends its wings, and reels so that one might imagine it ready to fall at each step. If approached when wounded and on the water, it swims off with speed, and when overtaken, it suddenly turns about, opens its large bill, snaps it violently several times in succession, causing it to emit a smart noise in the manner of owls, strikes at you, and bites very severely. While I was at Mr. Bullow's, his Negro hunter waded after one whose wing had been broken. The Pelican could not be seized without danger, and I was surprised to see the hunter draw his butcher's knife, strike the long blade through the open pouch of the bird, hook it, as it were, by the lower mandible, and at one jerk swing it up into the air with extreme dexterity, after which he broke its neck and dragged it ashore.

The pouch measures from six to ten inches in depth, according to the age of the bird after the first moult. The superb male whose portrait is before you, and which was selected from among a great number, had it about the last mentioned size, and capable of holding a gallon of water, were the mandibles kept horizontal. This membrane is dried and used for keeping snuff, gunpowder and shot. When fresh it may be extended so as to become quite thin and transparent, like a bladder.

This Pelican seldom seizes fish that are longer than its bill, and the size of those on which it ordinarily feeds is much smaller. Indeed, several which I examined, had in the stomach upwards of a hundred fishes, which were only from two to three inches in length. That organ is long, slender, and rather fleshy. In some I found a great number of live blue-coloured worms, measuring two and a half inches in length, and about the thickness of a crow-quill. The gut is about the size of a swan's quill, and from ten to twelve feet in length, according to the age of the individual.

At all periods the Brown Pelican keeps in flocks, seldom amounting to more than fifty or sixty individuals of both sexes, and of different ages. At the approach of the pairing time, or about the middle of April, the old males and females separate from the rest, and remove to the inner keys or to large estuaries, well furnished with mangroves of goodly size. The young birds, which are much more numerous, remain along the shores of the open sea, unless during heavy gales.

Now let us watch the full grown birds. Some skirmishes have taken place, and the stronger males, by dint of loud snappings of their bill, some hard tugs of the neck and head, and some heavy beats with their wings, have driven away the weaker, which content themselves with less prized belles. The females, although quiet and gentle on ordinary occasions, are more courageous than the males, who, however, are assiduous in their attentions, assist in forming the nest, feed their mates while sitting, and even share the labour of incubation with them. Now see the mated birds, like the citizens of a newly laid out town in some part of our western country, breaking the dry sticks from the trees, and conveying them in their bills to yon mangrove isle. You see they place all their mansions on the south-west side, as if to enjoy the benefit of all the heat of that sultry climate. Myriads of mosquitoes buzz around them, and alight on the naked parts of their body, but this seems to give them no concern. Stick after stick is laid, one crossing another, until a strong platform is constructed. Now roots and withered plants are brought, with which a basin is formed for the eggs. Not a nest, you observe, is placed very low; the birds prefer the tops of the mangroves, although they do not care how many nests are on one tree, or how near the trees are to each other. The eggs, of which there are never more than three, are rather elliptical, and average three inches and one-eighth in length, by two inches and one-eighth in their greatest breadth. The shell is thick and rather rough, of a pure white colour, with a few faint streaks of a rosy tint, and blotches of a very pale hue, from the centre towards the crown of the egg.

The young are at first covered with cream-coloured down, and have the bill and feet disproportionately large. They are fed with great care, and so abundantly, that the refuse of their food, putrid and disgusting, lies in great quantities round them; but neither young nor old regard this, however offensive it may be to you. As the former grow the latter bring larger fish to them. At first the food is dropped in a well macerated state into their extended throats; afterwards the fish is given to them entire; and finally the parent birds merely place it on the edge of the nest. The young increase in size at a surprising rate. When half fledged they seem a mere mass of fat, their partially indurated bill has acquired considerable length, their wings droop by their sides, and they would be utterly unable to walk. The Vultures at this period often fall upon them and devour them in the absence of their parents. The Indians also carry them off in considerable numbers; and farther eastward, on the Halifax river, for instance, the Negroes kill all they can find, to make gombo soup of them during the winter. The crows, less powerful, but quite as cunning, suck the eggs; and many a young one which has accidentally fallen from the nest, is sure to be picked up by some quadruped, or devoured by the Shark or Balacuda. When extensive depredations have thus been made, the birds abandon their breeding places, and do not return to them. The Pelicans in fact are, year after year, retiring from the vicinity of man, and although they afford but very unsavoury food at any period of their lives, will yet be hunted beyond the range of civilization, just as our best of all game, the Wild Turkey, is now, until to meet with them the student of nature will have to sail round Terra del Fuego, while he may be obliged to travel to the Rocky Mountains before he find the other bird. Should you approach a settlement of the Pelicans and fire a few shots at them, they all abandon the place, and leave their eggs or young entirely at your disposal.

At all seasons, the Negroes of the plantations on the eastern coast of the Floridas lie in wait for the Pelicans. There, observe that fellow, who, with rusty musket, containing a tremendous charge of heavy shot, is concealed among the palmettoes, on the brink of a kind of embankment formed by the shelly sand. Now comes a flock of Pelicans, forcing their way against the breeze, unaware of the danger into which they rush, for there, a few yards apart, several Negroes crouch in readiness to fire; and let me tell you, good shots they are. Now a blast forces the birds along the shore; off goes the first gun, and down comes a Pelican; shot succeeds shot; and now the Negroes run up to gather the spoil. They skin the birds like so many racoons, cut off the head, wings, and feet; and should you come this way next year, you may find these remains bleached in the sun. Towards night, the sable hunters carry off their booty, marching along in Indian file, and filling the air with their extemporaneous songs. At home they perhaps salt, or perhaps smoke them; but in whatever way the Pelicans are prepared, they are esteemed good food by the sons of Africa.

The Brown Pelican is a strong and tough bird, although not so weighty as the white species. Its flesh is, in my opinion, always impure. It seems never satisfied with food, and it mutes so profusely, that not a spot of verdure can be seen on the originally glossy and deep-coloured mangroves on which it nestles; and I must say that, much as I admire it in some respects, I should be sorry to keep it near me as a pet.

During winter, when the mullets, a favourite fish with the Brown

Pelican, as it is with me, retires [sic] into deeper water, these birds advance farther to seaward, and may be seen over all parts of the Gulf of Mexico, and between the Florida Reefs and the opposite isles, especially during fine weather. They are very sensible to cold, and in this respect are tender birds. Now and then, at this season, they are seen on Lake Borgne and over Lake Pontchartrain, but never on the Mississippi beyond the rise of the tides, the space higher up being abandoned to the White Pelican. The keenness of their sight is probably equal to that of any hawk, and their hearing is also very acute. They are extremely silent birds, but when excited they utter a loud and rough grunt, which is far from musical. The young take two years to attain maturity. Several persons in the Floridas assured me that the Brown Pelicans breed at all seasons of the year; but as I observed nothing to countenance such an idea, I would give it as my opinion that they raise only one brood in the season.

Their bodies are greatly inflated by large air-cells; their bones, though strong, are very light; and they are tough to kill.

The Mangrove.

The species of Mangrove [Red Mangrove] represented in the plate is very abundant along the coast of Florida and on almost all the Keys, excepting the Tortugas. Those islands which are named Wet Keys are entirely formed of Mangroves, which raising their crooked and slender stems from a bed of mud, continue to increase until their roots and pendent branches afford shelter to the accumulating debris, when the earth is gradually raised above the surface of the water. No sooner has this taken place than the Mangroves in the central part of the island begin to decay, and in the course of time there is only an outer fringe or fence of trees, while the interior becomes overgrown with grass and low bushes. Meantime the Mangroves extend towards the sea, their hanging branches taking root wherever they come in contact with the bottom, and their seeds also springing up. I am at a loss for an object with which to compare these trees, in order to afford you an idea of them; yet if you will figure to yourself a tree reversed, and standing on its summit, you may obtain a tolerable notion of their figure and mode of growth. The stem, roots and branches are very tough and stubborn, and in some places the trees are so intertwined that a person might find it as easy to crawl over them as to make his way between them. They are evergreen, and their tops afford a place of resort to various species of birds at all seasons, while their roots and submersed branches give shelter to numberless testaceous mollusca and small fishes. The species represented is rarely observed on the coast of Florida of a greater height than twenty-five or thirty feet, and its average height is not above fifteen feet. The Land Mangrove [Black Mangrove], of which I have seen only a few, the finest of which were on Key West, is a tall tree, much larger and better shaped than the other, with narrower leaves and shorter fruits.

[From *Ornithological Biography*, Vol. III, pp. 376-384, 386.]

THE ORANGE-CROWNED WARBLER

Sylvia celata, Say.
Plate CLXXVIII. Male and Female.

[Orange-crowned Warbler,
Vermivora celata]

This species is seen in the company of *Sylvia coronata* and *Sylvia petechia,* both in the Southern States, where it passes the winter, and while crossing the Union, in early spring, on its way to those North-eastern Districts where it breeds. It leaves Louisiana, the Floridas, and the Carolinas, from the beginning to the end of April; is seen in the Middle States, about the 10th of May; and reaches the State of Maine and the British provinces by the end of that month. On its return, besides settling in the Southern States, it spreads over the provinces of Mexico, from whence individuals in spring migrate by the vast prairies, and along the shores of the western parts of the Union, entering Canada in that direction in the first days of June. The Orange-crowned Warbler is thus very widely distributed over North America. I met with none, however, between Halifax and Labrador, nor did I see one in the latter country.

In the summer months, it manifests a retiring disposition, keeping among the low brushwood that borders the rivers and lakes of the Northern Districts. While in the south, however, where it is rather

Plate CLXXVIII. *Orange-crowned Warbler*

common near the sea-shore, it is less cautious, and is seen, in considerable numbers, in the orange groves around the plantations, or even in the gardens, especially in East Florida. Like the *Sylvia petechia,* it plays about the piazzas, skipping on wing in front of the clapboarded house, in quest of its prey, which it expertly seizes without alighting, or without snapping its bill, except during the disputes that occur among the males, as the spring advances. You find it among the branches of the Pride-of-China, that ornaments the streets of the southern cities and villages, as well as on those bordering the roads. From these it descends into the smilaxes, rose-bushes, and other shrubs, all of which yield it food and shelter. At the approach of darkness, it enters among the foliage of the evergreen wild orange and wild peach, where, with the *Sylvia petechia* and *Sylvia coronata,* it quietly passes the night. Its principal food consists of insects, partly caught on the wing, but chiefly along the branches and twigs, where the little depredator seeks them out with great activity.

The flight of this bird is short, rather low, and is performed by gently curved glidings. When ascending, however, it becomes as it were uncertain and angular.

The Orange-crowned Warbler breeds in the eastern parts of Maine, and in the British provinces of New Brunswick and Nova Scotia. Its nest is composed of lichens detached from the trunks of trees, intermixed with short bits of fine grass, and is lined with delicate fibrous roots and a proportionally large quantity of feathers. The eggs, which are from four to six, are of a pale green colour, sprinkled with small black spots. The nest is placed not more than from three to five feet from the ground between the smaller forks of some low fir tree. Only one brood is raised in the season, and the birds commence their journey southward from the middle of August to the beginning of September.

In autumn, it nearly loses the orange spot on its head, there being then merely a dull reddish patch, which is only seen on separating the feathers. In the breeding season, the part in question becomes as bright as you see it in the plate, in which are represented a pair of these birds, on a twig of the great huckleberry, which grows in East Florida.

The Huckleberry

This plant . . . is very abundant in the pine barrens of the Floridas, where it is in full flower in February, and attains a height of from four to eight feet.

[From *Ornithological Biography,* Vol. II, pp. 449-450, 451.]

John James Audubon

THE SANDERLING

Tringa arenaria, Bonap. [Sanderling, *Crocethia alba*]
Plate CCXXX. Male and Female.

Although the Sanderling extends its rambles along our Atlantic shores, from the eastern extremities of Maine to the southernmost Keys of the Floridas, it is only an autumnal and winter visitor. It arrives in the more Eastern Districts about the 1st of August, on the sea-shores of New York and New Jersey rarely before the 10th of August, and seldom reaches the extensive sand-banks of East Florida previous to the month of November. Along the whole of this extended coast, it is more or less abundant, sometimes appearing in bands composed of a few individuals, and at times in large flocks, but generally mingling with other species of small shore-birds. Thus I have seen Turnstones and Knots mixed with the Sanderlings, but in such cases they are perhaps wanderers, which have not succeeded in meeting with companions of their own species, that associate with the birds of which I here speak.

The Sanderling obtains its food principally by probing the moist sands of the sea-shores with its bill held in an oblique position. At every step it inserts this instrument with surprising quickness, to a greater or less depth, according to the softness of the sand, sometimes introducing it a quarter of an inch, sometimes to the base. The holes thus made may be seen on the borders of beaches, when the tide is fast receding, in rows of twenty, thirty, or more; in certain spots less numerous; for it appears that when a place proves unproductive of the food for which they are searching, they very soon take to their wings and remove to another, now and then in so hurried a manner that one might suppose they had been suddenly frightened. The contents of the stomach of those which I shot while thus occupied, were slender sea-worms, about an inch in length, together with minute shell-fish and gravel. At other times, when they were seen following the receding waves, and wading up to the belly in the returning waters, I found in them small shrimps and other crustacea.

In their flight the Sanderlings do not perform so many evolutions as Sandpipers usually display. They generally alight about a hundred yards of the place from which they started, and run for a yard or so, keeping their wings partially extended. They move on the sand with great activity, running so as to keep pace with a man walking at a moderate rate. Their flight is rapid and straighter than that of other small species, and when on wing they seldom exhibit each surface of the body alternately, as many others are wont to do.

I have thought that the migrations of this bird are carried on under night; but of this I am by no means certain, although I observed some small flocks, composed of a few dozen individuals, crossing the Gulf of St. Lawrence, at a little height over the water, in the month of June. The lateness of the season induced me to hope that I might find some nests of the Sanderling on the coast of Labrador; but in this I was disappointed, although some young birds were seen at Bras d'Or, in little parties of four or five individuals. This was early in August, and they were already on their way southward.

The Sanderling affords good eating, especially the young, and the sportsman may occasionally kill six or seven at a shot, provided he fires the moment the flock has alighted, for immediately after the birds spread abroad in search of food.

The female may easily be distinguished from the male, by her superior size; but in the colouring of birds of both sexes, I have observed as much difference as in the Turnstone. Even during winter, some are more or less marked with black and brownish-red, while others, which, however, I easily ascertained to be younger birds, were of an almost uniform light grey above, each feather edged with dull

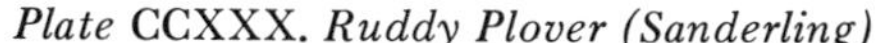

Plate CCXXX. *Ruddy Plover (Sanderling)*

white; but in all those which I have examined, whether old birds in the full spring or summer dress, in which I have shot some in May, in the Middle Districts, or young birds in autumn and during winter, I have seen no difference in the colours of the bill, legs, and toes. My plate of this species represents two birds in winter plumage, which were obtained in East Florida in the month of December. The figure of a fine male, which, being on another sheet of paper, was overlooked during my absence from London, you will find in Plate CCLXXXV of "The Birds of America."

[From *Ornithological Biography*, Vol. III, pp. 231-232.]

ANHINGA OR SNAKE-BIRD

Plotus Anhinga, Linn. [Anhinga, *Anhinga anhinga*]
Plate CCCXVI. Male and Female.

Many writers have described what they have been pleased to call the habits of the Anhinga; nay, some have presumed to offer comments upon them, and to generalize and form theories thereon, or even to inform us gravely and oracularly what they ought to be, when the basis of all their fancies was merely a dried skin and feathers appended. Leaving these ornithologists for the present to amuse themselves in their snug closets, I proceed to detail the real habits of this curious bird, as I have observed and studied them in Nature.

The Snake-Bird is a constant resident in the Floridas, and the lower parts of Louisiana, Alabama, and Georgia. Few remain during winter in South Carolina, or in any district to the eastward of that State; but some proceed as far as North Carolina in spring, and breed along the coast. I have found it in Texas in the month of May, on the waters of Buffalo Bayou, and the St. Jacinto River, where it breeds, and where, as I was told, it spends the winter. It rarely ascends the Mississippi beyond the neighbourhood of Natchez, from which most of the individuals return to the mouths of that great stream, and the numerous lakes, ponds, and bayous in its vicinity, where I have observed the species at all seasons, as well as in the Floridas.

Plate CCCXVI. *Black-bellied Darter (Anhinga)*

Being a bird which, by its habits, rarely fails to attract the notice of the most indifferent observer, it has received various names. The Creoles of Louisiana, about New Orleans, and as far up the Mississippi as Pointe Coupé, call it "Bec à Lancette," on account of the form of its bill; whilst at the mouths of the river it bears the name of "Water Crow." In the southern parts of Florida, it is called the "Grecian Lady," and in South Carolina it is best known by the name of "Cormorant." Yet in all these parts, it bears also the name of "Snake-Bird;" but it is nowhere with us called the "Black-bellied Darter," which, by the way, could only be with strict propriety applied to the adult male.

Those which, on the one hand, ascend the Mississippi, and, on the other, visit the Carolinas, arrive at their several places of resort early in April, in some seasons even in March, and there remain until the beginning of November. Although this bird is occasionally seen in the immediate vicinity of the sea, and at times breeds not far from it, I never met with an individual fishing in salt water. It gives a decided preference to rivers, lakes, bayous, or lagoons in the interior, always however in the lowest and most level parts of the country. The more retired and secluded the spot, the more willingly does the Snake-Bird remain about it. Sometimes indeed I have suddenly come on some in such small ponds, which I discovered by mere accident, and in parts of woods so very secluded, that I was taken by surprise on seeing them. The Floridas therefore are peculiarly adapted for this species, as there the torpid waters of the streams, bayous, and lakes are most abundantly supplied with various species of fish, reptiles, and insects, while the temperature is at all seasons congenial, and their exemption from annoyance almost unparalleled. Wherever similar situations occur in other parts of the Southern States, there the Anhingas are met with in numbers proportioned to the extent of the favourable localities. It is very seldom indeed that any are seen on rapid streams, and more especially on clear water, a single instance of such an occurrence being all that I have observed. Wherever you may chance to find this bird, you will perceive that it has not left itself without the means of escape; you will never find one in a pond or bayou completely enclosed by tall trees, so as to obstruct its passage; but will observe that it generally prefers ponds or lakes, surrounded by deep and almost impenetrable morasses, and having a few large trees growing out of the water near their centre, from the branches of which they can easily mark the approach of an enemy, and make their escape in good time. Unlike the Fish-hawk and Kings-fisher, the Anhinga however never plunges or dives from an eminence in procuring its prey, although from its habit of occasionally dropping in silence to the water from its perch, for the purpose of afterwards swimming about and diving in the manner of the Cormorant, some writers have been led to believe that it does so.

The Black-bellied Darter, all whose names I shall use, for the purpose of avoiding irksome repetitions, may be considered as indefinitely gregarious; by which I mean that you may see eight or more together at times, during winter especially, or only two, as in the breeding season. On a few occasions, whilst in the interior of the southernmost parts of Florida, I saw about thirty individuals on the same lake. While exploring the St. John's River of that country in its whole length, I sometimes saw several hundreds together. I procured a great number on that stream, on the lakes in its neighbourhood, and also on those near the plantation of Mr. Bulow, on the eastern side of the Peninsula. I observed that the young Darters, as well as those of the Cormorants, Herons, and many other birds, kept apart from the old individuals, which they however joined in spring, when they had attained their full beauty of plumage.

The Anhinga is altogether a diurnal bird, and, like the Cormorant, is fond of returning to the same roosting place every evening about dusk, unless prevented by molestation. At times I have seen from three to seven alight on the dead top branches of a tall tree, for the purpose of there spending the night; and this they repeated for several weeks, until on my having killed some of them and wounded others, the rest abandoned the spot, and after several furious contests with a party that roosted about two miles off, succeeding in establishing themselves among them. At such times they seldom sit very near each other, as Cormorants do, but keep at a distance of a few feet or yards, according to the nature of the branches. Whilst asleep, they stand with the body almost erect, but never bend the tarsus so as to apply it in its whole length, as the Cormorant does; they keep their head snugly covered among their scapulars, and at times emit a wheezing sound, which I supposed to be produced by their breathing. In rainy weather they often remain roosted the greater part of the day, and on such occasions they stand erect, with their neck and head stretched upwards, remaining perfectly motionless, as if to allow the water to glide off their plumage. Now and then, however, they suddenly ruffle their feathers, violently shake themselves, and again compressing their form, resume their singular position.

Their disposition to return to the same roosting places is so decided that, when chased from their places of resort, they seldom fail to betake themselves to them during the day; and in this manner they may easily be procured with some care. Whilst at Mr. Bulow's, I was almost daily in the habit of visiting a long, tortuous, bayou, many miles in extent, which at that season (winter) was abundantly supplied with Anhingas. There the Otter, the Alligator, and many species of birds, found an ample supply of food; and as I was constantly watching them, I soon discovered a roosting place of the Snake-Birds, which was a large dead tree. I found it impossible to get near them either by cautiously advancing in the boat, or by creeping among the briars, canes, and tangled palmettoes which profusely covered the banks. I therefore paddled directly to the place, accompanied by my faithful and sagacious Newfoundland dog. At my approach the birds flew off towards the upper parts of the stream, and as I knew that they might remain for hours, I had a boat sent after them with orders to the Negroes to start all that they could see. Dragging up my little bark, I then hid myself among the tangled plants, and, with my eyes bent on the dead tree, and my gun in readiness, I remained until I saw the beautiful bird alight and gaze around to see if all was right. Alas! it was not aware of its danger, but, after a few moments, during which I noted its curious motions, it fell dead into the water, while the reverberations consequent on the discharge of my gun alarmed the birds around, and by looking either up or down the bayou I could see many Anhingas speeding away to other parts. My dog, as obedient as the most submissive of servants, never stirred until ordered, when he would walk cautiously into the water, swim up to the dead bird, and having brought it to me, lie down gently in his place. In this manner, in the course of one day I procured fourteen of these birds, and wounded several others. I may here at once tell you that all the roosting places of the Anhinga which I have seen were over the water, either on the shore or in the midst of some stagnant pool; and this situation they seemed to select because there they can enjoy the first gladdening rays of the morning sun, or bask in the blaze of its noontide splendour, and also observe with greater ease the approach of their enemies, as they betake themselves to it after feeding, and remain there until hunger urges them to fly off. There, trusting to the extraordinary keenness of their beautiful bright eyes in spying the marauding sons of the forest, or the not less dangerous enthusiast, who, probably like yourself, would venture through mud and slime up to his very neck, to get within rifle shot of a bird so remarkable in form and manners, the Anhingas, or "Grecian Ladies," stand erect, with their wings and tail fully or partially spread out in the sunshine, whilst their long slender necks and heads are thrown as it were in every direction by the most curious and sudden jerks and bendings. Their bills are open, and you see that the intense heat of the atmosphere induces them to suffer their gular pouch to hang loosely. What delightful sights and scenes these have been to me, good Reader! With what anxiety have I waded toward these birds, to watch their movements, while at the same time I cooled my overheated body, and left behind on the shores myriads of hungry sand-flies, gnats, mosquitoes, and ticks, that had annoyed me for hours! And oh! how great has been my pleasure when, after several failures, I have at last picked up the spotted bird, examined it with care, and then returned to the gloomy shore, to note my observations! Great too is my pleasure in now relating to you the results of my long personal experience, together with that of my excellent friend Dr. Bachman, who has transmitted his observations on this bird to me.

Wilson, I am inclined to think, never saw a live Anhinga; and the notes, furnished by Mr. Abbot of Georgia, which he has published, are very far from being correct. In the supplementary volumes of American Ornithology published in Philadelphia, the Editor, who visited the Floridas, added nothing of importance beyond giving more accurate measurements of a single specimen than Wilson had given from the stuffed skins from which he made his figures, and which were in the museum of that city.

The peculiar form, long wings, and large fan-like tail of the Anhinga, would at once induce a person looking upon it to conclude that it was intended by nature rather for protracted and powerful flight, than for spending as it does more than half of its time by day in the water, where its progress, one might suppose, would be greatly impeded by the amplitude of these parts. Yet how different from such a supposition is the fact? The Anhinga in truth is the very first of all fresh-water divers. With the quickness of thought it disappears beneath the surface, and that so as scarcely to leave a ripple on the spot; and when your anxious eyes seek around for the bird, you are astonished to find it many hundred yards distant, the head perhaps merely above water for a moment; or you may chance to perceive the bill alone gently cutting the water, and producing a line of wake not observable beyond the distance of thirty yards from where you are standing. With habits like these it easily eludes all your efforts to procure it. When shot at while perched, however severely wounded they may be, they fall at once perpendicularly, the bill downward, the wings and tail closed, and then dive and make their way under water to such a distance that they are rarely obtained. Should you, however, see them again, and set out in pursuit, they dive along the shores, attach themselves to roots of trees or plants by the feet, and so remain until life is extinct. When shot dead on the trees, they sometimes cling so firmly to the branches that you must wait some minutes before they fall.

The generally received opinion or belief that the Anhinga always swims with its body sunk beneath the surface is quite incorrect; for it does so only when in sight of an enemy, and when under no apprehension of danger it is as buoyant as any other diving bird, such as a Cormorant, a Merganser, a Grebe, or a Diver. This erroneous opinion has, however, been adopted simply because few persons have watched the bird with sufficient care. When it first observes an enemy, it immediately sinks its body deeper, in the manner of the birds just mentioned, and the nearer the danger approaches, the more does it sink, until at last it swims off with the head and neck only above the surface, when these parts, from their form and peculiar sinous motion, somewhat resemble the head and part of the body of a snake. It is in fact from this circumstance that the Anhinga has received the name of Snake-Bird. At such a time, it is seen constantly turning its head from side to side, often opening its bill as if for the purpose of inhaling a larger quantity of air, to enable it the better to dive, and remain under water so long that when it next makes its appearance it is out of your reach. When fishing in a state of security it dives precisely like a Cormorant, returns to the surface as soon as it has procured a fish or other article of food, shakes it, if it is not too large often throws it up into the air, and receiving it conveniently in the bill, swallows it at once, and recommences its search. But I doubt much if it ever seizes on anything that it cannot thus swallow whole.

They have the curious habit of diving under any floating substances, such as parcels of dead weeds or leaves of trees which have accidentally been accumulated by the winds or currents, or even the green slimy substances produced by putrefaction. This habit is continued by the species when in a perfect state of domestication, for I have seen one kept by my friend John Bachman thus diving when within a few feet of a quantity of floating rice-chaff, in one of the tide-ponds in the neighbourhood of Charleston. Like the Common Goose, it invariably depresses its head while swimming under a low bridge, or a branch or trunk of a tree hanging over the water. When it swims beneath the surface of the water, it spreads its wings partially, but does not employ them as a means of propulsion, and keeps its tail always considerably expanded, using the feet as paddles either simultaneously or alternately. . . .

The Anhinga is shy and wary when residing in a densely peopled part of the country, which, however, is rarely the case, as I have already mentioned; but when in its favourite secluded and peaceful haunts, where it has seldom or never been molested, it is easily approached and without difficulty procured; nay, sometimes one will remain standing in the same spot and in the same posture, until you have fired several bullets from your rifle at it. Its mode of fishing is not to plunge from a tree or stump in pursuit of its prey, but to dive while swimming in the manner of Cormorants and many other birds. Indeed, it could very seldom see a fish from above the surface of the turbid waters which it prefers.

It moves along the branches of trees rather awkwardly; but still it walks there, with the aid of its wings, which it extends for that purpose, and not unfrequently also using its bill in the manner of a Parrot. On the land, it walks and even runs with considerable ease, certainly with more expertness than the Cormorant, though much in the same style. But it does not employ its tail to aid it, for, on the contrary, it carries that organ inclined upwards, and during its progress from one place to another, the movements of its head and neck are continued. These movements, which, as I have said, resemble sudden jerkings of the parts to their full extent, become extremely graceful during the love season, when they are reduced to gentle curvatures. I must not forget to say, that during all these movements, the gular pouch is distended, and the bird emits rough guttural sounds. If they are courting on wing, however, in the manner of

Cormorants, Hawks, and many other birds, they emit a whistling note, somewhat resembling that of some of our rapacious birds, and which may be expressed by the syllables *eek, eek, eek,* the first loudest, and the rest diminishing in strength. When they are on the water, their call-notes so much resemble the rough grunting cries of the Florida Cormorant, that I have often mistaken them for the latter.

The flight of the Anhinga is swift, and at times well sustained; but like the Cormorants, it has the habit of spreading its wings and tail before it leaves its perch or the surface of the water, thus frequently affording the sportsman a good opportunity of shooting it. When once on wing, they can rise to a vast height, in beautiful gyrations, varied during the love-season by zigzag lines chiefly performed by the male, as he plays around his beloved. At times they quite disappear from the gaze, lost as it were, in the upper regions of the air; and at other times, when much lower, seem to remain suspended in the same spot for several seconds. All this while, and indeed as long as they are flying, their wings are directly extended, their neck stretched to its full length, their tail more or less spread according to the movements to be performed, being closed when they descend, expanded and declined to either side when they mount. During their migratory expeditions, they beat their wings at times in the manner of the Cormorant, and at other times sail like the Turkey Buzzard and some Hawks, the former mode being more frequently observed when they are passing over an extent of woodland, the latter when over a sheet of water. If disturbed or alarmed, they fly with continuous beats of the wings, and proceed with great velocity. As they find difficulty in leaving their perch without previously expanding their wings, they are also, when about to alight, obliged to use them in supporting their body, until their feet have taken a sufficient hold of the branch on which they desire to settle. In this respect, they exactly resemble the Florida Cormorant.

There are facts connected with the habits of birds which might afford a pretty good idea of the relative temperatures of different parts of the country during a given season; and those observed with regard to the Anhinga seem to me peculiarly illustrative of this circumstance. I have found the "Grecian Lady" breeding on St. John's River in East Florida, near Lake George, as early as the 23rd of February; having previously seen many of them caressing each other on the waters, and again carrying sticks, fresh twigs, and other matters, to form their nests, and having also shot females with the eggs largely developed. Now, at the same period, perhaps not a single Anhinga is to be seen in the neighbourhood of Natchez, only a few about New Orleans, in the eastern parts of Georgia, and the middle maritime portions of South Carolina. In Louisiana this bird breeds in April or May, and in South Carolina rarely before June, my friend Bachman having found eggs, and young just hatched, as late as the 28th of that month. In North Carolina, where only a few pairs breed, it is later by a fortnight.

I have already expressed my opinion that birds which thus breed so much earlier in one section of the country than in another, especially when at great distances, may, after producing one or even two broods, in the same year, still have time enough to proceed toward higher latitudes for the purpose of again breeding. Actual observations have moreover satisfied me that individuals of the same species produced in warm latitudes have a stronger disposition toward reproduction than those of more northern climates. This being the case, and most birds endowed with the power of migrating, having a tendency to exercise it, may we not suppose that the pair of Anhingas which bred on the St. John's in February, might be inclined to breed again either in South Carolina or in the neighbourhood of Natchez, several months after. But, as yet, I have not been able to adduce positive proof of the accuracy of this opinion. . . .

Like all other carnivorous and piscivorous birds, the Anhinga can remain days and nights without food, apparently without being much incommoded. When overtaken on being wounded, and especially if brought to the ground, it seems to regard its enemies without fear. On several occasions of this kind, I have seen it watch my approach, or that of my dog, standing as erect as it could under the pain of its wounds, with its head drawn back, its bill open, and its throat swelled with anger until, when at a sure distance, it would dart its head forward and give a severe wound. One which had thus struck at my dog's nose, hung to it until dragged to my feet over a space of thirty paces. When seized by the neck, they scratch severely with their sharp claws, and beat their wings about you with much more vigour than you would suppose they could possess. Having witnessed the singular means employed by this bird in making its escape on sudden emergencies, I will here relate an instance, which evinces a kind of reason. Whilst ascending the St. John's river in East Florida, along with Captain Piercy of the U.S. Navy, our boat was rowed into a circular basin of clear shallow water, having a sandy bottom; such places being found occasionally in that country, produced by the flowing of springs from the more elevated sandy parts into the muddy rivers and lakes. We entered the cove by passing between the branches of low trees, overhung by others of great height. The first object that attracted my attention was a female Anhinga perched on the opposite side of the cove, and, as I did not wish that it should be shot, we merely advanced towards it, when it began to throw its head about, and watch our motions. The place was small, and the enclosing trees high. Though it might have flown upwards and escaped, it remained perched, but evidently perturbed and apprehensive of danger. When the boat was at a short distance, it suddenly threw itself backward, cutting a somerset as it were, and, covered by the branches, darted straight through the tangled forest, and was soon out of sight. Never before nor since have I seen or heard of Anhingas flying through the woods.

[From *Ornithological Biography,* Vol. IV, pp. 137-143, 144-147, 149-150.]

THE RED-BACKED SANDPIPER

Tringa alpina, Linn. [Dunlin, *Erolia alpina*]
Plate CCXC. Male in Summer, and Adult in Winter.

In autumn and winter, this species is abundant along the whole range of our coast, wherever the shores are sandy or muddy, from Maine to the mouths of the Mississippi; but I never found one far inland. Sometimes they collect into flocks of several hundred individuals, and are seen wheeling over the water near the shores or over the beaches, in beautiful order, and now and then so close together as to afford an excellent shot, especially when they suddenly alight in a mass near the sportsman, or when, swiftly veering, they expose their lower parts at the same moment. On such occasions a dozen or more may be killed at once, provided the proper moment is chosen.

There seems to be a kind of impatience in this bird that prevents it from remaining any length of time in the same place, and you may see it scarcely alighted on a sand-bar, fly off without any apparent reason to another, where it settles, runs for a few moments, and again starts off on wing. When searching for food they run with great agility, following the retiring waves, and retreating as they advance, probing the wet sands, and picking up objects from their surface, ever jerking up the tail, and now and then uttering a faint cry, pleasant to the ear, and differing from the kind of scream which they emit while on wing.

When I was in the Floridas in winter, I found this species abundant, and my party shot a great number of them, on account of the fatness and juiciness of their flesh. They all appeared to have their plumage greyer than those shot in the Carolinas at the same season, and not one exhibited the least redness on the back, although that colour is so conspicuous in spring before they leave us for the north. They usually take their departure from the south about the first of

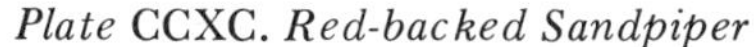

Plate CCXC. *Red-backed Sandpiper*

Plate CXXVI. *White-headed Eagle*

April, reach the Middle Districts by the fifteenth of that month, and in a few days assume their summer plumage. I have observed that at this season the male birds are frequently in the habit of raising their wings and running in that position for a few steps, when they close them, and nod to the nearest female. None of the other sex, however, seemed to take the least notice of this homage.

[From *Ornithological Biography,* Vol. III, p. 580.]

THE WHITE-HEADED EAGLE

Falco leucocephalus, Linn. [Bald Eagle,
Plate CXXVI. Young. *Haliaeetus leucocephalus*]

Although I have already given a long account of the adult of this species, in the first volume of my biographies, I have thought it necessary, not only to figure the young, but also to offer you some of the observations relative to the habits of this handsome and powerful bird, which I have collected in the course of my long rambles. These I select from among the many recorded in my journals, giving the preference to those which seem most likely to interest you.

St. Johns River, East Florida, 7th February 1832.—I observed four nests of the White-headed Eagle this day, while the United States' schooner Spark lay at anchor not far from the shore. They were at no great distance from each other, and all placed on tall live pine-trees. Our commander, Lieutenant Piercey of our Navy, having at that time little to do, as he lay waiting the flood-tide, a boat was manned, and several of us went on shore. On approaching the nearest nest, we saw two young birds standing erect on its edge, while their parents were perched on the branches above them. As we went nearer, the old ones flew off silently, while the young did not seem to pay the least attention to us, this being a part of the woods where probably no white man had ever before put his foot, and the Eaglets having as yet no experience of the barbarity of the race. The captain took the first shot: one of the birds was severely wounded, and tumbled half way from the nest towards the ground, when it recovered, flapped its wings, and suddenly sailed away until we lost sight of it as it flew into the woods. I marked its course, however. One of the sailors was told to shoot the other, which had not moved from its position; he missed it; and as I saw it make movements indicative of its surprise and fear, I fired, but wounded it so slightly in one pinion, that it was enabled to fly off in an irregular manner towards the river. This I judged was the first attempt it had ever made to fly. I followed its course with my eye, and after in vain waiting a long time for a shot at the old birds, I went in search of it, while the rest of the party pursued the other. After some time I reached our boat, and at the same instant was surprised to see the wounded bird perched on a low stump within half gun-shot. I fired, and the bird fell, but before I reached the spot, it flew off again and tumbled into the river, where, in this to it new and wonderful element, it flapped its wings, and made way so fast, that I took to the water and brought it ashore, my faithful Newfoundland dog Plato being on board, quite lamed by having brought me birds some days before from banks of *racoon oysters.* After all, it was necessary to knock the bird on the head, which done I returned to the party, none of whom had yet found their prey, they having disagreed as to the course it had taken. Being somewhat of a woodsman, I pointed towards the place where I thought the bird must be, and after a few hundred yards walking among palmettoes, Spanish bayonets, sword-grass, and other disagreeable undergrowth, we discovered the poor bird gasping in its last agonies. On examining their bodies we found both well supplied with shot, and I became more assured than ever of the hardiness of the species.

On the same river, 8th February—We visited another nest, on which, by the aid of a telescope, we saw three young ones in the posture described above. The bird first shot fell back in the nest and there remained: it was struck by a bullet. The next was so severely wounded that it clung outside the nest, until fired at a second time, when it fell. The third was killed, as it was preparing to fly off. Our axes being dull, the tree large, and a fair breeze springing up, we returned to the Spark, where in a few hours these young birds were skinned, cooked, and eaten, by those who had been "in at the death." They proved good eating, the flesh resembling veal in taste and tenderness. One of us only did not taste of the dish, simply I believe from prejudice. The contents of the stomachs of these young Eagles were large fragments of catfish heads and bones of quadrupeds and birds. We frequently saw old birds of the species sail down to the surface of the water, and rise holding in their talons heads of catfishes which abounded on the water and were rejected, as the inhabitants assured us, by the alligators, who content themselves with the best part, the tail, leaving the heads to such animals as can dissect them and escape the dangerous sharp bony guards placed near the gills, and which the fish has the power of firmly fixing at right angles as if they were a pair of small bayonets. Should this really be a general habit of the alligator, it indicates his faculty of gaining knowledge by experience, or of having it naturally implanted. I could easily distinguish the sex of all the young Eagles of this species which we procured. The females were not only larger, but almost black, whilst the males were much lighter and of less weight.

Some weeks afterwards, when young Eagles would have been thought a dainty even by our most prejudiced companions—for you must not suppose, reader, that every student of nature meets with "pigs ready roasted" in our woods—we saw an old White-headed Eagle perched on a tall tree at the edge of the river. While admiring its posture, by means of a telescope, and marking its eye keenly bent towards the water, it suddenly dropped like a stone from its perch, almost immersed its body into the stream, and rose with a large trout, with which it scrambled to the shore. Our captain, his first lieutenant, my assistant, and your humble servant, were present on this occasion, and saw it very composedly eat the fish, after shaking the water from its plumage. I must add that never before had I seen this bird plunge into the water, although I had several times seen it scrambling after small fishes in shallows and gravel banks.

February 29th.—I saw some Fish-Hawks defend themselves, and chase away from their nests the Bald Eagle. The former were incubating, and the latter, as well as some Turkey Buzzards, were anxiously trying to rob the nest, wherever they found the Fisher Bird absent from its tenement. The Fish-hawks at last collected from different parts of the river, and I felt great pleasure in seeing these brave birds actually drive away their cowardly enemies. The Fish-Hawk had only eggs in that country when the young of the Eagle were large and fully able to fly. . . .

Wilson figured and described the young of the White-headed Eagle under the name of the Sea Eagle, *Falco ossifragus,* although not without expressing doubts.

[From *Ornithological Biography,* Vol. II, pp. 160-162, 164.]

THE COMMON GALLINULE

Gallinula Chloropus, Lath.
Plate CCXLIV. Male.

[Common Gallinule,
Gallinula chloropus]

The two species of Gallinule which occur in the United States are confined within a comparatively small range in that extensive country, the southern portions of which appear to suit them better, at all seasons of the year, than the other districts. The Common Gallinule is extremely abundant during winter along the rivers, fresh-water creeks, lagoons, ponds and lakes, between the Gulf of Mexico and the eastern shores of the Floridas, while in spring and summer a good number migrate eastward into the Carolinas, and now and then a few stragglers may be seen on the fresh waters of the Middle Districts, beyond which none, to my knowledge, have ever been observed. They seldom ascend any of our southern streams to any considerable distance, few are ever met with many miles above Natchez on the Mississippi, and none are to be seen in the Western Country.

In general they are equally diurnal and nocturnal in their habits, and when undisturbed frequent the land as much as the water. In the lower parts of Louisiana and the Floridas, I have seen them seek their food and amuse themselves by day in the pastures and fields, and I have observed both them and the Gallinules of England enacting their courtship, while the sun was yet high above the horizon. In sight of man, however, they are timorous although not shy, and retreat from him among the grass and sedges bordering the water, to which they resort for safety. If shot at, or otherwise frightened, they run with speed, and either fly or swim off as fast as possible, to elude their enemy.

During my various temporary residences in London, I have often seen the Gallinules resort to the grounds in the Regent's Park at all hours of the day. They were there in a manner partially domesticated, and walked quite unconcernedly in the meadows, led their young over the water, and paid their addresses to each other, while fifty or more persons were amusing themselves with feeding the ducks and swans over the bridge leading to the inner circle, and within sight of these birds. While I was at Spring-Garden Spring in East Florida, in the early part of January, the Gallinules were seen in great numbers on every bayou leading towards the waters of the St. John, and at that early period the manifestations of their amatory propensity were quite remarkable. The male birds courted the females, both on the land and on the water; they frequently spread out their tail like a fan, and moved round each other, emitting a murmur-

Plate CCXLIV. *Common Gallinule*

ing sound for some seconds. The female would afterwards walk to the water's edge, stand in the water up to her breast, and receive the caresses of the male, who immediately after would strut on the water before her, jerking with rapidity his spread tail for a while, after which they would both resume their ordinary occupations. This was in the middle of the day, when I could have counted eight or ten pairs in sight.

The nest is formed with more labour than art, being composed of a quantity of withered rushes and plants, interwoven in a circular form, frequently from two to three inches thick in the centre, surrounded by an edge or brim four or five inches high. If not greatly disturbed, these birds raise several broods in a season, using the same nest, and making additions to it previous to depositing each new set of eggs. In Lower Louisiana I found it usually five or six feet from the water, among the rankest weeds, along the bayous and lakes, which are so numerous there. In some instances it was placed on a prostrate trunk of a tree over the water, when the materials of which it was composed were less abundant than in other circumstances. I never saw one floating loose, but have often heard people say they had occasionally seen a nest in that state, although I am not much disposed to give credit to such assertions. The number of eggs seldom exceeds eight or nine, and is more frequently from five to seven. As the bird lays more than once, its progeny is thus numerous. The Gallinules cover their eggs when they leave them, no doubt to protect them from crows and other enemies, but return to them as soon as food has been procured, although both sexes incubate. The eggs measure an inch and five-eighths, by an inch and one and a half eighths, and are of a dull darkish cream colour, spotted and dotted with various tints of reddish-brown and umber.

The females are as assiduous in their attentions to their young as the wild Turkey Hens; and, although the young take to the water as soon as hatched, the mother frequently calls them ashore, when she nurses and dries them under her body and wings. In this manner she looks after them until they are nearly a month old, when she abandons them and begins to breed again. The young, which are covered with hairy, shining, black down, swim beautifully, jerking their heads forward at each movement of their feet. They seem to grow surprisingly fast, and at the age of six or seven weeks are strong, active, and perhaps as well able to elude their enemies as the old birds are. Their food consists of grasses, seeds, water-insects, worms, and snails, along with which they swallow a good deal of sand or gravel. They walk and run over the broad leaves of water-lilies, as if on land, dive if necessary, and appear at times to descend into the water in search of food, although I cannot positively assert that they do so.

On more than one occasion, I have seen a flock of these young birds playing on the surface of the water like Ducks, beating it with their wings, and splashing it about in a curious manner, when their gambols would attract a garfish, which at a single dart would seize one of them and disappear. The rest affrighted would run as it were with inconceivable velocity on the surface of the water, make for the shore, and there lie concealed and silent for a quarter of an hour or so. In the streams and ponds of the Floridas, this species and some others of similar habits, suffer greatly from Alligators and Turtles, as well as from various kinds of fish, although, on account of their prolific nature, they are yet abundant.

This Gallinule seldom resorts to salt water, but at times is met with on the banks of bayous in which the water is brackish. This, however, happens only during winter. On land it walks somewhat like a chicken, and thirty, forty, or more individuals may be seen searching for worms and insects among the grass, which they also nip in the manner of the domestic fowl. On such occasions, the constantly repeated movements of their tail are rendered conspicuous by the pure white of the feathers beneath it, which, along with the white stripes on the flanks, and in spring the vivid red of the frontal plate, renders their general appearance quite interesting. In cases of danger, they run with great speed, and easily conceal themselves. On the water they sit very lightly, and swim with activity, the movements of their head and neck keeping pace with those of their feet. They pick up their food from either side, continually jerk their tail, and not unfrequently touch the water with it.

Although not a migratory bird, this species flies very well, whenever it has occasion to rise from the ground. Its wings, although concave, are large for its size, more so in fact than those of *Rallus crepitans,* which migrates to a considerable extent. But, in general, the Gallinules are averse from flying, unless when anxious to remove from one lake or stream to another, when they rise fifty or sixty feet in the air, and fly with ease and considerable velocity, by continued flappings, the neck and legs stretched out. At all other times when raised, they suffer their legs to dangle, proceed slowly to a short distance, and drop among the reeds, or if over the water, they dive and hide, leaving nothing but the bill projecting above the surface.

The young in autumn have not attained their full size; their colours are much duller than those of the old birds, particularly the stripes on the flanks and under the tail, which are of a dull cream colour instead of being pure white. The frontal plate is small, and almost covered by the feathers around it; the legs and feet are of a dingy green, and the red band on the tibia is scarcely apparent. In spring they acquire their full plumage, but the frontal plate increases in size for several years.

There are great differences as to size between birds of both sexes. The male from which I drew the figure in the plate, was of an average size, having been selected from a bagful procured expressly for the purpose. Our Gallinule corresponds so precisely with that of Europe, that I cannot hesitate in affirming that it is the same species.

[From *Ornithological Biography,* Vol. III, pp. 330-333.]

GLOSSY IBIS

Ibis Falcinellus, Vieill. [Glossy Ibis, *Plegadis falcinellus*]
Plate CCCLXXXVII. Male.

The first intimation of the existence of this beautiful species of Ibis within the limits of the United States is due to Mr. George Ord of Philadelphia, the friend and companion of the celebrated Alexander Wilson. It was described by him in the first volume of the Journal of the Academy of Natural Sciences of Philadelphia. He states that "on the seventh of May of the present year (1817), Mr. Thomas Say received from Mr. Oram, of Great Egg Harbour, a fine specimen of *Tantalus,* which had been shot there. It is the first instance which has come to my knowledge of this species having been found in the United States. I was informed that a recent specimen of this bird was, likewise in the month of May, presented to the Baltimore Museum, and that two individuals were killed in the district of

Plate CCCLXXXVII. *Glossy Ibis*

Columbia." In the sequel Mr. Ord compares it with Dr. Latham's account of the *Tantalus Mexicanus* of that author, and conjectures that it is the same.

It is not a little curious to see the changes of opinion that have taken place within these few years among naturalists who have thought of comparing American and European specimens of the birds which have been alleged to be the same in both continents. The Prince of Musignano, for example, who has given a figure of the very individual mentioned by Mr. Ord, thought at the time when he published the fourth volume of his continuation of Wilson's American Ornithology, that our Glossy Ibis was the one described by the older European writers under the name of *Ibis Falcinellus.* Now, however, having altered his notions so far as to seem desirous of proving that the same species of bird cannot exist on both the continents, he has latterly produced it anew under the name of *Ibis Ordi.* This new name I cannot with any degree of propriety adopt. I consider it no compliment to the discoverer of a bird to reject the name which he has given it, even for the purpose of calling it after himself.

The Glossy Ibis is of exceedingly rare occurrence in the United States, where it appears only at long and irregular intervals, like a wanderer who has lost his way. It exists in Mexico, however, in vast numbers. In the spring of 1837, I saw flocks of it in the Texas; but even there it is merely a summer resident, associating with the White Ibis, along the grassy margins of the rivers and bayous, and apparently going to and returning from its roosting places in the interior of the country. Its flight resembles that of its companion, the White Ibis, and it is probable that it feeds on the same kinds of crustaceous animals, and breeds on low bushes in the same great associations as that species, but we unfortunately had no opportunity of verifying this conjecture. Mr. Nuttall, in his Ornithology of the United States and Canada, says that "a specimen has occasionally been exposed for sale in the market of Boston."

I have given the figure of a male bird in superb plumage, procured in Florida, near a wood-cutter's cabin, a view of which is also given.

[From *Ornithological Biography*, Vol. IV, pp. 608-609.]

WILSON'S PLOVER

Charadrius Wilsonius, Ord.
Plate CCIX. Male and Female.

[Wilson's Plover, *Charadrius wilsonia*]

Reader, imagine yourself standing motionless on some of the sandy shores between South Carolina and the extremity of Florida, waiting with impatience for the return of day;—or, if you dislike the idea, imagine me there. The air is warm and pleasant, the smooth sea reflects the feeble glimmerings of the fading stars, the sound of living thing is not heard; nature, universal nature, is at rest. And here am I, inhaling the grateful sea-air, with eyes intent on the dim distance. See the bright blaze that issues from the verge of the waters! and now the sun himself appears, and all is life, or seems to be; for as the influence of the Divinity is to the universe, so is that of the sun to the things of this world. Far away beyond that treacherous reef, floats a gallant bark, that seems slumbering on the bosom of the waters like a silvery sea-bird. Gentle breezes now creep over the ocean, and ruffle its surface into tiny wavelets. The ship glides along, the fishes leap with joy, and on my ear comes the well known note of the bird which bears the name of one whom every ornithologist must honour. Long have I known the bird myself, and yet desirous of knowing it better, I have returned to this beach many successive seasons for the purpose of observing its ways, examining its nest, marking the care with which it rears its young, and the attachment which it manifests to its mate. Well, let the scene vanish! and let me present you with the results of my observations.

Wilson's Plover! I love the name because of the respect I bear towards him to whose memory the bird has been dedicated. How pleasing, I have thought, it would have been to me, to have met with him on such an excursion, and, after having procured a few of his own birds, to have listened to him as he would speak of a thousand interesting facts connected with his favourite science and my ever-pleasing pursuits. How delightful to have talked, among other things, of the probable use of the *double claws* which I have found attached to the toes of the species which goes by his name, and which are also seen in other groups of shore and sea birds. Perhaps he might have informed me why the claws of some birds are pectinated on one toe

Plate CCIX. *Wilson's Plover*

and not on the rest, and why that toe itself is so cut. But alas! Wilson was with me only a few times, and then *nothing* worthy of his attention was procured.

This interesting species, which always looks to me as if in form a miniature copy of the Black-bellied Plover, is a constant resident in the southern districts of the Union. There it breeds, and there too it spends the winter. Many individuals, no doubt, move farther south, but great numbers are at all times to be met with from Carolina to the mouths of the Mississippi, and in all these places I have found it the whole year round. Some go as far to the eastward as Long Island in the State of New York, where, however, they are considered as rarities; but beyond this, none, I believe, are seen along our eastern shores. This circumstance has seemed the more surprising to me, that its relative the Piping Plover proceeds as far as the Magdeleine Islands; and that the latter bird should also breed in the Carolinas a month earlier than Wilson's Plover ever does, seems to me not less astonishing.

Wilson's Plover begins to lay its eggs about the time when the young of the Piping Plover are running after their parents. Twenty or thirty yards from the uppermost beat of the waves, on the first of June, or some day not distant from it, the female may be seen scratching a small cavity in the shelly sand, in which she deposits four eggs, placing them carefully with the broad end outermost. The eggs, which measure an inch and a quarter by seven and a half eighths, are of a dull cream colour, sparingly sprinkled all over with dots of pale purple and spots of dark brown. The eggs vary somewhat in size, and in their ground colour, but less than those of many other species of the genus. The young follow their parents as soon as they are hatched, and the latter employ every artifice common to birds of this family, to entice their enemies to follow them and thus save their offspring.

The flight of this species is rapid, elegant, and protracted. While travelling from one sand-beach or island to another, they fly low over the land or water, emitting a fine clear soft note. Now and then, when after the breeding season they form into flocks of twenty or thirty, they perform various evolutions in the air, cutting backwards and forwards, as if inspecting the spot on which they wish to alight, and then suddenly descend, sometimes on the sea-beach, and sometimes on the more elevated sands at a little distance from it. They do not run so nimbly as the Piping Plovers, nor are they nearly so shy. I have in fact frequently walked up so as to be within ten yards or so of them. They seldom mix with other species, and they shew a decided preference to solitary uninhabited spots.

Their food consists principally of small marine insects, minute shellfish, and sandworms, with which they mix particles of sand. Towards autumn they become almost silent, and being then very plump, afford delicious eating. They feed fully as much by night as by day, and the large eyes of this as of other species of the genus, seem to fit them for nocturnal searchings.

The young birds assemble together, and spend the winter months apart from the old ones, which are easily recognised by their lighter tints. While in the Floridas, near St. Augustine, in the months of December and January, I found this species much more abundant than any other; and there were few of the Keys that had a sandy beach, or a rocky shore, on which one or more pairs were not observed.

[From *Ornithological Biography,* Vol. III, pp. 73-75.]

THE FLORIDA JAY

Corvus floridanus, Bartram.
Plate LXXXVII. Male and Female.

[Scrub Jay, *Aphelocoma coerulescens,* ssp. *A. coerulescens coerulescens* (Bosc)]

This beautiful and lively bird is a constant resident in the southwestern parts of Florida, from which country it seldom, if ever, removes to any great distance. It is never seen in the State of Louisiana, far less in that of Kentucky, and when Charles Bonaparte asserts that it occurs in these districts, we must believe that he has been misinformed. It is so confined to the particular portions of Florida which it inhabits, that even on the eastern shores of that peninsula few are to be seen. I have never observed it in any part of Georgia, or farther to the eastward.

The flight of the Florida Jay is generally performed at a short distance from the ground, and consists either of a single sailing sweep, as it shifts from one tree or bush to another, or of continuous flappings, with a slightly undulated motion, in the manner of the

Plate LXXXVII. *Florida Jay*

Magpie (*Corvus Pica*) or of the Canada Jay (*Corvus canadensis*). Its notes are softer than those of its relative the Blue Jay (*Corvus cristatus*), and are more frequently uttered. Its motions are also more abrupt and quicker. It is seen passing from one tree to another with expanded tail, stopping for a moment to peep at the intruder, and hopping off to another place the next minute. It frequently descends to the ground, along the edges of oozy or marshy places, to search for snails, of which, together with berries of various kinds, fruits and insects, its food consists. It is easily approached during the breeding season, but is more shy at other times. It is a great destroyer of the eggs of small birds, as well as of young birds, which it chases and kills by repeated blows of its bill on their heads, after which it tears their flesh with avidity.

The Florida Jay is easily kept in a cage, where it will feed on recent or dried fruits, such as figs, raisins, and the kernels of various nuts, and exhibits as much gaiety as the Blue Jay does in a similar state. Like the latter it secures its food between its feet, and breaks it into pieces before swallowing it, particularly the acorns of the Live Oak, and the snails which it picks up among the Sword Palmetto. No sooner have the seeds of that plant become black, or fully ripe, than the Florida Jay makes them almost its sole food for a time, and wherever a patch of these troublesome plants are to be seen, there also is the Jay to be met with. I have called the palmetto a troublesome plant, because its long, narrow, and serrated leaves are so stiff, and grow so close together, that it is extremely difficult to walk among them, the more so that it usually grows in places where the foot is seldom put without immediately sinking in the mire to a depth of several inches.

The nest of the Florida Jay is sparingly formed of dry sticks, placed across each other, and, although of a rounded shape, is so light that the bird is easily seen through it. It is lined with fibrous roots, placed in a circular manner. The eggs are from four to six, of a light olive colour, marked with irregular blackish dashes. Only one brood is raised in the season.

I had a fine opportunity of observing a pair of these birds in confinement, in the city of New Orleans. They had been raised out of a family of five, taken from the nest, and when I saw them had been two years in confinement. They were in full plumage, and extremely beautiful. The male was often observed to pay very particular attentions to the female at the approach of spring. They were fed upon rice, and all kinds of dried fruit. Their cage was usually opened after dinner, when both immediately flew upon the table, fed on the almonds which were given them, and drank claret diluted with water. Both affected to imitate particular sounds, but in a very imperfect manner. These attempts at mimicry probably resulted from their having been in company with parrots and other birds. They suffered greatly when moulting, becoming almost entirely bare, and requiring to be kept near the fire. The female dropped two eggs in the cage, but never attempted to make a nest, although the requisite materials were placed at her disposal.

I have represented a pair of Florida Jays on a branch of the Persimon tree, ornamented with its richly coloured fruits. This tree grows to a moderate height as well as girth. The wood is hard and compact. The leaves drop off at an early period. The fruit, when fully ripe, is grateful to the palate. The Persimon occurs in all parts of the United States, but abounds in the low lands of Florida and Louisiana, probably more than in any other portion of the Union.

The Persimon Tree

Leaves ovato-oblong, acuminate, smooth, venous; petioles downy; buds smooth. The flowers are pale yellow, and the fruits, which are of the size of a plum, are of a globular form, and when mature, of a dull yellowish colour. The bark of old trees is cracked, and of a dark colour. The wood is employed for various purposes, being fine-grained, hard and durable.

[From *Ornithological Biography*, Vol. I, pp. 444-445, 446.]

THE WOOD IBIS

Tantalus loculator, Linn. [Wood Stork, *Mycteria americana*]
Plate CCXVI. Male.

This very remarkable bird, and all others of the same genus that are known to occur in the United States, are constant residents in some

Plate CCXVI. *Wood Ibis*

part of our Southern Districts, although they perform short migrations. A few of them now and then stray as far as the Middle States, but instances of this are rare; and I am not aware that any have been seen farther to the eastward than the southern portions of Maryland, excepting a few individuals of the Glossy and the White Ibises, which have been procured in Pennsylvania, New Jersey, and New York. The Carolinas, Georgia, the Floridas, Alabama, Lower Louisiana, including Opellousas, and Mississippi, are the districts to which they resort by preference, and in which they spend the whole year. With the exception of the Glossy Ibis, which may be looked upon as a bird of the Mexican territories, and which usually appears in the Union singly or in pairs, they all live socially in immense flocks, especially during the breeding season. The country which they inhabit is doubtless the best suited to their habits; the vast and numerous swamps, lagoons, bayous, and submersed savannahs that occur in the lower parts of our Southern States, all abounding with fishes and reptiles; and the temperature of these countries being congenial to their constitutions.

In treating of the bird now under your notice, Mr. William Bartram says, "This solitary bird does not associate in flocks, but is generally seen alone." This was published by Wilson, and every individual who has since written on the subject, has copied the assertion without probably having any other reason than that he believed the authors of it to state a fact. But the habits of this species are entirely at variance with the above quotation, to which I direct your attention not without a feeling of pain, being assured that Mr. Bartram could have made such a statement only because he had few opportunities of studying the bird in question in its proper haunts.

The Wood Ibis is rarely met with single, even after the breeding season, and it is more easy for a person to see an hundred together at any period of the year, than to meet with one by itself. Nay, I have seen flocks composed of several thousands, and that there is a natural necessity for their flocking together I shall explain to you. This species feeds entirely on fish and aquatic reptiles, of which it destroys an enormous quantity, in fact more than it eats; for if they have been killing fish for half an hour and have gorged themselves, they suffer the rest to lie on the water untouched, when it becomes food for alligators, crows, and vultures, whenever these animals can lay hold of it. To procure its food, the Wood Ibis walks through shallow muddy lakes or bayous in numbers. As soon as they have discovered a place abounding in fish, they dance as it were all through it, until the water becomes thick with the mud stirred from the bottom by their feet. The fishes, on rising to the surface, are instantly struck by the beaks of the Ibises, which, on being deprived of life, they turn over and so remain. In the course of ten or fifteen minutes, hundreds of fishes, frogs, young alligators, and water-snakes cover the surface, and the birds greedily swallow them until they are completely gorged, after which they walk to the nearest margins, place themselves in long rows, with their breasts all turned towards the sun, in the manner of Pelicans and Vultures, and thus remain for an hour or so. When digestion is partially accomplished, they all take to wing, rise in spiral circlings to an immense height, and sail about for an hour or more, performing the most beautiful evolutions that can well be conceived. Their long necks and legs are stretched out to their full extent, the pure white of their plumage contrasts beautifully with the jetty black of the tips of their wings. Now in large circles they seem to ascend toward the upper regions of the atmosphere; now, they pitch towards the earth; and again, gently rising, they renew their gyrations. Hunger once more induces them to go in search of food, and, with extended front, the band sails rapidly towards another lake or bayou.

Mark the place, reader, and follow their course through canebrake, cypress-swamp, and tangled wood. Seldom do they return to the same feeding place on the same day. You have reached the spot, and are standing on the margin of a dark-watered bayou, the sinuosities of which lead your eye into a labyrinth ending in complete darkness. The tall canes bow to each other from the shores; the majestic trees above them, all hung with funereal lichen, gently wave in the suffocating atmosphere; the bullfrog, alarmed, shrinks back into the water; the alligator raises his head above its surface, probably to see if the birds have arrived, and the wily cougar is stealthily advancing toward one of the Ibises, which he expects to carry off into the thicket. Through the dim light your eye catches a glimpse of the white-plumaged birds, moving rapidly like spectres to and fro. The loud clacking of their mandibles apprises you of the havock they commit among the terrified inhabitants of the waters, while the knell-like sounds of their feet come with a feeling of dread. Move, gently or not, move at all, and you infallibly lose your opportunity of observing the actions of the birds. Some old male has long marked you; whether it has been with eye or with ear, no matter. The first stick your foot cracks, his hoarse voice sounds the alarm. Off they all go, battering down the bending canes with their powerful pinions, and breaking the smaller twigs of the trees, as they force a passage for themselves.

Talk to me of the stupidity of birds, of the dulness of the Wood Ibis! say it is fearless, easily approached, and easily shot. I listen, but it is merely through courtesy; for I have so repeatedly watched its movements, in all kinds of circumstances, that I am quite convinced we have not in the United States a more shy, wary, and vigilant bird than the Wood Ibis. In the course of two years spent, I may say, among them, for I saw some whenever I pleased during that period, I never succeeded in surprising one, not even under night, when they were roosting on trees at a height of nearly a hundred feet, and sometimes rendered farther secure by being over extensive swamps. . . .

The name of "Wood Ibis" given to this bird, is not more applicable to it than to any other species; for every one with which I am acquainted resorts quite as much to the woods at particular periods. All our species may be found on wet savannahs, on islands surrounded even by the waters of the sea, the Florida Keys for example, or in the most secluded parts of the darkest woods, provided they are swampy, or are furnished with ponds. I have found the Wood, the Red, the White, the Brown, and the Glossy Ibises, around ponds in the centre of immense forests; and in such places, even in the desolate pine-barrens of the Floridas; sometimes several hundred miles from the sea coast, on the Red River, in the State of Louisiana, and above Natchez, in that of Mississippi, as well as within a few miles of the ocean. Yet, beyond certain limits, I never saw one of these birds.

One of the most curious circumstances connected with this species is, that although the birds are, when feeding, almost constantly within the reach of large alligators, of which they devour the young, these reptiles never attack them; whereas if a Duck or a Heron comes within the reach of their tails, it is immediately killed and swallowed. The Wood Ibis will wade up to its belly in the water, round the edges of "alligators' holes," without ever being injured; but should one of these birds be shot, an alligator immediately makes towards it and pulls it under water. The gar-fish is not so courteous, but gives chase to the Ibises whenever an opportunity occurs. The Snapping Turtle is also a great enemy to the young birds of this species.

The flight of the Wood Ibis is heavy at its rising from the ground. Its neck at that moment is deeply curved downward, its wings flap heavily but with great power, and its long legs are not stretched out behind until it has proceeded many yards. But as soon as it has attained a height of eight or ten feet, it ascends with great celerity, generally in a spiral direction, in silence if not alarmed, or, if frightened, with a rough croaking guttural note. When fairly on wing, they proceed in a direct flight, with alternate flappings and sailings of thirty or forty yards, the sailings more prolonged than the flappings. They alight on trees with more ease than Herons generally do, and either stand erect or crouch on the branches, in the manner of the Wild Turkey, the Herons seldom using the latter attitude. When they are at rest, they place their bill against the breast, while the neck shrinks as it were between the shoulders. In this position you may see fifty on the same tree, or on the ground, reposing in perfect quiet for hours at a time, although some individual of the party will be constantly on the look-out, and ready to sound the alarm.

In the spring months, when these birds collect in large flocks, before they return to their breeding places, I have seen thousands together, passing over the woods in a line more than a mile in extent, and moving with surprising speed at the height of only a few yards above the trees. When a breeding place has once been chosen, it is resorted to for years in succession; nor is it easy to make them abandon it after they have deposited their eggs, although, if much annoyed, they never return to it after that season.

Besides the great quantity of fishes that these Ibises destroy, they also devour frogs, young alligators, wood-rats, young rails and grakles, fiddlers and other crabs, as well as snakes and small turtles. They never eat the eggs of the alligator, as has been alleged, although they probably would do so, could they demolish the matted nests of that animal, a task beyond the power of *any* bird known to me. I never saw one eat any thing which either it or some of its fellows had not killed. Nor will it eat an animal that has been dead for some time, even although it may have been killed by itself. When eating, the clacking of their mandibles may be heard at the distance of several hundred yards.

When wounded, it is dangerous to approach them, for they bite severely. They may be said to be very tenacious of life. Although usually fat, they are very tough and oily, and therefore are not fit for food. The Negroes, however, eat them, having, previous to cooking them, torn off the skin, as they do with Pelicans and Cormorants. My own attempts, I may add, were not crowned with success. Many of the Negroes of Louisiana destroy these birds when young, for the sake of the oil which their flesh contains, and which they use in greasing machines.

The French Creoles of that State name them "Grands Flamans," while the Spaniards of East Florida know them by the name of "Gannets." When in the latter country, at St Augustine, I was induced to make an excursion, to visit a large pond or lake, where I was assured there were Gannets in abundance, which I might shoot off the trees, provided I was careful enough. On asking the appearance of the Gannets, I was told that they were large white birds, with wings black at the end, a long neck, and a large sharp bill. The description so far agreeing with that of the Common Gannet or Solan Goose, I proposed no questions respecting the legs or tail, but went off. Twenty-three miles, Reader, I trudged through the woods, and at last came in view of the pond; when, lo! its borders and the trees around it were covered with Wood Ibises. Now, as the good people who gave the information spoke according to their knowledge, and agreeably to their custom of calling the Ibises Gannets, had I not gone to the pond, I might have written this day that Gannets are found in the interior of the woods in the Floridas, that they alight on trees, &c. which, if *once* published, would in all probability have gone down to future times through the medium of compilers, and all perhaps without acknowledgment.

The Wood Ibis takes four years in attaining full maturity, although birds of the second year are now and then found breeding. This is rare, however, for the young birds live in flocks by themselves, until they have attained the age of about three years. They are at first of a dingy brown, each feather edged with paler; the head is covered to the mandibles with short downy feathers, which gradually fall off as the bird advances in age. In the third year, the head is quite bare, as well as a portion of the upper part of the neck. In the fourth year, the bird is as you see it in the plate. The male is much larger and heavier than the female, but there is no difference in colour between the sexes.

[From *Ornithological Biography*, Vol. III, pp. 128-130, 131-131.]

Plate CCCXXIII. *Black Skimmer or Shearwater*

BLACK SKIMMER
OR RAZOR-BILLED SHEARWATER

Rhynchops nigra, Linn. [Black Skimmer, *Rhyncops nigra*]
Plate CCCXXIII. Male.

This bird, one of the most singularly endowed by nature, is a constant resident on all the sandy and marshy shores of our more southern states, from South Carolina to the Sabine River, and doubtless also in Texas, where I found it quite abundant in the beginning of spring. At this season parties of Black Skimmers extend their movements eastward as far as the sands of Long Island, beyond which however I have not seen them. Indeed in Massachusetts and Maine this bird is known only to such navigators as have observed it in the southern and tropical regions.

To study its habits therefore, the naturalist must seek the extensive sand-bars, estuaries, and mouths of the rivers of our Southern States, and enter the sinuous bayous intersecting the broad marshes along their coasts. There, during the warm sunshine of the winter days, you will see thousands of Skimmers, covered as it were with their gloomy mantles, peaceably lying beside each other, and so crowded together as to present to your eye the appearance of an immense black pall accidentally spread on the sand. Such times are their hours of rest, and I believe of sleep, as, although partially diurnal, and perfectly able to discern danger by day, they rarely feed then, unless the weather be cloudy. On the same sands, yet apart from them, equal numbers of our common Black-headed Gulls may be seen enjoying the same comfort in security. Indeed the Skimmers are rarely at such times found on sand or gravel banks which are not separated from the neighbouring shores by some broad and deep piece of water. I think I can safely venture to say that in such places, and at the periods mentioned, I have seen not fewer than ten thousand of these birds in a single flock. Should you now attempt to approach them, you will find that as soon as you have reached within twice the range of your long duck-gun, the crowded Skimmers simultaneously rise on their feet, and watch all your movements. If you advance nearer, the whole flock suddenly taking to wing, fill the air with their harsh cries, and soon reaching a considerable height, range widely around, until, your patience being exhausted, you abandon the place. When thus taking to wing in countless multitudes, the snowy white of their under parts gladdens your eye, but anon, when they all veer through the air, the black of their long wings and upper parts produces a remarkable contrast to the blue sky above. Their aërial evolutions on such occasions are peculiar and pleasing, as they at times appear to be intent on removing to a great distance, then suddenly round to, and once more pass almost over you, flying so close together as to appear like a black cloud, first ascending, and then rushing down like a torrent. Should they see that you are retiring, they wheel a few times close over the ground, and when assured that there is no longer any danger, they alight pell-mell, with wings extended upwards, but presently closed, and once more huddling together they lie down on the ground, to remain until forced off by the tide. When the Skimmers repose on the shores of the mainland during high-water, they seldom continue long on the same spot, as if they felt doubtful of security; and a person watching them at such times might suppose that they were engaged in searching for food.

No sooner has the dusk of evening arrived than the Skimmers begin to disperse, rise from their place of rest singly, in pairs, or in parties from three or four to eight or ten, apparently according to the degree of hunger they feel, and proceed in different directions along parts of the shores previously known to them, sometimes going up tide-rivers to a considerable distance. They spend the whole night on wing, searching diligently for food. Of this I had ample and satisfactory proof when ascending the St. John River in East Florida, in the United States' Schooner the Spark. The hoarse cries of the Skimmers never ceased more than an hour, so that I could easily know whether they were passing upwards or downwards in the dark. And this happened too when I was at least a hundred miles from the mouth of the river.

Being aware, previously to my several visits to the peninsula of the Floridas and other parts of our southern coasts where the Razor-bills are abundant, of the observations made on this species by M. Lesson, I paid all imaginable attention to them, always aided with an excellent glass, in order to find whether or not they fed on bivalve shell-fish found in the shallows of sand-bars and other places at low water; but not in one single instance did I see any such occurrence, and in regard to this matter I agree with Wilson in asserting that, while with us, these birds do not feed on shell-fish. . . .

While watching the movements of the Black Skimmer as it was searching for food, sometimes a full hour before it was dark, I have seen it pass its lower mandible at an angle of about 45 degrees into the water, whilst its *moveable* upper mandible was elevated a little above the surface. In this manner, with wings raised and extended, it ploughed as it were, the element in which its quarry lay to the extent of several yards at a time, rising and falling alternately, and that as frequently as it thought it necessary for securing its food when in sight of it; for I am certain that these birds never immerse their lower mandible until they have observed the object of their pursuit, for which reason their eyes are constantly directed downwards like those of Terns and Gannets. I have at times stood nearly an hour by the side of a small pond of salt water having a communication with the sea or a bay, while these birds would pass within a very few yards of me, then apparently quite regardless of my presence, and proceed fishing in the manner above described. Although silent at the commencement of their pursuit, they become noisy as the darkness draws on, and then give out their usual call notes, which resemble the syllables *hurk, hurk,* twice or thrice repeated at short intervals, as if to induce some of their companions to follow in their wake. I have seen a few of these birds glide in this manner in search of prey over a long salt-marsh bayou, or inlet, following the whole of its sinuosities, now and then lower themselves to the water, pass their bill along the surface, and on seizing a prawn or a small fish, instantly rise, munch and swallow it on wing. . . .

The flight of the Black Skimmer is perhaps more elegant than that of any water bird with which I am acquainted. The great length of its narrow wings, its partially elongated forked tail, its thin body and extremely compressed bill, all appear contrived to assure it that buoyancy of motion which one cannot but admire when he sees it on wing. It is able to maintain itself against the heaviest gale; and I believe no instance has been recorded of any bird of this species having been forced inland by the most violent storm. But, to observe the aërial movements of the Skimmer to the best advantage, you must visit its haunts in the love season. Several males, excited by the ardour of their desires, are seen pursuing a yet unmated female. The coy one, shooting aslant to either side, dashes along with marvellous speed, flying hither and thither, upwards, downwards, in all directions. Her suitors strive to overtake her; they emit their love-cries with vehemence; you are gladdened by their softly and tenderly enunciated *ha, ha,* or the *hack, hack, cae, cae,* of the last in the chase. Like the female they all perform the most curious zigzags, as they follow in close pursuit, and as each beau at length passes her in succession, he extends his wings for an instant, and in a manner struts by her side. Sometimes a flock is seen to leave a sand-bar, and fly off in a direct course, each individual apparently intent on distancing his companions; and then their mingling cries of *ha, ha, hack, hack, cae, cae,* fill the air. I once saw one of these birds fly round a whole flock that had alighted, keeping at the height of about twenty yards, but now and then tumbling as if its wings had suddenly failed, and again almost upsetting, in the manner of the Tumbler Pigeon. . . .

The Skimmer forms no other nest than a slight hollow in the sand.

The eggs, I believe, are always three, and measure an inch and three quarters in length, an inch and three-eighths in breadth. As if to be assimilated to the colours of the birds themselves, they have a pure white ground, largely patched or blotched with black or very dark umber, with here and there a large spot of a light purplish tint. They are as good to eat as those of most Gulls, but inferior to the eggs of Plovers and other birds of that tribe. The young are clumsy, much of the same colour as the sand on which they lie, and are not able to fly until about six weeks, when you now perceive their resemblance to their parents. They are fed at first by the regurgitation of the finely macerated contents of the gullets of the old birds, and ultimately pick up the shrimps, prawns, small crabs, and fishes dropped before them. As soon as they are able to walk about, they cluster together in the manner of the young of the Common Gannet, and it is really marvellous how the parents can distinguish them individually on such occasions. This bird walks in the manner of the Terns, with short steps, and the tail slightly elevated. When gorged and fatigued, both old and young birds are wont to lie flat on the sand, and extend their bills before them; and when thus reposing in fancied security, may sometimes be slaughtered in great numbers by the single discharge of a gun. When shot at while on wing, and brought to the water, they merely float, and are easily secured. If the sportsman is desirous of obtaining more, he may easily do so, as others pass in full clamour close over the wounded bird.

[From *Ornithological Biography,* Vol. IV, pp. 203-206, 208.]

THE NIGHT HERON

Ardea Nycticorax, Linn. [Black-crowned Night Heron,
Plate CCXXXVI. Adult Male and Young. *Nycticorax nycticorax*]

The Night Heron is a constant resident in the Southern States, where it is found in abundance in the low swampy tracts near the coast, from the mouth of Sabine River to the eastern boundaries of South Carolina. On the whole of that vast extent of country, it may be procured at all seasons. The adult birds keep farther south than the young, flocks of the latter remaining in South Carolina during the whole winter, and there the Night Herons are at that period more common than most other species of the family. In that State it is named "The Indian Pullet," in Lower Louisiana the Creoles call it "*Gros-bec*," the inhabitants of East Florida know it under the name of "Indian Hen," and in our Eastern States its usual appelation is "Qua Bird."

In the course of my winter rambles through East Florida, I met with several of the large places of resort of Night Herons, and, in particular, one remarkable for the vast number of birds congregated there. It is about six miles below the plantation of my friend John Bullow, Esq., on a bayou which opens into the Halifax River. There several hundred pairs appeared to be already mated, although it was

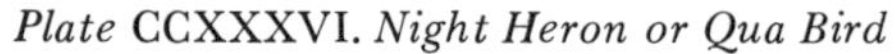

Plate CCXXXVI. *Night Heron or Qua Bird*

only the month of January; many of the nests of former years were still standing, and all appeared to live in peace and contentment. . . .

The Night Heron seldom advances very far into the country, but remains on the low swampy lands along the coast. It is rare to see one farther up the Mississippi than the mouth of the Arkansas, to which a few are at times induced to go while rambling along the great stream. I never saw one, or heard of any, whilst in Kentucky, and I doubt much if they are ever seen in the upper parts of the State of Tennessee. The distance of a hundred miles from the tide-mark appears to be the farthest extent of their inland movements. On the other hand, they are fond of resorting to the islands along the coast, on many of which they breed.

At the approach of spring, great numbers of those which have wintered far south, leave their places of sojourn and migrate eastward, although probably an equal number remain in the low lands of Louisiana and the Floridas during the whole year. There, indeed, I have found them with eggs in April and May, and as young birds just fledged were very abundant at the same places, I concluded that these eggs were of the second laying. By the middle of March, the number of Night Herons is seen to increase daily in the Carolinas, and, about a month later, some make their appearance in the Middle Districts, where many remain and breed. They are not abundant in the State of New York, are seen sparingly breeding in Massachusetts, while only a few proceed to Maine, and farther eastward they are looked upon as a great curiosity. In Nova Scotia, Newfoundland, and Labrador, this species is quite unknown. . . .

Excepting while breeding, this species is extremely shy and wary, especially the adults. To approach them from a distance after they have seen you, is no easy task. They seem to know the distance at which your gun can injure them, they watch all your movements, and at the proper moment leave their perches. Should you chance to crack a stick while advancing towards them, they start at once, give a few raps with their wings in the manner of the Common Pigeon, and fly off as if delighted at your disappointment. On the contrary, you may shoot them with ease, if you lie in wait near the places to which they resort to roost by day, and at which they generally arrive singly, or a few at a time, when, from your place of concealment among the trees, you may kill them the moment they alight over your head, and at a short distance. In this manner I have known forty or fifty procured by two sportsmen in the course of about two hours. You may also not unfrequently shoot them at any hour of the day, by starting them from secluded feeding-grounds, and thus I have shot a good many in different parts of the United States, and even in the Middle Districts. They are, however, rarely shot whilst on the ground, their hearing being still more acute than that of the American Bittern, which prefers squatting in the grass to flying off, when any noise is heard, whereas the Night Heron rises immediately.

This species breeds in communities around the stagnant ponds, either near rice plantations or in the interior of retired and secluded swamps, as well as on some of the sea islands covered with evergreen trees. Their heronries are formed either in low bushes, or in middle-sized or tall trees, as seems most convenient or secure. In the Floridas, they are partial to the mangroves that overhang the salt-water; in Louisiana, they prefer the cypresses; and in the Middle States, they find the cedars most suitable. In some breeding-places within a few miles of Charleston, which I visited in company with my friend John Bachman, the nests were placed on low bushes, and crowded together, some within a yard of the ground, others raised seven or eight feet above it, many being placed flat on the branches, while others were in the forks. Hundreds of them might be seen at once, as they were built on the side of the bushes fronting the water. Those which I found in the Floridas were all placed on the south-west sides of mangrove islands, but were farther apart from each other, some being only about a foot above high-water mark, while others were in the very tops of the trees, which, however, scarcely exceeded twenty feet in height. In some inland swamps in Louisiana, I saw them placed on the tops of tall cypress trees about a hundred feet high, and along with those of *Ardea Herodias, A. alba,* and some Anhingas. In the Jerseys I have found the Night Herons breeding on water oaks and cedars; and my friend Thomas Nuttall informs me, that "in a very secluded and marshy island, in Fresh Pond, near Boston, there likewise exists one of these ancient heronries; and though the birds have been frequently robbed of their eggs, in great numbers, by mischievous boys, they still lay again immediately after, and usually succeed in raising a second brood." The same accurate observer remarks, that "about the middle of October, the Qua Birds begin to retire from this part of Massachusetts, towards their southern winter quarters, although a few of the young birds still linger occasionally to the 29th or 30th of that month." This last observation is a farther evidence of the reluctance which the young of this species feel to go as far south during winter as the old birds.

The nest of the Night Heron is large, flattish, and formed of sticks placed in different directions, sometimes to the height of three or four inches. At times it is arranged with so little care, that the young upset it before they are able to fly. Many of the nests are annually repaired, and these birds, when they have once found an agreeable settlement, return regularly to it, until some calamity forces them to abandon it. The full number of the eggs is four, and they measure at an average two inches and one-sixteenth by an inch and a half. They are thin-shelled, and of a plain light sea-green colour. In about three weeks after the young are hatched, most of them leave the nest, and crawl about the branches, to which they cling firmly, ascending to the tops of the bushes or trees, and there awaiting the return of their parents with food. If you approach them at such times, the greatest consternation ensues both among the young and the old birds; the loud and incessant croaking which both have until then kept up, suddenly ceases; the parent birds rise in the air, sail around and above you, some alighting on the neighbouring trees; while the young scramble off in all directions to avoid being taken. So great at times is their terror, that they throw themselves into the water, and swim off with considerable rapidity, until they reach the shore, when they run and hide in every convenient place. Retire for half an hour, and you will be sure to hear the old and the young calling to each other; the noise gradually increases, and in a short time is as loud as ever. The stench emitted by the excrements with which the abandoned nests, the branches and leaves of the trees and bushes, and the ground, are covered, the dead young, the rotten and broken eggs, together with putrid fish and other matters, renders a visit to these places far from pleasant. Crows, Hawks and Vultures torment the birds by day, while Racoons and other animals destroy them by night. The young are quite as good for eating as those of the Common Pigeon, being tender, juicy, and fat, with very little of the fishy taste of many birds which, like them, feed on fishes and reptiles. At this period few if any of the old birds have the long feathers of the hind head, and these are not reproduced before the latter part of the following winter, when they seem to attain their extreme length in a few weeks.

The flight of the Night Heron is steady, rather slow, and often greatly protracted. They propel themselves by regular flappings of the wings, and, like the true Herons, draw in their head on the shoulders, while their legs stretch out behind, and with the tail form a kind of rudder. When alarmed they at times rise high in the air, and sail about for a while. They sail in the same manner before alighting on their feeding grounds, which they rarely do without having previously attended to their security by alighting on the neighbouring trees and looking about them. Their migrations are performed under night, when their passage is indicated by their loud hoarse notes resembling the syllable *qua*, uttered at pretty regular intervals. On these occasions they appear to fly faster than usual.

On the ground, this bird exhibits none of the grace observed in all the true Herons; it walks in a stooping posture, the neck much retracted, until it sees its prey, when, with a sudden movement, it stretches it out and secures its food. It is never seen standing motionless, waiting for its prey, like the true Herons, but is constantly moving about in search of it. Its feeding places are the sides of ditches, meadows, the shady banks of creeks, bayous, and ponds or rivers, as well as the extensive salt-marshes and mud-bars left exposed at low water; and I have observed it to alight in the ponds in the suburbs of Charleston towards evening, and feed there. In all such situations, excepting the last, this bird may often be seen by day, but more especially in the evening or morning twilight, wading up to its ankles, or, as we commonly say, its knee-joints. Its food consists of fishes, shrimps, tadpoles, frogs, water-lizards, and leeches, small crustacea of all kinds, water insects, moths, and even mice, which seem not less welcome to it than its more ordinary articles of food. When satisfied, it retires to some high tree on the banks of a stream or in the interior of a swamp, and there it stands, usually on one leg, for hours at a time, apparently dosing, though seldom sound asleep.

When wounded, this bird first tries to make its escape by hiding among the grass or bushes, squatting the moment it finds what it deems a secure place; but if no chance of a safe retreat occurs, it raises its crest, ruffles its feathers, and, opening its bill, prepares to defend itself. It can bite pretty severely, but the injury inflicted by its bill is not to be compared with that produced by its claws, which on such occasions it uses with much effect. If you seize it, it utters a loud, rough, continued sound, and tries to make its escape whenever it perceives the least chance.

The Night Heron undergoes three annual changes of plumage ere it attains its perfect state, although many individuals breed in the spring of the third year. After the first autumnal moult, the young is as you see it represented in the plate. In the second autumn, the markings of the neck and other parts have almost entirely disappeared; the upper parts of the head have become of a full blackish-green, mixing near the upper mandible with the dull brown of the first season, while the rest of the plumage has assumed a uniform dull ochreous greyish-brown. In the course of the following season, the bird exhibits the green of the shoulders and back, the head is equally richly coloured, and the frontal band between the upper mandible and the eye, and over the latter, is pure white. At this age it rarely has the slender white feathers of the hind head longer than an inch or two. The sides of the neck, and all the lower parts, have become of a purer greyish-white. The wings are now spotless in all their parts, and of a light brownish-grey, as is the tail. The following spring, the plumage is complete, and the bird is as represented in the plate. After this period, with the exception of losing its long crest-feathers after the young are hatched, it retains its colouring. No difference can be observed in the tints of the sexes, but the male is somewhat larger.

A very considerable difference in size is observable at all seasons in birds of this species. Some that are fully feathered, and therefore at least three years old, measure as much as four inches less than others of the same sex, and weigh less in proportion. These circumstances might suffice with some naturalists to attempt to form two species out of one, but in this they would certainly fail.

In the neighbourhood of New Orleans, and along the Mississippi, as far up as Natchez, the shooting of this species is a favourite occupation with the planters, who represent it as equalling any other bird in the delicacy of its flesh.

The frog, of which I have introduced a figure, is common in the retired swamps which the Night Heron frequents, and is often devoured by it. The flowering plants which you see, are abundant in the States of Georgia and South Carolina, as well as in the Floridas.

[From *Ornithological Biography*, Vol. III, pp. 275-280.]

John James Audubon

THE GREAT BLUE HERON

Ardea Herodias, Linn. [Great Blue Heron, *Ardea herodias*]
Plate CCXI. Male.

The State of Louisiana has always been my favourite portion of the Union, although Kentucky and some other States have divided my affections; but as we are on the banks of the fair Ohio, let us pause a while, good Reader, and watch the Heron. In my estimation, few of our waders are more interesting than the birds of this family. Their contours and movements are always graceful, if not elegant. Look on the one that stands near the margin of the pure stream:—see his reflection dipping as it were into the smooth water, the bottom of which it might reach had it not to contend with the numerous boughs of those magnificent trees. How calm, how silent, how grand is the scene! The tread of the tall bird himself no one hears, so carefully does he place his foot on the moist ground, cautiously suspending it for a while at each step of his progress. Now his golden eye glances over the surrounding objects, in surveying which he takes advantage of the full stretch of his graceful neck. Satisfied that no danger is near, he lays his head on his shoulders, allows the feathers of his breast to droop, and patiently awaits the approach of his finned prey. You might imagine what you see to be the statue of a bird, so motionless is it. But now, he moves; he has taken a silent step, and with great care he advances; slowly does he raise his head from his shoulders, and now, what a sudden start! his formidable bill has transfixed a perch, which he beats to death on the ground. See with what difficulty he gulps it down his capacious throat! and now his broad wings open, and away he slowly flies to another station, or perhaps to avoid his unwelcome observers.

The "Blue Crane" (by which name this species is generally known in the United States) is met with in every part of the Union. Although more abundant in the low lands of our Atlantic coast, it is not uncommon in the countries west of the Alleghany Mountains. I have found it in every State in which I have travelled, as well as in all our "Territories." It is well known from Louisiana to Maine, but seldom occurs farther east than Prince Edward's Island in the Gulf of St. Lawrence, and not a Heron of any kind did I see or hear of in Newfoundland or Labrador. Westward, I believe, it reaches to the very bases of the Rocky Mountains. It is a hardy bird, and bears the

Plate CCXI. *Great Blue Heron*

extremes of temperature surprisingly, being in its tribe what the Passenger Pigeon is in the family of Doves. During the coldest part of winter the Blue Heron is observed in the State of Massachusetts and in Maine, spending its time in search of prey about the warm springs and ponds which occur there in certain districts. They are not rare in the Middle States, but more plentiful to the west and south of Pennsylvania, which perhaps arises from the incessant war waged against them.

Extremely suspicious and shy, this bird is ever on the look-out. Its sight is as acute as that of any falcon, and it can hear at a considerable distance, so that it is enabled to mark with precision the different objects it sees, and to judge with accuracy of the sounds which it hears. Unless under very favourable circumstances, it is almost hopeless to attempt to approach it. You may now and then surprise one feeding under the bank of a deep creek or bayou, or obtain a shot as he passes unawares over you on wing; but to walk up towards one would be a fruitless adventure. I have seen many so wary, that, on seeing a man at any distance within a half a mile, they would take to wing; and the report of a gun forces one off his grounds from a distance at which you would think he could not be alarmed. When in close woods, however, and perched on a tree, they can be approached with a good chance of success.

The Blue Heron feeds at all hours of the day, as well as in the dark and dawn, and even under night, when the weather is clear, his appetite alone determining his actions in this respect; but I am certain that when disturbed during dark nights it feels bewildered, and alights as soon as possible. When passing from one part of the country to another at a distance, the case is different, and on such occasions they fly under night at a considerable height above the trees, continuing their movements in a regular manner.

The commencement of the breeding season varies, according to the latitude, from the beginning of March to the middle of June. In the Floridas it takes place about the first of these periods, in the Middle Districts about the 15th of May, and in Maine a month later. It is at the approach of this period only that these birds associate in pairs, they being generally quite solitary at all other times; nay, excepting during the breeding season, each individual seems to secure for itself a certain district as a feeding ground, giving chase to every intruder of its own species. At such times they also repose singly, for the most part roosting on trees, although sometimes taking their station on the ground, in the midst of a wide marsh, so that they may be secure from the approach of man. This unsocial temper probably arises from the desire of securing a certain abundance of food, of which each individual in fact requires a large quantity.

The manners of this Heron are exceedingly interesting at the approach of the breeding season, when the males begin to look for partners. About sunrise you see a number arrive and alight either on the margin of a broad sand-bar or on a savannah. They come from different quarters, one after another, for several hours; and when you see forty or fifty before you, it is difficult for you to imagine that half the number could have resided in the same district. Yet in the Floridas I have seen hundreds thus collected in the course of a morning. They are now in their full beauty, and no young birds seem to be among them. The males walk about with an air of great dignity, bidding defiance to their rivals, and the females utter their coaxing notes all at once, and as each male evinces an equal desire to please the object of his affection, he has to encounter the enmity of many an adversary, who, with little attention to politeness, opens his powerful bill, throws out his wings, and rushes with fury on his foe. Each attack is carefully guarded against, blows are exchanged for blows; one would think that a single well-aimed thrust might suffice to inflict death, but the strokes are parried with as much art as an expert swordsman would employ; and, although I have watched these birds for half an hour at a time as they fought on the ground, I never saw one killed on such an occasion; but I have often seen one felled and trampled upon, even after incubation had commenced. These combats over, the males and females leave the place in pairs. They are now mated for the season, at least I am inclined to think so, as I never saw them assemble twice on the same ground, and they become comparatively peaceable after pairing.

It is by no means a constant practice with this species to breed in communities, whether large or small; for although I have seen many such associations, I have also found many pairs breeding apart. Nor do they at all times make choice of the trees placed in the interior of a swamp, for I have found heronries in the pine-barrens of the Floridas, more than ten miles from any marsh, pond, or river. I have also observed nests on the tops of the tallest trees, while others were only a few feet above the ground: some also I have seen on the ground itself, and many on cactuses. In the Carolinas, where Herons of all sorts are extremely abundant, perhaps as much so as in the lower parts of Louisiana or the Floridas, on account of the numerous reservoirs connected with the rice plantations, and the still more numerous ditches which intersect the rice-fields, all of which contain fish of various sorts, these birds find it easy to procure food in great abundance. There the Blue Herons breed in considerable numbers, and if the place they have chosen be over a swamp, few situations can be conceived more likely to ensure their safety, for one seldom ventures into those dismal retreats at the time when these birds breed, the effluvia being extremely injurious to health, besides the difficulties to be overcome in making one's way to them.

Imagine, if you can, an area of some hundred acres, overgrown with huge cypress trees, the trunks of which, rising to a height of perhaps fifty feet before they send off a branch, spring from the midst of the dark muddy waters. Their broad tops, placed close together with interlaced branches, seem intent on separating the heavens from the earth. Beneath their dark canopy scarcely a single sunbeam ever makes its way; the mire is covered with fallen logs, on which grow matted grasses and lichens, and the deeper parts with nympheae and other aquatic plants. The Congo snake and water-moccasin glide before you as they seek to elude your sight, hundreds of turtles drop, as if shot, from the floating trunks of the fallen trees, from which also the sullen alligator plunges into the dismal pool. The air is pregnant with pestilence, but alive with musquitoes and other insects. The croaking of the frogs, joined with the hoarse cries of the Anhingas and the screams of the Herons, forms fit music for such a scene. Standing knee-deep in the mire, you discharge your gun at one of the numerous birds that are breeding high over head, when immediately such a deafening noise arises, that, if you have a companion with you, it were quite useless to speak to him. The frightened birds cross each other confusedly in their flight; the young attempting to secure themselves, some of them lose their hold, and fall into the water with a splash; a shower of leaflets whirls downwards from the tree-tops, and you are glad to make your retreat from such a place. Should you wish to shoot Herons, you may stand, fire, and pick up your game as long as you please; you may obtain several species, too, for not only does the Great Blue Heron breed there, but the White, and sometimes the Night Heron, as well as the Anhinga, and to such places they return year after year, unless they have been cruelly disturbed.

The nest of the Blue Heron, in whatever situation it may be placed, is large and flat, externally composed of dry sticks, and matted with weeds and mosses to a considerable thickness. When the trees are large and convenient, you may see several nests on the same tree. The full complement of eggs which these birds lay is three, and in no instance have I found more. Indeed, this is constantly the case with all the large species with which I am acquainted, from *Ardea coerulea* to *Ardea occidentalis;* but the smaller species lay more as they diminish in size, the Louisiana Heron having frequently four, and the Green Heron five, and even sometimes six. Those of the Great Blue Heron are very small compared with the size of the bird, measuring only two and a half inches by one and seven-twelfths; they are of a dull bluish-white, without spots, rather rough, and of a regular oval form.

The male and the female sit alternately, receiving food from each other, their mutual affection being as great as it is towards their young, which they provide for so abundantly, that it is not uncommon to find the nest containing a quantity of fish and other food, some fresh, and some in various stages of putrefaction. As the young advance they are less frequently fed, although still as copiously supplied whenever opportunity offers; but now and then I have observed them, when the nests were low, standing on their haunches, with their legs spread widely before them, and calling for food in vain. The quantity which they require is now so great that all the exertions of the old birds appear at times to be insufficient to satisfy their voracious appetite; and they do not provide for themselves until fully able to fly, when their parents chase them off, and force them to shift as they can. They are generally in good condition when they leave the nest; but from want of experience they find it difficult to procure as much food as they have been accustomed to, and soon become poor. Young birds from the nest afford tolerable eating; but the flesh of the old birds is by no means to my taste, nor so good as some epicures would have us to believe, and I would at any time prefer that of a Crow or young Eagle.

The principal food of the Great Blue Heron is fish of all kinds; but it also devours frogs, lizards, snakes, and birds, as well as small quadrupeds, such as shrews, meadow-mice, and young rats, all of which I have found in its stomach. Aquatic insects are equally welcome to it, and it is an expert flycatcher, striking at moths, butterflies, and libellulae, whether on the wing or when alighted. It destroys a great number of young Marsh-Hens, Rails, and other birds; but I never saw one catch a fiddler or a crab; and the only seeds that I have found in its stomach were those of the great water-lily of the Southern States. It always strikes its prey through the body, and as near the head as possible. When the animal is strong and active, it kills it by beating it against the ground or a rock, after which it swallows it entire. While on the St. John's River in East Florida, I shot one of these birds, and on opening it on board, found in its stomach a fine perch quite fresh, but of which the head had been cut off. The fish, when cooked, I found excellent, as did Lieutenant Piercy and my assistant Mr. Ward, but Mr. Leehman would not so much as taste it. When on a visit to my friend John Bulow, I was informed by him, that although he had several times imported gold fishes from New York, with the view of breeding them in a pond, through which ran a fine streamlet, and which was surrounded by a wall, they all disappeared in a few days after they were let loose. Suspecting the Heron to be the depredator, I desired him to watch the place carefully with a gun; which was done, and the result was, that he shot a superb specimen of the present species, in which was found the last gold fish that remained.

In the wild state it never, I believe, eats dead fish of any sort, or indeed any other food than that killed by itself. Now and then it strikes at a fish so large and strong as to endanger its own life; and I once saw one on the Florida coast, that, after striking a fish, when standing in the water to the full length of its legs, was dragged along for several yards, now on the surface, and again beneath. When, after a severe struggle, the Heron disengaged itself, it appeared quite overcome, and stood still near the shore, his head turned from the sea, as if afraid to try another such experiment. The number of fishes, measuring five or six inches, which one of these birds devours in a day, is surprising: Some which I kept on board the Marion would swallow, in the space of half an hour, a bucketful of young mullets; and when fed on the flesh of green turtles, they would eat several pounds at a meal. I have no doubt that, in favourable circumstances, one of them could devour several hundreds of small fishes in a day. A Heron that was caught alive on one of the Florida keys, near Key West, looked so emaciated when it came on board, that I had it killed to discover the cause of its miserable condition. It was an adult female that had bred that spring; her belly was in a state of mortification, and on opening her, we found the head of a fish measuring several inches, which, in an undigested state, had lodged among the entrails of the poor bird. How long it had suffered could only be guessed, but this undoubtedly was the cause of the miserable state in which it was found.

I took a pair of young Herons of this species to Charleston. They were nearly able to fly when caught, and were standing erect a few yards from the nest, in which lay a putrid one that seemed to have been trampled to death by the rest. They offered little resistance, but grunted with a rough uncouth voice. I had them placed in a large coop, containing four individuals of the *Ardea occidentalis,* who immediately attacked the new-comers in the most violent manner, so that I was obliged to turn them loose on the deck. I had frequently observed the great antipathy evinced by the majestic white species towards the blue in the wild state, but was surprised to find it equally strong in young birds which had never seen one, and were at that period smaller than the others. All my endeavours to remove their dislike were unavailing, for when placed in a large yard, the White Herons attacked the Blue, and kept them completely under. The latter became much tamer, and were more attached to each other. Whenever a piece of turtle was thrown to them, it was dexterously caught in the air and gobbled up in an instant, and as they became more familiar, they ate bits of biscuit, cheese, and even rhinds of bacon.

When wounded, the Great Blue Heron immediately prepares for defence, and woe to the man or dog who incautiously comes within reach of its powerful bill, for that instant he is sure to receive a severe wound, and the risk is so much the greater that birds of this species commonly aim at the eye. If beaten with a pole or long stick, they throw themselves on their back, cry aloud, and strike with their bill and claws with great force. I have shot some on trees, which, although quite dead, clung by their claws for a considerable time before they fell. I have also seen the Blue Heron giving chase to a Fish Hawk, whilst the latter was pursuing its way through the air towards a place where it could feed on the fish which it bore in its talons. The Heron soon overtook the Hawk, and at the very first lounge made by it, the latter dropped its quarry, when the Heron sailed slowly towards the ground, where it no doubt found the fish. On one occasion of this kind, the Hawk dropped the fish in the water, when the Heron, as if vexed that it was lost to him, continued to harass the Hawk, and forced it into the woods.

The flight of the Great Blue Heron is even, powerful, and capable of being protracted to a great distance. On rising from the ground or on leaving its perch, it goes off in silence with extended neck and dangling legs, for eight or ten yards, after which it draws back its neck, extends its feet in a straight line behind, and with easy and measured flappings continues its course, at times flying low over the marshes, and again, as if suspecting danger, at a considerable height over the land or the forest. It removes from one pond or creek, or even from one marsh to another, in a direct manner, deviating only on apprehending danger. When about to alight, it now and then sails in a circular direction, and when near the spot it extends its legs, and keeps its wings stretched out until it has effected a footing. The same method is employed when it alights on a tree, where, however, it does not appear to be as much at its ease as on the ground. When suddenly surprised by an enemy, it utters several loud discordant notes, and mutes the moment it flies off.

This species takes three years in attaining maturity, and even after that period it still increases in size and weight. When just hatched they have a very uncouth appearance, the legs and neck being very long, as well as the bill. By the end of a-week the head and neck are sparingly covered with long tufts of silky down, of a dark grey colour, and the body exhibits young feathers, the quills large with soft blue sheaths. The tibio-tarsal joints appear monstrous, and at this period the bones of the leg are so soft, that one may bend them to a considerable extent without breaking them. At the end of four weeks, the body and wings are well covered with feathers of a dark slate colour, broadly margined with ferruginous, the latter colour shewing plainly on the thighs and the flexure of the wing; the bill has grown wonderfully, the legs would not now easily break, and the birds are able to stand erect on the nest or on the objects near it. They are now seldom fed oftener than once a-day, as if their parents were intent on teaching them that abstinence without which it would often be difficult for them to subsist in their after life. At the age of six or seven weeks they fly off, and at once go in search of food, each by itself.

In the following spring, at which time they have grown much, the elongated feathers of the breast and shoulders are seen, the males shew the commencement of the pendent crest, and the top of the head has become white. None breed at this age, in so far as I have been able to observe. The second spring, they have a handsome appearance, the upper parts have become light, the black and white marks are much purer, and some have the crest three or four inches in length. Some breed at this age. The third spring, the Great Blue Heron is as represented in the plate.

The males are somewhat larger than the females, but there is very little difference between the sexes in external appearance. This species moults in the Southern States about the beginning of May, or as soon as the young are hatched, and one month after the pendent crest is dropped, and much of the beauty of the bird is gone for the season. The weight of a full grown Heron of this kind, when it is in good condition, is about eight pounds; but this varies very much according to circumstances, and I have found some having all the appearance of old birds that did not exceed six pounds. The stomach consists of a long bag, thinly covered by a muscular coat, and is capable of containing several fishes at a time. The intestine is not thicker than the quill of a swan, and measures from eight and a half to nine feet in length.

[From *Ornithological Biography,* Vol. III, pp. 87-95.]

THE WHOOPING CRANE

Grus americana, Temm.
Plate CCXXVI. Male.

[Whooping Crane, *Grus americana*
Sandhill Crane, *Grus canadensis*]

The wariness of this species [Sandhill Crane] is so remarkable, that it takes all the cunning and care of an Indian hunter to approach it at times, especially in the case of an old bird. The acuteness of their sight and hearing is quite wonderful. If they perceive a man approaching, even at the distance of a quarter of a mile, they are sure to take to wing. Should you accidentally tread on a stick and break it, or suddenly cock your gun, all the birds in the flock raise their heads and emit a cry. Shut the gate of a field after you, and from that moment they all watch your motions. To attempt to crawl towards them, even among long grass, after such an intimation, would be useless; and unless you lie in wait for them, and be careful

Plate CCXXVI. *Hooping Crane*

ntain a perfect silence, or may have the cover of some large heaps of brushwood, or fallen logs, you may as well stay at . They generally see you long before you perceive them, and so s they are aware that you have not observed them, they remain ; but the moment that, by some inadvertency, you disclose to your sense of their presence, some of them sound an alarm. For rt, Reader, I would as soon undertake to catch a deer by fair run ng, as to shoot a Sand-hill Crane that had observed me. Sometimes, indeed, towards the approach of spring, when they are ready to depart for their breeding grounds, the voice of one will startle and urge to flight all within a mile of the spot. When this happens, all the birds around join into a great flock, gradually rise in a spiral manner, ascend to a vast height, and sail off in a straight course.

When wounded, these birds cannot be approached without caution, as their powerful bill is capable of inflicting a severe wound. Knowing this as I do, I would counsel any sportsman not to leave his gun behind, while pursuing a wounded Crane. One afternoon in winter, as I was descending the Mississippi, on my way to Natchez, I saw several Cranes standing on a large sand-bar. The sight of these beautiful birds excited in me a desire to procure some of them. Accordingly, taking a rifle and some ammunition, I left the flat-bottomed boat in a canoe, and told the men to watch for me, as the current was rapid at that place, the river being there narrowed by the sand-bar. I soon paddled myself to the shore, and having observed, that, by good management, I might approach the Cranes under cover of a huge stranded tree, I landed opposite to it, drew up my canoe, and laying myself flat on the sand, crawled the best way I could, pushing my gun before me. On reaching the log, I cautiously raised my head opposite to a large branch, and saw the birds at a distance somewhat short of a hundred yards. I took, as I thought, an excellent aim, although my anxiety to shew the boatmen how good a marksman I was rendered it less sure than it might otherwise have been. I fired, when all the birds instantly flew off greatly alarmed, excepting one which leaped into the air, but immediately came down again, and walked leisurely away with a drooping pinion. As I rose on my feet, it saw me, I believe, for the first time, cried out lustily, and ran off with the speed of an ostrich. I left my rifle unloaded, and in great haste pursued the wounded bird, which doubtless would have escaped had it not made towards a pile of drift wood, where I overtook it. As I approached it, panting and almost exhausted, it immediately raised itself to the full stretch of its body, legs, and neck, ruffled its feathers, shook them, and advanced towards me with open bill, and eyes glancing with anger. I cannot tell you whether it was from feeling almost exhausted with the fatigue of the chase; but, however it was, I felt unwilling to encounter my antagonist, and keeping my eye on him, moved backwards. The farther I removed, the more he advanced, until at length I fairly turned my back to him, and took to my heels, retreating with fully more speed than I had pursued. He followed, and I was glad to reach the river, into which I plunged up to the neck, calling out to my boatmen, who came up as fast as they could. The Crane stood looking angrily on me all the while, immersed up to his belly in the water, and only a few yards distant, now and then making thrusts at me with his bill. There he stood until the people came up; and highly delighted they were with my situation. However, the battle was soon over, for, on landing, some of them struck the winged warrior on the neck with an oar, and we carried him on board.

While in the Floridas, I saw only a few of these birds [Whooping Cranes] alive, but many which had been shot by the Spaniards and Indians, for the sake of their flesh and beautiful feathers, of which latter they make fans and fly-brushes. None of these birds remain there during summer; and William Bartram, when speaking of this species, must have mistaken the Wood Ibis for it. . . .

Those [Sandhill Cranes] which resort to plantations, situated in the vicinity of large marshes, covered with tall grasses, cat's tails, and other plants, spend the night on some hillock, standing on one leg, the other being drawn under the body, whilst the head is thrust beneath the broad feathers of the shoulder. In returning towards the feeding grounds, they all emit their usual note, but in a very low undertone, leaving their roost at an earlier or later hour, according to the state of the weather. When it is cold and clear, they start very early; but when warm and rainy, not until late in the morning. Their motions toward night are determined by the same circumstances. They rise easily from the ground after running a few steps, fly low for thirty or forty yards, then rise in circles, crossing each other in their windings, like Vultures, Ibises, and some other birds. If startled or shot at, they utter loud and piercing cries. These cries, which I cannot compare to the sounds of any instrument known to me, I have heard at the distance of three miles, at the approach of spring, when the males were paying their addresses to the females, or fighting among themselves. They may be in some degree represented by the syllables *kewrr, kewrr, kewrooh;* and strange and uncouth as they are, they have always sounded delightful in my ear. . . .

In captivity the Whooping Crane becomes extremely gentle, and feeds freely on grain and other vegetable substances. . . . Having myself kept one alive, I will give you an account of its habits.

It was nearly full-grown when I obtained it, and its plumage was changing from greyish-brown to white. Its figure you will see in the plate to which this article refers. I received it as a present from Captain Clack of the United States Navy, commander of the Erie sloop of war. It had been wounded in the wing, on the coast of Florida, but the fractured limb had been amputated and soon healed. During a voyage of three months, it became very gentle, and was a great favourite with the sailors. I placed it in a yard, in company with a beautiful Snow Goose. This was at Boston. It was so gentle as to suffer me to caress it with the hand, and was extremely fond of searching for worms and grubs about the wood-pile, probing every hole it saw with as much care and dexterity as an Ivory-billed Woodpecker. It also watched with all the patience of a cat the motions of some mice which had burrows near the same spot, killed them with a single blow, and swallowed them entire, one after another, until they were extirpated. I fed it on corn and garbage from the kitchen, to which were added bits of bread and cheese, as well as some apples. It would pick up the straws intended to keep its feet from being soiled, and arrange them round its body, as if intent on forming a nest. For hours at a time, it would stand resting on one foot in a very graceful posture; but what appeared to me very curious was, that it had a favourite leg for this purpose; and in fact none of my family ever found it standing on the other, although it is probable that this happened in consequence of the mutilation of the wing, the leg employed being that of the injured side. The stump of its amputated wing appeared to be a constant source of trouble, particularly at the approach of the winter: it would dress the feathers about it, and cover it with so much care, that I really felt for the poor fellow. When the weather became intensely cold, it regularly retired at the approach of night under a covered passage, where it spent the hours of darkness; but it always repaired to this place with marked reluctance, and never until all was quiet and nearly dark, and it came out, even when the snow lay deep on the ground, at the first appearance of day. Now and then it would take a run, extend its only wing, and, uttering a loud cry, leap several times in the air, as if anxious to return to its haunts. At other times it would look upwards, cry aloud as if calling to some acquaintance passing high in the air, and again use its ordinary note whenever its companion the Snow Goose sent forth her own signals. It seldom swallowed its food without first carrying it to the water, and dipping it several times, and now and then it would walk many yards for that express purpose. Although the winter was severe, the thermometer some mornings standing as low as 10°, the bird fattened and looked extremely well. So strong was the natural suspicion of this bird, that I frequently saw it approach some cabbage leaves with measured steps, look at each sideways before it would touch one of them, and after all, if it by accident tossed the leaf into the air when attempting to break it to pieces, it would run off as if some dreaded enemy were at hand.

[From *Ornithological Biography*, Vol. III, pp. 205-208, 209-210.]

THE WHOOPING CRANE

Grus Americana, Temm. [Sandhill Crane, *Grus canadensis*]
Plate CCLXI. Young.

The specimen from which the figure in this plate was drawn, was that mentioned at p. 209 [p. 181], as having been presented to me by Captain Clack [a specimen mix-up]. . . . In this state, the Whooping Crane has been considered as a distinct species, to which the name of Brown or Canada Crane, *Grus canadensis,* has been given.

On referring to one of my journals, written on the Gulf of Mexico, I find it stated that one of these birds came on board one dark night, and, after passing the man at the helm, fell into the yawl hanging at the stern of the ship, where in the morning it was discovered and secured. Although to appearance in good health, it refused every kind of food, and in a few days died. Knowing the great power of flight of this species, I could only conjecture that some disease operating powerfully at the moment, had caused the bird to take refuge in the boat.

[From *Ornithological Biography*, Vol. III, p. 441.]

Plate CCLXI. *Hooping Crane (Sandhill Crane)*

John James Audubon

THE DUSKY PETREL

Puffinus obscurus, Cuv.
Plate CCXCIX. Male.

[Audubon's Shearwater,
Puffinus lherminieri]

On the 26th of June 1826, while becalmed on the Gulf of Mexico, off the western shores of Florida, I observed that the birds of this species, of which some had been seen daily since we left the mouth of the Mississippi, had become very numerous. The mate of the vessel killed four at one shot, and, at my request, brought them on board. From one of them I drew the figure which has been engraved. The notes made at the time are now before me, and afford me the means of presenting you with a short account of the habits of this bird.

They skim very low over the sea in search of the floating bunches of marine plants, usually called the Gulf Weed, so abundant here as sometimes to occupy a space of half an acre or more. In proceeding, they flap their wings six or seven times in succession, and then sail for three or four seconds with great ease, having their tail much spread, and their long wings extended at right angles with the body. On approaching a mass of weeds, they raise their wings obliquely, drop their legs and feet, run as it were on the water, and at length alight on the sea, where they swim with as much ease as ducks, and dive freely, at times passing several feet under the surface in pursuit of the fishes, which, on perceiving their enemy, swim off, but are frequently seized with great agility. Four or five, sometimes fifteen or twenty of these birds, will thus alight, and, during their stay about the weeds, dive, flutter, and swim, with all the gaiety of a flock of ducks newly alighted on a pond. Many gulls of different kinds hover over the spot, vociferating their anger and disappointment at not being so well qualified for supplying themselves with the same delicate fare. No sooner have all the fishes disappeared than the Petrels rise, disperse, and extend their flight in search of more, returning perhaps in a while to the same spot. I heard no sound or note from any of them, although many came within twenty yards of the ship and alighted there. Whenever an individual settled in a spot, many others flew up directly and joined it. At times, as if by way of resting themselves, they alighted, swam lightly, and dipped their bills frequently in the water, in the manner of Mergansers.

I preserved the skins of the four specimens procured. One of them I sent to the Academy of Natural Sciences of Philadelphia, by Cap-

Plate CCXCIX. *Dusky Petrel*

tain John R. Butler, of the ship Thalia, then bound from Havannah to Minorca. Two others were presented to my excellent friend Dr. Traill, on my first becoming acquainted with him at Liverpool.

I found the wings of this species strong and muscular for its size, this structure being essentially requisite for birds that traverse such large expanses of water, and are liable to be overtaken by heavy squalls. The stomach resembles a leather purse, four inches in length, and was much distended with fishes of various kinds, partially digested or entire. The aesophagus is capable of being greatly expanded. Some of the fishes were two and a half inches in length, and one in depth. The flesh of this Petrel was fat, but tough, with a strong smell, and unfit for food; for, on tasting it, as is my practice, I found it to resemble that of the porpoises. No difference is perceptible in the sexes.

While on board the United States' Revenue Cutter the Marion, and in the waters of the Gulf Stream opposite Cape Florida, I saw a flock of these birds, which, on our sailing among them, would scarcely swim off from our bows, they being apparently gorged with food. As we were running at the rate of about ten knots, we procured none of them. I have also seen this species off Sandy Hook.

[From *Ornithological Biography*, Vol. III, pp. 620-621.]

John James Audubon

THE GREENSHANK

Totanus Glottis, Bechst. [Greenshank, *Totanus nebularia*]
Plate CCLXIX. Male.

While on Sand Key, which is about six miles distant from Cape Sable of the Floridas, in lat. 24° 57' north, and 81° 45' long. west of Greenwich, I shot three birds of this species on the 28th of May 1832. I had at first supposed them to be Tell-tale Godwits, as they walked on the bars and into the shallows much in the same manner, and, on obtaining them, imagined they were new; but on shewing them to my assistant Mr. Ward, who was acquainted with the Greenshank of Europe, he pronounced them to be of that species, and I have since ascertained the fact by a comparison of specimens. They were all male birds, and I observed no material difference in their plumage. We did not find any afterwards; but it is probable that we

Plate CCLXIX. *Greenshank*

had seen some previously, although we did not endeavour to procure them, having supposed them to be Tell-tales. Almost all the birds seen in the Floridas at this date had young or eggs; and this circumstance increased my surprise at finding all the three individuals to be males. They had been shot merely because they offered a tempting opportunity, being all close together, and it is not often that one can kill three Tell-tales at once.

[From *Ornithological Biography,* Vol. III, p. 483. Since none of this species has been recorded in North America after Audubon's time, the Greenshank has been relegated to the Hypothetical List of the A.O.U.]

LOUISIANA HERON

Ardea Ludoviciana, Wils. [Louisiana Heron, *Hydranassa tricolor*]
Plate CCXVII. Male.

Delicate in form, beautiful in plumage, and graceful in its movements, I never see this interesting Heron, without calling it the Lady of the Waters. Watch its motions, as it leisurely walks over the pure sand beaches of the coast of Florida, arrayed in the full beauty of its spring plumage. Its pendent crest exhibits its glossy tints, its train falls gracefully over a well defined tail, and the tempered hues of its back and wings contrast with those of its lower parts. Its measured steps are so light that they leave no impression on the sand, and with its keen eye it views every object around with the most perfect accuracy. See, it has spied a small fly lurking on a blade of grass, it silently runs a few steps, and with the sharp point of its bill it has already secured the prey. The minnow just escaped from the pursuit of some larger fish has almost rushed upon the beach for safety; but the quick eye of the Heron has observed its motions, and in an instant it is swallowed alive. Among the herbage yet dripping with dew the beautiful bird picks its steps. Not a snail can escape its keen search, and as it moves around the muddy pool, it secures each water lizard that occurs. Now the sun's rays have dried up the dews, the flowers begin to droop, the woodland choristers have ended their morning concert, and like them, the Heron, fatigued with its exertions, seeks a place of repose under the boughs of the nearest bush, where it may in safety await the coolness of the evening. Then for a short while it again searches for food. Little difficulty does it experience in this; and at length, with the last glimpse of day, it opens its wings, and flies off towards its well-known roosting-place, where it spends the night contented and happy.

This species, which is a constant resident in the southern parts of the peninsula of the Floridas, seldom rambles far from its haunts during the winter season, being rarely seen at that period beyond Savannah in Georgia to the eastward. To the west it extends to the broad sedgy flats bordering the mouths of the Mississippi, along the whole Gulf of Mexico, and perhaps much farther south. In the beginning of spring, it is found abundantly in the Carolinas, and sometimes as far east as Maryland, or up the Mississippi as high as Natchez. You never find it far inland: perhaps forty miles would be a considerable distance at any time of the year. It is at all seasons a social bird, moving about in company with the Blue Heron or the White Egret. It also frequently associates with the larger species, and breeds in the same places, along with the White Heron, the Yellow-crowned Heron, and the Night Heron; but more generally it resorts to particular spots for this purpose, keeping by itself, and assembling in great numbers. Those which visit the Carolinas, or the country of the Mississippi, make their appearance there about the first of April, or when the Egrets and other species of Heron seek the same parts, returning to the Floridas or farther south about the middle of September, although I have known some to remain there during mild winters. When this is the case, all the other species may be met with in the same places, as the Louisiana Heron is the most delicate in constitution of all. Whilst at St. Augustine in Florida, in the month of January, I found this species extremely abundant there; but after a hard frost of a few days, they all disappeared, leaving the other Herons, none of which seemed to be affected by the cold, and returned again as soon as the Fahrenheit thermometer rose to 80°. There they were in full livery by the end of February, and near Charleston by the 5th of April.

Although timid, they are less shy than most other species, and more easily procured. I have frequently seen one alight at the distance of a few yards, and gaze on me as if endeavouring to discover

Plate CCXVII. *Louisiana Heron*

my intentions. This apparent insensibility to danger has given rise to the appellation of *Egrette folle,* which is given to them in Lower Louisiana.

The flight of this beautiful Heron is light, rather irregular, swifter than that of any other species, and capable of being considerably protracted. They usually move in long files, rather widely separated, and in an undulating manner, with constant flappings. When proceeding towards their roosts, or when on their migrations, they pass as high over the country as other species; on the former occasion, they pass and repass over the same tract, thus enabling the gunner easily to shoot them, which he may especially calculate on doing at the approach of night, when they are gorged with food, and fly lower than in the morning. They may, however, be still more surely obtained on their arriving at their roosting place, where they alight at once among the lowest branches. On being shot at, they seldom fly to a great distance, and their attachment to a particular place is such that you are sure to find them there during the whole period of their stay in the country, excepting the breeding time. At the cry of a wounded one, they assail you in the manner of some Gulls and Terns, and may be shot in great numbers by any person fond of such sport.

On the 29th of April, while wading around a beautiful key of the Floridas, in search of certain crustaceous animals called the sea Cray-fish [Florida lobster], my party and I suddenly came upon one of the breeding places of the Louisiana Heron. The southern exposures of this lovely island were overgrown with low trees and bushes matted together by thousands of smilaxes and other creeping plants, supported by various species of cactus. Among the branches some hundred pairs of these lovely birds had placed their nests, which were so low and so close to each other, that without moving a step one could put his hand into several. The birds thus taken by surprise rose affrighted into the air, bitterly complaining of being disturbed in their secluded retreat. The nests were formed of small dried sticks crossing each other in various ways. They were flat, had little lining, and each contained three eggs, all the birds being then incubating. Observing that many eggs had been destroyed by the Crows and Buzzards, as the shells were scattered on the ground, I concluded that many of the Herons had laid more than once, to make up their full complement of eggs; for my opinion is, that all our species, excepting the Green Heron, never lay more nor less than three, unless an accident should happen. The eggs of the Louisiana Heron measure one inch and six and a half twelfths in length, an inch and a quarter in breadth; they are nearly elliptical, of a beautiful pale blue colour inclining to green, smooth, and with a very thin shell. The period of incubation is twenty-one days. Like all other species of the genus, this raises only one brood in the season. The little island of which I have spoken lies exposed to the sea, and has an extent of only a few acres. The trees or bushes with which it is covered seemed to have been stunted by the effect produced by their having been for years the receptacles of the Herons' nests.

On the 19th May, in the same year, I found another breeding place of this species not far from Key West. The young birds, which stood on all the branches of the trees and bushes on the southern side of the place, were about the size of our Little Partridge. Their notes, by which we had been attracted to the spot, were extremely plaintive, and resembled the syllables, *wiee, wiee, wiee.* When we went up to them, the old birds all flew to another key, as if intent on drawing us there; but in vain, for we took with us a good number of their young. It was surprising to see the little fellows moving about among the branches, clinging to them in all sorts of curious positions, and persevering in forcing their way toward the water, when over which they at once dropped, and swam off from us with great vigour and speed. When seized with the hand, they defended themselves to the utmost. At this early period, they plainly shewed the sprouting features of the crest. Many Crow Blackbirds had nests on the same mangroves, and a Fish-Hawk also had formed its nest there at a height of not more than five feet from the water. On the 24th of May, these Herons were fully fledged, and able to fly to a short distance. In this state we, with some difficulty, procured one alive. Its legs and feet were green, the bill black, but its eyes, like those of an adult bird, were of a beautiful red hue. Many were caught afterwards and taken as passengers on board the Marion. They fed on any garbage thrown to them by the sailors; but whenever another species came near them, they leaped towards its bill, caught hold of it as if it had been a fish, and hung to it until shaken off by their stronger associates. On several occasions, however, the *Ardea occidentalis* [Great White Heron] shook them off violently, and after beating them on the deck, swallowed them before they could be rescued!

[From *Ornithological Biography,* Vol. III, pp. 136-139]

THE GREAT WHITE HERON

Ardea occidentalis.
Plate CCLXXXI.

[Great White Heron,
Ardea occidentalis]

On the 24th of April 1832, I landed on Indian Key in Florida, and immediately after formed an acquaintance with Mr. Egan, of whom I have already several times spoken. He it was who first gave me notice of the species which forms the subject of this article, and of which I

Plate CCLXXXI. *Great White Heron*

cannot find any description. The next day after that of my arrival, when I was prevented from accompanying him by my anxiety to finish a drawing, he came in with two young birds alive, and another lying dead in a nest, which he had cut off from a mangrove. You may imagine how delighted I was, when at the very first glance I felt assured that they were different from any that I had previously seen. The two living birds were of a beautiful white, slightly tinged with cream-colour, remarkably fat and strong for their age, which the worthy Pilot said could not be more than three weeks. The dead bird was quite putrid and much smaller. It looked as if it had accidentally been trampled to death by the parent birds ten or twelve days before, the body being almost flat and covered with filth. The nest with the two live birds was placed in the yard. The young Herons seemed quite unconcerned when a person approached them, although on displaying one's hand to them, they at once endeavoured to strike it with their bill. My Newfoundland dog, a well-trained and most sagacious animal, was whistled for and came up; on which the birds rose partially on their legs, ruffled all their feathers, spread their wings, opened their bills, and clicked their mandibles in great anger, but without attempting to leave the nest. I ordered the dog to go near them, but not to hurt them. They waited until he went within striking distance, when the largest suddenly hit him with its bill, and hung to his nose. Plato, however, took it all in good part, and merely brought the bird towards me, when I seized it by the wings, which made it let go its hold. It walked off as proudly as any of its tribe, and I was delighted to find it possessed of so much courage. These birds were left under the charge of Mrs. Egan, until I returned from my various excursions to the different islands along the coast.

On the 26th of the same month, Mr. Thruston took me and my companions in his beautiful barge to some keys on which the Florida Cormorants were breeding in great numbers. As we were on the way we observed two tall white Herons standing on their nests; but although I was anxious to procure them alive, an unfortunate shot from one of the party brought them to the water. They were, I was told, able to fly, but probably had never seen a man before. While searching that day for nests of the Zenaida Dove, we observed a young Heron of this species stalking among the mangroves that bordered the key on which we were, and immediately pursued it. Had you been been looking on, good Reader, you might have enjoyed a hearty laugh, although few of us could have joined you. Seven or eight persons were engaged in the pursuit of this single bird, which, with extended neck, wings, and legs, made off among the tangled trees at such a rate, that, anxious as I was to obtain it alive, I several times thought of shooting it. At length, however, it was caught, its bill was securely tied, its legs were drawn up, and fastened by a strong cord, and the poor thing was thus conveyed to Indian Key, and placed along with its kinsfolk. On seeing it, the latter immediately ran towards it with open bills, and greeted it with a most friendly welcome, passing their heads over and under its own in the most curious and indeed ludicrous manner. A bucketful of fish was thrown to them, which they swallowed in a few minutes. After a few days, they also ate pieces of pork-rhind, cheese, and other substances.

While sailing along the numerous islands that occur between Indian Key and Key West, I saw many birds of this species, some in pairs, some single, and others in flocks; but on no occasion did I succeed in getting within shot of one. Mr. Egan consoled me by saying that he knew some places beyond Key West where I certainly should obtain several, were we to spend a day and a night there for the purpose. Dr. Benjamin Strobel afterwards gave me a similar assurance. In the course of a week after reaching Key West, I in fact procured more than a dozen birds of different ages, as well as nests and eggs, and their habits were carefully examined by several of my party.

At three o'clock one morning, you might have seen Mr. Egan and myself, about eight miles from our harbour, paddling as silently as possible over some narrow and tortuous inlets, formed by the tides through a large flat and partially submersed key. There we expected to find many White Herons; but our labour was for a long time almost hopeless, for, although other birds occurred, we had determined to shoot nothing but the Great White Heron, and none of that species came near us. At length, after six or seven hours of hard labour, a Heron flew right over our heads, and to make sure of it, we both fired at once. The bird came down dead. It proved to be a female, which had either been sitting on her eggs or had lately hatched her young, her belly being bare, and her plumage considerably worn. We now rested a while, and breakfasted on some biscuit soaked in molasses and water, reposing under the shade of the mangroves, where the mosquitoes had a good opportunity of breaking their fast also. We went about from one key to another, saw a great number of White Herons, and at length, towards night, reached the Marion, rather exhausted, and having a solitary bird. Mr. Egan and I had been most of the time devising schemes for procuring others with less trouble, a task which might easily have been accomplished a month before, when, as he said, the birds were "sitting hard." He asked if I would return that night at twelve o'clock to the last key which we had visited. I mentioned the proposal to our worthy Captain, who, ever willing to do all in his power to oblige me, when the service did not require constant attendance on board, said that if I would go, he would accompany us in the gig. Our guns were soon cleaned, provisions and ammunition placed in the boats, and after supping we talked and laughed until the appointed time.

"Eight Bells" made us bound on our feet, and off we pushed for the islands. The moon shone bright in the clear sky; but as the breeze had died away, we betook ourselves to our oars. The state of the tide was against us, and we had to drag our boats several miles over the soapy shallows; but at last we found ourselves in a deep channel beneath the hanging mangroves of a large key, where we had observed the Herons retiring to roost the previous evening. There we lay quietly until daybreak. But the mosquitoes and sandflies! Reader, if you have not been in such a place, you cannot easily conceive the torments we endured for a whole hour, when it was absolutely necessary for us to remain perfectly motionless. At length day dawned, and the boats parted, to meet on the other side of the key. Slowly and silently each advanced. A Heron sprung from its perch almost directly over our heads. Three barrels were discharged,—in vain; the bird flew on unscathed; the pilot and I had probably been too anxious. As the bird sped away, it croaked loudly, and the noise, together with the report of our guns, roused some hundreds of these Herons, which flew from the mangroves, and in the grey light appeared to sail over and around us like so many spectres. I almost despaired of procuring any more. The tide was now rising, and when we met with the other boat we were told, that if we had waited until we could have shot at them while perched, we might have killed several; but that now we must remain until full tide, for the birds had gone to their feeding grounds.

The boats parted again, and it was now arranged that whenever a Heron was killed, another shot should be fired exactly one minute after, by which each party would be made aware of the success of the other. Mr. Egan, pointing to a nest on which stood two small young birds, desired to be landed near it. I proceeded into a narrow bayou, where we remained quiet for about half an hour, when a Heron flew over us and was shot. It was a very fine old male. Before firing my signal shot, I heard a report from afar, and a little after mine was discharged I heard another shot, so I felt assured that two birds had been killed. When I reached the Captain's boat I found that he had in fact obtained two; but Mr. Egan had waited two hours in vain near the nest, for none of the old birds came up. We took him from his hiding place, and brought the Herons along with us. It was now nearly high water. About a mile from us, more than a hundred Herons stood on a mud-bar up to their bellies. The pilot said that now was our best chance, as the tide would soon force them to fly, when they would come to rest on the trees. So we divided, each choosing his own place, and I went to the lowest end of the key, where it was separated from another by a channel. I soon had the pleasure of observing all the Herons take to wing, one after another, in quick succession. I then heard my companions' guns, but no signal of success. Obtaining a good chance as I thought, I fired at a remarkably large bird, and distinctly heard the shot strike it. The Heron merely croaked, and pursued its course. Not another bird came near enough to be shot at, although many had alighted on the neighbouring key, and stood perched like so many newly finished statues of the purest alabaster, forming a fine contrast to the deep blue sky. The boats joined us. Mr. Egan had one bird, the Captain another, and both looked at me with surprise. We now started for the next key, where we expected to see more. When we had advanced several hundred yards along its low banks, we found the bird at which I had shot lying with extended wings in the agonies of death. It was from this specimen that the drawing was made. I was satisfied with the fruits of this day's excursion. On other occasions I procured fifteen more birds, and judging that number sufficient, I left the Herons to their occupations.

This species is extremely shy. Sometimes they would rise when at the distance of half a mile from us, and fly quite out of sight. If pursued, they would return to the very keys or mud-flats from which they had risen, and it was almost impossible to approach one while perched or standing in the water. Indeed, I have no doubt that half a dozen specimens of *Ardea Herodias* [Great Blue Heron] could be procured for one of the present, in the same time and under similar circumstances.

The Great White Heron is a constant resident on the Florida Keys, where it is found more abundant during the breeding season than anywhere else. They rarely go as far eastward as Cape Florida, and are not seen on the Tortugas, probably because these islands are destitute of mangroves. They begin to pair early in March, but many do not lay their eggs until the middle of April. Their courtships were represented to me as similar to those of the Great Blue Heron. Their nests are at times met with at considerable distances from each other, and although many are found on the same keys, they are placed farther apart than those of the species just mentioned. They are seldom more than a few feet above high-water-mark, which in the Floridas is so low, that they look as if only a yard or two above the roots of the trees. From twenty to thirty nests which I examined were thus placed. They were large, about three feet in diameter, formed of sticks of different sizes, but without any appearance of lining, and quite flat, being several inches thick. The eggs are always three, measure two inches and three quarters in length, one inch and eight-twelfths in breadth, and have a rather thick shell, of a uniform plain light bluish-green colour. Mr. Egan told me that incubation continues about thirty days, that both birds sit, (the female, however, being most assiduous,) and with their legs stretched out before them, in the same manner as the young when two or three weeks old. The latter, of which I saw several from ten days to a month old, were pure white, slightly tinged with cream colour, and had no indications of a crest. Those which I carried to Charleston, and which were kept for more than a year, exhibited nothing of the kind. I am unable to say how long it is before they attain their full plumage as represented in the plate, when, as you see, the head is broadly but loosely and shortly tufted, the feathers of the breast pendent, but not remarkably long, and there are none of the narrow feathers seen in other species over the rump or wings.

These Herons are sedate, quiet, and perhaps even less animated that the *A. Herodias.* They walk majestically, with firmness and great elegance. Unlike the species just named, they *flock* at their feeding grounds, sometimes a hundred or more being seen together; and what is still more remarkable is, that they betake themselves to the mud-flats or sand-bars at a distance from the Keys on which they roost and breed. They seem, in so far as I could judge, to be diurnal, an opinion corroborated by the testimony of Mr. Egan, a person of great judgment, sagacity and integrity. While on these banks, they stand motionless, rarely moving towards their prey, but waiting until it comes near, when they strike it and swallow it alive, or when large beat it on the water, or shake it violently, biting it severely all the while. They never leave their feeding grounds until driven off by the tide, remaining until the water reaches their body. So wary are they, that although they may return to roost on the same keys, they rarely alight on trees to which they have resorted before, and if repeatedly disturbed they do not return, for many weeks at least. When roosting, they generally stand on one foot, the other being drawn up, and, unlike the Ibises, are never seen lying flat on trees, where, however, they draw in their long neck, and place their head under their wing.

I was often surprised to see that while a flock was resting by day in the position just described, one or more stood with outstretched necks, keenly eyeing all around, now and then suddenly starting at the sight of a Porpoise or Shark in chase of some fish. The appearance of a man or a boat, seemed to distract them; and yet I was told that nobody ever goes in pursuit of them. If surprised, they leave their perch with a rough croaking sound, and fly directly to a great distance, but never inland.

The flight of the Great White Heron is firm, regular, and greatly protracted. They propel themselves by regular slow flaps, the head being drawn in after they have proceeded a few yards, and their legs extended behind, as is the case with all other Herons. They also now and then rise high in the air, where they sail in wide circles, and they never alight without performing this circling flight, unless when going to feeding grounds on which other individuals have already settled. It is truly surprising that a bird of so powerful a flight never visits Georgia or the Carolinas, nor goes to the Mainland. When you see them about the middle of the day on their feeding grounds they "loom" to about double their size, and present a singular appearance. It is difficult to kill them unless with buck-shot, which we found ourselves obliged to use.

When I left Key West, on our return towards Charleston, I took with me two young birds that had been consigned to the care of my friend Dr. B. Strobel, who assured me that they devoured more than their weight of food per day. I had also two young birds of the *Ardea Herodias* alive. After bringing them on board, I placed them all together in a very large coop; but was soon obliged to separate the two species, for the white birds would not be reconciled to the blue, which they would have killed. While the former had the privilege of the deck for a few minutes, they struck at the smaller species, such as the young of *Ardea rufescens* and *A. Ludoviciana*, some of which they instantly killed and swallowed entire, although they were abundantly fed on the flesh of green Turtles. None of the sailors succeeded in making friends with them.

On reaching Indian Key, I found those which had been left with Mrs. Egan, in excellent health and much increased in size, but to my surprise observed that their bills were much broken, which she assured me had been caused by the great force with which they struck at the fishes thrown to them on the rocks of their enclosure,—a statement which I found confirmed by my own observation in the course of the day. It was almost as difficult to catch them in the yard, as if they had never seen a man before, and we were obliged to tie their bills fast, to avoid being wounded by them while carrying them on board. They thrived well, and never manifested the least animosity towards each other. One of them which accidentally walked before the coop in which the Blue Herons were, thrust its bill between the bars, and transfixed the head of one of these birds, so that it was instantaneously killed.

When we arrived at Charleston, four of them were still alive. They were taken to my friend John Bachman, who was glad to see them. He kept a pair, and offered the other to our mutual friend Dr. Samuel Wilson, who accepted them, but soon afterwards gave them to Dr. Gibbes of Columbia College, merely because they had killed a number of Ducks. My friend Bachman kept two of these birds for many months; but it was difficult for him to procure fish enough for them, as they swallowed a bucketful of mullets in a few minutes, each devouring about a gallon of these fishes. They betook themselves to roosting in a beautiful arbour in his garden; where at night they looked with their pure white plumage like beings of another world. It is a curious fact, that the points of their bills, of which an inch at least had been broken, grew again, and were as regularly shaped at the end of six months as if nothing had happened to them. In the evening or early in the morning, they would frequently set, like pointer dogs, at moths which hovered over the flowers, and with a well-directed stroke of their bill seize the fluttering insect and instantly swallow it. On many occasions, they also struck at chickens, grown fowls and ducks, which they would tear up and devour. Once a cat which was asleep in the sunshine, on the wooden steps of the viranda, was pinned through the body to the boards, and killed by one of them. At last they began to pursue the younger children of my worthy friend, who therefore ordered them to be killed. One of them was beautifully mounted by my assistant Mr. Henry Ward, and is now in the Museum of Charleston. Dr. Gibbes was obliged to treat his in the same manner; and I afterwards saw one of them in his collection. Of the fifteen skins of this species which I carried to Philadelphia, one was presented to the Academy of Natural Sciences of that beautiful city, another was given in exchange for various skins, and two I believe are now in the possession of George Cooper, Esq. of New York. Two were sent along with other specimens to Mr. Selby of Twizel House, Northumberland. On my arrival in England, I presented a pair to His Royal Highness the Duke of Sussex, who gave them to the British Museum, where I have since seen them mounted. I also presented a specimen to the Zoological Society of London.

Mr. Egan kept for about a year one of these birds, which he raised from the nest, and which, when well grown, was allowed to ramble along the shores of Indian Key in quest of food. One of the wings had been cut, and the bird was known to all the resident inhabitants, but was at last shot by some Indian Hunter, who had gone there to dispose of a collection of sea shells.

Some of the Herons feed on the berries of certain trees during the latter part of autumn and the beginning of winter. Dr. B. B. Strobel observed the Night Heron eating those of the "Gobo-limbo," [gumbo-limbo] late in September at Key West.

Among the varied and contradictory descriptions of Herons, you will find it alleged that these birds seize fish while on wing by plunging the head and neck into the water; but this seems to me extremely doubtful. Nor, I believe, do they watch for their prey while perched on trees. Another opinion is, that Herons are always thin, and unfit for food. This, however, is by no means generally the case in America, and I have thought these birds very good eating when not too old.

[From *Ornithological Biography*, Vol. III, pp. 542-550.]

THE REDDISH EGRET

Ardea rufescens, Gmel.
Plate CCLVI. Adult and Young.

[Reddish Egret,
Dichromanassa rufescens]

While sailing towards the Florida Keys, my mind was agitated with anticipations of the delight I should experience in exploring a region whose productions were very imperfectly known. Often did I think of the Heron named after Titian Peale, by my learned friend the Prince of Musignano. Mr. Peale had procured only a single specimen, and in the winter season, but whether or not the species was abundant on the Keys of Florida remained to be discovered. No sooner had I been landed and formed an acquaintance with Mr. Egan, the pilot of whom I have often spoken, who was well acquainted with the haunts of many of the birds of those islands, than I asked him respecting the various Herons which might be found there or on the shores of the mainland. Before answering me, he counted his fingers slowly, and then said that he could recollect only "twelve sorts;" "but," added he, "these birds change their colours so curiously, that it is past wonder with me to believe that any one man could know them without watching them as I have done for many years." I then inquired if I was in good time to procure all the sorts which he knew. He answered in the affirmative; but felt some doubt as to my procuring the eggs of one kind at least, which breed earlier than the rest, and was pure white from the shell, and the largest of all. Thinking the species to which he alluded might be the *Ardea alba* of Linnaeus, I asked if it had long thread-like feathers over the tail during the breeding season. "Oh no, Sir," said he, "it never has; it is as tall as

Plate CCLVI. *Purple Heron (Reddish Egret)*

yourself, and when you see some on the wing, you will be pleased, for their wings are as large as those of the Brown Pelican. The one I guess you mean, mostly goes farther to the eastward to breed, along with a very small one, also always white, with the feathers over the tail as you say, and curled upwards. These are the only three sorts that are white." I begged him to describe the colours of the others, which he did so well that I recognized ten species in all; but the large white one, and another of a grey and purple colour, were unknown to me, and I told him so, stating at the same time how anxious I was to procure them if possible. "If possible! nothing in the world can be more easy, for if they have no eggs left, they have young ones enough to load your schooner. I can take you straight to their breeding place."

You may suppose, Reader, how my spirits were raised by this intelligence, and how surprised I was that Peale's Egret was not in the number of the Florida Herons. We speedily embarked in Mr. Thruston's boat, spread our sails to the breeze, and passed several keys, on which we procured two young birds of the large white species, which I saw at once was unknown to me, but of which you will find an account in this volume. As we approached the next island, I saw twenty or thirty pairs of Herons, some of which were pure white, others of a light blue colour, but so much larger than the Blue Heron, *Ardea caerulea* [Little Blue Heron], that I asked the pilot what they were, when he answered, "the very fellows I want to shew you, and you may soon see them close enough, as you and I will shoot a few by way of amusement." Before half an hour had elapsed, more than a dozen were lying at my feet. Some of them were as white as driven snow, the rest of a delicate purplish tint, inclining to grey on the back and wings, with heads and necks of a curious reddish colour. Males and females there were, but they were all of one species, for my companion assured me that "this sort bred before they turned to their natural colours," by which he meant before attaining their full plumage at the age of three years. Well, the immature birds were the very same as the individual to which, as the representative of a new species, the name of Peale's Egret had been given. This I saw at once, for so good is the representation of it in the fourth volume of Bonaparte's American Ornithology, that from the mere recollection of it I was enabled to recognise the bird at once. You may imagine the pleasure I felt, as well as that which I experienced on becoming better acquainted with this species, which I found in many places both with eggs and with young.

The Reddish Egret is a constant resident on the Florida Keys, to which it is so partial at all seasons that it never leaves them. Some individuals are seen as far east as Cape Florida, and westward along the Gulf of Mexico. Whether it may ever betake itself to fresh water I cannot say, but I never found one in such a situation. It is a more plump bird for its size than most other Herons, and in this respect resembles the Night Heron and the Yellow-crowned species, but possesses all the gracefulness of the tribe to which it belongs. In walking it lifts its feet high, and proceeds at a quiet pace, but sometimes briskly; it alights with ease on trees, and walks well on the larger branches. It rarely feeds from the edges of the water, but resorts to the shallows of the extensive mud or sand flats, so numerous about the keys. There, twenty or thirty, sometimes so many as a hundred, may be seen wading up to the heel (or knee-joint as it is usually called) in pursuit of prey, or standing in silence awaiting the approach of an animal on which it feeds, when it strikes it, and immediately swallows it, if not too large; but if so, it carries it to the shore, beats it, and tears it to pieces, rarely, however, using its feet for that purpose, and certainly never employing its pectinated claws, which no Heron that I know ever uses for any other object than that of scratching its head, or perhaps of securing its steps on rocky bottoms. These birds remain on the flats thus employed, until the advance of the tide forces them to the land.

The flight of this Heron is more elevated and regular than that of the smaller species. During the love season, it is peculiarly graceful and elegant, especially when one unmated male is pursuing another, a female being in sight. They pass through the air with celerity, turn and cut about in curious curves and zigzags, the stronger bird frequently erecting its beautiful crest, and uttering its note, at the moment when it expects to give its rival a thrust. When these aerial combats take place between old and immature birds, their different colours form a striking contrast, extremely pleasing to the beholder. While travelling to and from their feeding grounds, or from one key to another, they propel themselves by easy, well-sustained, and regular flappings of their extended wings, the neck reposing on the shoulders, the legs stretched out behind like a rudder, while their beautiful thready trains float in the breeze. On approaching a landing place, they seldom fail to perform a few circumvolutions, in order to see that all around is quiet, for they are more shy and wary than the smaller Herons, and almost as suspicious as the two larger species, *Ardea occidentalis,* and *A. Herodias;* and this becomes apparent as soon as they discontinue the feeding of their young, when you find it extremely difficult to approach them. After this period I rarely shot one, unless I happened to come upon it unawares, or while it was passing over me when among the mangroves.

About the beginning of April, these Herons begin to pair. The males chase each other on the ground, as well as in the air, and on returning to their chosen females erect their crest and plumes, swell out their necks, pass and repass before them, and emit hollow rough sounds, which it is impossible for me to describe. It is curious to see a party of twenty or thirty on a sand-bar, presenting as they do a mixture of colours from pure white to the full hues of the old birds of either sex; and still more curious perhaps it is to see a purple male paying his addresses to a white female, while at hand a white male is caressing a purple female, and not far off are a pair of white, and another of purple birds. Nay, reader, until I had witnessed these remarkable circumstances, I felt some distrust respecting the statement of the worthy pilot. I am even now doubtful if all the young breed the first spring after their birth, and am more inclined to think that they do not, on account of the large flocks of white birds of this species which during the breeding time kept apart from those that had nests, but which on examination were not found to be barren birds, although they had the crests and pendent feathers less elongated than those white individuals that were actually breeding.

By the middle of April, they construct their nests, which they place for the most part on the south-western sides of the mangroves immediately bordering the keys, never on the trees at a distance from the water, and rarely very close together. Some are placed on the top branches, others a foot or two above the highest tide-mark; many of them are annually repaired, perhaps all that stand the winter gales. The nest, which is quite flat, is large for the size of the bird, and is formed of dry sticks, interspersed with grass and leaves. The eggs are three, average an inch and three quarters in length, one and three-eighths in breadth, have an elliptical form, and a smooth shell, of a uniform rather pale sea-green colour. They afford excellent eating.

Both sexes incubate, but I did not ascertain the time required for hatching.

The young while yet naked are of a dark colour, there being only a few scanty tufts of long soft down on the head and other parts; but when the feathers begin to sprout they became white. Being abundantly and carefully fed, at first by regurgitation, they grow fast, and soon become noisy. When about a month old, they are fed less frequently, and the fish is merely dropt before them or into their open throats; soon after they sit upright on the nest, with their legs extended forward, or crawl about on the branches, as all other Herons are wont to do. They are now sensible of danger, and when a boat is heard coming towards them they hide among the branches, making towards the interior of the keys, where it is extremely difficult to follow them. On one occasion, when I was desirous of procuring some of them alive, to take to Charleston, it took more than an hour to catch eight or nine of them, for they moved so fast and stealthily through the mangroves, always making for the closest and most tangled parts, that a man was obliged to keep his eyes constantly on a single individual, which it was very difficult to do, on account of the number of birds crossing each other in every direction. They do not fly until they are six or seven weeks old, and even then do not venture beyond the island on which they have been reared. In captivity, those which we had procured feed freely, and soon became tolerably docile. They were supplied with pieces of green turtle and other species of the tribe, and some of them reached Charleston in good health. One continued alive for nearly two years with my friend the Rev. John Bachman. It was allowed to walk in the garden and poultry-yard, and ate an enormous quantity of small fish and all sorts of garbage, contenting itself, when better food was scarce, with the entrails of fowls, and even fed freely on moistened corn-meal or mush. It caught insects with great dexterity, and was very gentle and familiar, frequently going into the kitchen, where it was a great favourite. It had acquired a crest and a few of the pendent feathers of the back by the month of January, when about twenty-two months old. One cold night, it was accidentally neglected, and in the morning was found dead, having shared the fate of so many thousands of pet birds in all parts of the world. On being opened, it was found to be a male. Although I have not been able to trace the gradual changes of colour which this species undergoes, I have little doubt that it will be found to attain maturity the third spring after birth.

The Reddish Egret rarely associates with others; nor does it suffer them to nestle on the same island with itself. In this respect, it differs from all other Herons with which I am acquainted; for although the Great White Heron, *A. occidentalis*, has a decided antipathy to the Great Blue Heron, still it now and then allows a few to breed on the north side of its island. The present species is as strictly marine as the Great White Heron; and these are the only two that are so, for all the others feed on fresh-water fishes, not less than on those obtained in salt-water; as well as on other food of various kinds. [The Reddish Egret is occasionally reported in Florida Keys. Neither species is strictly marine.] Like all others, the Reddish Egret loses its ornaments soon after incubation, when old and young mix, and follow their occupations together. When wounded, it strikes with its bill, scratches with its claws, and, throwing itself on its back, emits its rough and harsh notes, keeping all the while its crest erected and expanded, and its feathers swelled out. Its principal food consists of fishes of various sizes, of which it consumes a great number, and of which it finds no difficulty in procuring a sufficiency, as all the waters of those portions of the Floridas that are inhabited by it are very profusely stocked. I was told that, although still plentiful in the Floridas, this species was much more so when the keys were first settled. I was present when a person killed twenty-eight in succession in about an hour, the poor birds hovering above their island in dismay, and unaware of the destructive power of their enemy.

The remarkable circumstance of this bird's changing from white to purple will no doubt have some tendency to disconcert the systematists, who, it seems, pronounce all the birds which they name Egrets to be always white; but how much more disconcerted must they be when they see that among the Herons peculiarly so named, which they say are always coloured, the largest known to exist in the United States is pure white. It is not at present my intention to say what an Egret is, or what a Heron is; but it can no longer be denied that the presence or absence of a loose crest, floating plume, and a white colour, are insufficient for establishing essential characters separating Egrets from Herons, which in fact display the most intimate connection, the one group running into the other in an almost imperceptible gradation. Hoping that an account of the extent of the migrations of the twelve species of Heron that occur in the United States, and whose habits I have studied for many years under the most favourable circumstances, may prove acceptable, I now lay one before you, arranging the species according to size, without regard to the rank they hold in systematic works.

1. The Great White Heron. *Ardea occidentalis.* A constant resident on the southern keys of Florida; entirely maritime; never goes farther eastward than Cape Florida, though in winter the younger birds migrate southward, and perhaps pass beyond the extremities of the Gulf of Mexico.

2. The Great Blue Heron. *Ardea Herodias.* A constant resident in the Floridas; migrates throughout the Union, and as far along the Atlantic coast as the southernmost islands of the Gulf of St. Lawrence in summer; breeds in all the districts, and at the approach of winter returns to the Southern States.

3. The White Heron [Common Egret]. *Ardea alba.* Resident in the Floridas; migrates to the eastward sometimes as far as Massachusetts, and up the Mississippi as far as the city of Natchez; never seen far inland.

4. The Purple Heron [Reddish Egret]. *Ardea rufescens.* Resident on the Florida Keys; entirely maritime; never seen farther eastward than Cape Florida; the young sometimes remove southward in winter.

5. The American Bittern. *Ardea minor.* A winter resident in the Floridas; many migrate over the greater part of the Union and beyond its northern limits; never seen in Kentucky; return before winter to the Southern States.

6. The [Black-crowned] Night Heron. *Ardea Nycticorax.* Resident in the Floridas; migrates eastward as far as Maine, up the Mississippi as high as Memphis; none seen in Kentucky; returns to the Southern States at the approach of winter, and occurs at the distance of a hundred miles inland.

7. The Yellow-crowned [Night] Heron. *Ardea violacea.* A few spend the winter in the Floridas; it rarely migrates farther eastward than New Jersey; proceeds up the Mississippi to Natchez; never goes far inland; the greatest number winter beyond the southern limits of the United States.

8. The [Little] Blue Heron. *Ardea caerulea.* Resident in the Flor-

idas; migrates eastward as far as Long Island; proceeds up the Mississippi about a hundred miles above Natchez; never goes far inland.

9. The Louisiana Heron. *Ardea Ludoviciana.* Resident in the Floridas; rarely seen as far east as New Jersey; seldom passes Natchez on the Mississippi; never goes far inland.

10. The White [Snowy] Egret. *Ardea candidissima.* Resident in the Floridas; migrates eastward as far as New York, up the Mississippi as far as Memphis; never goes far inland; returns to the Southern States as soon as the young are able to travel.

11. The Green Heron. *Ardea virescens.* Resident in the Floridas; disperses over the Union; goes far inland; the greater number return at the approach of winter to the Southern States.

12. The Least Bittern. *Ardea exilis.* Resident in the Floridas; migrates as far as Maine, and throughout the Western Country, far up the Missouri; returns early in autumn to the Southern States.

You will see from the above statement, that the Herons are almost similar to our Pigeons in respect to the extent of their migrations, which must appear the more remarkable on account of their comparative size, *Ardea Herodias* and *A. virescens* corresponding in a great degree to the *Columba migratoria* and *C. carolinensis.*

[From *Ornithological Biography,* Vol. III, pp. 411-417.]

THE PIPERY FLYCATCHER

Muscicapa dominicensis, Briss. [Gray Kingbird, *Tyrannus dominicensis*]
Plate CLXX. Male.

Having landed on one of the Florida Keys, I scarcely had time to cast a glance over the diversified vegetation which presented itself, when I observed a pair of birds mounting perpendicularly in the air twittering with a shrill continued note new to me. The country itself was new: it was what my mind had a thousand times before conceived a tropical scene to be. As I walked over many plants, curious and highly interesting to me, my sensations were joyous in the highest degree, for I saw that in a few moments I should possess a new

Plate CLXX. *Gray Tyrant (Pipery Flycatcher)*

subject, on which I could look with delight, as one of the great Creator's marvellous works.

I was on one of those yet unknown islets, which the foot of man has seldom pressed. A Flycatcher unknown to me had already presented itself, and the coing of a Dove never before heard come on my ear. I felt some of that pride, which doubtless pervades the breast of the discoverer of some hitherto unknown land. Although desirous of obtaining the birds before me, I had no wish to shoot them at that moment. My gun lay loosely on my arms, my eyes were rivetted on the Flycatchers, my ears open to the soft notes of the Doves. Reader, such are the moments, amid days of toil and discomfort, that compensate for every privation. It is on such occasions that the traveller feels most convinced, that the farther he proceeds, the better will be his opportunities of observing the results of the Divine conception. What else, I would ask of you, can be more gratifying to the human intellect!

Delighted and amused I stood for a while contemplating the beautiful world that surrounded me, and from which man would scarcely retire with willingness, had not the Almighty ordained it otherwise. But action had now to succeed, and I quickly procured some of the Flycatchers. Their habits too, I subsequently studied for weeks in succession, and the result of my observations I now lay before you.

About the 1st of April, this species reaches the Florida Keys, and spreads over the whole of them, as far as Cape Florida, or perhaps somewhat farther along the eastern coast of the Peninsula. It comes from Cuba, where the species is said to be rather abundant, as well as in the other West India Islands. Its whole demeanour so much resembles that of the Tyrant Flycatcher, that were it not for its greater size, and the difference of its notes, it might be mistaken for that bird, as I think it has been on former occasions by travellers less intent than I, on distinguishing species. At the season when I visited the Floridas, there was not a Key ever so small without at least a pair of them.

Their flight is performed by a constant flutter of the wings, unless when the bird is in chase, or has been rendered shy, when it exhibits a power and speed equal to those of any other species of the genus. During the love season, the male and female are seen rising from a dry twig together, either perpendicularly, or in a spiral manner, crossing each other as they ascend, twittering loudly, and conducting themselves in a manner much resembling that of the Tyrant Flycatcher. When in pursuit of insects, they dart at them with great velocity. Should any large bird pass near their stand, they immediately pursue it, sometimes to a considerable distance. I have seen them, after teasing a Heron or Fish Crow, follow them nearly half a mile, and return exulting to the tree on which they had previously been perched. Yet I frequently observed that the approach of a White-headed Pigeon or Zenaida Dove, never ruffled their temper. To the Grakles they were particularly hostile, and on all occasions drove them away from their stand, or the vicinity of their nest, with unremitting perseverance. The reason in this case, and in that of the Fish Crow, was obvious, for these birds sucked their eggs or destroyed their young whenever an opportunity occurred. This was also the case with the Mangrove Cuckoo.

This species is careless of the approach of man, probably because it is seldom disturbed by him. I have been so near some of them as to see distinctly the colour of their eyes. No sooner, however, had it begun to build its nest, than it flew about me or my companions, as if much exasperated at our being near, frequently snapping its beak with force, and in various ways loudly intimating its disapprobation of our conduct. Then as if we retired from the neighbourhood of its nest, it flew upwards, chattering notes of joy.

They fix their nest somewhat in the manner of the King Bird, that is, on horizontal branches, or in the large fork of a mangrove, or bush of any other species, without paying much attention to its position, with respect to the water, but with very singular care to place it on the western side of the tree, or of the islet. I found it sometimes not more than two feet above high water, and at other times twenty. It is composed externally of light dry sticks, internally of a thin layer of slender grasses or fibrous roots, and has some resemblance to that of the Carolina Pigeon in this respect that, from beneath, I could easily see the eggs through it. These were regularly four in all the nests that I saw, of a white colour, with many dots towards the larger end. The young I have never seen, my visit to those Keys having been in some measure abridged through lack of provisions.

On one of the Keys to which I went, although of small size, I saw several nests, and at least a dozen of these birds all peaceably enjoying themselves. The sexes present no external difference. According to report, they retire from these islands about the beginning of November, after which few land birds of any kind are seen on them.

After I had arrived at Charlestown in South Carolina, on returning from my expedition to the Floridas, a son of Paul Lee, Esq. a friend of the Rev. John Bachman, called upon us, asserting that he had observed a pair of Flycatchers in the College Yard, differing from all others with which he was acquainted. We listened, but paid little regard to the information, and deferred our visit to the trees in the College Yard. A week after, young Lee returned to the charge, urging us to go to the place, and see both the birds and their nest. To please this amiable youth Mr. Bachman and I soon reached the spot; but before we arrived the nest had been destroyed by some boys. The birds were not to be seen, but a Common King Bird happening to fly over us, we jeered our young observer, and returned home. Soon after the Flycatchers formed another nest, in which they reared a brood, when young Lee gave intimation to Mr. Bachman, who, on visiting the place, recognised them as of the species described in this article. Of this I was apprised by letter after I had left Charleston, for the purpose of visiting the northern parts of the Union. The circumstance enforced upon me the propriety of never suffering an opportunity of acquiring knowledge to pass, and of never imagining for a moment that another may not know something that has escaped your attention.

Since that time, three years have elapsed. The birds have regularly returned every spring to the College-yard, and have there reared, in peace, two broods each season, having been admired and respected by the collegians, after they were apprised that the species had not previously been found in the State. It thus furnishes another of the now numerous instances of new species entering the Union from the south, to increase our Fauna, and enliven our hours.

The branch on which I have represented a Male in full plumage, is that of a species rather rare on the Florida Keys, although, as I was assured it abounds in Cuba. It blooms during the season when this bird builds its nest. The flower is destitute of scent; the fruit is a long narrow legume, containing numerous seeds, placed at equal distances.

[From *Ornithological Biography,* Vol. II, pp. 392-395.]

THE ROSEATE TERN

Sterna Dougallii, Mont. [Roseate Tern, *Sterna dougallii*]
Plate CCXL. Adult.

On the 28th of April 1832, it was my lot to be on the beautiful rocky islet named Indian Key, where I spent a few hours of the night in unsuccessful attempts to procure repose, which was effectually banished by the consciousness of my being in a portion of the country not yet examined by any industrious student of nature, and in which I expected to find much that would prove interesting. The rain fell in torrents, and the rattling of the large drops on the shingles of the veranda in which my hammock had been slung, together with the chillness of the air, contributed to keep me awake. Finding it useless to remain in bed, I roused my companions; it was just four o'clock, and in a few minutes all the people in the house were up, and breakfast preparing. Before six the rain abated, and as I was determined not to lose a day, the guns were mustered, we made our way to the boats, and pushed off through a gentle shower in quest of unknown birds! In about an hour the rain ceased, the sky gradually cleared, and the sun soon dried our clothes. About this time we observed a great number of Terns on a sand bar, which we approached. The birds were not shy, so that we obtained an opportunity of firing two guns at them, when we leaped out, and on wading to the shore picked up thirty-eight Roseate Terns and several of another species.

Beautiful, indeed, are Terns of every kind, but the Roseate excels the rest, if not in form, yet in the lovely hue of its breast. I had never seen a bird of this species before, and as the unscathed hundreds arose and danced as it were in the air, I thought them the Humming Birds of the sea, so light and graceful were their movements. Now they flocked together and hovered over us, again with a sudden dash they plunged towards us in anger; even their cries of wrath sounded musical, and although I had carried destruction among them, I felt delighted. As I have just said, I had not before seen a Roseate Tern, not even the skin of one stuffed with tow; the species was not in the Synopsis of my friend Bonaparte, and now I had my cap filled to the brim with specimens. You may rest assured that I took precious care of those which I had procured, but not another individual was robbed of life on that excursion. The other Terns were as new to me.

Plate CCXL. *Roseate Tern*

I observed the form of their black bill and feet, the yellow tip of the former, and wrapped them up with care, while I tried to recollect the name they bore in books. To have found hundreds of the Roseate Tern in the Floridas, while I had anxious but slender hopes of meeting it on the coast of Labrador, was to me quite astonishing. So it was, however, and I determined to ransack every key and sand-beach, to try to find its breeding-ground. Nor were my desires ungratified.

The Roseate Tern spends the breeding season along the southern shores of the Floridas in considerable numbers. At different times in the course of nearly three months which I spent among the keys, I saw flocks of twenty, thirty, or more pairs, breeding on small detached rocky islands, scantily furnished with grass, and in the company of hundreds of Sandwich Terns. The two species appeared to agree well together, and their nests were intermingled. The full number of eggs of the present species is three. They differ considerably in size and markings; their average length, however, is an inch and three quarters, their breadth an inch and one-eighth; they are of a longish oval shape, rather narrowed at the small end, of a dull buff or clay colour, sparingly sprinkled and spotted with different tints of umber and light purple. They were deposited on the bare rocks, among the roots of the grasses, and left in fair weather to the heat of the sun. Like those of the Common Tern and other species, they are delicious eating. The eggs of the Sandwich Tern were more attended to during the day, but toward night both species sat on their eggs. I did not see any of the young, but procured a good number of those of the preceding year, which kept apart from the old birds, but had in all respects the same habits.

The Roseate Tern is at all times a noisy, restless bird; and on approaching its breeding place, it incessantly emits its sharp shrill cries, resembling the syllable *crāk*. Its flight is unsteady and flickering, like that of the Arctic or Lesser Terns, but rather more buoyant and graceful. They would dash at us and be off again with astonishing quickness, making great use of their tail on such occasions. While in search of prey, they carry the bill in the manner of the Common Tern, that is perpendicularly downward, plunge like a shot, with wings nearly closed, so as to immerse part of the body, and immediately reascend. They were seen dipping in this manner eight or ten times in succession, and each time generally secured a small fish. Their food consisted of fishes, and a kind of small molluscous animal which floats near the surface, and bears the name of "sailor's button." They usually kept in parties of from ten to twenty, followed the shores of the sand-bars and keys, moving backwards and forwards much in the manner of the Lesser Tern, and wherever a shoal of small fish was found, there they would hover and dash headlong at them for several minutes at a time.

The wreckers informed me that this species returns regularly to these islands each spring, about the 10th of April, and goes off southward early in September. These birds, with their favourite companions the Sandwich Terns, habitually resorted to the sand-bars each day, to rest for an hour or two. I have never seen them on any part of our middle or eastern coast, and am of opinion that they rarely proceed farther eastward than the Capes of Florida, and that they are more attached to the immediate vicinity of the shores than the larger species, which more generally fly out to some distance. The delicate and beautiful rosy tint of the breast soon fades after death. Those specimens which were not skinned immediately after being procured did not retain it for a week, and in none of them was it perceptible, without separating the feathers, at the end of a month. In winter it disappears, as well as the glossy black of the head. The length of the outer tail-feathers varies considerably; but I could perceive no decided difference of size or colour in the sexes, although I thought the females somewhat smaller than the males.

[From *Ornithological Biography*, Vol. III, pp. 296-298.]

THE FLORIDA CORMORANT

Phalacrocorax floridanus.
Plate CCLII. Male.

[Double-crested Cormorant,
Phalacrocorax auritus,
ssp *P. auritus floridanus* (Audubon)]

The Florida Cormorant, *P. Floridanus* is a constant resident in the southern parts of the country from which it derives its name, and is more especially abundant there in early spring and summer, breeding on the keys and along the salt-water inlets of the southern extremity of the peninsula, from which considerable numbers are now known

Plate CCLII. *Florida Cormorant*

to visit the waters of the Mississippi and even of the Ohio, while others proceed as far eastward as Cape Hatteras, all returning to the Floridas on the approach of cold weather.

The Florida Cormorant seldom goes far out to sea, but prefers the neighbourhood of the shores, being found in the bays, inlets, and large rivers. I never met with one at a greater distance from land than five miles. It is at all seasons gregarious, although it is not always found in large flocks. The birds of this species never suffer others of the same genus to resort to their breeding places, although they sometimes associate with individuals belonging to different genera. The *P. Carbo* appropriates to itself the upper shelves of the most rugged and elevated rocks, whose bases are washed by the sea; *P. dilophus* breeds on flat rocky islands at some distance from the shores of the mainland; and the Florida Cormorant nestles on trees. In the many breeding places of all these species which I have visited, I never found individuals of one intermingled with those of another, although the Large Cormorant did not seem averse from having the Peregrine Falcon in its vicinity, while the Double-crested allowed a few Gannets or Guillemots to nestle beside it, and the Florida Cormorant associated with Herons, Frigate Pelicans, Grakles, or Pigeons.

This species seldom flies far over land, but follows the sinuosities of the shores or the waters of rivers, although its course towards a given point should thus be three times as long. It is the only one of the three species that, in as far as I have observed in America, alights on trees. My learned friend, the Prince of Musignano, mentions in his valuable Synopsis of the Birds of the United States, a species of Cormorant under the name of *P. Graculus,* which he describes as being when adult greenish-black, with a few scattered white streaks on the neck, in winter bronzed, and having a golden-green crest, the head, neck, and thighs with short small white feathers, and adds that it "inhabits both continents and both hemispheres: not uncommon in spring and autumn in the Middle States: very common in the Floridas, where it breeds, though very abundant in the arctic and antarctic circles." Unfortunately no dimensions are given, except of the bill, which is said to be three and a half inches long. The Florida Cormorant, however, does not at any season present these characters, and therefore conceiving it to be different from any hitherto described, I have taken the liberty of giving it a name, while the figure and description will enable the scientific to form a distinct idea of it, and thus to confirm the species, or restore to it its previous appellation, should it have received one.

On the 26th of April 1832, I and my party visited several small Keys, not many miles distant from the harbour in which our vessel lay. Mr. Thruston had given us his beautiful barge, and accompanied us with his famous pilot, fisherman and hunter, Mr. Egan. The Keys were separated by narrow and tortuous channels, from the surface of the clear waters of which were reflected the dark mangroves, on the branches of which large colonies of Cormorants had already built their nests, and were sitting on their eggs. There were many thousands of these birds, and each tree bore a greater or less number of their nests, some five or six, others perhaps as many as ten. The leaves, branches, and stems of the trees, were in a manner whitewashed with their dung. The temperature in the shade was about 90° Fahr., and the effluvia which impregnated the air of the channels were extremely disagreeable. Still the mangroves were in full bloom, and the Cormorants in perfect vigour. Our boat being secured, the people scrambled through the bushes, in search of the eggs. Many of the birds dropped into the water, dived, and came up at a safe distance; others in large groups flew away affrighted; while a great number stood on their nests and the branches, as if gazing upon beings strange to them. But alas! they soon became too well acquainted with us, for the discharges from our guns committed frightful havock among them. The dead were seen floating on the water, the crippled making towards the open sea, which here extended to the very Keys on which we were, while groups of a hundred or more swam about a little beyond reach of our shot, awaiting the event, and the air was filled with those whose anxiety to return to their eggs kept them hovering over us in silence. In a short time the bottom of our boat was covered with the slain, several hats and caps were filled with eggs; and we may now intermit the work of destruction. You must try to excuse these murders, which in truth might not have been nearly so numerous, had I not thought of you quite as often while on the Florida Keys, with a burning sun over my head, and my body oozing at every pore, as I do now while peaceably scratching my paper with an iron-pen, in one of the comfortable and quite cool houses of the most beautiful of all the cities of old Scotland.

The Florida Cormorant begins to pair about the first of April, and commences the construction of its nest about a fortnight after. Many do not lay quite so early, and I found some going through their preparations until the middle of May. Their courtships are performed on the water. On the morning, beautiful but extremely hot, of the 8th of that month, while rambling over one of the Keys, I arrived at the entrance of a narrow and rather deep channel, almost covered over by the boughs of the mangroves and some tall canes, the only tall canes I had hitherto observed among those islands. I paused, looked at the water, and observing it to be full of fish, felt confident that no shark was at hand. Cocking both locks of my gun, I quietly waded in. Curious sounds now reached my ears, and as the fishes did not appear to mind me much, I proceeded onward among them for perhaps a hundred yards, when I observed that they had all disappeared. The sounds were loud and constantly renewed, as if they came from a joyous multitude. The inlet suddenly became quite narrow, and the water reached to my arm-pits. At length I placed myself behind some mangrove trunks, whence I could see a great number of Cormorants not more than fifteen or twenty yards from me. None of them, it seemed, had seen or heard me; they were engaged in going through their nuptial ceremonies. The males while swimming gracefully round the female would raise their wings and tail, draw their head over their back, swell out their neck for an instant, and with a quick forward thrust of the head utter a rough guttural note, not unlike the cry of a pig. The female at this moment would crouch as it were on the water, sinking into it, when her mate would sink over her until nothing more than his head was to be seen, and soon afterwards both sprung up and swam joyously round each other, croaking all the while. Twenty or more pairs at a time were thus engaged. Indeed, the water was covered with Cormorants, and, had I chosen, I might have shot several of them. I now advanced slowly towards them, when they stared at me as you might stare at a goblin, and began to splash the water with their wings, many diving. On my proceeding they all dispersed, either plunging beneath or flying off, and making rapidly towards the mouth of the inlet. Only a few nests were on the mangroves, and I looked upon the spot as analogous to the tournament grounds of the Pinnated Grouse, although no battles took place in my presence. A few beautiful Herons were sitting peaceably on their nests, the musquitoes were very abundant, large ugly blue land-crabs crawled among the mangroves, hurrying towards their retreats, and I retired, as I had arrived, in perfect silence. While proceeding I could not help remarking the instinctive knowledge of the fishes, and thought how curious it was that, as soon as they had observed the Cormorants' hole, none had gone farther, as if they were well aware of the danger, but preferred meeting me as I advanced towards the birds. I emerged from the water almost exhausted with heat, my eyes aching from the perspiration; but the refreshing sea-breeze now reached me, and cooled my feverish frame. Thankful, Reader, did I then feel, and thankful do I feel now, having survived so many encounters of this kind.

The nest of the Florida Cormorant is of rather a small size, being only eight or nine inches in diameter. It is formed of sticks crossing each other, and is flat, without any appearance of finishing. All the nests are placed on a western exposure, and are usually completely covered with excrement, as are also frequently the eggs, which are three or four, and differ in size, their average length, however, being two inches and a quarter, their greatest breadth one inch and three and a half eighths. They are rendered rather rough by the coating of calcareous matter which surrounds them; but when this is removed, the real shell is found to be of a uniform fine light bluish-green tint. I was unable to ascertain the period of incubation. The young are at first blind, naked, black, and extremely uncouth. On placing some which were quite small on the water, they instantly dived, rose again, and swam about at random, diving on the least noise. If you approach them when about a month old, they throw themselves from the nest and plunge into the water. When undisturbed, they remain in the nest until they are fully fledged and able to fly, after which they undergo various changes, and are not perfect until nearly two years old.

Soon after they are left to shift for themselves, great numbers go to search for food in the quiet waters of inland streams. Thousands may now be seen on the lakes of the interior of the Floridas, and on the large rivers there. At this season many proceed as far as the Capes of North Carolina, the Mississippi, the Arkansas, the Yazoo, and other streams, including the fair Ohio, on which they are at times seen early in October, when they begin to return to the places of their nativity. During several weeks which I spent on the St. John's River, while on board the United States' schooner-of-war the Spark, I was surprised to see the number of these Cormorants already returning towards the keys, so much so that had I been the discoverer of that stream under similar circumstances, I should in all probability have named it Cormorant River. While we were at anchor near its mouth, they passed close to us in long single files almost continually, and, on reaching the sea, bore away towards the south along the shores. . . .

When in fresh water streams they fish principally in the eddies, and as soon as one of them is depopulated, or proves unworthy of their farther search, they rise and fly about a foot above the surface to another place, where they continue to fish. In the inner lakes of the Floridas they fish at random any where, and this is equally the case around the Keys, and on the bays and inlets along the coast. In fine calm weather, when the sun is pouring down a flood of light and heat, the Cormorants in flocks betake themselves to some clean sand-bar or rocky isle, or alight on trees, where they spread out their wings, and bask at times for hours, in the manner of vultures and Pelicans.

The Florida Cormorant, like all the other species with which I am acquainted, swims deep, and dives with great expertness, so that it is almost useless to follow one when wounded, unless it has been greatly injured. On seeing an enemy approach, it first beats the water with its wings, as if in play, or as it would do if washing itself, raises both wings for a minute or more, then paddles off, and takes to wing. When on a lake, they prefer diving to flying, swim with all but the neck and head under water, in the manner of the Anhinga or Snake-bird, and easily dive without shewing their backs.

They procure their food entirely by diving from the surface of the water, never from on wing, as some compilers assert; nay, the very form of their bill, and the want of air-cells, such as plunging birds are usually provided with, prevent them from darting from above into the water, as is the habit of Gannets and other birds, which seek for food on wing, go far out to sea, and stand gales such as the Cormorant, which rarely venture out of sight of the shores, does not dare to encounter, or of those which, like Gulls, pass swiftly in curved lines over the surface, picking up their prey. On emerging, these Cormorants usually swallow their prey if it has been so seized as to enable them to do so with ease; if not, they throw it up to a short distance in the air, receive it with open bill, and gulp it head foremost. If the fish is large, they swim or fly to the shore, or alight on a tree with it, and there beat and tear it to pieces, after which they swallow it. Their appetite is scarcely satiable, and they gorge themselves to the utmost at every convenient opportunity.

The flight of this species is perhaps more rapid than that of the others mentioned above, and is performed by continued flappings when the bird is travelling, but by alternate flappings and sailings of great elegance during the beginning of the breeding season, or when they collect in large flocks in lowering weather, sometimes also when about to alight. Their food consists chiefly of fish, and they generally prefer those of small size. While on the Florida Keys, I procured five specimens of the Hippocampus, fresh and uninjured, from the gullets of some of these Cormorants. They are hard to kill, and live to a great age.

They are easily treated in captivity; but their awkward movements on the ground, where they often use the tail as a support, render them less pleasing objects than other feathered pets. Besides, they eat and mute inordinately, and instead of charming you with songs, utter no sound excepting a grunt. Their flesh is dark, generally tough, and has a rank fishy taste, which can suit the palate only of refined epicures, some of whom I have heard pronounce it excellent. The Indians and Negroes of the Floridas kill the young when nearly able to fly, and after skinning them, salt them for food. I have seen them offered for sale in the New Orleans market, the poorer people there making gombo soup of them.

A bird of this species, which I shot near its breeding place, and which, on being examined, proved to be a female, had the feathers of the tail covered with delicate slender sea-weeds of a bright green colour, such as I have often observed on marine turtles, and which appeared to have actually grown there.

The slender feathers on the sides of the head fall off by the time incubation has commenced, and do not appear during winter, as is alleged by authors when speaking of the crests or appendages of Cormorants, nor do they last more than a few weeks, as is also the case in the Egrets and Herons.

[From *Ornithological Biography*, Vol. III, pp. 387-394.]

THE ZENAIDA DOVE

Columba zenaida, Bonap.
Plate CLXII. Male and Female.

[Zenaida Dove, *Zenaida aurita*,
ssp *Z. aurita zenaida* (Bonaparte)]

The impressions made on the mind in youth, are frequently stronger than those at a more advanced period of life, and are generally retained. My Father often told me, that when yet a child, my first attempt at drawing was from a preserved specimen of a dove, and many times repeated to me that birds of this kind are usually remarkable for the gentleness of their disposition, and that the manner in which they prove their mutual affection, and feed their offspring, was undoubtedly intended in part to teach other beings a lesson of connubial and parental attachment. Be this as it may, hypothesis or not, I have always been especially fond of doves. The timidity and anxiety which they all manifest, on being disturbed during incuba-

Plate CLXII. *Zenaida Dove*

tion, and the continuance of their mutual attachment for years, are distinguishing traits in their character. Who can approach a sitting dove, hear its notes of remonstrance, or feel the feeble strokes of its wings, without being sensible that he is committing a wrong act?

The cooing of the Zenaida Dove is so peculiar, that one who hears it for the first time naturally stops to ask, "What bird is that?" A man who was once a pirate assured me that several times, while at certain wells dug in the burning shelly sands of a well known Key, which must here be nameless, the soft and melancholy cry of the doves awoke in his breast feelings which had long slumbered, melted his heart to repentance, and caused him to linger at the spot in a state of mind which he only who compares the wretchedness of guilt within him with the happiness of former innocence, can truly feel. He said he never left the place without increased fears of futurity, associated as he was, although I believe by force, with a band of the most desperate villains that ever annoyed the navigation of the Florida coasts. So deeply moved was he by the notes of any bird, and especially by those of a dove, the only soothing sounds he ever heard during his life of horrors, that through these plaintive notes, and them alone, he was induced to escape from his vessel, abandon his turbulent companions, and return to a family deploring his absence. After paying a parting visit to those wells, and listening once more to the cooings of the Zenaida Dove, he poured out his soul in supplications for mercy, and once more became what one has said to be "the noblest work of God," an honest man. His escape was effected amidst difficulties and dangers, but no danger seemed to him to be compared with the danger of one living in the violation of human and divine laws, and now he lives in peace in the midst of his friends.

The Zenaida Dove is a transient visitor of the Keys of East Florida. Some of the fishermen think that it may be met with there at all seasons, but my observations induce me to assert the contrary. It appears in the islands near Indian Key about the 15th of April, continues to increase in numbers until the month of October, and then returns to the West India Islands, whence it originally came. They begin to lay their eggs about the first of May. The males reach the Keys on which they breed before the females, and are heard cooing as they ramble about in search of mates, more than a week before the latter make their appearance. In autumn, however, when they take their departure, males, females, and young set out in small parties together.

The flight of this bird resembles that of the little Ground Dove more than any other. It very seldom flies higher than the tops of the mangroves, or to any considerable distance at a time, after it has made choice of an island to breed on. Indeed, this species may be called a Ground Dove too; for, although it alights on trees with ease, and walks well on branches, it spends the greater portion of its time on the ground, walking and running in search of food with lightness and celerity, carrying its tail higher than even the Ground Dove, and invariably roosting there. The motions of its wings, although firm, produce none of the whistling sound, so distinctly heard in the flight of the Carolina Dove [Mourning Dove]; nor does the male sail over the female while she is sitting on her eggs, as is the habit of that species. When crossing the sea, or going from one Key to another, they fly near the surface of the water; and, when unexpectedly startled from the ground, they remove to a short distance, and alight amongst the thickest grasses or in the heart of the low bushes. So gentle are they in general, that I have approached some so near that I could have touched them with my gun, while they stood intently gazing on me, as if I were an object not at all to be dreaded.

Those Keys which have their interior covered with grass and low shrubs, and are girt by a hedge of mangroves, or other trees of inferior height, are selected by them for breeding; and as there are but few of this description, their places of resort are well known, and are called Pigeon or "*Dove Keys.*" It would be useless to search for them elsewhere. They are by no means so abundant as the White-headed Pigeons, which place their nest on any kind of tree, even on those whose roots are constantly submersed. Groups of such trees occur of considerable extent, and are called "Wet Keys."

The Zenaida Dove always places her nest on the ground, sometimes artlessly at the foot of a low bush, and so exposed that it is easily discovered by any one searching for it. Sometimes, however, it uses great discrimination, placing it between two or more tufts of grass, the tops of which it manages to bend over, so as completely to conceal it. The sand is slightly scooped out, and the nest is composed of slender dried blades of grass, matted in a circular form, and imbedded amid dry leaves and twigs. The fabric is more compact than the nest of any other pigeon with which I am acquainted, it being sufficiently solid to enable a person to carry the eggs or young in it with security. The eggs are two, pure white, and translucent. When sitting on them, or when her young are still small, this bird rarely removes from them, unless an attempt be made to catch her, which she however evades with great dexterity. On several occasions of this kind, I have thought that the next moment would render me the possessor of one of these doves alive. Her beautiful eye was steadily bent on mine, in which she must have discovered my intention, her body was gently made to retire sidewise to the farther edge of her nest, as my hand drew nearer to her, and just as I thought I had hold of her, off she glided with the quickness of thought, taking to wing at once. She would then alight within a few yards of me, and watch my motions with so much sorrow, that her wings drooped, and her whole frame trembled as if suffering from intense cold. Who could stand such a scene of despair? I left the mother to her eggs or offspring.

On one occasion, however, I found two young birds of this species about half grown, which I carried off, and afterwards took to Charleston, in South Carolina, and presented to my worthy friend the Rev. John Bachman. When I robbed this nest, no parent bird was near. The little ones uttered the usual lisping notes of the tribe at this age, and as I put their bills in my mouth, I discovered that they might be easily raised. They were afterwards fed from the mouth with Indian corn meal, which they received with avidity, until placed under the care of a pair of common tame pigeons, which at once fostered them.

The cooing of this species so much resembles that of the Carolina Dove, that, were it not rather soft, and heard in a part of the world where the latter is never seen, you might easily take it for the notes of that bird. Morning is the time chosen by the Zenaida Dove to repeat her tender tales of love, which she does while perched on the low large branch of some tree, but never from the ground. Heard in the wildest solitudes of the Keys, these notes never fail to remind one that he is in the presence and under the protection of the Almighty Creator.

During mid-day, when the heat is almost insufferable in the central parts of the Keys resorted to by these birds, they are concealed and mute. The silence of such a place at noon is extremely awful. Not a breath of air is felt, nor an insect seen, and the scorching rays of the sun force every animated being to seek for shelter and repose.

From what I have said of the habits of the Zenaida Dove, you may easily conceive how difficult a task it is to procure one. I have had full experience of the difficulty, and entire satisfaction in surmounting it, for in less than an hour, with the assistance of Captain Day, I shot nineteen individuals, the internal and external examination of which enabled me to understand something of their structure.

The flesh is excellent, and they are generally very fat. They feed on grass seeds, the leaves of aromatic plants, and various kinds of berries, not excepting those of a tree which is extremely poisonous, —so much so, that if the juice of it touch the skin of a man, it destroys it like aquafortis. Yet these berries do not injure the health of the birds, although they render their flesh bitter and unpalatable for a time. For this reason, the fishermen and wreckers are in the habit of examining the crops of the doves previous to cooking them. This, however, only takes place about the time of their departure from the Keys, in the beginning of October. They add particles of shell or gravel to their food.

From my own observations, and the report of others, I am inclined to believe that they raise only two broods each season. The young, when yet unfledged, are of a deep leaden or purplish-grey colour, the bill and legs black, nor is it until the return of spring that they attain their full plumage. The male is larger than the female, and richer in the colouring of its plumage. Their feathers fall off at the slightest touch, and like all other pigeons, when about to die, they quiver their wings with great force.

The branch on which I have represented these birds, belonged to a low shrub abundant in the Keys where they are found. The flower has a musty scent, and is of short duration.

This species resorts to certain wells, which are said to have been dug by pirates, at a remote period. There the Zenaida Doves and other birds are sure to be seen morning and evening. The loose sand thrown up about these wells suits them well to dust in, and clean their apparel.

Purple-flowered Anona

This plant [Pond apple or custard apple] is very abundant on many of the outer Keys of the Floridas. It grows among other shrubs, seldom exceeding seven or eight feet in height, and more frequently not more than four or five. The leaves are obovate, rounded at the base, thick, glossy above, downy beneath. The outer petals are larger, and not unlike the divided shell of a hickory or pig nut; the inner ovate, deep purple, with a white band at the base. I did not see the fruit, which I was told is not unpalatable when ripe, it being then about the size of a common walnut, and of a black colour.

[From *Ornithological Biography,* Vol. II, pp. 354-358, 359.]

Plate CCCLXXVII. *Scolopaceus Courlan*

SCOLOPACEOUS COURLAN

Aramus Scolopaceus, Vieill. [Limpkin, *Aramus guarauna*]
Plate CCCLXXVII. Male.

This very remarkable bird appears to be entirely confined to that section of the Peninsula of Florida known by the name of "Everglades," and the swampy borders of the many bayous and lagoons issuing from that great morass. Few are found farther north than "Spring-garden Spring," of which I have given you an account. I have heard of its having been in one instance procured on one of the Florida Keys, by Mr. Titian Peale, whose specimen, which was a young male, has been described and figured in the continuation of Wilson's American Ornithology. None were seen by me on any of these islands, and our worthy Pilot told me, that in the course of the many years which he had spent in that country he had never met with one off the main-land. It did not occur to me on any part of the coast, while I was proceeding to the Texas, nor is it to be found in that country, which seems very strange, when I look at this bird, and compare it with the Rail family, which is so abundant along the whole of that coast, and to which it is very nearly allied in some of its habits, more especially to the Fresh-water Marsh Hen, *Rallus elegans.*

The flight of the Scolopaceous Courlan is heavy and of short duration; the concavity and shortness of its wings, together with the nature of the places which it inhabits, probably rendering it slow to remove from one spot to another on wing, it being in a manner confined among tall plants, the roots of which are frequently under water. When it rises spontaneously it passes through the air at a short distance above the weeds, with regular beats of the wings, its neck extended to its full length, and its long legs dangling beneath, until it suddenly drops to the ground. Few birds then excel it in speed, as it proceeds, if pursued, by long strides, quickly repeated, first in a direct course, along paths formed by itself when passing and repassing from one place to another, and afterwards diverging so as to ensure its safety even when chased by the best dogs, or other not less eager enemies inhabiting the half-submersed wilderness which it has chosen for its residence. When accidentally surprised, it rises obliquely out of its recess, with the neck greatly bent downward, and although its legs dangle for a while, they are afterwards extended behind in the manner of those of the Heron tribe. At such times these birds are easily shot; but if they are only wounded, it would be vain to pursue them. Although of considerable size and weight, they are enabled, by the great length and expansion of their toes to walk on the broad leaves of the larger species of Nymphaea found in that country. They swim with the same buoyancy as the Coots, Gallinules, and Rails.

The nest of this bird is placed among the larger tufts of the tallest grasses that grow at short distances from the bayous, many of which are influenced by the low tides of the Gulf. It is so well fastened to the stems of the plants, in the same manner as that of *Rallus crepitans,* as to be generally secure from inundation; and is composed of rank weeds matted together, and forming a large mass, with a depression in the centre. The eggs, which rarely exceed five or six, are large for the size of the bird. The young are hatched early in May, and follow their parents soon after birth, being covered with coarse tufty feathers, of a black colour.

The Ever-glades abound with a species of large greenish snail [apple or pomacea snail], on which these birds principally feed; and, from the great number of empty shells which are found at the foot of the nest and around it, it is probable that the sitting bird is supplied with food by her mate. Their notes, when uttered while they are on wing, are a sort of cackle, but when on the ground, much louder, especially during the pairing season, or when they are started by the report of a gun. The flesh of the young is pretty good eating. Although it is alleged that this bird occasionally alights on trees, I have never seen it in such a situation.

[From *Ornithological Biography*, Vol. IV, pp. 543-544.]

BLUE HERON

Ardea coerulea, Linn. [Little Blue Heron,
Plate CCCVII. Adult Male and Young. *Florida caerulea*]

Along with a few other Herons, this is, comparatively speaking, confined within narrow limits along our southern coast in winter. It occurs, however, in most parts of the Floridas, where it is a constant resident, and whence, at the approach of summer, vast multitudes are seen proceeding northward, in search of suitable places in which they may rear their young in security. Many, however, go southward, beyond the limits of the United States, and proceed coastwise to Texas and Mexico to spend the winter, especially the younger birds, when still in that singular white plumage which differs so much from that of the young of every other known species of this genus, except that of the Reddish Egret (*A. rufescens*). At New Orleans, where it arrives at the same period, both from Mexico and the Floridas, its first appearance in spring is about the beginning of March; at which time also multitudes leave the Floridas on their way eastward, to settle in Georgia, the Carolinas, and other States farther east, as far as Long Island in that of New York. Beyond this, I believe, no birds of the species have been met with. They rarely, if ever, proceed far inland, or leave the shores of our large rivers and estuaries. On the Mississippi, the swamps and lakes on the borders of which are so well adapted to the habits of these birds, few individuals are ever seen above Natchez. About the beginning of September, by which time the young are able to shift for themselves, they return southward.

When in the Floridas, during winter, I observed that the Blue Herons associated with other species, particularly the White Heron [Common Egret], *Ardea alba*, and the Louisiana Heron, *Ardea Ludoviciana,* all of which were in the habit of roosting together in the thick evergreen low bushes that cover the central parts of the islands along the coast. Their passage to and from their feeding places, is as regular as the rising and setting of the sun, and, unless frequently disturbed, they betake themselves every night to the same locality, and almost to the same spot. In the morning, they rise with one accord from the roosts on which they have been standing all night on

Plate CCCVII. *Blue Crane or Heron*

one leg, the other drawn up among the feathers of the abdomen, their neck retracted, and their head and bill buried beneath their scapulars. On emerging from their retreats, they at once proceed to some distant place in search of food, and spend the day principally on the head waters of the rivers, and the fresh-water lakes of the interior, giving a decided preference to the soft mud banks, where small crabs or fiddlers are abundant, on which they feed greedily, when the inland ponds have been dried up, and consequently no longer supply them with such fishes as they are wont to feed upon.

There, and at this season, Reader, you may see this graceful Heron, quietly and in silence walking along the margins of the water, with an elegance and grace which can never fail to please you. Each regularly-timed step is lightly measured, while the keen eye of the bird seeks for and watches the equally cautious movements of the objects towards which it advances with all imaginable care. When at a proper distance, it darts forth its bill with astonishing celerity, to pierce and secure its prey; and this it does with so much precision, that, while watching some at a distance with a glass, I rarely observed an instance of failure. If fish is plentiful, on the shallows near the shore, when it has caught one, it immediately swallows it, and runs briskly through the water, striking here and there, and thus capturing several in succession. Two or three dashes of this sort, afford sufficient nourishment for several hours, and when the bird has obtained enough it retires to some quiet place, and remains there in an attitude of repose until its hunger returns. During this period of rest, however, it is as watchful as ever, and on hearing the least noise, or perceiving the slightest appearance of danger, spreads its wings, and flies off to some other place, sometimes to a very distant one. About an hour before sunset, they are again seen anxiously searching for food. When at length satisfied, they rise simultaneously from all parts of the marsh, or shore, arrange themselves into loose bodies, and ascending to the height of fifty or sixty yards in the air, fly in a straight course towards their roosting place. I saw very few of these birds during the winter, on or near the river St. John in Florida; but on several occasions met with some on small ponds in the pine barrens, at a considerable distance from any large stream, whither they had been attracted by the great number of frogs.

The flight of the Blue Heron is rather swifter than that of the Egret, *Ardea candidissima,* and considerably more so than that of the

Great Blue Heron, *Ardea Herodias,* but very similar to that of the Louisiana Heron, *Ardea Ludoviciana.* When the bird is traveling, the motion is performed by flappings in quick succession, which rapidly propel it in a direct line, until it is about to alight, when it descends in circular sailings of considerable extent towards the spot selected. During strong adverse winds, they fly low, and in a continuous line, passing at the necessary distance from the shores to avoid danger, whether at an early or a late hour of the day. I recollect that once, on such an occasion, when, on the 15th of March, I was in company with my friend John Bachman, I saw a large flock about sunset arising from across the river, and circling over a large pond, eight miles distant from Charleston. So cautious were they, that although the flock was composed of several hundred individuals, we could not manage to get so much as a chance of killing one. I have been surprised to see how soon the Blue Herons become shy after reaching the districts to which they remove for the purpose of breeding from their great rendezvous the Floridas, where I never experienced any difficulty in procuring as many as I wished. . . .

The Blue Heron breeds earlier or later according to the temperature of the district to which it resorts for that purpose, and therefore earlier in Florida, where, however, considerable numbers remain, during the whole year than in other parts of the United States. Thus I have found them in the southern parts of that country, sitting on their eggs, on the 1st of March, fully a month earlier than in the vicinity of Bayou Sara, on the Mississippi, where they are as much in advance of those which betake themselves, in very small numbers indeed, to our Middle Districts, in which they rarely begin to breed before the fifteenth of May.

The situations which they choose for their nests are exceedingly varied. I have found them sitting on their eggs on the Florida Keys, and on the islands in the Bay of Galveston, in Texas, in nests placed amidst and upon the most tangled cactuses, so abundant on those curious isles, on the latter of which the climbing Rattlesnake often gorges itself with the eggs of this and other species of Heron, as well as with their unfledged young. In the Lower parts of Louisiana, it breeds on low bushes of the water-willow, as it also does in South Carolina; whereas, on the islands on the coast of New Jersey, and even on the mainland of that State, it places its nest on the branches of the cedar and other suitable trees. Wherever you find its breeding place, you may expect to see other birds in company with it, for like all other species, excepting perhaps the Louisiana Heron, it rarely objects to admit into its society the Night Heron, the Yellow-crowned Heron, or the White Egret.

The heronries of the southern portions of the United States are often of such extraordinary size as to astonish the passing traveller. I confess that I myself might have been as sceptical on this point as some who, having been accustomed to find in all places the Heron to be a solitary bird, cannot be prevailed on to believe the contrary, had I not seen with my own eyes the vast multitudes of individuals of different species breeding together in peace in certain favourable localities. . . .

The nest of the Blue Heron, wherever situated, is loosely formed of dry sticks, sometimes intermixed with green leaves of various trees, and with grass or moss, according as these materials happen to be plentiful in the neighbourhood. It is nearly flat, and can scarcely be said to have a regular lining. Sometimes you see a solitary nest fixed on a cactus, a bush, or a tree; but a little beyond this you may observe from six to ten, placed almost as closely together as you would have put them had you measured out the space necessary for containing them. Some are seen low over the water, while others are placed high; for, like the rest of its tribe, this species is rather fond of placing its tenement over or near the liquid element.

[From *Ornithological Biography*, Vol. IV, pp. 58-60, 61-62.]

THE WHITE IBIS

Ibis alba, Vieill. [White Ibis, *Eudocimus albus*]
Plate CCXXII. Adult Male, and Young.

Sandy Island, of which I have already spoken in my second volume, is remarkable as a breeding-place for various species of water and land birds. It is about a mile in length, not more than a hundred yards broad, and in form resembles a horse-shoe, the inner curve of which looks toward Cape Sable in Florida, from which it is six miles distant. At low water, it is surrounded to a great distance by mud

Plate CCXXII. *White Ibis*

flats abounding in food for wading and swimming birds, while the plants, the fruits, and the insects of the island itself, supply many species that are peculiar to the land. Beside the White Ibis, we found breeding there the Brown Pelican, the Purple, the Louisiana, the White, and the Green Herons, two species of Gallinule, the Cardinal Grosbeak, Crows, and Pigeons. The vegetation consists of a few tall mangroves, thousands of wild plum trees, several species of cactus, some of them nearly as thick as a man's body, and more than twenty feet high, different sorts of smilax, grape-vines, cane, palmettoes, Spanish bayonets, and the rankest nettles I ever saw,—all so tangled together, that I leave you to guess how difficult it was for my companions and myself to force a passage through them in search of birds' nests, which, however, we effected, although the heat was excessive, and the stench produced by the dead birds, putrid eggs, and the natural effluvia of the Ibises, was scarcely sufferable. But then, the White Ibis was there, and in thousands; and, although I already knew the bird, I wished to study its manners once more, that I might be enabled to present you with an account of them, which I now proceed to do,—endeavouring all the while to forget the pain of the numerous scratches and lacerations of my legs caused by the cactuses of Sandy Island.

As we entered that well-known place, we saw nests on every bush, cactus, or tree. Whether the number was one thousand or ten I cannot say, but this I well know:—I counted forty-seven on a single plum-tree. These nests of the White Ibis measure about fifteen inches in their greatest diameter, and are formed of dry twigs intermixed with fibrous roots and green branches of the trees growing on the island, which this bird easily breaks with its bill; the interior, which is flat, being finished with leaves of the cane and some other plants. The bird breeds only once in the year, and the full number of its eggs is three. They measure two inches and a quarter in length, with a diameter of one inch and five-eighths, are rough to the touch, although not granulated, of a dull white colour, blotched with pale yellow, and irregularly spotted with deep reddish-brown. They afford excellent eating, although when boiled they do not look inviting, the white resembling a livid-coloured jelly, and the yolk being of a reddish-orange, the former wonderfully transparent, instead of being opaque like that of most other birds. The eggs are deposited from the 10th of April to the 1st of May, and incubation is general by the 10th of the latter month. The young birds, which are at first covered with thick down of a dark grey colour, are fed by regurgitation. They take about five weeks to be able to fly, although they leave the nest at the end of three weeks, and stand on the branches, or on the ground, waiting the arrival of their parents with food, which consists principally of small fiddler crabs and crayfish. On some occasions, I have found them at this age miles away from the breeding-places, and in this state they are easily caught. As soon as the young are able to provide for themselves, the old birds leave them, and the different individuals are then seen searching for food apart. While nestling or in the act of incubating, these Ibises are extremely gentle and unwary, unless they may have been much disturbed, for they almost allow you to touch them on the nest. The females are silent all the while, but the males evince their displeasure by uttering sounds which greatly resemble those of the White-headed Pigeon, and which may be imitated by the syllables *crooh, croo, croo.* The report of a gun scarcely alarms them at first, although at all other periods these birds are shy and vigilant in the highest degree.

The change in the colouring of the bill, legs, and feet of this bird, that takes place in the breeding season, is worthy of remark, the bill being then of a deep orange-red, and the legs and feet of a red nearly amounting to carmine. The males at this season have the gular pouch of a rich orange colour, and somewhat resembling in shape that of the Frigate Pelican, although proportionally less. During the winter, these parts are of a dull flesh colour. The irides also lose much of their clear blue, and resume in some degree the umber colour of the young birds. I am thus particular in these matters, because it is doubtful if any one else has ever paid attention to them.

While breeding, the White Ibises go to a great distance in search of food for their young, flying in flocks of several hundreds. Their excursions take place at particular periods, determined by the decline of the tides, when all the birds that are not sitting go off, perhaps twenty or thirty miles, to the great mud flats, where they collect abundance of food, with which they return the moment the tide begins to flow. As the birds of this genus feed by night as well as by day, the White Ibis attends the tides at whatever hour they may be. Some of those which bred on Sandy Key would go to the keys next the Atlantic, more than forty miles distant, while others made for the Ever Glades; but they never went off singly. They rose with common accord from the breeding-ground, forming themselves into long lines, often a mile in extent, and soon disappeared from view. Soon after the turn of the tide we saw them approaching in the same order. Not a note could you have heard on those occasions; yet if you disturb them when far from their nests, they utter loud hoarse cries resembling the syllables *hunk, hunk, hunk,* either while on the ground or as they fly off.

The flight of the White Ibis is rapid and protracted. Like all other species of the genus, these birds pass through the air with alternate flappings and sailings; and I have thought that the use of either mode depended upon the leader of the flock, for, with the most perfect regularity, each individual follows the motion of that preceding it, so that a constant appearance of regular undulations is produced through the whole line. If one is shot at this time, the whole line is immediately broken up, and for a few minutes all is disorder; but as they continue their course, they soon resume their former arrangement. The wounded bird never attempts to bite or to defend itself in any manner, although, if only winged, it runs off with more speed than is pleasant to its pursuer.

At other times the White Ibis, like the Red and the Wood Ibises, rises to an immense height in the air, where it performs beautiful evolutions. After they have thus, as it were, amused themselves for some time, they glide down with astonishing speed, and alight either on trees or on the ground. Should the sun be shining, they appear in their full beauty, and the glossy black tips of their wings form a fine contrast with the yellowish-white of the rest of their plumage.

This species is as fond of resorting to the ponds, bayous, or lakes that are met with in the woods, as the Wood Ibis itself. I have found it breeding there at a distance of more than three hundred miles from the sea, and remaining in the midst of the thickest forests until driven off to warmer latitudes by the approach of winter. This is the case in the State of Mississippi, not far from Natchez, and in all the swampy forests around Bayou Sara and Pointe Coupée, as well as the interior of the Floridas. When disturbed in such places, these Ibises fly at once to the tops of the tallest trees, emitting their hoarse *hunk,* and watch your motions with so much care that it is extremely difficult to get within shot of them.

The manner in which this bird searches for its food is very curious. The Woodcock and the Snipe, it is true, are probers as well as it, but their task requires less ingenuity than is exercised by the White or the Red Ibis. It is also true that the White Ibis frequently seizes on small crabs, slugs and snails, and even at times on flying insects; but its usual mode of procuring food is a strong proof that cunning enters as a principal ingredient in its instinct. The Cray-fish often burrows to the depth of three or four feet in dry weather, for before it can be comfortable it must reach the water. This is generally the case during the prolonged heats of summer, at which time the White Ibis is most pushed for food. The bird, to procure the Cray-fish, walks with remarkable care towards the mounds of mud which the latter throws up while forming its hole, and breaks up the upper part of the fabric, dropping the fragments into the deep cavity that has been made by the animal. Then the Ibis retires a single step, and patiently waits the result. The Cray-fish, incommoded by the load of earth, instantly sets to work anew, and at last reaches the entrance of its burrow; but the moment it comes in sight, the Ibis seizes it with his bill.

Whilst at Indian Key, I observed an immense quantity of beautiful tree snails, of a pyramidal or shortly conical form, some pure white, others curiously marked with spiral lines of bright red, yellow and black. They were crawling vigorously on every branch of each bush where there was not a nest of the White Ibis; but wherever that bird had fixed its habitation, not a live snail was to be seen, although hundreds lay dead beneath. Was this caused by the corrosive quality of the bird's ordure?

There is a curious though not altogether general difference between the sexes of this species as to the plumage:—the male has five of its primaries tipped with glossy black for several inches, while the female, which is very little smaller than the male, has only four marked in this manner. On examining more than a hundred individuals of each sex, I found only four exceptions, which occurred in females that were very old birds, and which, as happens in some other species, might perhaps have been undergoing the curious change exhibited by ducks, pheasants, and some other birds, the females of which when old sometimes assume the livery of the males.

Much, as you are aware, good Reader, has been said respecting the "oil bags" of birds. I dislike controversy, simply because I never saw the least indications of it in the ways of the Almighty Creator. Should I err, forgive me, but my opinion is, that these organs were not made without an object. Why should they consist of matter so conveniently placed, and so disposed as to issue under the least pressure, through apertures in the form of well defined tubes? The White Ibis, as well as the Wood Ibis, and all the other species of this genus, when in full health, has these oil bags of great size, and, if my eyes have not deceived me, makes great use of their contents. Should you feel anxious to satisfy yourself on this subject, I request of you to keep some Ibises alive for several weeks, as I have done, and you will have an opportunity of judging. And again, tell me if the fat contained in these bags is not the very best *lip salve* that can be procured.

[From *Ornithological Biography*, Vol. III, pp. 173-177.]

AMERICAN FLAMINGO

Phoenicopterus ruber, Linn.
Plate CCCCXXXI. Adult Male.

[American Flamingo,
Phoenicopterus ruber]

On the 7th of May 1832, while sailing from Indian Key, one of the numerous islets that skirt the south-eastern coast of the Peninsula of Florida, I for the first time saw a flock of Flamingoes. It was on the afternoon of one of those sultry days which, in that portion of the country, exhibit towards evening the most glorious effulgence that can be conceived. The sun, now far advanced toward the horizon, still shone with full splendour, the ocean around glittered in its quiet beauty, and the light fleecy clouds that here and there spotted the heavens, seemed flakes of snow margined with gold. Our bark was propelled almost as if by magic, for scarcely was a ripple raised by her bows as we moved in silence. Far away to seaward we spied a flock of Flamingoes advancing in "Indian line," with well-spread wings, outstretched necks, and long legs directed backwards. Ah! Reader, could you but know the emotions that then agitated my breast! I thought I had now reached the height of all my expectations, for my voyage to the Floridas was undertaken in a great measure for the purpose of studying these lovely birds in their own beautiful islands. I followed them with my eyes, watching as it were every beat of their wings; and as they were rapidly advancing towards us, Captain Day, who was aware of my anxiety to procure some, had every man stowed away out of sight and our gunners in readiness. The pilot, Mr. Egan, proposed to offer the first taste of his "groceries" to the leader of the band. As I have more than once told you, he was a first-rate shot, and had already killed many Flamingoes. The birds were now, as I thought, within a hundred and fifty yards; when suddenly, to our extreme disappointment, their chief veered away, and was of course followed by the rest. Mr. Egan, however, assured us that they would fly round the Key, and alight not far from us, in less than ten minutes, which in fact they did, although to me these minutes seemed almost hours. "Now they come," said the pilot, "keep low." This we did; but, alas! the Flamingoes were all, as I suppose, very old and experienced birds, with the exception of one, for on turning round the lower end of the Key, they spied our boat again, sailed away without flapping their wings, and alighted about four hundred yards from us, and upwards of one hundred from the shore, on a "soap flat" of vast extent, where neither boat nor man could approach them. I however watched their motions until dusk, when we reluctantly left the spot and advanced toward Indian Key. Mr. Logan then told me that these birds habitually returned to their feeding-grounds toward evening, that they fed during the greater part of the night, and were much more nocturnal in their habits than any of the Heron tribe.

When I reached Key West, my first inquiries, addressed to Dr. Benjamin Strobel, had reference to the Flamingoes, and I felt gratified by learning that he had killed a good number of them, and that he would assist us in procuring some. As on that Key they are fond of resorting to the shallow ponds formerly kept there as reservoirs of water, for the purpose of making salt, we visited them at different times, but always without success; and, although I saw a great number of them in the course of my stay in that country, I cannot even at this moment boast of having had the satisfaction of shooting a single individual.

A very few of these birds have been known to proceed eastward of the Floridas beyond Charleston in South Carolina, and some have been procured there within eight or ten years back. None have ever been observed about the mouths of the Mississippi; and to my great surprise I did not meet with any in the course of my voyage to the Texas, where, indeed, I was assured they had never been seen, at least as far as Galveston Island. The western coast of Florida, and some portions of that of Alabama, in the neighbourhood of Pensacola, are the parts to which they mostly resort; but they are said to be there always extremely shy, and can be procured only by waylaying them in the vicinity of their feeding-grounds toward evening, when, on one occasion, Dr. Strobel shot several in the course of a few hours. Dr. Leitner also procured some in the course of his botanical excursions along the western coast of the Floridas, where he was at last murdered by some party of Seminole Indians, at the time of our last disastrous war with those children of the desert.

Flamingoes, as I am informed, are abundant on the Island of Cuba, more especially on the southern side of some of its shores, and where many islets at some distance from the mainland afford them ample protection. In their flight they resemble Ibises, and they usually move in lines, with the neck and legs fully extended, alternately flapping their wings for twenty or thirty yards and sailing over a like

Plate CCCCXXXI. *American Flamingo*

space. Before alighting they generally sail round the place for several minutes, when their glowing tints become most conspicuous. They very rarely alight on the shore itself, unless, as I am told, during the breeding season, but usually in the water, and on shallow banks, whether of mud or of sand, from which however they often wade to the shores. Their walk is stately and slow, and their cautiousness extreme, so that it is very difficult to approach them, as their great height enables them to see and watch the movements of their various enemies at a distance. When travelling over the water, they rarely fly at a greater height than eight or ten feet; but when passing over the land, no matter how short the distance may be, they, as well as Ibises and Herons, advance at a considerable elevation. I well remember that on one occasion, when near Key West, I saw one of them flying directly towards a small hummock of mangroves, to which I was near, and towards which I made, in full expectation of having a fine shot. When the bird came within a hundred and twenty yards, it rose obliquely, and when directly over my head, was almost as far off. I fired, but with no other effect than that of altering its course, and inducing it to rise still higher. It continued to fly at this elevation until nearly half a mile off, when it sailed downwards, and resumed its wonted low flight.

[From *Ornithological Biography,* Vol. V, pp. 255-257.]

THE SEMIPALMATED SNIPE, OR WILLET

Totanus semipalmatus, Temm. [Willet, *Catoptrophorus semipalmatus*]
Plate CCLXXIV. Male and Female.

In the Middle States, the Semipalmated Snipe is known to every fisherman gunner by the name of "Willet;" and from the Carolinas southward by that of "Stone Curlew." In the latter districts, during autumn and winter, it resorts to the stony shores of estuaries, the banks of racoon oysters, and the extensive salt-marshes so common there along the coast. On the 1st of May 1832, while rambling over some large and partially submersed islets of the Floridas called Duck Keys [25 miles west of Indian Key], scantily covered with bushes and some mangroves, I saw a good number of these birds in company with the Great Marbled Godwit. The Willets were all paired and very clamorous, although we found none of their nests. To my great surprise, I saw them alight on the bushes and trees with as much ease as if they had been land birds, stand erect, open their wings to the sun, and await our approach, exhibiting, when thus perched, much less shyness than when on the ground. Until then I had never observed such a habit in this bird, and indeed had felt surprised at seeing the Bartram Snipe, *Totanus Bartramius,* alight on fences and trees. Nothing of this kind is mentioned by Wilson, who, however, speaks of both species as if he were well acquainted with their habits. A few days after my visit to the Duck Keys, some nests containing eggs were found on other islets not far distant. . . .

The Semipalmated Snipe is at all times a shy and wary bird, so that in approaching it the sportsman requires to use the greatest caution. The method which I found most effectual was to employ a well-trained dog, and conceal myself among the rankest herbage of

Plate CCLXXIV. *Semipalmated Snipe or Willet*

the marshes. The Willets rarely failed to fly close over the dog, and as he now and then, playfully, as it were, approached me, the birds came within shooting distance. On such occasions, if one is brought down, another may follow, provided the sportsman is quick; but, after being thus shot at, the Willets generally take a long circuit, and remove towards some clear spot near the water, where they alight and watch your motions. The cries of one suffice to alarm all within hearing, and you see all of them with outstretched legs and necks running away as you approach. Often at the very instant when you are preparing to shoot, they all rise on wing, fly across some bay or creek, and betake themselves to the marsh, where they are safe from your pursuit.

During winter you frequently see these birds in the Southern States along the naked shores. The moment they see you the cry of alarm is sounded, and the flock, which now consists of one, two, or perhaps three families, suffer you to come almost within shot, as if purposely to tantalize you, but at this moment fly off circuitously over the water, and alight at the distance of some hundred yards. At such times you may procure them by floating your boat quietly along the shores; but the experiment rarely succeeds on the same flock more than once. When they are on large racoon-oyster beds, it is almost impossible to approach them; and if there should be a few Curlews or Oyster-catchers among them, it were better for you to go in search of some other game.

The flight of this species is strong, rapid, and greatly protracted. Its movements on wing greatly resemble those of the Oyster-catcher, and, unless during the breeding season, are performed low over the waters. They seldom rise without emitting their usual notes, which resemble the syllables *will-willet,* or *will, will, willet,* and are different from the softer and more prolonged whistling notes which they emit during the love season. They generally travel in flocks, even in spring, and congregate for the purpose of breeding, being attracted when passing by the notes of those which have already arrived at a chosen spot. The males and females remain together until autumn, when several families join and live peaceably together. When wounded and brought to the water, they swim tolerably well, but do not dive, although they now and then, on being approached, try to submerse themselves.

The Willets retire to the interior of the larger salt-marshes for the purpose of forming their nests and raising their broods in security.

There, in the vicinity of the shallow pools, which frequently occur in such places, the bird prepares a nest on the ground, among the rank grass, of which the tenement itself is composed. It is usually raised to the height of from three to five inches, and is, I believe, annually augmented or repaired. Wilson says that this augmentation or raising of the nest is carried on whilst the Willet is laying and sitting; but this I have never observed. The eggs, usually four in number, are placed with the broad end outwards, as is the case with those of most birds of this tribe. They measure two inches and one-eighth in length, by one inch and a half in breadth, are much flattened at the larger end, and more or less pointed at the other. The shell is smooth, of a dull yellowish-olive tint, irregularly spotted and blotched with dark umber. The eggs afford excellent eating. Both birds incubate, sitting alternately day and night. The young run about on leaving the shell, and are carefully fed by their parents. They are of a greyish hue, and covered with down, but soon shew feathers, grow rapidly, become fat and juicy, and by the time they are able to fly, afford excellent food. At the first moult they acquire their full plumage.

The food of the Willet consists of aquatic insects, small crabs, and fiddlers, which they procure either by pursuing them on foot or by probing for them in their burrows, along the mud bars, and in the crevices of the creeks and salt-water ditches. I have also observed it turning over stones and shells to seek for worms beneath them.

The males are smaller than the females. I have presented you with figures of the adult both in the winter and summer plumage.

[From *Ornithological Biography*, Vol. III, pp. 510-513.]

WHITE-HEADED PIGEON

Columba leucocephala, Linn.
Plate CLXXVII. Male and Female.

[White-crowned Pigeon,
Columba leucocephala]

The White-headed Pigeon arrives on the Southern Keys of the Floridas, from the Island of Cuba, about the 20th of April, sometimes not until the 1st of May, for the purpose of residing there for a season, and rearing its young. On the 30th of April, I shot several

Plate CLXXVII. *White-crowned Pigeon*

immediately after their arrival from across the Gulf Stream. I saw them as they approached the shore, skimming along the surface of the waters, flying with great rapidity, much in the manner of the common house species, but not near each other like the Passenger Pigeon. On nearing the land, they rose to the height of about a hundred yards, surveyed the country in large circles, then with less velocity gradually descended, and alighted in the thickest parts of the mangroves and other low trees. None of them could be easily seen in those dark retreats, and we were obliged to force them out, in order to shoot them, which we did at this time on the wing.

In creeping among the bushes to obtain a view of them whilst alighted, I observed that the more I advanced, the more they retired from me. This they did by alighting on the ground from the trees, among which they could not well make way on wing, although they could get on with much ease below, running off and hiding at every convenient spot that occurred. These manoeuvres lasted only a few days, after which I could see them perched on the tops of the trees, giving a preference perhaps to dry branches, but not a marked one, as some other species are wont to do.

They are at all times extremely shy and wary, more so in fact than any species with which I am acquainted. The sight of a man is to them insupportable, perhaps on account of the continued war waged against them, their flesh being juicy, well flavoured, and generally tender, even in old birds. Never could I get near one of them so long as it observed me. Indeed the moment they perceive a man, off they go, starting swiftly with a few smart raps of the wings, and realighting in a close covert for a while, or frequently flying to another key, from which they are sure to return to that left by them, should you pursue them. It is thus a most toilsome task to procure specimens of these birds.

Their shyness is but partially given up even during their love season, or while sitting on their eggs, for the moment they see you they get off slyly from the nest, walk on the branches for some distance, and take to wing without any noise, flying low along the edge of the mangroves, into which they throw themselves as soon as a place of safety offers itself, seldom on such occasions flying off to other keys. Their return to the nest is not immediate, the heat of these latitudes not requiring the same care in incubation as the comparative cold of more northern regions. I have waited their return sometimes as much as half an hour, without success.

By the first of May [June or July is more correct], the young squabs are nearly able to fly, and it is at this period that the greatest havoc is made among them. The fishermen and the wreckers visit the keys principally resorted to by this species, rifle all the nests they can find, and sometimes also shoot the old birds.

The key on which I first saw this bird, lies about twenty-five [fifty] miles south of Indian Key, and is named Bahia-honda Duck

Key. The farther south [west] we proceeded the more we saw, until we reached the low, sandy, sterile keys, called the Tortugas, on none of which did I see a pigeon of any kind. During my visit to the Floridas, our party procured a great number of White-headed Pigeons. They were all either adult, or full-plumed birds, having the upper part of the head pure white, with a deep rich brown edging at the lateral parts of the crown. On our return from the Tortugas to Key West, our vessel anchored close to a small key, in a snug harbour protected from the sea winds by several long and narrow islands well known to the navigators of those seas. Captain Day and myself visited this little key, which was not much more than an acre in extent, the same afternoon. No sooner had we landed, than, to our delight, we saw a great number of White-headed Pigeons rise, fly around the key several times, and all realight upon it. The Captain posted himself at one end of the key, I at the other, while the sailors walked about to raise the birds. In less than two hours we shot thirty-six of them, mostly on the wing. Their attachment to this islet resulted from their having nests with eggs on it. Along with them we found Grakles, Red-winged Starlings, Flycatchers, and a few Zenaida Doves. Having shot most of the Pigeons, examined their nests, collected their eggs, and written memoranda, we proceeded to other keys in search of other species, of which you will have an account in my next volume, they being all water birds.

The next morning we thought of calling at this little key on our way, and were surprised to find than many new comers had arrived there before us. They were, however, very shy, and we procured only seventeen in all. I felt convinced that this spot was a favourite place of resort to these birds. It being detached from all other keys, furnished with rank herbaceous plants, cactuses, and low shrubs, and guarded by a thick hedge of mangroves, no place could be better adapted for breeding; and, at each visit we paid it, White-headed Pigeons were procured. Allow me here, kind reader, to tell you that the number of that strange species of crabs called *soldiers* was so great, that our game could not be suffered to lie a few minutes on the ground without being either much mangled or carried into their subterranean retreats; so that, with all our care, we were actually deprived by them of several birds which we had shot. These curious crabs, which belong to the genus *Pagurus,* crawl up the trees, and no doubt often destroy the eggs or young of the Pigeons.

The principal difference between Pigeons and Doves, as to their habits, is, according to my observation, that the former generally build their nests close together on the same trees, which the latter never do. For this reason I would place the present species among the Doves.

The nest is placed high or low, according to circumstances; but there are never two on the same tree. I have found it on the top shoots of a cactus, only a few feet from the ground, on the upper branches of a mangrove, or quite low, almost touching the water, and hanging over it. In general the nest resembles that of the *Columba migratoria,* but it is more compact, and better lined. The outer part is composed of small dry twigs, the inner of fibrous roots and grasses. The eggs are two, opaque, white, rather roundish, and as large as those of the domestic Pigeon. From the appearance of the eggs in the ovaria of females having young at the time, I would infer that this species has several broods during each season; and perhaps they may breed in Cuba, after their return from the Florida Keys. None of these birds are found on the mainland, although it is at no great distance.

A rather extraordinary fact relating to the habits of this species, is that many of these birds, which breed in Cuba, or some of the Bahama Islands, come to the Florida Keys for the purpose of procuring food for their young, to which they return several times daily. This is particularly observed at the time when the Sea Grape is fully ripe, or during the month of June. The numbers of these Pigeons that resort to the Keys, attract several species of Hawks during the breeding season, amongst which the Peregrine and the Red-shouldered are conspicuous. On none of the Keys unvisited by this species, did I see a Hawk of any kind.

The White-headed Pigeon exhibits little of the pomposity of the common domestic species, in its amorous moments. The male, however, struts before the female with elegance, and the tones of his voice are quite sufficient to persuade her of the sincerity of his attachment. During calm and clear mornings, when nature appears in all her purity and brightness, the cooing of this Pigeon may be heard at a considerable distance, mingling in full concord with the softer tones of the Zenaida Dove. The bird standing almost erect, full-plumed, and proud of his beauty, emits at first a loud *croohoo,* as a prelude, and then proceeds to repeat his *coo-coo-coo.* These sounds are continued during the period of incubation, and are at all times welcome to the ear of the visitor of these remarkable islands. When approached suddenly, it emits a hollow, guttural sound, precisely resembling that of the Common Pigeon on such occasions.

The young birds are at first almost black, but have tufts of a soft buff-coloured down distributed mostly over the head and shoulders. While yet squabs they have no appearance of white on the head, and they take about four months before they acquire their perfect plumage. Smaller size, and a less degree of brilliancy, distinguish the female from the male. About the beginning of October they abound on [abandon] the Keys, and return to the West India Islands.

I have only to add the following particulars to what I have already detailed of the history of this species. While standing perched in a nearly upright posture, they have a continued movement of the head, with a frequent jerking upwards of the tail. Their flight may be compared to that of the European Cushat, being very swift and noiseless, after a few hard flaps at starting. In captivity they are easily managed, and readily breed. I saw several of them with my friends Dr. Wilson and Mr. John Bachman.

I have placed a pair of these Pigeons on a low, flowering tree [Geiger Tree], which is rather scarce on the Keys. It is in full bloom during the whole year, and its leaves, I thought, correspond with the colour of the birds, while the brilliant hue of its flowers forms a strong contrast.

The Rough-leaved Cordia

This plant, on account of its large tubular scarlet flowers, is one of the most beautiful of the West Indian trees. I saw only two individuals at Key West, where, as was supposed, they had been introduced from Cuba. They were about fifteen feet high, the stem having a diameter of only five or six inches. They were in full bloom in the early part of May, and their broad deep green leaves, and splendid red blossoms, mingled with the variety of plants around me, rendered their appearance delightful. Both trees were private property, and grew in a yard opposite to that of Dr. Strobel, through whose influence I procured a large bough, from which the drawing was made, with the assistance of Mr. Lehman. I was informed that they continued in flower nearly the whole summer.

[From *Ornithological Biography,* Vol. II, pp. 443-447, 448.]

THE GROUND DOVE

Columba passerina, Linn. [Ground Dove,
Plate CLXXXII. Male, Female, and Young. *Columbigallina passerina*]

Before I proceed to describe the habits of this interesting bird, allow me to present you with the result of my observations relative to the geographical distribution of the birds of the genus Columba, which are either resident in the United States, or visit them annually.

The *Passenger Pigeon* ranges over the whole of the United States, excepting perhaps the southernmost portions of the Floridas, and extends to Newfoundland, where it is well known.

The *Carolina Dove* ranges from Louisiana to the middle parts of the State of Massachusetts, but is never seen in Maine. It reaches up the Mississippi, as far as Prairie du Chien, and in that direction extends to the borders of Upper Canada.

The *Ground Dove* is met with from the lower parts of Louisiana to Cape Hatteras, following the coast quite round the Floridas, but very seldom seen at any great distance in the interior. It is unknown in the State of Mississippi; and I will venture to add, that one of these birds has never been seen in Kentucky, although some writers have alleged that they occur there. They are more abundant on the sea islands of Georgia, and the middle portions of the coast of East Florida, than any where else. A search for them an hundred miles inland would in all probability prove fruitless.

The *White-Headed Pigeon* is confined to about three hundred miles of the Florida Keys. It seldom, if ever, visits the mainland. It remains with us about seven months of the year.

The *Zenaida Dove* seldom reaches farther east, along the Florida Keys, than Cape [Florida] Light-House. It never visits the Main. Its residence with us is shorter than that of the White-Headed Pigeon by a full month.

The *Key West Pigeon* has never been met with elsewhere than on the island of that name. It remains there about five months only.

The same is the case with the Blue-headed Ground Pigeon, commonly called the Cuba Partridge, which is the rarest of all the species known to me that resort to the Floridas.

In the above account, I have placed the species according to the number of individuals of each that occur in our country, beginning with the Passenger Pigeon, which is the most numerous, and ending

Plate CLXXXII. *Ground Dove*

with the Blue-headed Pigeon, which is the rarest; and I beg of you, kind reader, to recollect that hear-say has no part as a foundation for the results in this statement. I may also inform you, that curiosity, in part, prompted me to present it, it having been written in 1832, with the view of seeing if any of these birds shall become more or less numerous, or extend or diminish their range.

The flight of the Ground Dove is low, easy, and accompanied with a whistling sound, produced by the action of the wings, when the bird is surprised and forced to fly. It is less protracted than that of any other species with which I am acquainted in the United States, with the exception of the Blue-headed Pigeon. The crossing of the Gulf Stream by the latter bird is more surprising than the extended flight of the European Quail. The Ground Dove seldom flies more than a hundred yards at a time, and indeed is extremely attached to the spot which it has selected for the season. You may drive it to the opposite end of a large field, and yet, in a few hours after, it may be found in the place whence you raised it. Although it alights on trees or low bushes, on the branches of which it walks with ease, and on which its nest is most frequently placed, the ground is its usual resort. There it runs with facility, keeping its tail considerably elevated, as if to save it from being soiled. It is also fond of alighting on fences, where it is easily observed, and where it may be heard cooing for half an hour at a time.

These Pigeons are met with in groups of four or five, and it is seldom that more than a dozen are seen together. They prefer the thinly grassed sandy portions of cotton fields, pea-patches, and such places. In East Florida they are seen in the villages, and resort to the orange groves about them, where they frequently breed. I have often found them in the inner court of the famous Spanish fort of St. Augustine, where I have been surprised to see them rise almost perpendicularly, to reach above the parapets, by which they insured their escape. They are easily caught in traps, and at that place are sold at 6 1/4 cents each. They readily become domesticated, and indeed so very gentle are they, that I have seen a pair which, having been caught at the time when their young were quite small, and placed in an aviary, at once covered the little ones, and continued to nourish them until full-grown. They afterwards raised a second brood in the same nest, and shewed great spirit in keeping the Jays and Starlings from their charge. In this aviary, which belonged to Dr. Wilson of Charleston, several other species bred, among which were the Carolina Dove, the Cardinal Bird, the Blue Grosbeak, the White-throated Sparrow, the Towhe Bunting, the Common Partridge, and the Wood Duck. The Ground Doves were fed on rice and other small grain.

The nest of this species is large for the size of the bird, and compact. Its exterior is composed of dry twigs, its interior of grasses disposed in a circular form. It is usually placed in low bushes or hedges, or in orange trees in orchards. Early in April the female deposits her two pure white eggs; and sometimes three, but more generally two broods are reared in a season. The male struts before the female in the manner of the Barbary Ringed Dove.

A few of these birds remain all the year in the vicinity of Charleston, but the greater number retire either to the sea islands or to the Floridas. I met with them on the Keys resorted to by the Zenaida Dove, and saw some on Sandy Island, which lies six miles south from Cape Sable, the extreme point of the peninsula. They were so gentle that I approached them within less than two yards. Their nest was placed on the top of a cactus, not more than two feet high. I took some pleasure in destroying a pair of Fish Crows, that were waiting an opportunity to deprive them of their young.

In a wild state, the food of this species consists of grass-seeds and various small berries, with which they pick up a large proportion of gravel to assist digestion. They are extremely fond of dusting themselves in the sand, lying down upon it for a long time, in the manner of Partridges and other Gallinaceous birds, to which indeed they are closely allied. Their flesh is excellent.

[From *Ornithological Biography,* Vol. II, pp. 471-474.]

ROSEATE SPOONBILL

Platalea Ajaja, Linn. [Roseate Spoonbill, *Ajaia ajaja*]
Plate CCCXXI. Adult Male.

This beautiful and singular bird, although a constant resident in the southern extremities of the peninsula of Florida, seldom extends its journeys in an eastern direction beyond the State of North Carolina.

Plate CCCXXI. *Roseate Spoonbill*

Indeed it is of extremely rare occurrence there, and even in South Carolina, my friend John Bachman informs me that he has observed only three individuals in the course of twenty years. He once obtained a specimen in full plumage about ten miles north of Charleston. It is rarely seen in the interior of the country, at any distance from the waters of the Atlantic, or those of the Gulf of Mexico. A specimen sent to Wilson at Philadelphia from the neighbourhood of the city of Natchez, in the State of Mississippi, appears to have lost itself, as during my stay in that section of the country I never heard of another; nor have I ever met with one of these birds farther up the Mississippi than about thirty miles from its mouths. Although rather abundant on some parts of the coast of Florida, I found it more so along the Bay of Mexico, particularly in Galveston Bay in the Texas, where, as well as on the Florida Keys, it breeds in flocks. The Spoonbills are so sensible of cold, that those which spend the winter on the Keys, near Cape Sable in Florida, rarely leave those parts for the neighbourhood of St. Augustine before the first days of March. But after this you may find them along most of the water courses running parallel to the coast, and distant about half a mile or a mile from it. I saw none on any part of the St. John's River; and from all the answers which I obtained to my various inquiries respecting this bird, I feel confident that it never breeds in the interior of the peninsula, nor is ever seen there in winter.

The Roseate Spoonbill is found for the most part along the marshy and muddy borders of estuaries, the mouths of rivers, ponds, or sea islands or keys partially overgrown with bushes, and perhaps still more commonly along the shores of those singular salt-water bayous so abundant within a mile or so of the shores, where they can reside and breed in perfect security in the midst of an abundance of food. It is more or less gregarious at all seasons, and it is rare to meet with fewer than half a dozen together, unless they have been dispersed by a tempest, in which case one of them is now and then found in a situation where you would least expect it. At the approach of the breeding season, these small flocks collect to form great bodies, as is the manner of the Ibises, and resort to their former places of residence, to which they regularly return, like Herons. During the moult, which takes place in Florida late in May, the young of the preceding year conceal themselves among the close branches of the mangroves and other trees growing over narrow inlets, between secluded keys, or on bayous, where they spend the whole day, and whence it is difficult to start them. Toward night they return to their feeding grounds, generally keeping apart from the old birds. In the same country the old birds pass through their spring moult early in March, after which they are truly beautiful, presenting the appearance which I have attempted to represent in the plate before you. The sight of a flock of fifteen or twenty of these full-dressed birds is extremely pleasing to the student of nature, should he conceal himself from their view, for then he may observe their movements and manners to advantage. Now, they all stand with their wings widely extended to receive the sun's rays, or perhaps to court the cooling breeze, or they enjoy either seated on their tarsi. Again, they all stalk about with graceful steps along the margin of the muddy pool, or wade in the shallows in search of food. After a while they rise simultaneously on wing, and gradually ascend in a spiral manner to a great height, where you see them crossing each other in a thousand ways, like so many Vultures or Ibises. At length, tired of this pastime, or perhaps urged by hunger, they return to their feeding grounds in a zigzag course, and plunge through the air, as if displaying their powers of flight before you. These birds fly with their necks stretched forward to their full length, and their legs and feet extended behind, moving otherwise in the manner of Herons, or with easy flappings, until about to alight, when they sail with expanded wings, passing once or twice over the spot, and then gently coming to the ground, on which they run a few steps. When travelling to a distant place they proceed in regular ranks, but on ordinary occasions they fly in a confused manner. When the sun is shining, and they are wheeling on wing previous to alighting, their roseate tints exhibit a richer glow, which is surpassed only by the brilliancy of the Scarlet Ibis, and American Flamingo.

This beautiful bird is usually fond of the company of our different Herons, whose keen sight and vigilance are useful to it in apprising it of danger, and allowing it to take flight in due time. When the Spoonbills are by themselves and feeding, they can easily be approached by those who, like yourself perhaps, are expert at crawling over the mud on hands and knees, through the tall and keen-edged saw-grass. I well recollect my own success when, after having seen three of these precious birds alight on their feeding grounds, about a quarter of a mile from where I stood, I managed after something short of half an hour to get within shot of them. Then, after viewing them for a while unseen, I touched one of my triggers, and two of them fell upon the surface of the shallow water. The other might, I believe, have been as easily shot, for it stood, as I have seen Wild Turkey cocks do on like occasions, looking with curious intensity as it were upon its massacred friends, until, seeing me get up and wade towards them, it hurriedly extended its broad wings, and flew off towards the sea-shore. When wounded in the wing, they make towards deeper water, and, if closely pursued, will swim to some distance, but without ever attempting to dive, and when at last seized, offer no resistance. On the contrary, if their wings are uninjured, though they may otherwise be severely wounded, they rise and fly to a great distance, or drop while on the way. I have considered these birds as tough to kill, and, when on open ground, even without being in company with Herons, as difficult of approach. They are as nocturnal as the night Heron, and, although they seek for food at times during the middle of the day, their principal feeding time is from near sunset until daylight. To all such feeding grounds as are exposed to the tides, they betake themselves when it is low water, and search for food along the shallow margins until driven off by the returning tide. Few birds are better aware of the hours at which the waters are high or low, and when it is near ebb you see them wending their way to the shore. Whenever a feeding place seems to be productive, the Spoonbills are wont to return to it until they have been much disturbed, and persons aware of this fact may waylay them with success, as at such times one may shoot them while passing over head. To procure their food, the Spoonbills first generally alight near the water, into which they then wade up to the tibia, and immerse their bills in the water or soft mud, sometimes with the head and even the whole neck beneath the surface. They frequently withdraw these parts however, and look around to ascertain if danger is near. They move their partially opened mandibles laterally to and fro with a considerable degree of elegance, munching the fry, insects, or small shell-fish, which they secure, before swallowing them. When there are many together, one usually acts as sentinel, unless a Heron should be near; and in either case you may despair of approaching them. I have never seen one of these birds feeding in fresh water, although I have been told that this is sometimes the case. To all those keys in the Floridas in which ponds have been dug for the making of salt, they usually repair in the evening for the purpose of feeding; but the shallow inlets in the great salt marshes of our southern coasts are their favourite places of resort.

The Roseate Spoonbills alight on trees with as much facility as Herons, and even walk on their large branches. They usually nestle on the tops of the mangroves, placing their nests at the distance of a few yards from each other. They are formed of sticks of considerable size and are flat, like most of those of the Heron tribe. The eggs are laid about the middle of April, and are usually three. They measure two inches and five-eighths in length, an inch and seven-eighths in their greatest breadth, are slightly granulated, almost equally rounded at both ends, and have a pure white colour. I have never seen the young when recently hatched; but when able to fly they are greyish-white. The bill is then quite smooth, of a yellowish-green colour, as are the legs and feet, as well as the skin on part of the head. Young birds in their second year have the wings and the lower wing-coverts of a pale roseate tint, the bill more richly coloured, and the legs and feet dark brownish-red, or purplish. At this age, they are unadorned with the curling feathers on the breast; but in the third spring the bird is perfect, although it increases in size for several seasons after. I have never seen one of these birds of the bright red colour assigned to them by some authors. . . .

The feathers of the wings and tail of the Roseate Spoonbill are manufactured into fans by the Indians and Negroes of Florida; and at St. Augustine these ornaments form in some degree a regular article of trade. Their flesh is oily and poor eating.

[From *Ornithological Biography,* Vol. IV, pp. 188-191, 192-193.]

THE BLUE-HEADED PIGEON

Columba cyanocephala, Linn.
Plate CLXXII. Male and Female.

[Blue-headed Quail-Dove,
Starnoenas cyanocephala]

A few of these birds migrate each spring from the Island of Cuba to the Keys of Florida, but are rarely seen, on account of the deep tangled woods in which they live. Early in May 1832, while on a shooting excursion with the commander of the United States Revenue Cutter, the Marion, I saw a pair of them on the western side of Key West. They were near the water, picking gravel, but on our approaching them they ran back into the thickets, which were only a few yards distant. Several fishermen and wreckers informed us that they were more abundant on the "Mule Keys;" but although a large party and myself searched these islands for a whole day, not one did we discover there. I saw a pair which I was told had been caught when young on the latter Keys, but I could not obtain any other information respecting them, than that they were fed on cracked corn and rice, which answered the purpose well.

I have represented three of these Pigeons on the ground, with some of the creeping plants which grew in the place where I saw the pair mentioned above. . . .

The beautiful Cyperus [wild Poinsettia] represented in this plate is

Plate CLXXII. *Blue-headed Pigeon*

quite abundant on all the dry Keys of the Floridas, and is also found in many parts of the interior of the peninsula.

[From *Ornithological Biography,* Vol. II, pp. 411, 412. *The A.O.U. Check-List of North American Birds* states, "Audubon's sight record of this Cuban species on the Florida Keys unsatisfactory," and so places it in its Hypothetical List.]

THE MANGO HUMMING BIRD

Trochilus mango, Linn.
Plate CLXXXIV. Male and Female.

[Blue-throated Mango,
Anthracothorax nigricollis]

I am indebted to my learned friend the Reverend John Bachman for this species of Humming Bird, of which he received a specimen from our mutual friend Dr. Strobel, and afterwards presented it to me.

"Hitherto," says he, "it has been supposed that only one species of Humming Bird (the *Trochilus Colubris*) ever visits the United

Plate CLXXXIV. *Mangrove Humming Bird*

States. Although this is a genus consisting of upwards of a hundred species, all of which are peculiar to the Continent of America and the adjoining islands, yet with few exceptions they are confined to the tropics. In those warm climates, where the Bignonias and other tubular flowers that bloom throughout the year, and innumerable insects that sport in the sun-shine, afford an abundance of food, these lively birds are the greatest ornaments of the gardens and forests. Such in most cases is the brilliancy of their plumage, that I am unable to find apt objects of comparison unless I resort to the most brilliant gems and the richest metals. So rapid is their flight that they seem to outstrip the wind. Almost always on the wing, we scarcely see them in any other position. Living on the honeyed sweets of the most beautiful flowers, and the minute insects concealed in their corollas, they come to us as etherial beings, and it is not surprising that they should have excited the wonder and admiration of mankind.

"It affords me great pleasure to introduce to the lovers of Natural History a second species of Humming Bird as an inhabitant of the United States. The specimen which is now in my possession, was obtained by Dr. Strobel at Key West in East Florida. He informed me that he had succeeded in capturing it from a bush where he had found it seated, apparently wearied after its long flight across the Gulf of Mexico, probably from some of the West India Islands, or the coast of South America. Whether this species is numerous in any part of Florida, I have had no means of ascertaining. The interior of that territory, as its name indicates, is the land of flowers, and consequently well suited to the peculiar habits of this genus; and as it has seldom been visited by ornithologists, it is possible that not only this, but several other species of Humming Birds, may yet be discovered as inhabitants of our southern country.

"I have not seen the splendid engravings of this genus by Messrs. Vieillot and Audebert, in which the *Trochilus Mango* is said to be figured; but from the description contained in Latham's Synopsis and Shaw's Zoology, I have no hesitation in pronouncing it an individual of this species."

The female figures introduced in the plate were taken from a specimen procured at Charleston; but whether it had been found in the United States or not, could not be ascertained.

[From *Ornithological Biography,* Vol. II, pp. 480-481.]

THE MANGROVE CUCKOO

Coccyzus Seniculus, Nuttall. [Mangrove Cuckoo, *Coccyzus minor*]
Plate CLXIX. Male.

A few days after my arrival at Key West in the Floridas, early in the month of May, Major Glassel of the United States' Army presented me with a specimen of this bird, which had been killed by one of the soldiers belonging to the garrison. I had already observed many Cuckoos in the course of my walks through the tangled woods of that curious island; but as they seemed to be our Common Yellow-billed species, I passed them without paying much attention to them. The moment this specimen was presented to me however, I knew that it was a species unknown to me, and thought, as I have on many occasions had reason to do, how vigilant the student of nature ought to be, when placed in a country previously unvisited by him. The bird was immediately drawn, and I afterwards shot several others, all precisely corresponding with it.

The habits of the Mangrove Cuckoo I found to be much the same as those of our two other well known species. Like them, it is fond of sucking the eggs of all kinds of birds in the absence of their owners, and also feeds on fruits and various species of insects. It is, however, more vigilant and shy, and does not extend its migrations northward beyond the eastern capes of the Floridas, appearing, indeed, to confine itself mostly to the islets covered with mangroves, among the sombre foliage of which trees it usually builds its nest and rears its young. It retires southward in the beginning of September, according to the accounts of it which I received in the country.

The nest is slightly constructed of dry twigs, and is almost flat, nearly resembling that of the Yellow-billed Cuckoo, which I have already described. The eggs are of the same number and form as those of that species, but somewhat larger. It raises two broods in the season, and feeds its young on insects until they are able to go abroad.

The White-headed Pigeon is frequently robbed of its eggs by this plunderer, and it is alleged by the fishermen and wreckers that it destroys the squabs when yet very young, but I saw no instance of this barbarous propensity. One which had been caught in its nest, and which I saw placed in a cage, refused all kinds of food, and soon died. This, however proved to me the great affection which they have towards their eggs. Their flight is much like that of the other species

Plate CLXIX. *Mangrove Cuckoo*

described by me, perhaps only more rapid and elevated when they are proceeding to some distant place.

The Seven Years' Apple

The plant, on a twig of which I have represented the Mangrove Cuckoo, is found on all the Florida Keys, and at times is seen growing in large patches on the mud flats that exist between the outer islets and the mainland. The leaves are thick, glossy above, furred, and of a dull brown colour beneath.

[From *Ornithological Biography*, Vol. II, pp. 390-391.]

THE KEY WEST PIGEON

Columba montana, Linn. [Key West Quail-Dove,
Plate CLXVII. Male and Female. *Geotrygon chrysia*]

It was at Key West that I first saw this beautiful Pigeon. The Marion was brought to anchor close to, and nearly opposite, the little town of the same name, some time after the setting of the sun. The few flickering lights I saw nearly fixed the size of the place in my imagination. In a trice, the kind captain and I were seated in his gig, and I felt the onward movement of the light bark as if actually on wing, so well timed was the pulling of the brave tars who were taking us to the shore. In this place I formed acquaintance with Major Glassel of the United States Artillery, and his family, of Dr. Benjamin Strobel, and several other persons, to whom I must ever feel grateful for the kind attention which they paid to me and my assistants, as well as for the alacrity with which they aided me in procuring rare specimens not only of birds, but also of shells and plants, most of which were unknown to me. Indeed—I cannot too often repeat it—the facilities afforded me by our Government, during my latter journeys and voyages, have been so grateful to my feelings, that I have frequently thought that circumstance alone quite sufficient to induce even a less ardent lover of nature to exert himself to the utmost in repaying the favour.

Major Glassel sent one of his serjeants with me to search the whole island, with which he was perfectly acquainted. The name of this soldier was Sykes, and his life, like mine, had been a chequered one; for there are few pleasures unaccompanied with pains, real or imaginary, and the worthy sergeant had had his share of both. I soon discovered that he was a perfect woodsman, for although we traversed the densest thickets, in close and gloomy weather, he conducted me quite across the island, in as masterly a manner as ever did an Indian on a like occasion.—But perhaps, kind reader, a copy of my journal for that day, may afford you a clearer idea of our search for rare birds, than any other means that I could devise. Before I proceed, however, allow me to state, that, while at Charleston, in South Carolina, I saw at my friend Bachman's house the head of a Pigeon which Dr. Strobel had sent from Key West, and which I perceived did not belong to the Zenaida Dove. Serjeant Sykes had seen the Pigeon, and acquainted as he was with the birds of the country, he gave some hope that we might procure a few of them that very day;—and now, for my Journal.

"*May* 6. 1832.—When I reached the garrison, I found the sergeant waiting for me. I gave him some small shot, and we set off, not in full run, nor even at a dog-trot, but with the slowness and carefulness usually employed by a lynx or a cougar when searching for prey. We soon reached the thickets, and found it necessary to move in truth very slowly, one foot warily advanced before the other, one hand engaged in opening a passage, and presently after occupied in securing the cap on the head, in smashing some dozens of hungry musquitoes, or in drawing the sharp thorn of a cactus from a leg or foot, in securing our gun-locks, or in assisting ourselves to rise after a fall occasioned by stumbling against the projecting angle of a rock. But we pushed on, squeezed ourselves between the stubborn branches, and forced our way as well as we could, my guide of course having the lead. Suddenly I saw him stoop, and observing the motion of his hand, immediately followed his example. Reduced by his position to one half of his natural height, he moved more briskly, inclined to the right, then to the left, then pushed forward, and raising his piece as he stopped, immediately fired. "I have it," cried he. "What?" cried I. "The pigeon"—and he disappeared. The heat was excessive, and the brushwood here was so thick and tangled, that had not Mr. Sykes been a United States soldier, I should have looked upon him as bent on retaliating on behalf of "the eccentric naturalist;" for, although not more than ten paces distant from me, not a glimpse of him could I obtain. After crawling to the spot I found him smoothing the feathers of a Pigeon which I had never seen, nay the most beautiful yet found in the United States. How I gazed on its resplendent plumage!—how I marked the expression of its rich-coloured, large and timid eye, as the poor creature was gasping its last breath! — Ah, how I looked on this lovely bird! I handled it, turned it, examined its feathers and form, its bill, its legs and claws, weighed it by estimate, and after a while formed a winding sheet for it of a piece of paper. Did ever an Egyptian pharmacopolist employ more care in embalming the most illustrious of the Pharaohs, than I did in trying to preserve from injury this most beautiful of the woodland cooers!

I never felt, nor did my companion, that our faces and hands were covered with musquitoes; and although the perspiration made my eyes smart, I was as much delighted as ever I had been on such an occasion. We travelled onward, much in the same manner, until we reached the opposite end of the island; but not another bird did we meet this day.

As we sat near the shore gazing on the curious light pea-green colour of the sea, I unfolded my prize, and as I now more quietly observed the brilliant changing metallic hues of its plumage, I could not refrain from exclaiming—"But who will draw it?" for the obvious difficulties of copying nature struck me as powerfully as they ever

Plate CLXVII. *Key-west Dove (Key West Pigeon)*

had done, and brought to my memory the following passage:—"La nature se joue du pinceau des hommes;—lorsqu' on croit qu'il a atteint sa plus grande beauté, elle sourit et s'embellit encore!"

We returned along the shore of this curious island to the garrison, after which Major Glassel's barge conveyed me on board of the Marion.

I have taken upon myself to name this species the Key West Pigeon, and offer it as a tribute to the generous inhabitants of that island, who favoured me with their friendship. . . .

The cooing of this species is not so soft or prolonged as that of the Common Dove, or of the Zenaida Dove, and yet not so emphatical as that of any true Pigeon with which I am acquainted. It may be imitated by pronouncing the following syllables:—*Whoe-whoe-oh-oh-oh.* When suddenly approached by man, it emits a guttural gasping-like sound, somewhat in the manner of the Common Tame Pigeon on such an occasion. They alight on the lower branches of shrubby trees, and delight in the neighborhood of shady ponds, but always inhabit, by preference, the darkest solitudes.

The nest of the Key West Pigeon is formed of light dry twigs, and much resembles in shape that of the Carolina Dove. Sometimes you find it situated on the ground, when less preparation is used. Some nests are placed on the large branches of trees quite low, while others are fixed on slender twigs. On the 20th May, one of these nests was found containing two pure white eggs, about the size of those of the White-headed Pigeon, nearly round, and so transparent that I could see the yolk by holding them to the light. How long incubation continues, or if they raise more than one brood in a season, I am unable to say.

Towards the middle of July they become sufficiently abundant at Key West, to enable sportsmen to shoot as many as a score in a day; for, as soon as the young are able to follow their parents, they frequently resort to the roads to dust themselves, and are then easily approached. Dr. Strobel told me he had procured more than a dozen of these birds in the course of a morning, and assured me that they were excellent eating.

Their food consists of berries and seeds of different plants, and when the sea-grape is ripe, they feed greedily upon it. They all depart for Cuba, or the other West India Islands, about the middle of October.

Until my arrival at Key West, this species was supposed to be the

Zenaida Dove. The young, when fully feathered, are of a dark-grey colour above, lighter below, the bill and legs of a deep leaden hue. I am inclined to believe that they attain their full beauty of plumage the following spring.

So much are these birds confined to the interior of the undergrowth, that their loves are entirely prosecuted there; nor do they on such occasions elevate themselves in the air, as is the manner of the Carolina Dove. . . .

The plants represented in this plate grew on Key West, in sheltered situations. That with purple flowers is a Convolvulus, the other an Ipomaea. The blossoms are partially closed at night, and although ornamental, are destitute of odour.

[From *Ornithological Biography,* Vol. II, pp. 382-385, 386.]

THE BOOBY GANNET

Sula fusca, Briss. [Brown Booby, *Sula leucogaster*]
Plate CCVII. Male.

As the Marion was nearing the curious islets of the Tortugas, one of the birds that more particularly attracted my notice was of this species. The nearer we approached the land, the more numerous did they become, and I felt delighted with the hope that ere many days should elapse, I should have an opportunity of studying their habits. As night drew her sombre curtain over the face of nature, some of these birds alighted on the top-yard of our bark, and I observed ever afterwards that they manifested a propensity to roost at as great a height as possible above the surrounding objects, making choice of the tops of bushes, or even upright poles, and disputing with each other the privilege. The first that was shot at, was approached with considerable difficulty: it had alighted on the prong of a tree which had floated and been fastened to the bottom of a rocky shallow at some distance from shore; the water was about four feet deep and quite rough; sharks we well knew were abundant around us; but the desire to procure the bird was too strong to be overcome by such obstacles. In an instant, the pilot and myself were over the sides of

Plate CCVII. *Booby Gannet*

the boat, and onward we proceeded with our guns cocked and ready. The yawl was well manned, and its crew awaiting the result. After we had struggled through the turbulent waters about a hundred yards, my companion raised his gun and fired; but away flew the bird with a broken leg, and we saw no more of it that day. Next day, however, at the same hour, the Booby was seen perched on the same prong, where, after resting about three hours, it made off to the open sea, doubtless in search of food.

About eight miles to the north-east of the Tortugas Light-house, lies a small sand-bar a few acres in extent, called Booby Island, on account of the number of birds of this species that resort to it during the breeding-season, and to it we accordingly went. We found it not more than a few feet above the surface of the water, but covered with Boobies, which lay basking in the sunshine, and pluming themselves. Our attempt to land on the island before the birds should fly off, proved futile, for before we were within fifty yards of it, they had all betaken themselves to flight, and were dispersing in various directions. We landed, however, distributed ourselves in different parts, and sent the boat to some distance, the pilot assuring us that the birds would return. And so it happened. As they approached, we laid ourselves as flat as possible in the sand, and although none of them alighted, we attained our object, for in a couple of hours we procured thirty individuals of both sexes and of different ages, finding little difficulty in bringing them down as they flew over us at a moderate height. The wounded birds that fell on the ground made immediately for the water, moving with more ease than I had expected from the accounts usually given of the awkward motions of these birds on the land. Those which reached the water swam off with great buoyancy, and with such rapidity, that it took much rowing to secure some of them, while most of those that fell directly into the sea with only a wing broken, escaped. The island was covered with their dung, the odour of which extended to a considerable distance leeward. In the evening of the same day we landed on another island, named after the Noddy, and thickly covered with bushes and low trees. to which thousands of that species of Tern resort for the purpose of breeding. There also we found a great number of Boobies. They were perched on the top-branches of the trees, on which they had nests, and here again we obtained as many as we desired. They flew close over our heads, eyeing us with dismay but in silence; indeed, not one of these birds ever emitted a cry, except at the moment when they rose from their perches or from the sand. Their note is harsh and guttural, somewhat like that of a strangled pig, and resembling the syllables *hork, hork.*

The nest of the Booby is placed on the top of a bush at a height of from four to ten feet. It is large and flat, formed of a few dry sticks, covered and matted with sea-weeds in great quantity. I have no doubt that they return to the same nest many years in succession, and repair it as occasion requires. In all the nests which I examined, only one egg was found, and as most of the birds were sitting, and some of the eggs had the chick nearly ready for exclusion, it is probable that these birds raise only a single young one, like the Common Gannet or Solan Goose. The egg is of a dull white colour, without spots, and about the size of that of a common hen, but more elongated, being 2 3/8 inches in length, with a diameter of 1 3/4. In some nests they were covered with filth from the parent bird, in the manner of the Florida Cormorant. The young, which had an uncouth appearance, were covered with down; the bill and feet of a deep livid blue or indigo colour. On being touched, they emitted no cry, but turned away their heads at every trial. A great quantity of fish lay beneath the trees in a state of putrefaction, proving how abundantly the young birds were supplied by their parents. Indeed, while we were on Noddy Island, there was a constant succession of birds coming in from the sea with food for their young, consisting chiefly of flying-fish and small mullets, which they disgorged in a half macerated state into the open throats of their offspring. Unfortunately the time afforded me on that coast was not sufficient to enable me to trace the progress of their growth. I observed, however, that none of the birds which were still brown had nests, and that they roosted apart, particularly on Booby Island, where also many barren ones usually resorted, to lie on the sand and bask in the sun.

The flight of the Booby is graceful and extremely protracted. They pass swiftly at a height of from twenty yards to a foot or two from the surface, often following the troughs of the waves to a considerable distance, their wings extended at right angles to the body; then, without any apparent effort, raising themselves and allowing the rolling waters to break beneath them, when they tack about, and sweep along in a contrary direction in search of food, much in the manner of the true Petrels. Now, if you follow an individual, you see that it suddenly stops short, plunges headlong into the water, pierces with its powerful beak and secures a fish, emerges again with inconceivable ease, after a short interval rises on wing, performs a few wide circlings, and makes off toward some shore. At this time its flight is different, being performed by flappings for twenty or thirty paces, with alternate sailings of more than double that space. When overloaded with food, they alight on the water, where, if undisturbed, they appear to remain for hours at a time, probably until digestion has afforded them relief.

The range to which this species confines itself along our coast, seldom extends beyond Cape Hatteras to the eastward, but they become more and more numerous the farther south we proceed. They breed abundantly on all such islands or keys as are adapted for the purpose, on the southern and western coasts of the Floridas and in the Gulf of Mexico, where I was told they breed on the sandbars. Their power of wing seems sufficient to enable them to brave the tempest, while during a continuance of fair weather they venture to a great distance seaward, and I have seen them fully 200 miles from land.

The expansibility of the gullet of this species enables it to swallow fishes of considerable size, and on such occasions their mouth seems to spread to an unusual width. In the throats of several individuals that were shot as they were returning to their nests, I found mullets measuring seven or eight inches, that must have weighed fully half a pound. Their body beneath the skin, is covered with numerous air-cells, which probably assist them in raising or lowering themselves while on wing, and perhaps still more so when on the point of performing the rapid plunge by which they secure their prey.

Their principal enemies during the breeding-season are the American Crow and the Fish Crow, both of which destroy their eggs, and the Turkey Buzzard, which devours their young while yet unfledged. They breed during the month of May, but I have not been able to ascertain if they raise more than one brood in the season. The adult birds chase away those which are yet immature during the period of incubation. It would seem that they take several years in attaining their perfect state.

When procured alive, they feed freely, and may be kept any length of time, provided they are supplied with fish. No other food, however, could I tempt them to swallow, excepting slices of turtle, which after all they did not seem to relish. In no instance did I observe one drinking. Some authors have stated that the Frigate Pelican and the Lestris force the Booby to disgorge its food that they may obtain it;

but this I have never witnessed. Like the Common Gannet, they may be secured by fastening a fish to a soft plant, and sinking it a few feet beneath the surface of the water, for if they perceive the bait, which they are likely to do if they pass over it, they plunge headlong upon it, and drive their bill into the wood.

When a Booby has alighted on the spar of a vessel, it is no easy matter to catch it, unless it is much fatigued; but if exhausted and asleep, an expert seaman may occasionally secure one. I was informed that after the breeding-season, these birds roost on trees in company with the Brown Pelican and a species of Tern, *Sterna stolida,* and spend their hours of daily rest on the sandbanks. Our pilot, who, as I have mentioned in my second volume, was a man of great observation, assured me that while at Vera Cruz, he saw the fishermen there go to sea, and return from considerable distances, simply by following the course of the Boobies.

The bills and legs of those which I procured in the brown plumage, and which were from one to two years of age, were dusky blue. These were undergoing moult on the 14th of May. At a more advanced age, the parts mentioned become paler, and when the bird has arrived at maturity, are as represented in my plate. I observed no external difference between the sexes in the adult birds. The stomach is a long dilatable pouch, thin, and of a yellow colour. The body is muscular, and the flesh, which is of a dark colour, tough, and having a disagreeable smell, is scarcely fit for food.

I am unable to find a good reason for those who have chosen to call these birds *boobies.* Authors, it is true, generally represent them as extremely *stupid;* but to me the word is utterly inapplicable to any bird with which I am acquainted. The Woodcock, too, is said to be stupid, as are many other birds; but my opinion, founded on pretty extensive observation, is, that it is only when birds of any species are unacquainted with man, that they manifest that kind of *ignorance* or *innocence* which he calls *stupidity,* and by which they suffer themselves to be imposed upon. A little acquaintance with him soon enables them to perceive enough of his character to induce them to keep aloof. This I observed in the Booby Gannet, as well as in the Noddy Tern, and in certain species of land birds of which I have already spoken. After my first visit to Booby Island in the Tortugas, the Gannets had already become very shy and wary, and before the Marion sailed away from those peaceful retreats of the wandering sea-birds, the *Boobies* had become so knowing, that the most expert of our party could not get within shot of them.

[From *Ornithological Biography*, Vol. III, pp. 63-67.]

THE NODDY TERN

Sterna stolida, Linn. [Noddy Tern, *Anous stolidus*]
Plate CCLXXV.

About the beginning of May, the Noddies collect from all parts of the Gulf of Mexico, and the coasts of Florida, for the purpose of returning to their breeding places, on one of the Tortugas called Noddy Key. They nearly equal in number the Sooty Terns, which also breed on an island a few miles distant. The Noddies form regular nests of twigs and dry grass, which they place on the bushes or low trees, but never on the ground. On visiting their island on the 11th of May 1832, I was surprised to see that many of them were repairing and augmenting nests that had remained through the winter, while others were employed in constructing new ones, and some were already sitting on their eggs. In a great many instances, the repaired nests formed masses nearly two feet in height, and yet all of them had only a slight hollow for the eggs, broken shells of which were found among the entire ones, as if they had been purposely placed there. The birds did not discontinue their labours, although there were nine or ten of us walking among the bushes, and when we had gone a few yards into the thicket, thousands of them flew quite low over us, some at times coming so close as to enable us to catch a few of them with the hand. On one side might be seen a Noddy carrying a stick in its bill, or a bird picking up something from the ground to add to its nest; on the other several were seen sitting on their eggs unconscious of danger, while their mates brought them food. The greater part rose on wing as we advanced, but re-alighted as soon as we had passed. The bushes were rarely taller than ourselves, so that we could easily see the eggs in the nests. This was quite a new sight to me, and not less pleasing than unexpected.

The Noddy, like most other species of Terns, lays three eggs, which average two inches in length, by an inch and three-eighths in breadth, and are of reddish-yellow colour, spotted and patched with dull red and faint purple. They afford excellent eating, and our sailors seldom failed to collect bucketfuls of them daily during our stay at the Tortugas. The wreckers assured me that the young birds remain along with the old through the winter, in which respect the Noddy, if this account be correct, differs from other species, the young of which keep by themselves until spring.

At the approach of a boat, the Noddies never flew off their island, in the manner of the Sooty Terns. They appeared to go farther out to sea than those birds, in search of their food, which consists of fishes mostly caught amid the floating sea-weeds, these Terns seizing them, not by plunging perpendicularly downwards, as other species do, but by skimming close over the surface in the manner of Gulls, and also by alighting and swimming round the edges of the weeds.

Plate CCLXXV. *Noddy Tern*

This I had abundant opportunities of seeing while on the Gulf of Mexico.

The flight of this bird greatly resembles that of the Night Hawk when passing over meadows or rivers. When about to alight on the water, the Noddy keeps its wings extended upwards, and touches it first with its feet. It swims with considerable buoyancy and grace, and at times immerses its head to seize on a fish. It does not see well by night, and it is perhaps for this reason that it frequently alights on the spars of vessels, where it sleeps so sound that the seamen often catch them. When seized in the hand, it utters a rough cry, not unlike that of a young American Crow taken from the nest. On such occasions, it does not disgorge its food, like the Cayenne Tern and other species, although it bites severely, with quickly repeated movements of the bill, which, on missing the object aimed at, snaps like that of our larger Flycatchers. Some which I kept several days, refused all kinds of food, became dull and languid, and at length died.

While hovering over us near their nests, these birds emitted a low querulous murmur, and, if unmolested, would attempt to alight on our heads. After a few visits, however, they became rather more careful of themselves, although the sitting birds often suffered us to put a hat over them. Like the Sooty Tern, this species incubates both day and night. The differences exhibited by Terns with respect to their mode of nestling and incubation, are great, even in the same neighbourhood, and under the same degree of atmospheric temperature. This species breeds on bushes or low trees, placing several nests on the same bush, or in fact as many as it will hold. The *Sterna fuliginosa* scoops out a slight hollow in the sand, under the bushes, without forming any nest, and incubates closely like the former. The Sandwich, the Cayenne, and the Roseate Terns, drop their eggs on the sand or the bare rock, and seldom sit upon them until evening, or during cloudy or rainy weather. The Cayenne, Sooty, and Noddy Terns differ greatly in their flight, their manner of feeding, and the extent of their migrations. The Tail of the Noddy is cuneate, instead of being forked, in which respect it differs essentially from that of the other species. Perhaps the naturalists who placed it in the same genus with the Roseate Tern, may have been nodding over their books.

Since writing the above account, I have read the article on this species by my esteemed friend Mr. Nuttall, and am surprised to find him state that "the Noddies breed in great numbers in the Bahama Islands, laying their eggs on the shelvings of rocks." No authority is given for this, which I regret, because had he given the fact as observed by himself, it would have astonished me as much as my account of the breeding of the Noddy in the Tortugas may astonish others.

[From *Ornithological Biography,* Vol. III, pp. 516-518.]

THE SOOTY TERN

Sterna fuliginosa, Lath. [Sooty Tern, *Sterna fuscata*]
Plate CCXXXV. Male.

Early in the afternoon of the 9th of May 1832, I was standing on the deck of the United States' revenue-cutter the Marion. The weather was very beautiful, although hot, and a favourable breeze wafted us onwards in our course. Captain Robert Day, who stood near me, on looking toward the south-west, ordered some person to be sent to the top to watch the appearance of land. A young lad was instantly seen ascending the rigging, and not many minutes after he had attained his post, we heard from him the cry of "land." It was the low keys of the Tortugas, toward which we had been steering. No change was made in the course of the "Lady of the Green Mantle," who glided along as if aware of the knowledge possessed by her commander. Now the light-house lantern appeared, like a bright gem glittering in the rays of the sun. Presently the masts and flags of several wreckers shewed us that they were anchored in the small but safe harbour. We sailed on, and our active pilot, who was also the first lieutenant of the Marion, pointed out to me a small island which he said was at this season the resort of thousands of birds, which he described by calling them "Black and White Sea Swallows," and again another islet, equally well stocked with another kind of Sea Swallow, which he added were called Noddies, because they frequently alighted on the yards of vessels at night, and slept there. He assured me that both species were on their respective breeding

Plate CCXXXV. *Sooty Tern*

grounds by millions, that the eggs of the first lay on the sand under bushes, at intervals of about a foot, while the nests of the last were placed as thickly on the bushes of their own chosen island. "Before we cast anchor," he added, "you will see them rise in swarms like those of bees when disturbed in their hive, and their cries will deafen you."

You may easily imagine how anxious I was to realize the picture; I expressed a wish to be landed on the island; but the kind officer replied, "My good Sir, you will soon be tired of their incessant noise and numbers, and will enjoy the procuring of Boobies much better." After various tacks, we made our way through the curious and extremely dangerous channels leading to the small harbour, where we anchored. As the chain grated the ear, I saw a cloud-like mass arise over the "Bird Key," from which we were only a few hundred yards distant; and in a few minutes the yawl was carrying myself and my assistant ashore. On landing, I felt for a moment as if the birds would raise me from the ground, so thick were they all round, and so quick the motion of their wings. Their cries were indeed deafening, yet not more than half of them took to wing on our arrival, those which rose being chiefly male birds, as we afterwards ascertained. We ran across the naked beach, and as we entered the thick cover before us, and spread in different directions, we might at every step have caught a sitting bird, or one scrambling through the bushes to escape from us. Some of the sailors, who had more than once been there before, had provided themselves with sticks, with which they knocked down the birds as they flew thick around and over them. In less than half an hour, more than a hundred Terns lay dead in a heap, and a number of baskets were filled to the brim with eggs. We then returned on board, and declined disturbing the rest any more that night. My assistant, Mr. H. Ward, of London, skinned upwards of fifty specimens, aided by Captain Day's servant. The sailors told me that the birds were excellent eating, but on this point I cannot say much in corroboration of their opinion, although I can safely recommend the eggs, for I considered them delicious, in whatever way cooked, and during our stay at the Tortugas we never passed a day without providing ourselves with a good quantity of them.

The next morning Mr. Ward told me that great numbers of the Terns left their island at two o'clock, flew off towards the sea, and returned a little before day, or about four o'clock. This I afterwards observed to be regularly the case, unless there happened to blow a gale, a proof that this species sees as well during the night as by day, when they also go to sea in search of food for themselves and their young. In this respect they differ from the *Sterna stolida,* which, when overtaken at sea by darkness, even when land is only a few miles distant, alight on the water, and frequently on the yards of vessels, where if undisturbed they sleep until the return of day. It is from this circumstance that they have obtained the name of Noddy, to which in fact they are much better entitled than the present species, which has also been so named, but of which I never observed any to alight on a vessel in which I was for thirty-five days in the Gulf of Mexico, at a time when that bird was as abundant during the day as the other species, of which many were caught at my desire by the sailors.

The present species rarely alights on the water, where it seems incommoded by its long tail; but the other, the *Sterna stolida,* which, in the shape of its tail, and in some of its habits, shews an affinity to the Petrels, not only frequently alights on the sea, but swims about on floating patches of the Gulf Weed, seizing on the small fry and little crabs that are found among the branches of that plant, or immediately beneath them.

I have often thought, since I became acquainted with the habits of the bird which here occupies our attention, that it differs materially from all the other species of the same genus that occur on our coasts. The *Sterna fuliginosa* never dives headlong and perpendicularly as the smaller species are wont to do, such as *St. Hirundo* [Common Tern], *St. arctica* [Arctic], *St. minuta* [Least], *St. Dougallii* [Roseate] or *St. nigra* [Black], but passes over its prey in a curved line, and picks it up. Its action I cannot better compare to that of any other bird than the Night Hawk, while plunging over its female. I have often observed this Tern follow and hover in the wake of a porpoise, while the latter was pursuing its prey, and at the instant when by a sudden dash it frightens and drives toward the surface the fry around it, the Tern as suddenly passes over the spot, and picks up a small fish or two.

Nor is the flight of this Tern characterized by the buoyancy and undecidedness, if I may so speak, of the other species mentioned above, it being as firm and steady as that of the Cayenne Tern, excepting during the movements performed in procuring its food. Like some of the smaller gulls, this bird not unfrequently hovers close to the water to pick up floating objects, such as small bits of fat pork and greasy substances thrown overboard purposely for making the experiment. It is not improbable that the habits peculiar to this species, the Noddy, and one or two others, of which I shall have occasion to speak elsewhere, may tend to induce systematic writers to place them in a new "subgenus."

There is a circumstance connected with the habits of the two species of which I now more particularly speak, which, although perhaps somewhat out of place, I cannot refrain from introducing here. It is that the *Sterna stolida always forms a nest on trees or bushes,* on which that bird alights with as much ease as a Crow or Thrush; whereas the *Sterna fuliginosa* never forms a nest of any sort, but deposits its eggs in a slight cavity which it scoops in the sand under the trees. But, reader, let us return to the Bird Key.

Early the next morning I was put on shore, and remained there until I had completed my observations on the Terns. I paid no attention to their lamentable cries, which were the less piercing that on this occasion I did not molest them in the least. Having seated myself on the shelly sand, which here formed the only soil, I remained almost motionless for several hours, in consequence of which the birds alighted about me, at the distance of only a few yards, so that I could plainly see with what efforts and pains the younger females deposited their eggs. Their bill was open, and their pantings indicated their distress, but after the egg had been expelled, they immediately walked off in an awkward manner, until they reached a place where they could arise without striking the branches of the bushes near them, when they flew away. Here and there, in numerous places within twenty yards of me, females, having their complement of eggs, alighted, and quietly commenced the labour of incubation. Now and then a male bird also settled close by, and immediately disgorged a small fish within the reach of the female. After some curious reciprocal nods of their heads, which were doubtless intended as marks of affection, the caterer would fly off. Several individuals, which had not commenced laying their eggs, I saw scratch the sand with their feet, in the manner of the common fowl, while searching for food. In the course of this operation, they frequently seated themselves in the shallow basin to try how it fitted their form, or find out what was still wanted to ensure their comfort. Not the least semblance of a quarrel did I observe between any two of these interesting creatures; indeed, they all appeared as if happy members of a single family; and as if to gratify my utmost wishes, a few of them went through the process of courtship in my presence. The male birds frequently threw their heads over their back as it were, in the manner of several species of gulls; they also swelled out their throats, walked round the females, and ended by uttering a soft puffing sound as they caressed them. Then the pair for a moment or two walked round each other, and at length rose on wing and soon disappeared. Such is one of the many sights it has been my good fortune to witness, and by each of them have I been deeply impressed with a sense of the pervading power of the Deity.

The Sooty Tern always lays three eggs as its full number, and in no instance, among thousands of the nests which were on the Bird Key, did I find one more when the female was sitting close. I was desirous of ascertaining whether the male and the female incubate alternately; but this I was unable to do, as the birds frequently left their eggs for half an hour or even three quarters at a time, but rarely longer. This circumstance, together with the very slight difference in size and colour between the sexes, was the cause of my failure.

It was curious to observe their actions whenever a large party landed on the island. All those not engaged in incubation would immediately rise in the air and scream aloud; those on the ground would then join them as quickly as they could, and the whole forming a vast mass, with a broad extended front, would as it were charge us, pass over for fifty yards or so, then suddenly wheel round, and again renew their attack. This they would repeat six or eight times in succession. When the sailors, at our desire, all shouted as loud as they could, the phalanx would for an instant become perfectly silent, as if to gather our meaning; but the next moment, like a huge wave breaking on the beach, it would rush forward with deafening noise.

When wounded and seized by the hand, this bird bites severely, and utters a plaintive cry differing from its usual note, which is loud and shrill, resembling the syllables *oo-ee, oo-ee.* Their nests are all scooped near the roots or stems of the bushes, and under the shade of their boughs, in many places within a few inches of each other. There is less difference between their eggs, than is commonly seen in those of water birds, both with respect to size and colouring. They generally measure two inches and one-eighth, by one and a-half, have a smooth shell, with the ground of a pale cream colour, sparingly marked with various tints of lightish umber, and still lighter marks of purple, which appear as if within the shell. The Lieutenant, N. Lacoste, Esq. informed me that shortly after the young are hatched, they ramble pell-mell over the island, to meet their parents, and be fed by them; that these birds have been known to collect there for the purpose of breeding, since the oldest wreckers on that coast can recollect; and that they usually arrive in May, and remain until the beginning of August, when they retire southward to spend the winter months. I could not however obtain a sufficiently accurate description of the different states of plumage which they go through, so as to enable me to describe them in the manner I should wish to do. All that I can say is, that before they take their departure, the young are greyish-brown above, dull white beneath, and have the tail very short.

At Bird Key we found a party of Spanish Eggers from Havannah. They had already laid in a cargo of about eight tons of the eggs of this Tern and the Noddy. On asking them how many they supposed they had, they answered that they never counted them, even while selling them, but disposed of them at seventy-five cents per gallon; and that one turn to market sometimes produced upwards of two hundred dollars, while it took only a-week to sail backwards and forwards and collect their cargo. Some eggers, who now and then come from Key West, sell their eggs at twelve and a half cents the dozen; but wherever these eggs are carried, they must soon be disposed of and eaten, for they become putrid in a few weeks.

On referring to my journals once more, I find the following remarks with reference to the Sooty Tern. It would appear that at some period not very remote, the Noddy, *Sterna stolida,* must have had it in contemplation to appropriate to itself its neighbour's domains; as on examination of this island, several thousand nests of that bird were found built on the tops of the bushes, although no birds of the species were about them. It is therefore probable that if such an attempt was made by them, they were defeated and forced to confine themselves to the neighbouring island, where they breed by themselves, although it is only a few miles distant. That such interferences and conflicts now and then occur among different species of birds, has often been observed by other persons, and in several instances by myself, particularly among Herons. In these cases, right or wrong, the stronger party never fails to dislodge the weaker, and keep possession of the disputed ground.

[From *Ornithological Biography,* Vol. III, pp. 263-268.]

THE TROPIC BIRD

Phaeton aethereus, Linn.
Plate CCLXII. Adult Male and Female.

[White-tailed Tropicbird,
Phaethon lepturus]

The specimens from which the figures in the plate were taken, were obtained on the Tortugas, in the summer of 1832, by my kind friend Robert Day, Esq. of the United States' Revenue Cutter, the Marion. They were shot out of a flock of eight or ten, and were in fine condition. I have represented the Male and Female, in what I suppose to be their full summer or breeding plumage; but not having had an opportunity of studying the habits of this remarkable bird, I am unable to give any information respecting them.

[From *Ornithological Biography,* Vol. III, p. 442.]

Plate CCLXII. *Tropic Bird*

BLACK-HEADED, OR LAUGHING GULL

Larus Atricilla, Linn. [Laughing Gull, *Larus atricilla*]
Plate CCCXIV. Male in spring, and Young.

Before entering upon the peculiar habits of this Gull, allow me, good-natured Reader, to present you with some general observations on the genus to which it belongs.

At the approach of autumn, it frequently happens that the young birds of several species associate together, congregating at times in vast numbers, and especially during low tides, on the outer margins of sand-bars situated in estuaries. There you may hear them keeping up an almost incessant cackle, and see them running about dressing their plumage, or patiently waiting the rising of the waters, on which much desired event taking place, they generally disperse, and fly off to search for food. If disturbed while thus reposing, they shew greater shyness, perhaps, than at any other time, and the loud note of alarm from one of the group soon reaches your ear. Look at them now, Reader, as they simultaneously spread their wings, and after a step or two launch into the air, gradually ascend, and in silence rise to a great height, performing extended gyrations, and advancing toward the open sea.

It seldom happens that when one of the larger species is shot, its companions will come to the rescue, as is the case with the smaller, such as the Kittiwake, and the present species. I have thought it remarkable how keenly and aptly Gulls generally discover at once the intentions towards them of individuals of our own species. To the peaceable and industrious fisherman they scarcely pay any regard, whether he drags his heavy net along the shore, or patiently waits until his well-baited hook is gulped below the dancing yet well-anchored bark, over the side of which he leans in constant and anxious expectation. At such a time indeed, if the fisher has had much success, and his boat displays a good store, Gulls will almost assail him like so many beggars, and perhaps receive from him a trifling yet dainty morsel. But, on the opposite side of the bay, see how carefully and suspiciously the same birds are watching every step of the man who, with a long gun held in a trailing position, tries

Plate CCCXIV. *Black-headed Gull*

to approach the flock of sleeping Wigeons. Why, not one of the Gulls will go within three times the range of his murderous engine; and, as if to assure him of their knowledge of his designs, they merely laugh at him from their secure station.

When congregated during the love-season, their loquacity has never failed to remind me of the impetuous, unmusical, and yet not unpleasant notes of our thieving Red-winged Starlings. But when apart, and at all times excepting the periods of pairing or breeding, or while some of the smaller species are chased by their vigilant enemies the Jagers, they are usually silent birds, especially when on wing. In rainy or squally weather, they skim low over the water, or the land, always against the wind, passing at times within a few feet of the surface. Again, at such times, I have observed Gulls of every species with which I am acquainted, suddenly give a shake or two to their wings, and stop as it were for a moment in their flight, as if they had espied something worthy of their attention below; but, on closely observing them, I have become convinced that such manoeuvres were performed only with the view of readjusting their whole plumage, which had perhaps been disarranged by a side current of wind.

All Gulls are wonderfully tenacious of life. When wounded or closely pursued, they are very apt to disgorge their food, or to sustain themselves against the agonies of death with uncommon vigour. They appear indeed to be possessed of extraordinary powers of respiration, through means of which they revive at the very moment when you might conceive them to have actually reached the last gasp. I have seen cases in which individuals of this tribe, after having been strongly squeezed for several minutes across the body, and after their throats had been crammed with cotton or tow, recovered as soon as the pressure was remitted, and immediately attempted to bite with as much eagerness as when first seized, when, by the by, they are wont to mute, as well as when suddenly surprised and taking to wing. In certain states of the atmosphere, Gulls, as well as other birds, appear much larger than they actually are; and on such occasions, they, of course, seem nearer than you would find them to be; for which reason, I would advise you, Reader, to be on your guard, for you may be strangely misled as to the distance at which you suppose the bird to be, and pull your trigger merely to send your shot into the sand, far short from the Gulls or other light-coloured birds in view.

Much confusion appears to exist among authors regarding our Laughing Gull, and this, in my humble opinion, simply because not one of them has studied it, in its native haunts, and at all seasons, since the period when it was briefly characterized by our great master Linnaeus, who, after all that has been said against him, has not yet had his equal. Alexander Wilson, who, it seems, knew something of the habits of this bird, thought it however identical with the *Larus ridibundus* of Europe, as is shewn by the synonymes which he has given. Others, who only examined some dried skins, without knowing so much as the day or even the year in which they had been shot, or their sex, or whether the feathers before them had once belonged to a bird that was breeding, or barren, when it was procured, described its remains perhaps well enough for their own purpose, but certainly not with all the accuracy which is necessary to establish once and for ever a distinct species of bird. Others, not at all aware that most Gulls, and the present species in particular, assume, in the season of pairing, and in a portion of the breeding time, beautiful rosy tints in certain parts of their plumage, which at other periods are pure white, have thought that differences of this sort, joined to those of the differently-sized spots observable in particular specimens, and not corresponding with the like markings in other birds of the same size and form, more or less observable at different periods on the tips of the quills, were quite sufficient to prove that the young bird, and the breeding bird, and the barren bird, of one and the same species, differed specifically from the old bird, or the winter-plumage bird. But, Reader, let us come to the point at once.

At the approach of the breeding season, or, as I like best to term it, the love season, this species becomes first hooded, and the white feathers of its breast, and those of the lower surface of its wings, assume a rich blush of roseate tint. If the birds procured at that time are several years old and perfect in their powers of reproduction, which is easily ascertained on the spot, their primary quills shew little or no white at their extremities, and their hood descends about three quarters of an inch lower on the throat than on the hind part of the head, provided the bird be a male. But should they be barren birds, *the hood will be wanting,* that portion of their plumage remaining as during winter, and although the primaries will be black, or nearly so, each of them will be broadly tipped, or marked at the end, with a white spot, which in some instances will be found to be fully half an inch in size; yet the tail of these birds, as if to prove that they are adults, is as purely white to its extreme tip, as in those that are breeding; but neither the breast, nor the under wing-coverts, will exhibit the rosy tint of one in the full perfection of its powers.

The males of all the Gulls with which I am acquainted, are larger than the females; and this difference of size is observable in the young birds even before they are fully fledged. In all of these, however, putting aside their sex, I have found great differences of size to exist, sometimes as much as two inches in length, with proportional differences in the bills, tarsi, and toes; and this, in specimens procured from one flock of these gulls at a single discharge of the gun, and at different seasons of the year. The colour of their bills too is far from being always alike, being brownish-red in some, purplish or of a rich and deep carmine in others. As to the white spots on the extremities of the primary quills of birds of this family, I would have you, Reader, never to consider them as affording essential characters. Nay, if you neglect them altogether, you will save yourself much trouble, as they will only mislead you by their interminable changes, and you may see that the spots on one wing are sometimes different in size and number from those on the other wing of the same specimen. If all this be correct, as I assure you it must be, being the result of numberless observations made in the course of many years, in the very places of resort of our different Gulls, will you not agree with me, Reader, that the difficulty of distinguishing two very nearly allied species must be almost insuperable when one has nothing better than a few dried skins for objects of observation and comparison?

The Black-headed Gull may be said to be a constant resident along the southern coast of the United States, from South Carolina to the Sabine River; and I have found it abundant over all that extent both in winter and in summer, but more especially on the shores and keys of the Floridas, where I found it breeding, as well as on some islands in the Bay of Galveston in Texas. A very great number of these birds however remove, at the approach of spring, towards the Middle and Eastern Districts, along the shores of which they breed in considerable numbers, particularly on those of New Jersey and Long Island, as well as on several islands in the Sound. They constantly evince a dislike to rocky shores, and therefore are seldom seen beyond Massachusetts, in which State indeed they are exceedingly rare.

None were observed by any members of my party on the Magdalene Islands, or on the coasts of Labrador or Newfoundland. I never met with any of them on the Mississippi above New Orleans, although they are plentiful in that neighbourhood during winter, and until the breeding season commences; and I think that this species never travels beyond the influence of the tide-waters of any stream. Wilson, in speaking of it, says that it is seen on the newly ploughed fields, and around the houses of the farmers of New Jersey; but the habit of visiting ploughed grounds I have not observed in any one of the American Gulls, although I have frequently noticed it in some of the European species, particularly *Larus canus, L. ridibundus,* and *L. argentatus.*

At all periods of the year, the Black-headed Gulls keep in flocks formed of many families; and in the breeding season, or even as soon as their courtships have commenced, they assemble by hundreds of pairs, or even by thousands. At this time they are so clamorous as to stun your ear with their laughing-like cries, though at other seasons they are generally silent, unless when suddenly alarmed, or when chased by the Jager. Their loves are conducted with extreme pomposity: they strut and bow to the females, throwing their head backwards, like all other Gulls, although in a less degree and with a less curious motion than Cormorants. You see them first stretching their heads forwards; then with open bill, vibrating tongue, and eyes all glowing, they emit their loud laughing notes, which, in a general sense, resemble those of many other species, though they are not precisely similar to those of any. But before I proceed with my account of their manners, I will give you the result of some curious observations which I made on them in Florida.

Previously to my visit to that interesting peninsula, I had not unfrequently noticed indications of strong amatory propensities in several species of Gulls, but never to the extent exhibited by the present species, many of which I saw copulating in the latter part of autumn and in winter, fully three months before the usual time of depositing their eggs in that country. Similar observations were made on *Larus argentatus* [Herring Gull], on the coast of Maine, and on *Larus marinus* [Great Black-backed Gull], in the Bay of Fundy. Nay, even in Europe I have seen this extraordinary tendency to reproduce out of season, as it were. On some such occasions, when I was at St. Augustine, in the month of December, I have observed four or five males of the present species paying their addresses to one female, who received their courtesies with evident welcome. Yet the females in that country did not deposit eggs until the 20th day of April. The most surprising fact of all was, that, although these birds were paired, and copulated regularly, by the 1st of February, not one had acquired the spring or summer plumage, or the dark coloured hood, or the rosy tint of the breast, nor lost the white spots on the tips of their primary quills. This change, however, was apparent by the 5th of March, became daily stronger, and was perfected by the 15th of that month. A few exceptions occurred among the numbers procured at these periods, but the generality of the birds were as above described. . . .

Now, Reader, though I am growing old, I yet feel desirous of acquiring knowledge regarding the habits of our birds, and should much like to learn from you the reasons why these gulls went off in lines from their breeding grounds, and returned in an extended front? Was it, in the latter case, because they were afraid of passing their nests unknowingly; or, in the former, under the necessity of following an experienced leader, who, under the stimulus of an empty maw, readily undertook the office, but who, like many other bon-vivants, became in the evening too dull to be of use to his companions?

This species breeds, according to the latitude, from the 1st of March to the middle of June; and I have thought that on the Tortuga Keys, it produced two broods each season. . . .

The Black-headed Gull frequently associates with the Razor-billed Shearwater, *Rhynchops nigra*, in winter; and I can safely say that I have seen more than a thousand of each kind alight on the same points of estuaries and mouths of rivers; the Gulls standing or sitting by themselves, at no great distance from the Razor-bills. Now and then they would all suddenly rise on wing as if frightened, perform a few evolutions in the air, and again settle on the very same spot, still, however, keeping separate. While thus in the company of the Razor-bills, the Gulls are with great difficulty approached, the former being exceedingly wary, and almost always rising when a person draws near, the Gulls immediately following them, and the two great flocks making off to some distant point, generally not very accessible. If taken up on being wounded, these gulls are apt to bite severely. If, on being shot at, they fall on the water, they swim fast and lightly, their companions all the while soaring above, and plunging towards them, as if intent on rescuing them. This great sympathy often proves fatal to them, for if the gunner is inclined, he may shoot them down without any difficulty, and the more he kills the more his chances are increased.

On the 10th of May 1832, it was my good fortune to be snugly on board the "Lady of the Green Mantle," or, in other words, the fine revenue cutter the Marion. The Gulls that laughed whilst our anchors were swiftly descending towards the marvellous productions of the deep, soon had occasion to be sorrowful enough. As they were in great numbers, officers and men, as well as the American Woodsman, gazing upon them from the high decks of the gallant bark, had ample opportunities of observing their motions. They were all busily engaged on wing, hovering here and there around the Brown Pelicans, intent on watching their plunges into the water, and all clamorously teasing their best benefactors. As with broadly extended pouch and lower mandible, the Pelican went down headlong, so gracefully followed the gay rosy-breasted Gull, which, on the brown bird's emerging, alighted nimbly on its very head, and with a gentle stoop instantly snatched from the mouth of its purveyor the glittering fry that moment entrapped!

Is this not quite strange, Reader? Aye, truly it is. The sight of these manoeuvres rendered me almost frantic with delight. At times, several gulls would attempt to alight on the head of the same Pelican, but finding this impossible, they would at once sustain themselves around it, and snatch every morsel that escaped from the pouch of the great bird. So very dexterous were some of the Gulls at this sport, that I have seen them actually catch a little fish as it leaped from the yet partially open bill of the Pelican. And now, Reader, I will conclude this long article with some fragments from my journals.

Tortugas, May 1832.—Whilst here, I often saw the Black-headed Gull of Wilson, sucking the eggs of *Sterna fuliginosa,* and *Sterna stolida.* Our sailors assured me that these gulls also eat the young of these two species of Terns when newly hatched.

[From *Ornithological Biography,* Vol. IV, pp. 118-124, 125-126.]

THE FRIGATE PELICAN

Tachypetes Aquilus, Vieill. [Magnificent Frigatebird,
Plate CCLXXI. Adult. *Fregata magnificens*]

Previous to my visit to the Florida Keys, I had seen but few Frigate Birds, and those only at some distance, while I was on the Gulf of Mexico, so that I could merely recognise them by their mode of flight. On approaching Indian Key, however, I observed several of them, and as I proceeded farther south, their numbers rapidly increased; but on the Tortugas very few were observed. This bird rarely travels farther eastward than the Bay of Charleston in South Carolina, although it is abundant at all seasons from Cape Florida to Cape Sable, the two extreme points of the peninsula. How far south it may be found I cannot tell.

The Frigate Pelicans may be said to be as gregarious as our Vultures: You see them in small or large flocks, according to circumstances. Like our Vultures, they spend the greater part of the day on wing, searching for food; and like them also, when gorged or roosting, they collect in large flocks, either to fan themselves or to sleep close together. They are equally lazy, tyrannical, and rapacious, domineering over birds weaker than themselves, and devouring the young of every species, whenever an opportunity offers, in the absence of the parents; in a word, they are most truly Marine Vultures.

About the middle of May, a period which to me appeared very late for birds found in so warm a climate as that of the Florida Keys, the Frigate Pelicans assemble in flocks of from fifty to five hundred pairs or more. They are seen flying at a great height over the islands on which they have bred many previous seasons, courting for hours together; after which they return towards the mangroves, alight on them, and at once begin to repair the old nests or construct new ones. They pillage each other's nests of their materials, and make excursions for more to the nearest keys. They break the dry twigs of trees with ease, passing swiftly on wing, and snapping them off by a single grasp of their powerful bill. It is indeed a beautiful sight to see them when thus occupied, especially when several are so engaged, passing and repassing with the swiftness of thought over the trees whose tops are blasted; their purpose appears as if accomplished by magic. I know only two other birds that perform the same action: one of them is the Forked-tailed Hawk [Swallow-tailed Kite], the

Plate CCLXXI. *Frigate Pelican*

other our swift or Chimney Swallow; but neither of them is so expert as the Frigate Pelican. It sometimes happens that this bird accidentally drops a stick while travelling towards its nest, when, if this should happen over the water, it plunges after it and seizes it with its bill before it has reached the waves.

The nests are usually placed on the south side of the keys, and on such trees as hang over the water, some low, others high, several in a single tree, or only one, according to the size of the mangrove, but in some cases lining the whole side of the island. They are composed of sticks crossing each other to the height of about two inches, and are flattish but not very large. When the birds are incubating, their long wings and tail are seen extending beyond the nest for more than a foot. The eggs are two or three, more frequently the latter number, measure two inches and seven-eighths in length, two in breadth, being thus of a rather elongated form, and have a thick smooth shell, of a greenish-white colour, frequently soiled by the filth of the nests. The young are covered with yellowish-white down, and look at first as if they had no feet. They are fed by regurgitation, but grow tardily, and do not leave the nest until they are able to follow their parents on wing.

At that period the plumage of the young females is marbled with grey and brown, with the exception of the head and the lower parts, which are white. The tail is about half the length it attains at the first moult, and is brownish-black, as are the primaries. After the first change of plumage, the wings become longer, and their flight is almost as elegant and firm as that of older birds.

The second spring plumage of this sex is brownish-black on the upper parts, that colour extending over the head and around the neck in irregular patches of brown, continued in a sharp angle towards the breast, but separated on its sides by the white that ascends on either side of the neck towards the head. The lower tail-coverts are brownish-black, as are the lower parts of the belly and flanks; the shoulders alone remaining as at first. The tail and wings are perfect.

The third spring, the upper parts of the head and neck are of a purer brownish-black, which extends down to the extremity of the angle, as are the feathers of the belly and the lower tail-coverts, the dark colour reaching now to within five inches of the angle on the breast. The white of the intermediate space has become much purer;

here and there light tints of bronze appear; the feet, which at first were dull yellow, have become of a rich reddish-orange, and the bill is pale blue. The bird is now capable of breeding, although its full plumage is not obtained until the next moult, when the colours become glossy above, and the white of the breast pure.

The changes which the males undergo are less remarkable. They are at first, when fully fledged, entirely of the colour seen on the upper parts of the young females; and the tint is merely improved afterwards, becoming of a deeper brownish-black, and acquiring purer reflections of green, purple and bronze, which in certain lights are seen on every part of the head, neck and body, and in very old males on the wings and tail. They also commence breeding the third spring. But I now return to the habits of this interesting bird.

The Frigate Pelican is possessed of a power of flight which I conceive superior to that of perhaps any other bird. However swiftly the Cayenne Tern, the smaller Gulls or the Jager move on wing, it seems a matter of mere sport to it to overtake any of them. The Goshawk, the Peregrine, and the Gyr Falcon, which I conceive to be the swiftest of our hawks, are obliged to pursue their victim, should it be a Green-winged Teal or Passenger Pigeon, at times for half a mile, at the highest pitch of their speed, before they can secure them. The bird of which I speak comes from on high with the velocity of a meteor, and on nearing the object of its pursuit, which its keen eye has spied while fishing at a distance, darts on either side to cut off all retreat, and with open bill forces it to drop or disgorge the fish which it has just caught. See him now! Yonder, over the waves leaps the brilliant dolphin, as he pursues the flying-fishes, which he expects to seize the moment they drop into the water. The Frigate Bird, who has marked them, closes his wings, dives toward them, and now ascending, holds one of the tiny things across his bill. Already fifty yards above the sea, he spies a porpoise in full chase, launches towards the spot, and in passing seizes the mullet that had escaped from its dreaded foe; but now, having obtained a fish too large for his gullet, he rises, munching it all the while, as if bound for the skies. Three or four of his own tribe have watched him and observed his success. They shoot towards him on broadly extended pinions, rise in wide circles, smoothly, yet as swiftly as himself. They are now all at the same height, and each as it overtakes him, lashes him with its wings, and tugs at his prey. See! one has fairly robbed him, but before he can secure the contested fish it drops. One of the other birds has caught it, but he is pursued by all. From bill to bill, and through the air, rapidly falls the fish, until it drops quite dead on the waters, and sinks into the deep. Whatever disappointment the hungry birds feel, they seem to deserve it all.

Sights like these you may every day see, if you take ship and sail for the Florida Keys. I have more to tell you, however, and of things that to me were equally pleasing. While standing in the cool veranda of Major Glassel of the United States army, at Key West, I observed a Frigate Pelican that had forced a Cayenne Tern, yet in sight, to drop a fish, which the broad-winged warrior had seized as it fell. This fish was rather large for the Tern, and might probably be about eight inches in length. The Frigate Pelican mounted with it across his bill about a hundred yards, and then tossing it up caught it as it fell, but not in the proper manner. He therefore dropped it, but before it had fallen many yards, caught it again. Still it was not in a good position, the weight of the head, it seemed, having prevented the bird from seizing it by that part. A second time the fish was thrown upwards, and now at last was received in a convenient manner, that is with its head downwards, and immediately swallowed.

When the morning light gladdens the face of nature, and while the warblers are yet waiting in silence the first rays of the sun, whose appearance they will hail with songs of joy, the Frigate Bird, on extended pinions, sails from his roosting place. Slowly and gently, with retracted neck he glides, as if desirous of quietly trying the renovated strength of his wings. Toward the vast deep he moves, rising apace, and before any other bird views the bright orb emerging from the waters. Pure is the azure of the heavens, and rich the deep green of the smooth sea below; there is every prospect of the finest weather; and now the glad bird shakes his pinions; and far up into the air, far beyond the reach of man's unaided eye, he soars in his quiet but rapid flight. There he floats in the pure air, but thither can fancy alone follow him. Would that I could accompany him! But now I see him again, with half-closed wings, gently falling towards the sea. He pauses a while, and again dives through the air. Thrice, four times, has he gradually approached the surface of the ocean; now he shakes his pinions as violently as the swordsman whirls his claymore; all is right; and he sweeps away, shooting to this side and that, in search of prey.

Mid-day has arrived, and threatening clouds obscure the horizon; the breeze, ere felt, ruffles the waters around; a thick mist advances over the deep; the sky darkens, and as the angry blasts curl the waves, the thunder mutters afar; all nature is involved in gloom, and all is in confusion, save only the Man-of-war Bird, who gallantly meets the gale. If he cannot force his way against the storm, he keeps his ground, balancing himself like a hawk watching his prey beneath; but now the tempest rages, and rising obliquely, he shoots away, and ere long surmounts the tumultuous clouds, entering a region calm and serene, where he floats secure until the world below has resumed its tranquillity.

I have frequently observed the Frigate Bird scratch its head with its feet while on wing; and this happening one day, when the bird fell through the air, as it is accustomed to do at such times, until it came within shot, I killed it when almost over my head, and immediately picked it up. I had been for years anxious to know what might be the use of the pectinated claws of birds; and on examining both its feet with a glass, I found the racks crammed with insects, such as occur on the bird's head, and especially around the ears. I also observed that the pectinated claws of birds of this species were much longer, flatter, and more comb-like than those of any other species with which I am acquainted. I now therefore feel convinced, that, however useful this instrument may be on other occasions, it is certainly employed in cleansing parts of the skin of birds which cannot be reached by the bill.

At times these birds may be seen chasing and jostling each other as if engaged in a frolic, after which they bear away on extended wings, and fly in a direct course until out of sight. But although their flight is easy and powerful, in a degree not surpassed by any other bird, they move with great difficulty on the ground. They can rise, however, from a sand-bar, no matter how low and level it may be. At such times, as well as when sitting on the water, which it occasionally does, the bird raises its wings almost perpendicularly, spreads its tail half erect, and at the first flap of the former, and simultaneous stroke of the latter, on the ground or the water, bounces away. Its feet, however, are of little service beyond what I have mentioned, and the supporting of its body when it has alighted on a branch, on which it rarely stands very erect, although it moves sideways on it, as Parrots sometimes do. It never dives, its bill in form resembling that of the Cormorants, which also never plunge from on wing in pursuit of fish, and only dip into the water when dropping from a perch or a rock to escape danger, as the Anhingas and some other birds are also accustomed to do.

When the Frigate Pelican is in want of a dead fish, a crab, or any floating garbage suited to its appetite, it approaches the water in the manner of Gulls, holding its wings high, and beating them until the bill has performed its duty, which being accomplished, the bird immediately rises in the air and devours its prey.

These birds see well at night, although they never go to sea excepting by day. At various times I have accidentally sailed by mangrove keys on which hundreds were roosted, and apparently sound asleep, when, on my firing a gun for the purpose of starting whatever birds might be there, they would all take to wing and sail as beautifully as during day, returning to the trees as the boats proceeded. They are by no means shy; indeed they seem unaware of danger from a gun, and rarely all go off when a party is shooting at them, until a considerable number has been obtained. The only difficulty I experienced in procuring them was on account of the height to which they so soon rose on leaving the trees; but we had excellent guns, and our worthy pilot's "Long Tom" distinguished itself above the rest. At one place, where we found many hundreds of them, they sailed for nearly half an hour over our heads, and about thirty were shot, some of them at a remarkable height, when we could hear the shot strike them, and when, as they fell to the water, the sound of their great wings whirling through the air resembled that produced by a sail flapping during a calm. When shot at and touched ever so slightly, they disgorge their food in the manner of Vultures, Gulls and some Terns; and if they have fallen and are approached, they continue to vomit the contents of their stomach, which at times are extremely putrid and nauseous. When seized, they evince little disposition to defend themselves, although ever so slightly wounded, but struggle and beat themselves until killed. Should you, however, place your fingers within their open bill, you might not withdraw them scatheless.

They are extremely silent, and the only note which I heard them utter was a rough croaking one. They devour the young of the Brown Pelican when quite small, as well as those of other birds whose nests are flat and exposed during the absence of the parent birds; but their own young suffer in the same manner from the still more voracious Turkey Buzzard. The notion that the Frigate Bird forces the Pelicans and Boobies to disgorge their prey is erroneous. The Pelican, if attacked or pursued by this bird, could alight on the water or elsewhere, and by one stroke of its sharp and powerful bill destroy the rash aggressor. The Booby would in all probability thrust its strong and pointed bill against the assailant with equal success. The Cayenne Tern, and other species of that genus, as well as several small Gulls, all abundant on the Florida coasts, are its purveyors, and them it forces to disgorge or drop their prey. Those of the deep are the dolphins, porpoises, and occasionally the sharks. Their sight is wonderfully keen, and they now and then come down from a great height to pick up a dead fish only a few inches long floating on the water. Their flesh is tough, dark, and, as food, unfit for any other person than one in a state of starvation.

I have given a figure of a very beautiful old male in spring plumage, which was selected from a great number of all ages. I have also represented the feet of an individual between two and three years old, on account of the richness of their colour at that age, whereas in the adult males they are quite black.

[From *Ornithological Biography*, Vol. III, pp. 495-501.]

THE SANDWICH TERN

Sterna cantiaca, Gmel. — [Sandwich Tern,
Plate CCLXXIX. Adult and Young. — *Thalasseus sandvicensis*]

On the 26th of May 1832, while sailing along the Florida Keys in Mr. Thruston's barge, accompanied by his worthy pilot and my assistant, I observed a large flock of Terns, which, from their size and other circumstances, I would have pronounced to be Marsh Terns, had not the difference in their manner of flight convinced me that they were of a species hitherto unknown to me. The pleasure which one feels on such an occasion cannot easily be described, and all that it is necessary for me to say on the subject at present is, that I begged to be rowed to them as quickly as possible. A nod and a wink from the

Plate CCLXXIX. *Sandwich Tern*

pilot satisfied me that no time should be lost, and in a few minutes all the guns on board were in requisition. The birds fell around us; but as those that had not been injured remained hovering over their dead and dying companions, we continued to shoot until we procured a very considerable number. On examining the first individual picked up from the water, I perceived from the yellow point of its bill that it was different from any that I had previously seen, and accordingly shouted "A prize! a prize! a new bird to the American Fauna!" And so it was, good Reader, for no person before had found the Sandwich Tern on any part of our coast. A large basket was filled with them, and we pursued our course. On opening several individuals, I found in the females eggs nearly ready for being laid. The males, too, manifested the usual symptoms of increased action in the organs distinctive of the sex. I felt a great desire to discover their breeding grounds, which I had the pleasure of doing in a few days after.

The vigour and activity of this bird while on wing afforded me great pleasure. Indeed its power of flight exceeds that of the Marsh Tern, which I consider as a closely allied species. While travelling, it advances by regular sharp flappings of its wings, which propel it forward much in the manner of the Passenger Pigeon, when, single and remote from a flock, it pushes on with redoubled speed. While plunging after the small mullets and other diminutive fishes that form the principal part of its food, it darts perpendicularly downwards with all the agility and force of the Common and Arctic Terns, nearly immersing its whole body at times, but rising instantly after, and quickly regaining a position from which it can advantageously descend anew. Should the fish disappear, as the bird is descending, the latter instantly recovers itself without plunging into the water. Its cries are sharp, grating, and loud enough to be heard at the distance of half a mile. They are repeated at intervals while it is travelling, and kept up incessantly when one intrudes upon it in its breeding grounds, on which occasion it sails and dashes over your head, chiding you with angry notes more disagreeable than pleasant to your ear. . . .

I never saw the Sandwich Tern on any other portion of our coasts than between the Florida Keys and Charleston, and from whence it first came there, or how it went thence to Europe, is an enigma which may perhaps never be solved. On asking the Wreckers if they had been in the habit of seeing these birds, they answered in the affirmative, and added that they paid them pretty frequent visits during the breeding season, on account of their eggs as well as of the young, which, when nearly able to fly, they said were also good eating. According to their account, this species spends the whole winter near and upon the keys, and the young keep separate from the old birds.

[From *Ornithological Biography,* Vol. III, pp. 531-533.]

THE GREAT MARBLED GODWIT

Limosa Fedoa, Vieill. [Marbled Godwit,
Plate CCXXXVIII. Male and Female. *Limosa fedoa*]

This fine bird is found during winter on all the large muddy flats of the coast of Florida that are intermixed with beds of racoon oysters. As the tide rises it approaches the shores, and betakes itself to the wet savannahs. At this season it is generally seen in flocks of five or six, searching for food in company with the Tell-tale, the Yellow-shanks, the Long-billed Curlew, and the White Ibis. While feeding, it probes the mud and wet sand, often plunging its bill to its whole length, in the manner of the Common Snipe and the Woodcock. It is fond of the small crabs called fiddlers, many of which it obtains both by probing their burrows, and running after them along the edges of the salt meadows and marshes. Sometimes you see it wading in the water up to its body, and when about to lose ground, it rises and extends its wings, still continuing to search for fry, until forced to fly off by the increased depth of the water, when it alights on the shore and recommences its operations. While feeding on the banks, it appears to search for food between and under the oysters with singular care, at times pushing the bill sidewise into the soft mud beneath the shells. Towards the middle of the day, the separate flocks come together, assembling on some large sand-bar, where they remain for hours, trimming their plumage, after which many of them continue some time motionless, standing on one leg. Suddenly, however, they are all seen to stretch their wings upwards, their bleating notes are heard, and the next moment the flock rises, and disperses in small

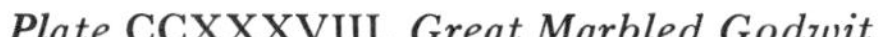

Plate CCXXXVIII. *Great Marbled Godwit*

parties, each of which proceeds in a different direction in search of food.

Few birds are more shy or vigilant than the Great Marbled Godwit. It watches the movements of the gunner with extreme care, particularly while in small flocks, in which case it rarely happens that one can approach them, and they are more commonly shot by coming unawares over the concealed sportsman. When in large flocks I have known them to be neared, and killed in great numbers. On such occasions, they walk towards each other, until they are quite close, when they stand still. Then is the time for the gunner, who has driven them before him as it were, to the extremity of a mud or sand-bar, to fire with a certainty of obtaining something worth his trouble, for besides the number killed by his first shot, he is likely to commit equal havock with the second, as they fly off in a dense mass.

On the 31st of May 1832, I saw an immense number of these birds on an extensive mud-bar bordering one of the Keys of Florida, about six miles south of Cape Sable [Sandy Key]. When I landed with my party, the whole, amounting to some thousands, collected in the manner mentioned above. Four or five guns were fired at once, and the slaughter was such, that I was quite satisfied with the number obtained, both for specimens and for food. For this reason, we refrained from firing at them again, although the temptation was at times great, as they flew over and wheeled round us for a while, until at length they alighted at some distance and began to feed. Those which we killed were plump, and afforded excellent eating. I was much surprised to find these Godwits so far south, but next morning, when none were to be seen excepting some wounded birds which we had not pursued, I concluded that the flock, which was the largest I have seen, had merely alighted there for the day.

The flight of this bird is regular and rather quick, although in the latter respect not to be compared with that of the Curlews. When flying to a considerable distance, or migrating, they usually proceed in extended lines, presenting an irregular front, which rarely preserves its continuity for any length of time, but undulates and breaks as the birds advance. The beat of their wings is regular, and they rarely utter any cries on such occasions.

This species enters the United States, on its return from its northern breeding-grounds, about the middle of August, and probably travels along the coast at that period as well as when proceeding northward, none having been seen by me or my party in Labrador or Newfoundland, and their passage having been observed only on the Atlantic shores of Nova Scotia, and the whole line of our coast, on different parts of which some of the flocks alight, and rest for a few weeks, both in spring and in autumn. I may add, that I never saw one of these birds beyond the distance of a few miles from the sea-shore.

[From *Ornithological Biography*, Vol. III, pp. 287-288.]

Waterway leading from Spring Garden

Episodes

SPRING GARDEN

Having heard many wonderful accounts of a certain spring near the sources of the St. John's River in East Florida, I resolved to visit it, in order to judge for myself. On the 6th of January 1832, I left the plantation of my friend John Bulow, accompanied by an amiable and accomplished Scotch gentleman, an engineer employed by the planters of those districts in erecting their sugar-house establishments. We were mounted on horses of the Indian breed, remarkable for their activity and strength, and were provided with guns and some provisions. The weather was pleasant, but not so our way, for no sooner had we left the "King's Road," which had been cut by the Spanish [English] government for a goodly distance, than we entered a thicket of scrubby oaks, succeeded by a still denser mass of low palmettoes, which extended about three miles, and among the roots of which our nags had great difficulty in making good their footing. After this we entered the Pine Barrens, so extensively distributed in this portion of the Floridas. The sand seemed to be all sand and nothing but sand, and the palmettoes at times so covered the narrow Indian trail which we followed, that it required all the instinct or sagacity of ourselves and our horses to keep it. It seemed to us as if we were approaching the end of the world. The country was perfectly flat, and, so far as we could survey it, presented the same wild and scraggy aspect. My companion, who had travelled there before, assured me that, at particular seasons of the year, he had crossed the barrens when they were covered with water fully knee-deep, when, according to his expression, they "looked most awful;" and I readily believed him, as we now and then passed through muddy pools, which reached the saddle-girths of our horses. Here and there large tracts covered with tall grasses, and resembling the prairies of the western wilds, opened to our view. Wherever the country happened to be sunk a little beneath the general level, it was covered with cypress trees, whose spreading arms were hung with a profusion of Spanish moss. The soil in such cases consisted of black mud, and was densely covered with bushes, chiefly of the Magnolia family.

We crossed in succession the heads of three branches of Haw Creek, of which the waters spread from a quarter to half a mile in breadth, and through which we made our way with extreme difficulty. While in the middle of one, my companion told me, that once when in the very spot where we then stood, his horse chanced to place his fore-feet on the back of a large alligator, which, not well pleased at being disturbed in his repose, suddenly raised his head, opened his monstrous jaws, and snapped off part of the lips of the affrighted pony. You may imagine the terror of the poor beast, which, however, after a few plunges, resumed its course, and succeeded in carrying its rider through in safety. As a reward for this achievement, it was ever after honoured with the appellation of "Alligator."

We had now travelled about twenty miles, and, the sun having reached the zenith, we dismounted to partake of some refreshment. From a muddy pool we contrived to obtain enough of tolerably clear water to mix with the contents of a bottle, the like of which I would strongly recommend to every traveller in these swampy regions; our horses, too, found something to grind among the herbage that surrounded the little pool; but as little time was to be lost, we quickly remounted, and resumed our disagreeable journey, during which we had at no time proceeded at a rate exceeding two miles and a half in the hour.

All at once, however, a wonderful change took place:—the country became more elevated and undulating; the timber was of a different nature, and consisted of red and live oaks, magnolias, and several kinds of pine. Thousands of "mole-hills," or the habitations of an animal here called "the salamander," and "goffer's burrows," presented themselves to the eye, and greatly annoyed our horses, which every now and then sank to the depth of a foot, and stumbled at the risk of breaking their legs, and what we considered fully as valuable, our necks. We now saw beautiful lakes of the purest water, and passed along a green space, having a series of them on each side of us. These sheets of water became larger and more numerous the farther we advanced, some of them extending to a length of several miles, and having a depth of from two to twenty feet of clear water; but their shores being destitute of vegetation, we observed no birds near them. Many tortoises, however, were seen basking in the sun, and all, as we approached, plunged into the water. Not a trace of man did we observe during our journey, scarcely a bird, and not a single quadruped, not even a rat; nor can one imagine a poorer and more desolate country than that which lies between the Halifax River, which we had left in the morning, and the undulated grounds at which we had now arrived.

But at length we perceived the tracks of living beings, and soon after saw the huts of Colonel Rees's negroes. Scarcely could ever African traveller have approached the city of Timbuctoo with more excited curiosity than we felt in approaching this plantation. Our Indian horses seemed to participate in our joy, and trotted at a smart rate towards the principal building, at the door of which we leaped from our saddles, just as the sun was withdrawing his ruddy light. Colonel Rees was at home, and received us with great kindness. Refreshments were immediately placed before us, and we spent the evening in agreeable conversation.

The next day I walked over the plantation, and examining the country around, found the soil of good quality, it having been reclaimed from swampy ground of a black colour, rich and very productive. The greater part of the cultivated land was on the borders of a lake, which communicates with others, leading to the St. John's River, distant about seven miles, and navigable so far by vessels not exceeding fifty or sixty tons. After breakfast, our amiable host shewed us the way to the celebrated spring, the sight of which afforded me pleasure sufficient to counter-balance the tediousness of my journey.

This spring presents a circular basin, having a diameter of about sixty feet, from the centre of which the water is thrown up with great force, although it does not rise to a height of more than a few inches above the general level. A kind of whirlpool is formed, on the edges of which are deposited vast quantities of shells, with pieces of wood, gravel, and other substances, which have coalesced into solid masses having a very curious appearance. The water is quite transparent, although of a dark colour, but so impregnated with sulphur, that it emits an odour which to me was highly nauseous. Its surface lies fifteen or twenty feet below the level of the woodland lakes in the neighbourhood, and its depth, in the autumnal months, is about seventeen feet, when the water is lowest. In all the lakes, the same species of shells as those thrown up by the spring, occur in abundance, and it seems more than probable that it is formed of the water collected from them by infiltration, or forms the subterranean outlet of some of them. The lakes themselves are merely reservoirs, containing the residue of the waters which fall during the rainy seasons, and contributing to supply the waters of the St. John River, with which they all seem to communicate by similar means. This spring pours its waters into "Rees's Lake," through a deep and broad channel, called Spring Garden Creek. This channel is said to be in some places fully sixty feet deep, but it becomes more shallow as you advance towards the entrance of the lake, at which you are surprised to find yourself on a mud flat covered only by about fifteen inches of water, under which the depositions from the spring lie to a depth of four or five feet in the form of the softest mud, while under this again is a bed of fine white sand. When this mud is stirred up by the oars of your boat or otherwise, it appears of a dark green colour, and smells strongly of sulphur. At all times it sends up numerous bubbles of air, which probably consist of sulphuretted hydrogen gas.

The mouth of this curious spring is calculated to be two and a half feet square; and the velocity of its water, during the rainy season, is three feet per second. This would render the discharge per hour about 499,500 gallons. Colonel Rees showed us the remains of another spring of the same kind, which had dried up from some natural cause.

My companion the Engineer having occupation for another day, I requested Colonel Rees to accompany me in his boat towards the River St. John, which I was desirous of seeing, as well as the curious country in its neighbourhood. He readily agreed, and, after an early breakfast next morning, we set out, accompanied by two servants to manage the boat. As we crossed Rees's Lake, I observed that its north-eastern shores were bounded by a deep swamp, covered by a rich growth of tall cypresses, while the opposite side presented large marshes and islands ornamented by pines, live-oaks, and orange trees. With the exception of a very narrow channel, the creek was covered with nympheae, and in its waters swam numerous alligators, while Ibises, Gallinules, Anhingas, Coots, and Cormorants, were seen pursuing their avocations on its surface or along its margins. Over our heads the Fish Hawks were sailing, and on the broken trees around we saw many of their nests.

We followed Spring Garden Creek for about two miles and a half, and passed a mud bar, before we entered "Dexter's Lake." The bar was stuck full of unios [freshwater mussels] in such profusion, that each time the Negroes thrust their hands into the mud they took up several. According to their report, these shellfish are quite unfit for food. In this lake the water had changed its hue, and assumed a dark chestnut colour, although it was still transparent. The depth was very uniformly five feet, and the extent of the lake was about eight miles by three. Having crossed it, we followed the creek, and soon saw the entrance of Woodruff's Lake, which empties its still darker waters into the St. John's River.

I here shot a pair of curious Ibises which you will find described in my fourth volume and landed on a small island covered with wild orange trees, the luxuriance and freshness of which were not less pleasing to the sight, than the perfume of their flowers was to the smell. The group seemed to me like a rich bouquet formed by nature to afford consolation to the weary traveller, cast down by the dismal scenery of swamps, and pools, and rank grass, around him. Under the shade of these beautiful ever-greens, and amidst the golden fruits that covered the ground, while the humming birds fluttered over our heads, we spread our cloth on the grass, and with a happy and thankful heart I refreshed myself with the bountiful gifts of an ever-careful Providence. Colonel Rees informed me that this charming retreat was one of the numerous *terrae incognitae* of this region of lakes, and that it should henceforth bear the name of "Audubon's Isle."

In conclusion, let me inform you, that the spring has been turned to good account by my general host Colonel Rees, who, aided by my amiable companion the Engineer, has directed its current so as to turn a mill, which suffices to grind the whole of his sugar cane.

[From *Ornithological Biography*, Vol. II, pp. 263-267.]

John James Audubon

ST. JOHN'S RIVER IN FLORIDA

Soon after landing at St. Augustine, in East Florida, I formed acquaintance with Dr. Simmons, Dr. Pocher, Judge Smith, the Misses Johnson, and other individuals, my intercourse with whom was as agreeable as beneficial to me. Lieutenant Constantine Smith, of the United States army, I found of a congenial spirit, as was the case with my amiable but since deceased friend, Dr. Bell of Dublin. Among the planters who extended their hospitality to me, I must particularly mention General Hernandez, and my esteemed friend John Bulow, Esq. To all these estimable individuals I offer my sincere thanks.

While in this part of the peninsula, I followed my usual avocations, although with little success, it then being winter. I had letters from the Secretaries of the Navy and Treasury of the United States, to the commanding officers of vessels of war of the revenue service, directing them to afford me any assistance in their power; and the schooner Spark having come to St. Augustine, on her way to the St. John's River, I presented my credentials to her commander Lieutenant Piercy, who readily and with politeness, received me and my assistants on board. We soon after set sail, with a fair breeze. The strict attention to duty on board even this small vessel of war, afforded matter of surprise to me. Every thing went on with the regularity of a chronometer; orders were given, answered to, and accomplished, before they had ceased to vibrate on the ear. The neatness of the crew equalled the cleanliness of the white planks of the deck; the sails were in perfect condition; and, built as the Spark was, for swift sailing, on she went, gambolling from wave to wave.

I thought that, while thus sailing, no feeling but that of pleasure could exist in our breasts; but, alas! how fleeting are our enjoyments. When we were almost at the entrance of the river, the wind changed, the sky became clouded, and, before many minutes had elapsed, the little bark was lying to "like a duck," as her commander expressed himself. It blew a hurricane:—let it blow, reader. At break of day we were again at anchor within the bar of St. Augustine.

Our next attempt was successful. Not many hours after we had crossed the bar, we perceived the star-like glimmer of the light in the great lantern at the entrance of the St. John's River. This was before day-light; and, as the crossing of the sand-banks or bars, which occur at the mouths of all the streams of this peninsula is difficult, and can be accomplished only when the tide is up, one of the guns was fired as a signal for the government pilot. The good man, it seemed, was unwilling to leave his couch, but a second gun brought him in his canoe alongside. The depth of the channel was barely sufficient. My eyes, however, were not directed towards the waters, but on high, where flew some thousands of snowy Pelicans, which had fled affrighted from their resting-grounds. How beautifully they performed their broad gyrations, and how matchless, after a while, was the marshalling of their files, as they flew past us!

On the tide we proceeded apace. Myriads of Cormorants covered the face of the waters, and over it Fish-Crows innumerable were already arriving from their distant roosts. We landed at one place to search for the birds whose charming melodies had engaged our attention, and here and there some young Eagles we shot, to add to our store of fresh provisions! The river did not seem to me equal in beauty to the fair Ohio; the shores were in many places low and swampy, to the great delight of the numberless Herons that moved along in gracefulness, and the grim alligators that swam in sluggish sullenness. In going up a bayou, we caught a great number of the young of the latter for the purpose of making experiments upon them.

After sailing a considerable way, during which our commander and officers took the soundings, as well as the angles and bearings of every nook and crook of the sinuous stream, we anchored one evening at a distance of fully one hundred miles from the mouth of the river. The weather, although it was the 12th of February, was quite warm, the thermometer on board standing at 75°, and on shore at 90°. The fog was so thick that neither of the shores could be seen, and yet the river was not a mile in breadth. The "blind musquitoes" covered every object, even in the cabin, and so wonderfully abundant were these tormentors, that they more than once fairly extinguished the candles whilst I was writing my journal, which I closed in despair, crushing between the leaves more than a hundred of the little wretches. Bad as they are, however, these blind musquitoes do not bite. As if purposely to render our situation doubly uncomfortable, there was an establishment for jerking beef, on the nearer shores to the windward of our vessel, from which the breeze came laden with no sweet odours.

In the morning when I arose, the country was still covered with thick fogs, so that although I could plainly hear the notes of the birds on shore, not an object could I see beyond the bowsprit, and the air was as close and sultry as on the previous evening. Guided by the scent of the jerkers' works, we went on shore, where we found the vegetation already far advanced. The blossoms of the jessamine, ever pleasing, lay steeped in dew; the humming bee was collecting her winter's store from the snowy flowers of the native orange; and the little warblers frisked along the twigs of the smilax. Now, amid the tall pines of the forest, the sun's rays began to force their way, and as the dense mists dissolved in the atmosphere, the bright luminary at length shone forth. We explored the woods around, guided by some friendly live-oakers who had pitched their camp in the vicinity. After a while the Spark again displayed her sails, and as she silently glided along, we spied a Seminole Indian approaching us in his canoe. The poor, dejected son of the woods, endowed with talents of the highest order, although rarely acknowledged by the proud usurpers of his native soil, has spent the night in fishing, and the morning in procuring the superb-feathered game of the swampy thickets; and with both he comes to offer them for our acceptance. Alas! thou fallen one, descendant of an ancient line of freeborn hunters, would that I could restore to thee thy birthright, thy natural independence, the generous feelings that were once fostered in thy brave bosom. But the irrevocable deed is done, and I can merely admire the perfect symmetry of his frame, as he dexterously throws on our deck the trouts and turkeys which he had captured. He receives a recompense, and without smile or bow, or acknowledgement of any kind, off he starts with the speed of an arrow from his own bow.

Alligators were extremely abundant, and the heads of the fishes which they had snapped off lay floating around on the dark waters. A rifle bullet was now and then sent through the eye of one of the largest, which, with a tremendous splash of its tail, expired. One morning we saw a monstrous fellow lying on the shore. I was desirous of obtaining him to make an accurate drawing of his head, and, accompanied by my assistant and two of the sailors, proceeded cautiously towards him. When within a few yards, one of us fired, and sent through his side an ounce ball, which tore open a hole large enough to receive a man's hand. He slowly raised his head, bent himself upwards, opened his huge jaws, swung his tail to and fro, rose on his legs, blew in a frightful manner, and fell to the earth. My assistant leaped on shore, and, contrary to my injunctions, caught hold of the animal's tail, when the alligator, awakening from its trance, with a last effort crawled slowly towards the water, and plunged heavily into it. Had he thought of once flourishing his tremendous weapon there might have been an end of his assailant's life, but he fortunately went in peace to his grave, where we left him, as the water was too deep. The same morning, another of equal size was observed swimming directly for the bows of our vessel, attracted by the gentle rippling of the water there. One of the officers, who had watched him, fired and scattered his brain through the air, when he tumbled and rolled at a fearful rate, blowing all the while most furiously. The river was bloody for yards around, but although the monster passed close by the vessel, we could not secure him, and after a while he sunk to the bottom.

Early one morning I hired a boat and two men, with the view of returning to St. Augustine by a short cut. Our baggage being placed on board, I bade adieu to the officers, and off we started. About four in the afternoon we arrived at the short cut, forty miles distant from our point of departure, and where we had expected to procure a waggon, but were disappointed. So we laid our things on the bank, and, leaving one of my assistants to look after them, I set out, accompanied by the other, and my Newfoundland dog. We had eighteen miles to go; and as the sun was only two hours high, we struck off at a good rate. Presently we entered a pine barren. The country was as level as a floor; our path, although narrow, was well beaten, having been used by the Seminole Indians for ages, and the weather was calm and beautiful. Now and then a rivulet occurred, from which we quenched our thirst, while the magnolias and other flowering plants on its banks relieved the dull uniformity of the woods. When the path separated into two branches, both seemingly leading the same way, I would follow one, while my companion took the other, and unless we met again in a short time, one of us would go across the intervening forest.

The sun went down behind a cloud, and the south-east breeze that sprung up at this moment, sounded dolefully among the tall pines. Along the eastern horizon lay a bed of black vapour, which gradually rose, and soon covered the heavens. The air felt hot and oppressive, and we knew that a tempest was approaching. Plato was now our guide, the white spots on his skin being the only objects that we could discern amid the darkness, and as if aware of his utility in this respect, he kept a short way before us on the trail. Had we imagined ourselves more than a few miles from the town, we would have made a camp, and remained under its shelter for the night; but conceiving that the distance could not be great, we resolved to trudge along.

Large drops began to fall from the murky mass overhead; thick, impenetrable darkness surrounded us, and to my dismay, the dog refused to proceed. Groping with my hands on the ground, I discovered that several trails branched out at the spot where he lay down; and when I had selected one, he went on. Vivid flashes of lightning streamed across the heavens, the wind increased to a gale, and the rain poured down upon us like a torrent. The water soon rose on the level ground so as almost to cover our feet, and we slowly advanced, fronting the tempest. Here and there a tall pine on fire presented a magnificent spectacle, illumining the trees around it, and surrounded with a halo of dim light, abruptly bordered with the deep black of the night. At one time we passed through a tangled thicket of low trees, at another crossed a stream flushed by the heavy rain, and again proceeded over the open barrens.

How long we thus, half-lost, groped our way, is more than I can tell you; but at length the tempest passed over, and suddenly the clear sky became spangled with stars. Soon after we smelt the salt-marshes, and walking directly towards them, like pointers advancing on a covey of partridges, we at last to our great joy descried the light of the beacon near St. Augustine. My dog began to run briskly around, having met with ground on which he had hunted before, and taking a direct course, led us to the great causeway that crosses the marshes at the back of the town. We refreshed ourselves with the produce of the first orange tree that we met with, and in half an hour more arrived at our hotel. Drenched with rain, steaming with perspiration, and covered to the knees with mud, you may imagine what figures we cut in the eyes of the good people whom we found snugly enjoying themselves in the sitting room. Next morning, Major Gates, who had received me with much kindness, sent a waggon with mules and two trusty soldiers for my companion and luggage.

[From *Ornithological Biography*, Vol. II, pp. 291-295.]

THE LIVE-OAKERS

The greater part of the forests of East Florida principally consists of what in that country are called "Pine Barrens." In these districts, the woods are rather thin, and the only trees that are seen in them are tall pines of rather indifferent quality, beneath which is a growth of rank grass, here and there mixed with low bushes and sword palmettoes. The soil is of a sandy nature, mostly flat, and consequently either covered with water during the rainy season, or parched in the summer and autumn, although you meet at times with ponds of stagnant water, where the cattle, which are abundant, allay their thirst, and around which resort the various kinds of game found in these wilds.

The traveller, who has pursued his course for many miles over the barrens, is suddenly delighted to see in the distance the appearance of a dark "hummock" of live oaks and other trees, seeming as if they had been planted in the wilderness. As he approaches, the air feels cooler and more salubrious, the song of numerous birds delights his ear, the herbage assumes a more luxuriant appearance, the flowers become larger and brighter, and a grateful fragrance is diffused around. These objects contribute to refresh his mind, as much as the sight of the waters of some clear spring, gliding among the undergrowth, seems already to allay his thirst. Over head festoons of innumerable vines, jessamines, and bignonias, link each tree with those around it, their slender stems being interlaced as if in mutual affection. No sooner, in the shade of these beautiful woods, has the traveller finished his mid-day repast, than he perceives small parties of men lightly accoutred, and each bearing an axe, approaching towards his resting place. They exchange the usual civilities, and immediately commence their labours, for they too have just finished their meal.

I think I see them proceeding to their work. Here two have stationed themselves on the opposite sides of the trunk of a noble and venerable live-oak. Their keen-edged and well-tempered axes seem to make no impression on it, so small are the chips that drop at each blow around the mossy and wide-spreading roots. There, one is ascending the stem of another, of which, in its fall, the arms have stuck among the tangled tops of the neighbouring trees. See how cautiously he proceeds, barefooted, and with a handkerchief round his head. Now he has climbed to the height of about forty feet from the ground; he stops, and squaring himself with the trunk on which he so boldly stands, he wields with sinewy arms his trusty blade, the repeated blows of which, although the tree be as tough as it is large, will soon sever it in two. He has changed sides, and his back is turned to you. The trunk now remains connected only by a thin stripe of wood. He places his feet on the part which is lodged, and shakes it with all his might. Now swings the huge log under his leaps, now it suddenly gives way, and as it strikes upon the ground its echoes are repeated through the hummock, and every wild turkey within hearing utters his gobble of recognition. The wood-cutter, however, remains collected and composed; but the next moment, he throws his axe to the ground, and assisted by the nearest grape-vine, slides down and reaches the earth in an instant.

Several men approach and examine the prostrate trunk. They cut at both its extremities, and sound the whole of its bark, to enable them to judge if the tree has been attacked by the white rot. If such has unfortunately been the case, there, for a century or more, this huge log will remain until it gradually crumbles; but if not, and if it is free of injury or "wind-shakes," while there is no appearance of the sap having already ascended, and its pores are altogether sound, they proceed to take its measurement. Its shape ascertained, and the timber that is fit for use laid out by the aid of models, which, like fragments of the skeleton of a ship, shew the forms and sizes required, the "hewers" commence their labours. Thus, reader, perhaps every known hummock in the Floridas is annually attacked, and so often does it happen that the white-rot or some other disease has deteriorated the quality of the timber, that the woods may be seen strewn with trunks that have been found worthless, so that every year these valuable oaks are becoming scarcer. The destruction of the young trees of this species caused by the fall of the great trunks is of course immense, and as there are no artificial plantations of these trees in our country, before long a good sized live-oak will be so valuable that its owner will exact an enormous price for it, even while it yet stands in the wood. In my opinion, formed on personal observation, Live-oak Hummocks are *not quite* so plentiful as they are represented to be, and of this I will give you *one* illustration.

On the 25th of February 1832, I happened to be far up the St.

John's River in East Florida, in the company of a person employed by our government in protecting the live-oaks of that section of the country, and who received a good salary for his trouble. While we were proceeding along one of the banks of that most singular stream, my companion pointed out some large hummocks of dark-leaved trees on the opposite side, which he said were entirely formed of live oaks. I thought differently, and as our controversy on the subject became a little warm, I proposed that our men should row us to the place, where we might examine the leaves and timber, and so decide the point. We soon landed, but after inspecting the woods, not a single tree of the species did we find, although there were thousands of large "swamp-oaks." My companion acknowledged his mistake, and I continued to search for birds.

One dark evening as I was seated on the banks of the same river, considering what arrangements I should make for the night, as it began to rain in torrents, a man who happened to see me, came up and invited me to go to his cabin, which he said was not far off. I accepted his kind offer, and followed him to his humble dwelling. There I found his wife, several children, and a number of men, who, as my host told me, were, like himself, Live-Oakers. Supper was placed on a large table, and on being desired to join the party, I willingly assented, doing my best to diminish the contents of the tin pans and dishes set before the company by the active and agreeable housewife. We then talked of the country, its climate and productions, until a late hour, when we laid ourselves down on bears' skins, and reposed till day-break.

I longed to accompany these hardy wood-cutters to the hummock where they were engaged in preparing live-oak timber for a man of war. Provided with axes and guns, we left the house to the care of the wife and children, and proceeded for several miles through a pine-barren, such as I have attempted to describe. One fine wild Turkey was shot, and when we arrived at the *Shantee* put up near the hummock, we found another party of wood-cutters waiting our arrival, before eating their breakfast, already prepared by a Negro man, to whom the turkey was consigned to be roasted for part of that day's dinner.

Our repast was an excellent one, and vied with a Kentucky breakfast: beef, fish, potatoes, and other vegetables, were served up, with coffee in tin cups, and plenty of biscuit. Every man seemed hungry and happy, and the conversation assumed the most humorous character. The sun now rose above the trees, and all, excepting the cook, proceeded to the hummock, on which I had been gazing with great delight, as it promised rare sport. My host, I found, was the chief of the party; and although he also had an axe, he made no other use of it than for stripping here and there pieces of bark from certain trees which he considered of doubtful soundness. He was not only well versed in his profession, but generally intelligent, and from him I received the following account, which I noted at the time.

The men who are employed in cutting the live oak, after having discovered a good hummock, build shantees of small logs, to retire to at night, and feed in by day. Their provisions consist of beef, pork, potatoes, biscuit, flour, rice, and fish, together with excellent whisky. They are mostly hale, strong, and active men, from the eastern parts of the Union, and receive excellent wages, according to their different abilities. Their labours are only of a few months' duration. Such hummocks as are found near navigable streams are first chosen, and when it is absolutely necessary, the timber is sometimes hauled five or six miles to the nearest water-course, where, although it sinks, it can, with comparative ease, be shipped to its destination. The best time for cutting the live oak is considered to be from the first of December to the beginning of March, or while the sap is completely down. When the sap is flowing, the tree is "bloom," and more apt to be "shaken." The white-rot, which occurs so frequently in the live-oak, and is perceptible only by the best judges, consists of round spots, about an inch and a half in diameter, on the outside of the bark, through which, at that spot, a hard stick may be driven several inches, and generally follows the heart up or down the trunk of the tree. So deceiving are these spots and trees to persons unacquainted with this defect, that thousands of trees are cut and afterwards abandoned. The great number of trees of this sort strewn in the woods would tend to make a stranger believe that there is much more good oak in the country than there really is; and perhaps, in reality, not more than one-fourth of the quantity usually reported, is to be procured.

The Live-oakers generally revisit their distant homes in the Middle and Eastern Districts, where they spend the summer, returning to the Floridas at the approach of winter. Some, however, who have gone there with their families, remain for years in succession; although they suffer much from the climate, by which their once good constitutions are often greatly impaired. This was the case with the individual above mentioned, from whom I subsequently received much friendly assistance in my pursuits.

[From *Ornithological Biography,* Vol. II, pp. 236-240.]

THE LOST ONE

A "Live-oaker" employed on the St. John's River, in East Florida, left his cabin, situated on the banks of that stream, and, with his axe on his shoulder, proceeded towards the swamp in which he had several times before plied his trade of felling and squaring the giant trees that afford the most valuable timber for naval architecture and other purposes.

At the season which is the best for this kind of labour, heavy fogs not unfrequently cover the country, so as to render it difficult for one to see farther than thirty or forty yards in any direction. The woods, too, present so little variety, that every tree seems the mere counterpart of every other; and the grass, when it has not been burnt, is so tall that a man of ordinary stature cannot see over it, whence it is necessary for him to proceed with great caution, lest he should unwittingly deviate from the ill-defined trail which he follows. To increase the difficulty, several trails often meet, in which case, unless the explorer be perfectly acquainted with the neighbourhood, it would be well for him to lie down, and wait until the fog should disperse. Under such circumstances, the best woodsmen are not unfrequently bewildered for a while; and I well remember that such an occurrence happened to myself, at a time when I had imprudently ventured to pursue a wounded quadruped, which led me some distance from the track.

The live-oaker had been jogging onwards for several hours, and became aware that he must have travelled considerably more than the distance between his cabin and the "hummock" which he desired to reach. To his alarm, at the moment when the fog dispersed, he saw the sun at its meridian height, and could not recognise a single object around him.

Young, healthy, and active, he imagined that he had walked with more than usual speed, and had passed the place to which he was bound. He accordingly turned his back upon the sun, and pursued a different route, guided by a small trail. Time passed, and the sun headed his course: he saw it gradually descend in the west; but all around him continued as if enveloped with mystery. The huge grey trees spread their giant boughs over him, the rank grass extended on all sides, not a living being crossed his path, all was silent and still, and the scene was like a dull and dreary dream of the land of oblivion. He wandered like a forgotten ghost that had passed into the land of spirits, without yet meeting one of his kind with whom to hold converse.

The condition of a man lost in the woods is one of the most perplexing that could be imagined by a person who has not himself been in a like predicament. Every object he sees, he at first thinks he recognises, and while his whole mind is bent on searching for more that may gradually lead to his extrication, he goes on committing greater errors the farther he proceeds. This was the case with the live-oaker. The sun was now setting with a fiery aspect, and by degrees it sunk in its full circular form, as if giving warning of a sultry morrow. Myriads of insects, delighted at its departure, now filled the air on buzzing wings. Each piping frog arose from the muddy pool in which it had concealed itself; the squirrel retired to its hole, the crow to its roost, and, far above, the harsh croaking voice of the heron announced that, full of anxiety, it was wending its way to the miry interior of some distant swamp. Now the woods began to resound to the shrill cries of the owl; and the breeze, as it swept among the columnar stems of the forest-trees, came laden with heavy and chilling dews. Alas, no moon with her silvery light shone on the dreary scene, and the Lost One, wearied and vexed, laid himself down on the damp ground. Prayer is always consolatory to man in every difficulty or danger, and the woodsman fervently prayed to his Maker, wished his family a happier night than it was his lot to experience, and with a feverish anxiety waited the return of day.

You may imagine the length of that dull, cold, moonless night. With the dawn of day came the usual fogs of those latitudes. The poor man started on his feet, and with a sorrowful heart, pursued a course which he thought might lead him to some familiar object, although, indeed, he scarcely knew what he was doing. No longer had he the trace of a track to guide him, and yet, as the sun rose, he calculated the many hours of day-light he had before him, and the farther he went continued to walk the faster. But vain were all his hopes; that day was spent in fruitless endeavors to regain the path that led to his home, and when night again approached, the terror that had been gradually spreading over his mind, together with the nervous debility induced by fatigue, anxiety, and hunger, rendered him almost frantic. He told me that at this moment he beat his breast, tore his hair, and had it not been for the piety with which his parents had in early life imbued his mind, and which had become habitual, would have cursed his existence. Famished as he now was, he laid himself on the ground, and fed on the weeds and grass that grew around him. That night was spent in the greatest agony and terror. "I knew my situation," he said to me. "I was fully aware that unless Almighty God came to my assistance, I must perish in those uninhabited woods. I knew that I had walked more than fifty miles, although I had not met with a brook, from which I could quench my thirst, or even allay the burning heat of my parched lips and blood-shot eyes. I knew that if I should not meet with some stream I must die, for my axe was my only weapon, and although deer and bears now and then started within a few yards or even feet of me, not one of them could I kill; and although I was in the midst of abundance, not a mouthful did I expect to procure, to satisfy the cravings of my empty stomach. Sir, may God preserve you from ever feeling as I did the whole of that day!"

For several days after, no one can imagine the condition in which he was, for when he related to me this painful adventure, he assured me that he had lost all recollection of what had happened. "God," he continued, "must have taken pity on me one day, for, as I ran wildly through those dreadful pine barrens, I met with a tortoise. I gazed upon it with amazement and delight, and, although I knew that were I to follow it undisturbed, it would lead me to some water, my hunger and thirst would not allow me to refrain from satisfying both, by eating its flesh, and drinking its blood. With one stroke of my axe the beast was cut in two, and in a few moments I dispatched all but the shell. Oh, Sir, how much I thanked God, whose kindness had put the tortoise in my way! I felt greatly renewed. I sat down at the foot of a pine, gazed on the heavens, thought of my poor wife and children, and again, and again thanked my God for my life, for now I felt less distracted in mind, and more assured that before long I must recover my way, and get back to my home."

The Lost One remained and passed the night, at the foot of the same tree under which his repast had been made. Refreshed by a sound sleep, he started at dawn to resume his weary march. The sun rose bright, and he followed the direction of the shadows. Still the dreariness of the woods was the same, and he was on the point of giving up in despair, when he observed a racoon lying squatted in the grass. Raising his axe, he drove it with such violence through the helpless animal, that it expired without a struggle. What he had done with the turtle, he now did with the racoon, the greater part of which he actually devoured at one meal. With more comfortable feelings, he then resumed his wanderings—his journey I cannot say,—for although in the possession of all his faculties, and in broad daylight, he was worse off than a lame man groping his way in the dark out of a dungeon, of which he knew not where the door stood.

Days, one after another, passed,—nay, weeks in succession. He fed now on cabbage-trees, then on frogs and snakes. All that fell in his way was welcome and savoury. Yet he became daily more emaciated, until at length he could scarcely crawl. Forty days had elapsed, by his own reckoning, when he at last reached the banks of the river. His clothes in tatters, his once bright axe dimmed with rust, his face begrimmed with beard, his hair matted, and his feeble frame little better than a skeleton covered with parchment, there he laid himself down to die. Amid the perturbed dreams of his fevered fancy, he thought he heard the noise of oars far away on the silent river. He listened, but the sounds died away on his ear. It was indeed a dream, the last glimmer of expiring hope, and now the light of life was about to be quenched for ever. But again, the sound of oars awoke him from his lethargy. He listened so eagerly, that the hum of a fly could not have escaped his ear. They were indeed the measured beats of oars, and now, joy to the forlorn soul! the sound of human voices thrilled to his heart, and awoke the tumultuous pulses of returning hope. On his knees did the eye of God see that poor man by the broad still stream that glittered in the sunbeams, and human eyes soon saw him too, for round that headland covered with tangled brushwood boldly advances the little boat, propelled by its lusty rowers. The Lost One raises his feeble voice on high;—it was a loud shrill scream of joy and fear. The rowers pause, and look around.

Another, but feebler scream, and they observe him. It comes,—his heart flutters, his sight is dimmed, his brain reels, he gasps for breath. It comes,—it has run upon the beach, and the Lost One is found.

This is no tale of fiction, but the relation of an actual occurrence, which might be embellished, no doubt, but which is better in the plain garb of truth. The notes by which I recorded it were written, in the cabin of the once lost live-oaker, about four years after the painful incident occurred. His amiable wife, and loving children, were present at the recital, and never shall I forget the tears that flowed from them as they listened to it, albeit it had long been more familiar to them than a tale thrice told. Sincerely do I wish, good reader, that neither you nor I may ever elicit such sympathy, by having undergone such sufferings, although no doubt such sympathy would be a rich recompense for them.

It only remains for me to say, that the distance between the cabin and the live-oak hummock to which the woodsman was bound, scarcely exceeded 8 miles, while the part of the river at which he was found, was 38 miles from his house. Calculating his daily wanderings at 10 miles, we may believe they amounted in all to 400. He must, therefore, have rambled in a circuitous direction, which people generally do in such circumstances. Nothing but the great strength of his constitution, and the merciful aid of his Maker, could have supported him for so long a time.

[From *Ornithological Biography*, Vol. II, pp. 69-73.]

THE FLORIDA KEYS (I)

As the "Marion" neared the inlet called "Indian Key," which is situated on the eastern coast of the peninsula of Florida, my heart swelled with uncontrollable delight. Our vessel once over the coral reef that every where stretches along the shore like a great wall, reared by an army of giants, we found ourselves in safe anchoring ground, within a few furlongs of the land. The next moment saw the oars of a boat propelling us towards the shore, and in brief time we stood on the desired beach. With what delightful feelings did we gaze on the objects around us!—the gorgeous flowers, the singular and beautiful plants, the luxuriant trees. The balmy air which we breathed filled us with animation, so pure and salubrious did it seem to be. The birds which we saw were almost all new to us; their lovely forms appeared to be arrayed in more brilliant apparel than I had ever before seen, and as they gambolled in happy playfulness among the bushes, or glided over the light green waters, we longed to form a more intimate acquaintance with them.

Students of nature spend little time in introductions, especially when they present themselves to persons who feel an interest in their pursuits. This was the case with Mr. Thruston, the Deputy Collector of the island, who shook us all heartily by the hand, and in a trice had a boat manned at our service. Accompanied by him, his pilot and fishermen, off we went, and after a short pull landed on a large key. Few minutes had elapsed, when shot after shot might be heard, and down came whirling through the air the objects of our desire. One thrust himself into the tangled groves that covered all but the beautiful coral beach that in a continued line bordered the island, while others gazed on the glowing and diversified hues of the curious inhabitants of the deep. I saw one of my party rush into the limpid element, to seize on a crab, that with claws extended upwards, awaited his approach, as if determined not to give way. A loud voice called him back to the land, for sharks are as abundant along these shores as pebbles, and the hungry prowlers could not have got a more savoury dinner.

The pilot, besides being a first-rate shot, possessed a most intimate acquaintance with the country. He had been a "conch-diver," and no matter what number of fathoms measured the distance between the surface of the water and its craggy bottom, to seek for curious shells in their retreat seemed to him more pastime than toil. Not a Cormorant or Pelican, a Flamingo, an Ibis, or Heron, had ever in his days formed its nest without his having marked the spot; and as to the Keys to which the Doves are wont to resort, he was better acquainted with them than many fops are with the contents of their pockets. In a word, he positively knew every channel that led to these islands, and every cranny along their shores. For years his employment had been to hunt those singular animals called Sea Cows or Marratees [manatees], and he had conquered hundreds of them, "merely," as he said, because the flesh and hide bring "a fair price" at Havannah. He never went anywhere to land without "Long Tom," which proved indeed to be a wonderful gun, and which made smart havoc when charged with "groceries," a term by which he designated the large shot he used. In like manner, he never paddled his light canoe without having by his side the trusty javelin, with which he unerringly transfixed such fishes as he thought fit either for market or for his own use. In attacking turtles, netting, or overturning them, I doubt if his equal ever lived on the Florida coast. No sooner was he made acquainted with my errand, than he freely offered his best services, and from that moment until I left Key West he was seldom out of my hearing.

While the young gentlemen who accompanied us were engaged in procuring plants, shells, and small birds, he tapped me on the shoulder, and with a smile said to me, "Come along, I'll shew you something better worth your while." To the boat we betook ourselves, with the Captain and only a pair of tars, for more he said would not answer. The yawl for a while was urged at a great rate, but as we approached a point, the oars were taken in, and the pilot alone sculling, desired us to make ready, for in a few minutes we should have "rare sport." As we advanced, the more slowly did we move, and the most profound silence was maintained, until suddenly coming almost in contact with a thick shrubbery of mangroves, we beheld, right before us, a multitude of pelicans. A discharge of artillery seldom produced more effect;—the dead, the dying, and the wounded, fell from the trees upon the water, while those unscathed flew screaming through the air in terror and dismay. "There," said he, "did not I tell you so; is it not rare sport?" The birds, one after another, were lodged under the gunwales, when the pilot desired the Captain to order the lads to pull away. Within about half a mile we reached the extremity of the key. "Pull away," cried the pilot, "never mind them on the wing, for those black rascals don't mind a little firing—now, boys, lay her close under the nests." And there we were, with four hundred cormorants' nests over our heads. The birds were sitting, and when we fired, the number that dropped as if dead and plunged into the water was such, that I thought by some unaccountable means or other we had killed the whole colony. You would have smiled at the loud laugh and curious gestures of the pilot. "Gentlemen," said he, "almost a blank shot!" And so it was, for, on following the birds as one after another peeped up from the water, we found only a few unable to take to wing. "Now," said the pilot, "had you waited until *I had spoken* to the black villains, you might have killed a score or more of them." On inspection, we found that our shots had lodged in the tough dry twigs of which these birds form their nests, and that we had lost the more favourable opportunity of hitting them, by not waiting until they rose. "Never mind," said the pilot, "if you wish it, you may load *The Lady of the Green Mantle* [the *Marion*] with them in less than a week. Stand still, my lads; and now, gentlemen, in ten minutes you and I will bring down a score of them." And so we did. As we rounded the island, a beautiful bird of the species called Peale's Egret, came up and was shot. We now landed, took in the rest of our party, and returned to Indian Key, where we arrived three hours before sunset.

The sailors and other individuals to whom my name and pursuits had become known, carried our birds to the pilot's house. His good wife had a room ready for me to draw in, and my assistant might have been seen busily engaged in skinning, while George Lehman was making a sketch of the lovely isle.

Time is ever precious to the student of nature. I placed several birds in their natural attitudes, and began to outline them. A dance had been prepared also, and no sooner was the sun lost to our eye, than males and females, including our captain and others from the vessel, were seen advancing gaily towards the house in full apparel. The birds were skinned, the sketch was on paper, and I told my young men to amuse themselves. As to myself, I could not join in the merriment, for, full of the remembrance of you, reader, and of the patrons of my work both in America and in Europe, I went on "grinding"—not on an organ, like the Lady of Bras d'Or, but on paper, to the finishing, not merely of my outlines, but of my notes respecting the objects seen this day.

The room adjoining that in which I worked, was soon filled. Two miserable fiddlers screwed their screeching silken strings—not an inch of catgut graced their instruments; and the bouncing of brave lads and fair lasses shook the premises to the foundation. One with a slip came down heavily on the floor, and the burst of laughter that followed echoed over the isle. Diluted claret was handed round to cool the ladies, while a beverage of more potent energies warmed their partners. After supper our captain returned to the Marion, and I, with my young men, slept in light swinging hammocks under the eaves of the piazza.

It was the end of April, when the nights were short, and the days therefore long. Anxious to turn every moment to account, we were on board Mr. Thruston's boat at three next morning. Pursuing our way through the deep and tortuous channels that everywhere traverse the immense muddy soap-like flats that stretch from the outward Keys to the Main, we proceeded on our voyage of discovery. Here and there we met with great beds of floating sea-weeds, which showed us that Turtles were abundant there, these masses being the refuse of their feeding. On talking to Mr. Thruston of the nature of these muddy flats, he mentioned that he had once been lost amongst their narrow channels for several days and nights, when in pursuit of some smugglers' boat, the owners of which were better acquainted with the place than the men who were along with him. Although in full sight of several of the Keys, as well as of the main land, he was unable to reach either, until a heavy gale raised the water, when he sailed directly over the flats, and returned home almost exhausted with fatigue and hunger. His present pilot often alluded to the circumstance afterwards, ending with a great laugh, and asserting that had he "been there, the rascals would not have escaped."

Coming under a Key on which multitudes of Frigate Pelicans had begun to form their nests, we shot a good number of them, and observed their habits. The boastings of our pilot were here confirmed by the exploits which he performed with his long gun, and on several occasions he brought down a bird from a height of fully a hundred yards. The poor birds, unaware of the range of our artillery, sailed calmly along, so that it was not difficult for "Long Tom," or rather for his owner, to furnish us with as many as we required. The day was spent in this manner, and towards night we returned, laden with booty, to the hospitable home of the pilot.

The next morning was delightful. The gentle sea-breeze glided over the flowery isle, the horizon was clear, and all was silent save the long breakers that rushed over the distant reefs. As we were proceeding towards some Keys, seldom visited by men, the sun rose from the bosom of the waters with a burst of glory that flashed on my soul the idea of that power which called into existence so magnificent an object. The moon, thin and pale, as if ashamed to shew her feeble light, concealed herself in the dim west. The surface of the waters shone in its tremulous smoothness, and the deep blue of the clear heavens was pure as the world that lies beyond them. The Heron heavily flew towards the land, like a glutton retiring at day-break, with well-lined paunch, from the house of some wealthy patron of good cheer. The Night Heron and the Owl, fearful of day, with hurried flight sought safety in the recesses of the deepest swamps; while the Gulls and Terns, ever cheerful, gambolled over the water, exulting in the prospect of abundance. I also exulted in hope, my whole frame seemed to expand; and our sturdy crew shewed, by their merry faces, that nature had charms for them too. How much of beauty and joy is lost to them who never view the rising sun, and of whose waking existence the best half is nocturnal!

Twenty miles our men had to row before we reached "Sandy Island," and as on its level shores we all leaped, we plainly saw the southernmost cape of the Floridas. The flocks of birds that covered the shelly beaches, and those hovering over head, so astonished us that we could for a while scarcely believe our eyes. The first volley procured a supply of food sufficient for two days' consumption. Such tales, you have already been told, are well enough at a distance from the place to which they refer; but you will doubtless be still more surprised when I tell you that our first fire among a crowd of the Great Godwits laid prostrate sixty-five of these birds. Rose-coloured Curlews stalked gracefully beneath the mangroves; Purple Herons rose at almost every step we took, and each cactus supported the nest of a White Ibis. The air was darkened by whistling wings, while, on the waters, floated Gallinules and other interesting birds. We formed a kind of shed with sticks and grass, the sailor cook commenced his labours, and ere long we supplied the deficiencies of our fatigued frames. The business of the day over, we secured ourselves from insects by means of musquito-nets, and were lulled to rest by the cacklings of the beautiful Purple Gallinules!

In the morning we rose from our sandy beds, and—

[From *Ornithological Biography,* Vol. II, pp. 312-316.]

THE FLORIDA KEYS (II)

I left you abruptly, perhaps uncivilly, reader, at the dawn of day, on Sandy Island, which lies just six miles from the extreme point of

South Florida. I did so because I was amazed at the appearance of things around me, which in fact looked so different then from what they seemed at night, that it took some minutes' reflection to account for the change. When we laid ourselves down in the sand to sleep, the waters almost bathed our feet; when we opened our eyes in the morning, they were at an immense distance. Our boat lay on her side, looking not unlike a whale reposing on a mud-bank. The birds in myriads were probing their exposed pasture-ground. There great flocks of Ibises fed apart from equally large collections of Godwits, and thousands of Herons gracefully paced along, ever and anon thrusting their javelin bills into the body of some unfortunate fish confined in a small pool of water. Of Fish-Crows, I could not estimate the number, but from the havoc they made among the crabs, I conjecture that these animals must have been scarce by the time of next ebb. Frigate Pelicans chased the Jager, which himself had just robbed a poor Gull of its prize, and all the Gallinules ran with spread wings from the mud-banks to the thickets of the island, so timorous had they become when they perceived us.

Surrounded as we were by so many objects that allured us, not one could we yet attain, so dangerous would it have been to venture on the mud; and our pilot having assured us that nothing could be lost by waiting, spoke of our eating, and on this hint told us that he would take us to a part of the island where "our breakfast would be abundant although uncooked." Off we went, some of the sailors carrying baskets, others large tin pans and wooden vessels, such as they use for eating their meals in. Entering a thicket of about an acre in extent, we found on every bush several nests of the Ibis, each containing three large and beautiful eggs, and all hands fell to gathering. The birds gave way to us, and ere long we had a heap of eggs that promised delicious food. Nor did we stand long in expectation, for, kindling a fire, we soon prepared, in one way or another, enough to satisfy the cravings of our hungry maws. Breakfast ended, the pilot looking at the gorgeous sunrise, said: "Gentlemen, prepare yourselves for fun, the tide is acoming."

Over these enormous mud-flats, a foot or two of water is quite sufficient to drive all the birds ashore, even the tallest Heron or Flamingo, and the tide seems to flow at once over the whole expanse. Each of us provided with a gun, posted himself behind a bush, and no sooner had the water forced the winged creatures to approach the shore, than the work of destruction commenced. When it at length ceased, the collected mass of birds of different kinds looked not unlike a small haycock. Who could not with a little industry have helped himself to a few of their skins? Why, reader, surely no one as fond of these things as I am. Every one assisted in this, and even the sailors themselves tried their hand at the work.

Our pilot, good man, told us he was no hand at such occupations, and would go after something else. So taking Long Tom and his fishing-tackle, he marched off quietly along the shores. About an hour afterwards we saw him returning, when he looked quite exhausted, and on our inquiring the cause said, "There is a dew-fish yonder and a few balacoudas, but I am not able to bring them, or even to haul them here; please send the sailors after them." The fishes were accordingly brought, and as I had never seen a dewfish, I examined it closely, and took an outline of its form, which some days hence you may perhaps see. It exceeded a hundred pounds in weight, and afforded excellent eating. The balacouda is also a good fish, but at times a dangerous one, for, according to the pilot, on more than one occasion "some of these gentry" had followed him when waist-deep in the water, in pursuit of a more valuable prize, until in self-defence he had to spear them, fearing that "the gentlemen" might at one dart cut off his legs, or some other nice bit, with which he was unwilling to part.

Having filled our cask from a fine well long since dug in the sand of Cape Sable, either by Seminole Indians or pirates, no matter which, we left Sandy Isle about full tide, and proceeded homewards, giving a call here and there at different keys, with the view of procuring rare birds, and also their nests and eggs. We had twenty miles to go "as the birds fly," but the tortuosity of the channels rendered our course fully a third longer. The sun was descending fast, when a black cloud suddenly obscured the majestic orb. Our sails swelled by a breeze, that was scarcely felt by us, and the pilot, requesting us to sit on the weather gunwale, told us that we were "going to get it." One sail was hauled in and secured, and the other was reefed although the wind had not increased. A low murmuring noise was heard, and across the cloud that now rolled along in tumultuous masses, shot vivid flashes of lightning. Our experienced guide steered directly across a flat towards the nearest land. The sailors passed their quids from one cheek to the other, and our pilot having covered himself with his oil-jacket, we followed his example. "Blow, sweet breeze," cried he at the tiller, and "we'll reach the land before the blast overtakes us, for, gentlemen, it is a furious cloud yon."

A furious cloud indeed was the one which now, like an eagle on outstretched wings, approached so swiftly, that one might have deemed it in haste to destroy us. We were not more than a cable's length from the shore, when, with an imperative voice, the pilot calmly said to us, "Sit quite still, Gentlemen, for I should not like to lose you overboard just now; the boat can't upset, my word for that, if you will but sit still—here we have it!"

Reader, persons who have never witnessed a hurricane, such as not unfrequently desolates the sultry climates of the south, can scarcely form an idea of their terrific grandeur. One would think that, not content with laying waste all on land, it must needs sweep the waters of the shallows quite dry, to quench its thirst. No respite for an instant does it afford to the objects within the reach of its furious current. Like the scythe of the destroying angel, it cuts everything by the roots, as it were with the careless ease of the experienced mower. Each of its revolving sweeps collects a heap that might be likened to the full sheaf which the husbandman flings by his side. On it goes with a wildness and fury that are indescribable; and when at last its frightful blasts have ceased, Nature, weeping and disconsolate, is left bereaved of her beauteous offspring. In some instances, even a full century is required, before, with all her powerful energies, she can repair her loss. The planter has not only lost his mansion, his crops, and his flocks, but he has to clear his lands anew, covered and entangled as they are with the trunks and branches of trees that are everywhere strewn. The bark overtaken by the storm, is cast on the lee-shore, and if any are left to witness the fatal results, they are the "wreckers" alone, who, with inward delight, gaze upon the melancholy spectacle.

Our light bark shivered like a leaf the instant the blast reached her sides. We thought she had gone over; but the next instant she was on the shore. And now in contemplation of the sublime and awful storm, I gazed around me. The waters drifted like snow; the tough mangroves hid their tops amid their roots, and the loud roaring of the waves driven among them blended with the howl of the tempest. It was not rain that fell; the masses of water flew in a horizontal direction, and where a part of my body was exposed I felt as if a smart blow had been given me on it. But enough! – in half an hour it was over. The pure blue sky once more embellished the heavens, and although it was now quite night, we considered our situation a good one.

The crew and some of the party spent the night in the boat. The pilot, myself, and one of my assistants took to the heart of the mangroves, and having found high land, we made a fire as well as we could, spread a tarpauling, and fixing our insect bars over us, soon forgot in sleep the horrors that had surrounded us.

Next day the Marion proceeded on her cruize, and in a few more days, having anchored in another safe harbour, we visited other Keys, of which I will, with your leave, give you a short account.

The Deputy-Collector of Indian Isle gave me the use of his pilot for a few weeks, and I was the more gratified by this, that besides knowing him to be a good man and a perfect sailor, I was now convinced that he possessed a great knowledge of the habits of birds, and could without loss of time lead me to their haunts. We were a hundred miles or so farther to the south. Gay May like a playful babe gambolled on the bosom of his mother Nature, and every thing was replete with life and joy. The pilot had spoken to me of some birds which I was very desirous of obtaining. One morning, therefore, we went in two boats to some distant isle, where they were said to breed. Our difficulties in reaching that Key might to some seem more imaginary than real, were I faithfully to describe them. Suffice it for me to tell you that after hauling our boats and pushing them with our hands, for upwards of nine miles, over the flats, we at last reached the deep channel that usually surrounds each of the mangrove islands. We were much exhausted by the labour and excessive heat, but we were now floating on deep water, and by resting a short while under the shade of some mangroves, we were soon refreshed by the breeze that gently blew from the Gulf. We further repaired our strength by taking some food; and I may as well tell you here, that during all the time I spent in that part of the Floridas, my party restricted themselves to fish and soaked biscuit, while our only and constant beverage was water and mollasses. I found that in these warm latitudes, exposed as we constantly were to alternate heat and moisture, ardent spirits and more substantial food would prove dangerous to us. The officers, and those persons who from time to time kindly accompanied us, adopted the same regimen, and not an individual of us had ever to complain of so much as a headach.

But we were under the mangroves—at a great distance on one of the flats, the Heron which I have named *Ardea occidentalis* was seen moving majestically in great numbers. The tide rose and drove them away, and as they came towards us, to alight and rest for a time on the tallest trees, we shot as many as I wished. I also took under my charge several of their young alive.

At another time we visited the "Mule Keys." There the prospect was in many respects dismal in the extreme. As I followed their shores, I saw bales of cotton floating in all the coves, while spars of every description lay on the beach, and far off on the reefs I could see the last remains of a lost ship, her dismantled bulk. Several schooners were around her; they were wreckers. I turned me from the sight with a heavy heart. Indeed, as I slowly proceeded, I dreaded to meet the floating or cast ashore bodies of some of the unfortunate crew. Our visit to the Mule Keys was in no way profitable, for besides meeting with but a few birds in two or three instances, I was, whilst swimming in a deep channel of a mangrove isle, much nearer a large shark than I wish ever to be again.

"The service" requiring all the attention, prudence, and activity of Captain Day and his gallant officers, another cruize took place, of which you will find some account in the sequel; and while I rest a little on the deck of the Lady of the Green Mantle, let me offer my humble thanks to the Being who has allowed me the pleasure of thus relating to you, kind reader, a small part of my adventures.

[From *Ornithological Biography*, Vol. II, pp. 345-349.]

THE WRECKERS OF FLORIDA

Long before I reached the lovely islets that border the southeastern shores of the Floridas, the accounts I had heard of "The Wreckers" had deeply prejudiced me against them. Often had I been informed of the cruel and cowardly methods which it was alleged they employed to allure vessels of all nations to the dreaded reefs, that they might plunder their cargoes, and rob their crews and passengers of their effects. I therefore could have little desire to meet with such men under any circumstances, much less to become liable to receive their aid; and with the name of Wreckers, there were associated in my mind ideas of piratical depredations, barbarous usage, and even murder.

One fair afternoon, while I was standing on the polished deck of the United States' revenue cutter the Marion, a sail hove in sight, bearing in an opposite course, and "close-hauled" to the wind. The gentle rake of her masts, as she rocked to and fro in the breeze, brought to my mind the wavings of the reeds on the fertile banks of the Mississippi. By-and-by the vessel altering her course, approached us. The Marion, like a sea-bird, with extended wings, swept through the waters, gently inclining to either side, while the unknown vessel leaped as it were from wave to wave, like the dolphin in eager pursuit of his prey. In a short time, we were gliding side by side, and the commander of the strange schooner saluted our captain, who promptly returned the compliment. What a beautiful vessel! we all thought; how trim, how clean-rigged, and how well manned! She swims like a duck; and now with a broad sheer, off she makes for the reefs, a few miles under our lee. There, in that narrow passage, well known to her commander, she rolls, tumbles, and dances, like a giddy thing, her copper sheathing now gleaming, and again disappearing under the waves. But the passage is thrid, and now, hauling on the wind, she resumes her former course, and gradually recedes from the view. Reader, it was a Florida Wrecker!

When at the Tortugas, I paid a visit to several vessels of this kind, in company with my excellent friend Robert Day, Esq. We had observed the regularity and quickness of the men then employed at their arduous tasks, and as we approached the largest schooner, I admired her form, so well adapted to her occupation, her great breadth of beam, her light draught, the correctness of her water-line, the neatness of her painted sides, the smoothness of her well-greased masts, and the beauty of her rigging. We were welcomed on board with all the frankness of our native tars. Silence and order prevailed on her decks. The commander and the second officer led us into a spacious cabin, well lighted, and furnished with every convenience for fifteen or more passengers. The former brought me his collection of marine shells, and whenever I pointed to one that I had not seen before, offered it with so much kindness, that I found it necessary to be careful in expressing my admiration of any particular shell. He had also many eggs of rare birds, which were all handed over to me, with an assurance that before the month should expire, a new set could easily be procured, "for," said he, "we have much idle time on the reefs at this season." Dinner was served, and we partook of their fare, which consisted of fish, fowl, and other materials. These rovers, who were both from "down east," were stout, active men, cleanly and smart in their attire. In a short time we were extremely social and merry. They thought my visit to the Tortugas, in quest of birds, was rather a "curious fancy;" but, notwithstanding, they expressed their pleasure while looking at some of my drawings, and offered their services in procuring specimens. Expeditions far and near were proposed, and on settling that one of them was to take place on the morrow, we parted friends.

Early next morning, several of these kind men accompanied me to a small key called Booby Island, about ten miles distant from the lighthouse. Their boats were well manned, and rowed with long and steady strokes, such as whalers and men-of-war's men are wont to draw. The captain sang, and at times, by way of frolic, ran a race with our own beautiful bark. The Booby Isle was soon reached, and our sport there was equal to any we had elsewhere. They were capital shots, had excellent guns, and knew more about boobies and noddies than nine-tenths of the best naturalists in the world. But what will you say when I tell you the Florida Wreckers are excellent at a deer hunt, and that at certain seasons, "when business is slack," they are wont to land on some extensive key, and in a few hours procure a supply of delicious venison.

Some days afterwards, the same party took me on an expedition in quest of sea-shells. There we were all in water at times to the waist, and now and then much deeper. Now they would dip, like ducks, and on emerging would hold up a beautiful shell. This occupation they seemed to enjoy above all others.

The duties of the Marion having been performed, intimation of our intended departure reached the Wreckers. An invitation was sent to me to go and see them on board their vessels, which I accepted. Their object on this occasion was to present me with some superb corals, shells, live turtles of the Hawk-billed species, and a great quantity of eggs. Not a "pecayon" would they receive in return, but putting some letters in my hands, requested me to "be so good as to put them in the mail at Charleston," adding that they were for their wives "down east." So anxious did they appear to be to do all they could for me, that they proposed to sail before the Marion, and meet her under weigh, to give me some birds that were rare on the coast, and of which they knew the haunts. Circumstances connected with "the service" prevented this, however, and with sincere regret, and a good portion of friendship, I bade these excellent fellows adieu. How different, thought I, is often the knowledge of things acquired by personal observation, from that obtained by report!

I had never before seen Florida Wreckers, nor has it since been my fortune to fall in with any; but my good friend Dr. Benjamin Strobel, having furnished me with a graphic account of a few days which he spent with them, I shall present you with it in his own words.

"On the 12th day of September, while lying in harbour at Indian Key, we were joined by five wrecking vessels. Their licenses having expired, it was necessary to go to Key West to renew them. We determined to accompany them the next morning, and here it will not be amiss for me to say a few words respecting these far-famed Wreckers, their captains and crews. From all that I had heard, I expected to see a parcel of dirty, pirate-looking vessels, officered and manned by a set of black-whiskered fellows, who carried murder in their very looks. I was agreeably surprised on discovering the vessels were fine large sloops and schooners, regular clippers, kept in first-rate order. The captains generally were jovial, good-natured sons of Neptune, who manifested a disposition to be polite and hospitable, and to afford every facility to persons passing up and down the Reef. The crews were hearty, well-drest, and honest-looking men.

"On the 13th, at the appointed hour, we all set sail together, that is, the five Wreckers and the schooner Jane. As our vessel was not noted for fast sailing, we accepted an invitation to go on board of a Wrecker. The fleet got under weigh about eight o'clock in the morning, the wind light but fair, the water smooth, and the day fine. I can scarcely find words to express the pleasure and gratification which I this day experienced. The sea was of a beautiful, soft, pea-green colour, smooth as a sheet of glass, and as transparent, its surface agitated only by our vessels as they parted its bosom, or by the Pelican in pursuit of his prey, which rising for a considerable distance in the air, would suddenly plunge down with distended mandibles and secure his food. The vessels of our little fleet, with every sail set that could catch a breeze, and the white foam curling round the prows, glided silently along, like islands of flitting shadows, on an immovable sea of light. Several fathoms below the surface of the water, and under us, we saw great quantities of fish diving and sporting among the sea-grass, sponges, sea-feathers, and corals, with which the bottom was covered. On our right hand were the Florida Keys, which, as we made them in the distance, looked like specks upon the surface of the water, but as we neared them, rose to view as if by enchantment, clad in the richest livery of spring, each variety of colour and hue rendered soft and delicate by a clear sky and a brilliant sun over head. All was like a fairy scene; my heart leaped up in delighted admiration, and I could not but exclaim, in the language of Scott,

"Those seas behold,
Round thrice an hundred islands rolled."

The trade-wind played around us with balmy and refreshing sweetness; and, to give life and animation to the scene, we had a contest for the mastery between all the vessels of the fleet, while a deep interest was excited in favour of this or that vessel, as she shot ahead, or fell astern.

About three o'clock in the afternoon, we arrived off the Bay of Honda. The wind being light, and no prospect of reaching Key West that night, it was agreed that we should make a harbour here. We entered a beautiful basin and came to anchor about four o'clock. Boats were got out, and several hunting parties formed. We landed, and were soon on the scent, some going in search of shells, others of birds. An Indian, who had been picked up somewhere along the coast by a Wrecker, and who was employed as a hunter, was sent ashore in search of venison. Previous to his leaving the vessel, a rifle was loaded with a single ball, and put into his hands. After an absence of several hours, he returned with two deer, which he had killed at a single shot. He watched until they were both in range of his gun, side by side, when he fired and brought them down.

All hands having returned, and the fruits of our excursion being collected, we had wherewithal to make an abundant supper. Most of the game was sent on board the largest vessel, where we proposed supping. Our vessels were all lying within hail of each other, and as soon as the moon arose, boats were seen passing from vessel to vessel, and all were busily and happily engaged in exchanging civilities. One could never have supposed that these men were professional rivals, so apparent was the good-feeling that prevailed among them. About nine o'clock we started for supper; a number of persons had already collected, and as soon as we arrived on board the vessel, a German sailor, who played remarkably well on the violin, was summoned on the quarter-deck, when all hands, with a good will, cheerily danced to lively airs until supper was ready. The table was laid in the cabin, and groaned under its load of venison, wild ducks, pigeons, curlews, and fish. Toasting and singing succeeded the supper, and among other curious matters introduced, the following song was sung by the German fiddler, who accompanied his voice with his instrument. He is said to be the author of the song. I say nothing of the poetry, but merely give it as it came on my ear. It is certainly very characteristic.

THE WRECKER'S SONG

Come ye, goot people, von and all,
    Come listen to my song:
A few remarks I have to make,
    Which vont be very long.
'Tis of our vessel stout and goot,
As ever yet was built of woot,
Along the reef where the breakers roar,
De Wreckers on de Florida shore!

Key Tavernier's our rendezvous;
    At anchor there we lie,
And see the vessels in the Gulf,
    Carelessly passing by.
When night comes on we dance and sing,
Whilst the current some vessel is floating in;
When day-light comes, a ship's on shore,
Among de rocks where de breakers roar.

When day-light dawns, we're under weigh,
    And every sail is set,
And if the wind it should prove light,
    Why then, our sails we wet.
To gain her first each eager strives,
To save de cargo and de people's lives,
Amongst de rocks where de breakers roar,
De Wreckers on de Florida shore.

When we get 'longside, we find she's bilged:
    We know vel vat to do,
Save de cargo dat we can,
    De sails and rigging too;

Den down to Key West we soon vill go,
When quickly our salvage we shall know;
When every ting it is fairly sold,
Our money down to us it is told.

Den one week's cruize we'll have on shore,
Before we do sail again,
And drink success to de sailor lads
Dat are ploughing of de main.
And when you are passing by dis way,
On the Florida Reef should you chance to stray,
Why, we will come to you on de shore,
Amongst de rocks where de breakers roar.

Great emphasis was laid upon particular words by the singer, who had a broad German accent. Between the verses he played a symphony [interlude], remarking, "Gentlemens, I makes dat myself." The chorus was trolled by twenty or thirty voices, which, in the stillness of the night, produced no unpleasant effect.

[From *Ornithological Biography*, Vol. III, pp. 158-163.]

DEATH OF A PIRATE

In the calm of a fine moonlight night, as I was admiring the beauty of the clear heavens, and the broad glare of light that glanced from the trembling surface of the waters around, the officer on watch came up and entered into conversation with me. He had been a turtler in other years, and a great hunter to boot, and although of humble birth and pretensions, energy and talent, aided by education, had raised him to a higher station. Such a man could not fail to be an agreeable companion, and we talked on various subjects, principally, you may be sure, birds and other natural productions. He told me he once had a disagreeable adventure, when looking out for game, in a certain cove on the shores of the Gulf of Mexico; and, on my expressing a desire to hear it, he willingly related to me the following particulars, which I give you, not perhaps precisely in his own words, but as nearly so as I can remember.

"Towards evening, one quiet summer day, I chanced to be paddling along a sandy shore, which I thought well fitted for my repose, being covered with tall grass, and as the sun was not many degrees above the horizon, I felt anxious to pitch my musquito bar or net, and spend the night in this wilderness. The bellowing notes of thousands of bull-frogs in a neighbouring swamp might lull me to rest, and I looked upon the flocks of blackbirds that were assembling as sure companions in this secluded retreat.

I proceeded up a little stream, to insure the safety of my canoe from any sudden storm, when, as I gladly advanced, a beautiful yawl came unexpectedly in view. Surprised at such a sight in a part of the country then scarcely known, I felt a sudden check in the circulation of my blood. My paddle dropped from my hands, and fearfully indeed, as I picked it up, did I look towards the unknown boat. On reaching it, I saw its sides marked with stains of blood, and looking with anxiety over the gunwale, I perceived to my horror, two human bodies covered with gore. Pirates or hostile Indians I was persuaded had perpetrated the foul deed, and my alarm naturally increased; my heart fluttered, stopped, and heaved with unusual tremors, and I looked towards the setting sun in consternation and despair. How long my reveries lasted I cannot tell; I can only recollect that I was roused from them by the distant groans of one apparently in mortal agony. I felt as if refreshed by the cold perspiration that oozed from every pore, and I reflected that though alone, I was well armed, and might hope for the protection of the Almighty.

Humanity whispered to me that, if not surprised and disabled, I might render assistance to some sufferer, or even be the means of saving a useful life. Buoyed up by this thought, I urged my canoe on shore, and seizing it by the bow, pulled it at one spring high among the grass.

The groans of the unfortunate person fell heavy on my ear, as I cocked and reprimed my gun, and I felt determined to shoot the first that should rise from the grass. As I cautiously proceeded, a hand was raised over the weeds, and waved in the air in the most supplicating manner. I levelled my gun about a foot below it, when the next moment, the head and breast of a man covered with blood were convulsively raised, and a faint hoarse voice asked me for mercy and help! A death-like silence followed his fall to the ground. I surveyed every object around with eyes intent, and ears impressible by the slightest sound, for my situation that moment I thought as critical as any I had ever been in. The croaking of the frogs, and the last blackbirds alighting on their roosts, were the only sounds or sights; and I now proceeded towards the object of my mingled alarm and commiseration.

Alas! the poor being who lay prostrate at my feet, was so weakened by loss of blood, that I had nothing to fear from him. My first impulse was to run back to the water, and having done so, I returned with my cap filled to the brim. I felt at his heart, washed his face and breast, and rubbed his temples with the contents of a phial, which I kept about me as an antidote for the bites of snakes. His features, seamed by the ravages of time, looked frightful and disgusting; but he had been a powerful man, as the breadth of his chest plainly shewed. He groaned in the most appalling manner, as his breath struggled through the mass of blood that seemed to fill his throat. His dress plainly disclosed his occupation:—a large pistol he had thrust into his bosom, a naked cutlass lay near him on the ground, a red silk handkerchief was bound over his projecting brows, and over a pair of loose trowsers he wore fisherman's boots. He was, in short, a pirate.

My exertions were not in vain, for as I continued to bathe his temples, he revived, his pulse resumed some strength, and I began to hope that he might perhaps survive the deep wounds he had received. Darkness, deep darkness, now enveloped us. I spoke of making a fire. "Oh! for mercy's sake," he exclaimed, "don't." Knowing, however, that under existing circumstances it was expedient for me to do so, I left him, went to his boat, and brought the rudder, the benches, and the oars, which with my hatchet I soon splintered. I then struck a light, and presently stood in the glare of a blazing fire. The pirate seemed struggling between terror and gratitude for my assistance; he desired me several times in half English and Spanish to put out the flames, but after I had given him a draught of strong spirits, he at length became more composed. I tried to staunch the blood that flowed from the deep gashes in his shoulders and side. I expressed my regret that I had no food about me, but when I spoke of eating he sullenly waved his head.

My situation was one of the most extraordinary that I have ever been placed in. I naturally turned my talk towards religious subjects, but, alas, the dying man hardly believed in the existence of God. "Friend," said he, "for friend you seem to be, I have never studied the ways of Him of whom you talk. I am an outlaw, perhaps you will say a wretch—I have been for many years a Pirate. The instructions of my parents were of no avail to me, for I have always believed that I was born to be a most cruel man. I now lie here, about to die in the weeds, because I long ago refused to listen to their many admonitions. Do not shudder when I tell you—these now useless hands murdered the mother whom they had embraced. I feel that I have deserved the pangs of the wretched death that hovers over me; and I am thankful that one of my kind will alone witness my last gaspings."

A fond but feeble hope that I might save his life, and perhaps assist in procuring his pardon, induced me to speak to him on the subject. "It is all in vain, friend—I have no objection to die—I am glad that the villains who wounded me were not my conquerors—I want no pardon from *any one*—Give me some water, and let me die alone.

With the hope that I might learn from his conversation something that might lead to the capture of his guilty associates, I returned from the creek with another capful of water, nearly the whole of which I managed to introduce into his parched mouth, and begged him, for the sake of his future peace, to disclose his history to me. "It is impossible," said he, "there will not be time; the beatings of my heart tell me so. Long before day, these sinewy limbs will be motionless. Nay, there will hardly be a drop of blood in my body; and that blood will only serve to make the grass grow. My wounds are mortal, and I must and will die without what you call confession."

The moon rose in the east. The majesty of her placid beauty impressed me with reverence. I pointed towards her, and asked the Pirate if he could not recognise God's features there. "Friend, I see what you are driving at," was his answer,—"you, like the rest of our enemies, feel the desire of murdering us all.—Well—be it so—to die is after all nothing more than a jest; and were it not for the pain, no one, in my opinion, need care a jot about it. But, as you really have befriended me, I will tell you all that is proper."

Hoping his mind might take a useful turn, I again bathed his temples and washed his lips with spirits. His sunk eyes seemed to dart fire at mine—a heavy and deep sigh swelled his chest and struggled through his blood-choked throat, and he asked me to raise him for a little. I did so, when he addressed me somewhat as follows, for, as I have told you, his speech was a mixture of Spanish, French and English, forming a jargon, the like of which I had never heard before, and which I am utterly unable to imitate. However I shall give you the substance of his declaration.

"First tell me, how many bodies you found in the boat, and what sort of dresses they had on." I mentioned their number, and described their apparel. "That's right," said he, "they are the bodies of the scoundrels who followed me in that infernal Yankee barge. Bold rascals they were, for when they found the water too shallow for their craft, they took to it and waded after me. All my companions had been shot, and to lighten my own boat I flung them overboard; but as I lost time in this, the two ruffians caught hold of my gunwale, and struck on my head and body in such a manner, that after I had disabled and killed them both in the boat, I was scarce able to move. The other villains carried off our schooner and one of our boats, and perhaps ere now have hung all my companions whom they did not kill at the time. I have commanded my beautiful vessel many years, captured many ships, and sent many rascals to the devil. I always hated the Yankees, and only regret that I have not killed more of them.–I sailed from Matanzas.–I have often been in concert with others. I have money without counting, but it is buried where it will never be found, and it would be useless to tell you of it." His throat filled with blood, his voice failed, the cold hand of death was laid on his brow, feebly and hurriedly he muttered, "I am a dying man, farewell."

Alas! It is painful to see death in any shape; in this it was horrible, for there was no hope. The rattling of his throat announced the moment of dissolution, and already did the body fall on my arms with a weight that was insupportable. I laid him on the ground. A mass of dark blood poured from his mouth; then came a frightful groan, the last breathing of that foul spirit; and what now lay at my feet in the wild desert?–a mangled mass of clay!

The remainder of that night was passed in no enviable mood; but my feelings cannot be described. At dawn I dug a hole with the paddle of my canoe, rolled the body into it, and covered it. On reaching the boat I found several buzzards feeding on the bodies, which I in vain attempted to drag to the shore. I therefore covered them with mud and weeds, and launching my canoe, paddled from the cove with a secret joy for my escape, overshadowed with the gloom of mingled dread and abhorrence."

[From *Ornithological Biography*, Vol. II, pp. 185-189.]

John James Audubon

THE TURTLERS

The Tortugas are a group of islands lying about eighty miles from Key West, and the last of those that seem to defend the peninsula of the Floridas. They consist of five or six extremely low uninhabitable banks formed of shelly sand, and are resorted to principally by that class of men called Wreckers and Turtlers. Between these islands are deep channels, which, although extremely intricate, are well known to those adventurers, as well as to the commanders of the revenue cutters, whose duties call them to that dangerous coast. The great coral reef or wall lies about eight miles from these inhospitable isles, in the direction of the Gulf, and on it many an ignorant or careless navigator has suffered shipwreck. The whole ground around them is densely covered with corals, sea-fans, and other productions of the deep, amid which crawl innumerable testaceous animals, while shoals of curious and beautiful fishes fill the limpid waters above them. Turtles of different species resort to these banks, to deposit their eggs in the burning sand, and clouds of sea-fowl arrive every spring for the same purpose. These are followed by persons called "Eggers," who, when their cargoes are completed, sail to distant markets, to exchange their ill-gotten ware for a portion of that gold, on the acquisition of which all men seem bent.

The "Marion" having occasion to visit the Tortugas, I gladly embraced the opportunity of seeing those celebrated islets. A few hours before sunset the joyful cry of "land" announced our approach to them, but as the breeze was fresh, and the pilot was well acquainted with all the windings of the channels, we held on, and dropped anchor before twilight. If you have never seen the sun setting in those latitudes, I would recommend to you to make a voyage for the purpose, for I much doubt if, in any other portion of the world, the departure of the orb of day is accompanied with such gorgeous appearances. Look at the great red disk, increased to triple its ordinary dimensions! Now it has partially sunk beneath the distant line of waters, and with its still remaining half irradiates the whole heavens with a flood of golden light, purpling the far off clouds that hover over the western horizon. A blaze of refulgent glory streams through the portals of the west, and the masses of vapour assume the semblance of mountains of molten gold. But the sun has now disappeared, and from the east slowly advances the grey curtain which night draws over the world.

The Night-hawk is flapping its noiseless wings in the gentle sea-breeze; the Terns, safely landed, have settled on their nests; the Frigate Pelicans are seen wending their way to distant mangroves; and the Brown Gannet, in search of a resting-place, has perched on the yard of the vessel. Slowly advancing landward, their heads alone above the water, are observed the heavily laden Turtles, anxious to deposit their eggs in the well-known sands. On the surface of the gently rippling stream, I dimly see their broad forms, as they toil along, while at intervals may be heard their hurried breathings, indicative of suspicion and fear. The moon with her silvery light now illumines the scene, and the Turtle having landed, slowly and laboriously drags her heavy body over the sand, her "flappers" being better adapted for motion in the water than on shore. Up the slope, however, she works her way, and see how industriously she removes the sand beneath her, casting it out on either side. Layer after layer she deposits her eggs, arranging them in the most careful manner, and, with her hind-paddles, brings the sand over them. The business is accomplished, the spot is covered over, and with a joyful heart, the Turtle swiftly retires towards the shore, and launches into the deep.

But the Tortugas are not the only breeding places of the Turtles; these animals, on the contrary, frequent many other keys, as well as various parts of the coast of the mainland. There are four different species, which are known by the names of the *Green* Turtle, the *Hawk-billed* Turtle, the *Logger-head* Turtle, and the *Trunk* [leather-back] Turtle. The first is considered the best as an article of food, in which capacity it is well known to most epicures. It approaches the shores, and enters the bays, inlets and rivers, early in the month of April, after having spent the winter in the deep waters. It deposits its eggs in convenient places, at two different times in May, and once again in June. The first deposit is the largest, and the last the least, the total quantity being at an average about two hundred and forty. The Hawk-billed Turtle, whose shell is so valuable as an article of commerce, being used for various purposes in the arts, is the next with respect to the quality of its flesh. It resorts to the outer keys only, where it deposits its eggs in two sets, first in July, and again in August, although it "crawls" the beaches of these keys much earlier in the season, as if to look for a safe place. The average number of its eggs is about three hundred. The Loggerhead visits the Tortugas in April, and lays from that period until late in June three sets of eggs, each set averaging a hundred and seventy. The Trunk Turtle, which is sometimes of an enormous size, and which has a pouch like a pelican, reaches the shores latest. The shell and flesh are so soft that one may push his finger into them, almost as into a lump of butter. This species is therefore considered as the least valuable, and indeed is seldom eaten, unless by the Indians, who, ever alert when the turtle season commences, first carry off the eggs, and afterwards catch the Turtles themselves. The average number of eggs which it lays in the season, in two sets, may be three hundred and fifty.

The Loggerhead and the Trunk Turtles are the least cautious in choosing the places in which to deposit their eggs, whereas the two other species select the wildest and most secluded spots. The Green Turtle resorts either to the shores of the Main, between Cape Sable and Cape Florida, or enters Indian, Halifax, and other large rivers or inlets, from which it makes its retreat as speedily as possible, and betakes itself to the open sea. Great numbers, however, are killed by the Turtlers and Indians, as well as by various species of carnivorous animals, as cougars, lynxes, bears, and wolves. The Hawkbill, which is still more wary, and is always the most difficult to surprise, keeps to the sea islands. All the species employ nearly the same method in depositing their eggs in the sand, and as I have several times observed them in the act, I am enabled to present you with a circumstantial account of it.

On first nearing the shores, and mostly on fine calm moonlight nights, the Turtle raises her head above the water, being still distant thirty or forty yards from the beach, looks around her, and attentively examines the objects on the shore. Should she observe nothing likely to disturb her intended operations, she emits a loud hissing sound, by which such of her many enemies as are unaccustomed to it, are startled, and so are apt to remove to another place, although unseen by her. Should she hear any noise, or perceive indications of danger, she instantly sinks and goes off to a considerable distance; but should every thing be quiet, she advances slowly towards the beach, crawls over it, her head raised to the full stretch of her neck, and when she has reached a place fitted for her purpose, she gazes all round in silence. Finding "all well," she proceeds to form a hole in the sand, which she effects by removing it from *under* her body with her *hind* flappers, scooping it out with so much dexterity that the sides seldom if ever fall in. The sand is raised alternately with each flapper, as with a large ladle, until it has accumulated behind her, when supporting herself with her head and fore part on the ground fronting her body, she with a spring from each flapper, sends the sand around her, scattering it to the distance of several feet. In this manner the hole is dug to the depth of eighteen inches or sometimes more than two feet. This labour I have seen performed in the short period of nine minutes. The eggs are then dropped one by one, and disposed in regular layers, to the number of a hundred and fifty, or sometimes nearly two hundred. The whole time spent in this part of the operation may be about twenty minutes. She now scrapes the loose sand back over the eggs, and so levels and smooths the surface, that few persons on seeing the spot could imagine anything had been done to it. This accomplished to her mind, she retreats to the water with all possible dispatch, leaving the hatching of the eggs to the heat of the sand. When a turtle, a loggerhead for example, is in the act of dropping her eggs, she will not move although one should go up to her, or even seat himself on her back, for it seems that at this moment she finds it necessary to proceed at all events, and is unable to intermit her labour. The moment it is finished, however, off she starts; nor would it then be possible for one, unless he were as strong as a Hercules, to turn her over and secure her.

To upset a turtle on the shore, one is obliged to fall on his knees, and, placing his shoulder behind her forearm, gradually raise her up by pushing with great force, and then with a jerk throw her over. Sometimes it requires the united strength of several men to accomplish this; and, if the turtle should be of very great size, as often happens on that coast, even hand-spikes are employed. Some turtlers are so daring as to swim up to them while lying asleep on the surface of the water, and turn them over in their own element, when, however, a boat must be at hand to enable them to secure their prize. Few turtles can bite beyond the reach of their fore legs, and few, when once turned over, can, without assistance, regain their natural position; but, notwithstanding this, their flappers are generally secured by ropes so as to render their escape impossible.

Persons who search for turtles' eggs, are provided with a light stiff cane or a gun-rod, with which they go along the shores, probing the sand near the tracks of the animals, which, however, cannot always be seen, on account of the winds and heavy rains, that often obliterate them. The nests are discovered not only by men, but also by beasts of prey, and the eggs are collected, or destroyed on the spot in great numbers; as on certain parts of the shores hundreds of turtles are known to deposit their eggs within the space of a mile. They form a new hole each time they lay, and the second is generally dug near the first, as if the animal were quite unconscious of what had befallen it. It will readily be understood that the numerous eggs seen in a turtle on cutting it up could not be all laid the same season. The whole number deposited by an individual in one summer may amount to four hundred, whereas if the animal is caught on or near her nest, as I have witnessed, the remaining eggs, all small, without shells, and as it were threaded like so many large beads, exceed three thousand. In an instance where I found that number, the turtle weighed nearly four hundred pounds. The young, soon after being hatched, and when yet scarcely larger than a dollar, scratch their way through their sandy covering and immediately betake them themselves to the water.

The food of the Green Turtle consists chiefly of marine plants, more especially the Grasswrack *(Zostera marina)*, which they cut near the roots to procure the most tender and succulent parts. Their feeding grounds, as I have elsewhere said, are easily discovered by floating masses of these plants on the flats, or along the shores to which they resort. The Hawk-billed species feeds on sea-weeds, crabs, various kinds of shell-fish and fishes; the Loggerhead mostly on the fish of conch-shells of large size, which they are enabled, by means of their powerful beak, to crush to pieces with apparently as much ease as a man cracks a walnut. One which was brought on board the Marion, and placed near the fluke of one of her anchors, made a deep indentation in that hammered piece of iron that quite surprised me. The Trunk Turtle feeds on mollusca, fish, crustacea, sea urchins, and various marine plants.

All the species move through the water with surprising speed; but the Green and Hawk-billed in particular, remind you, by their celerity and the ease of their motions, of the progress of a bird in the air. It is therefore no easy matter to strike one with a spear, and yet this is often done by an accomplished turtler.

While at Key West and other islands on the coast, where I made the observations here presented to you, I chanced to have need to purchase some turtles, to feed my friends on board the Lady of the Green Mantle—not my friends her gallant officers, or the brave tars who formed her crew, for all of them had already been satiated with turtle soup, but my friends the Herons, of which I had a goodly number alive in coops, intending to carry them to John Bachman of Charleston, and other persons for whom I ever feel a sincere regard. So I went to a "crawl," accompanied by Dr. Benjamin Strobel, to inquire about prices, when, to my surprise, I found that the smaller the turtles, above ten pounds weight, the dearer they were, and that I could have purchased one of the loggerhead kind that weighed more than seven hundred pounds, for little more money than another of only thirty pounds. While I gazed on the large one, I thought of the soups the contents of its shell would have furnished for a "Lord Mayor's dinner," of the numerous eggs which its swollen body contained, and of the curious carriage which might be made of its shell,—a car in which Venus herself might sail over the Caribbean sea, provided her tender doves lent their aid in drawing the divinity, and provided no shark or hurricane came to upset it. The turtler assured me that although the "great monster" was in fact better meat than any other of a less size, there was no disposing of it, unless indeed it had been in his power to have sent it to some very distant market. I would willingly have purchased it, but I knew that if killed, its flesh could not keep much longer than a day, and on that account I bought eight or ten small ones, which "my friends" really relished exceedingly, and which served to support them for a long time.

Turtles such as I have spoken of, are caught in various ways on the coasts of the Floridas, or in estuaries and rivers. Some turtlers are in the habit of setting great nets across the entrance of streams, so as to answer the purpose either at the flow or at the ebb of the waters. These nets are formed of very large meshes, into which the turtles partially enter, when, the more they attempt to extricate themselves, the more they get entangled. Others harpoon them in the usual manner; but in my estimation no method is equal to that employed by Mr. Egan, the Pilot of Indian Isle.

That extraordinary turtler had an iron instrument which he called a *peg*, and which at each end had a point not unlike what nail-makers call a brad, it being four-cornered but flattish, and of a shape somewhat resembling the beak of an Ivory-billed Woodpecker, together with a neck and shoulder. Between the two shoulders of this instrument a fine tough line, fifty or more fathoms in length, was fastened by one end being passed through a hole in the centre of the peg, and the line itself was carefully coiled up, and placed in a convenient part of the canoe. One extremity of this peg enters a sheath of iron that loosely attaches it to a long wooden spear, until a turtle has been pierced through the shell by the other extremity. He of the canoe paddles away as silently as possible whenever he spies a turtle basking on the water, until he gets within a distance of ten or twelve yards, when he throws the spear so as to hit the animal about the place which an entomologist would choose, were it a large insect, for pinning it to a piece of cork. As soon as the turtle is struck, the wooden handle separates from the peg, in consequence of the looseness of its attachment. The smart of the wound urges on the animal as if distracted, and it appears that the longer the peg remains in its shell, the more firmly fastened it is, so great a pressure is exercised upon it by the shell of the turtle, which being suffered to run like a whale, soon becomes fatigued, and is secured by hauling in the line with great care. In this manner, as the Pilot informed me, eight hundred Green Turtles were caught by one man in twelve months.

Each turtler has his *crawl,* which is a square wooden building or pen, formed of logs, which are so far separated as to allow the tide to pass freely through, and stand erect in the mud. The turtles are placed in this inclosure, fed and kept there until sold. If the animals thus confined have not laid their eggs previous to their seizure, they drop them in the water, so that they are lost. The price of Green Turtles, when I was at Key West, was from four to six cents per pound.

The loves of the turtles are conducted in the most extraordinary manner; but as the recital of them must prove out of place here, I shall pass them over. There is, however, a circumstance relating to their habits, which I cannot omit, although I have it not from my own ocular evidence, but from report. When I was in the Floridas, several of the turtlers assured me, that any turtle taken from the depositing ground, and carried on the deck of a vessel several hundred miles, would, if then let loose, certainly be met with at the same spot, either immediately after, or in the following breeding season. Should this prove true, and it certainly may, how much will be enhanced the belief of the student in the uniformity and solidity of Nature's arrangements, when he finds that the turtle, like a migratory bird, returns to the same locality, with perhaps a delight similar to that experienced by the traveller, who, after visiting distant countries, once more returns to the bosom of his cherished family.

[From *Ornithological Biography,* Vol. II, pp. 370-376.]

A LONG CALM AT SEA

On the 17th of May, 1826, I left New Orleans on board the ship Delos, commanded by Joseph Hatch, Esq. of Kennebunk, bound for Liverpool. The steamer Hercules which towed the ship, left us several miles outside of the Balize, about ten hours after our departure; but there was not a breath of wind, the waters were smoother than the prairies of the Oppelousas, and notwithstanding our great display of canvas, we lay, like a dead whale, floating at the mercy of the currents. The weather was uncommonly fair, and the heat excessive; and in this helpless state we continued for many days. About the end of a week we had lost sight of the Balize, although I was assured by the commander, that all this while the ship had rarely answered the helm. The sailors whistled for wind, and raised their hands in all directions, anxious as they were to feel some motion in the air; but all to no purpose; it was a dead calm, and we concluded that Aeolus had agreed with Neptune to detain us, until our patience should be fairly tried, or our sport exhausted; for sport we certainly had, both on board and around the ship. I doubt if I can better contribute to your amusement at present, than by giving you a short account of the occurrences that took place, during this sleepy fit of the being on whom we depended for our progress toward merry England.

Vast numbers of beautiful dolphins glided by the side of the vessel, glancing like burnished gold through the day, and gleaming like meteors by night. The captain and his mates were expert at alluring them with baited hooks, and not less so at piercing them with five-pronged instruments, which they called grains; and I was delighted with the sport, because it afforded me an opportunity of observing and noting some of the habits of this beautiful fish, as well as several other kinds.

On being hooked, the Dolphin flounces vigorously, shoots off with great impetuosity to the very end of the line, when, being suddenly checked, it often rises perpendicularly several feet out of the water, shakes itself violently in the air, gets disentangled, and thus escapes. But when well secured, it is held in play for a while by the experienced fisher, soon becomes exhausted, and is hauled on board. Some persons prefer pulling them in at once, but they seldom succeed, as the force with which the fish shakes itself on being raised out of the water, is generally sufficient to enable it to extricate itself. Dolphins move in shoals, varying from four or five to twenty or more, hunting in packs in the waters, as wolves pursue their prey on land. The object of their pursuit is generally the Flying-fish, now and then the Bonita; and when nothing better can be had, they will follow the little Rudder-fish, and seize it immediately under the stern of the ship. The Flying-fishes, after having escaped for a while by dint of their great velocity, but on being again approached by the Dolphin, emerge from the water, and spreading their broad wing-like fins, sail through the air and disperse in all directions, like a covey of timid partridges before the rapacious falcon. Some pursue a direct course, others diverge on either side; but in a short time they all drop into their natural element. While they are travelling in the air, their keen and hungry pursuer, like a greyhound, follows in their wake, and performing a succession of leaps, many feet in extent, rapidly gains upon the quarry, which is often seized just as it falls into the sea.

Dolphins manifest a very remarkable sympathy with each other. The moment one of them is hooked or grained, those in company make up to it, and remain around until the unfortunate fish is pulled on board, when they generally move off together, seldom biting at any thing thrown out to them. This, however, is the case only with the larger individuals, which keep apart from the young, in the same manner as is observed in several species of birds; for when the smaller Dolphins are in large shoals, they all remain under the bows of a ship, and bite in succession at any sort of line, as if determined to see what has become of their lost companions, in consequence of which they are often all caught.

You must not suppose that the Dolphin is without its enemies. Who, in this world, man or fish, has not enough of them? Often it conceives itself on the very eve of swallowing a fish, which, after all, is nothing but a piece of lead, with a few feathers fastened to it, to make it look like a flying-fish, when it is seized and severed in two by the insidious Balacouda, which I have once seen to carry off by means of its sharp teeth, the better part of a Dolphin that was hooked, and already hoisted to the surface of the water.

The Dolphins caught in the Gulf of Mexico during this calm were suspected to be poisonous; and to ascertain whether this was really the case, our cook, who was an African negro, never boiled or fried one without placing beside it a dollar. If the silver was not tarnished by the time the Dolphin was ready for the table, the fish was presented to the passengers, with an assurance that it was perfectly good. But as not a single individual of the hundred that we caught had the property of converting silver into copper, I suspect that our African sage was no magician.

One morning, that of the 22d of June, the weather sultry, I was surprised, on getting out of my hammock, which was slung on deck, to find the water all around swarming with Dolphins, which were sporting in great glee. The sailors assured me that this was a certain "token of wind," and, as they watched the movements of the fishes, added, "aye, and of a fair breeze too." I caught several Dolphins in the course of an hour, after which scarcely any remained about the ship. Not a breath of air came to our relief all that day, no, nor even the next. The sailors were in despair, and I should probably have become despondent also, had not my spirits been excited by finding a very large Dolphin on my hook. When I had hauled it on board, I found it to be the largest I had ever caught. It was a magnificent creature. See how it quivers in the agonies of death! its tail flaps the hard deck, producing a sound like the rapid roll of a drum. How beautiful the changes of its colours! Now it is blue, now green, silvery, golden, and burnished copper! Now it presents a blaze of all the hues of the rainbow intermingled; but, alack! it is dead, and the play of its colours is no longer seen. It has settled into the deep calm that has paralyzed the energies of the blustering winds, and smoothed down the proud waves of the ocean.

The best bait for the Dolphin is a long stripe of shark's flesh. I think it generally prefers this to the semblance of the flying-fish, which indeed it does not often seize unless when the ship is under weigh, and it is made to rise to the surface. There are times, however, when hunger and the absence of their usual food will induce the Dolphins to dash at any sort of bait; and I have seen some caught by means of a piece of white linen fastened to a hook. Their appetite is as keen as that of the Vulture, and whenever a good opportunity occurs, they gorge themselves to such a degree that they become an easy prey to their enemies the Balacouda and the Bottle-nosed Porpoise. One that had been grained while lazily swimming immediately under the stern of our ship, was found to have its stomach completely crammed with flying-fish, all regularly disposed side by side, with their tails downwards,—by which I mean to say that the Dolphin always *swallows its prey tail foremost*. They looked in fact like so many salted herrings packed in a box, and were to the number of twenty-two, each six or seven inches in length.

The usual length of the Dolphins caught in the Gulf of Mexico is about three feet, and I saw none that exceeded four feet two inches. The weight of one of the latter size was only eighteen pounds; for this fish is extremely narrow in proportion to its length, although rather deep in its form. When just caught, the upper fin, which reaches from the forehead to within a short distance of the tail, is of a fine dark blue. The upper part of the body in its whole length is azure, and the lower parts are of a golden hue, mottled irregularly with deep blue spots. It seems that they at times enter very shallow water, as in the course of my last voyage along the Florida coast, some were caught in a seine, along with their kinsman the "Cavalier," of which I shall speak elsewhere.

The flesh of the Dolphin is rather firm, very white, and lies in flakes when cooked. The first caught are generally eaten with great pleasure, but when served many days in succession, they become insipid. It is not, as an article of food, equal to the Balacouda, which is perhaps as good as any fish caught in the waters of the Gulf of Mexico.

[From *Ornithological Biography,* Vol. III, pp. 491-494.]

STILL BECALMED

On the 4th of June we were still in the same plight, although the currents of the Gulf had borne us to a great distance from the place where, as I have informed you, we had amused ourselves with catching Dolphins. These currents are certainly very singular, for they carried us hither and thither, at one time rendering us apprehensive of drifting on the coast of Florida, at another threatening to send us to Cuba. Sometimes a slight motion in the air revived our hopes, swelled our sails a little, and carried us through the smooth waters like a skater gliding on ice; but in a few hours it was again a dead calm.

One day several small birds, after alighting on the spars, betook themselves to the deck. One of them, a female Rice Bunting, drew our attention more particularly, for, a few moments after her arrival, there came down, as if in her wake, a beautiful Peregrine Falcon. The plunderer hovered about for a while, then stationed himself on the end of one of the yard-arms, and suddenly pouncing on the little gleaner of the meadows, clutched her and carried her off in exultation. But, Reader, mark the date, and judge besides of my astonishment when I saw the Falcon feeding on the Finch while on wing, precisely with the same ease and composure as the Mississippi Kite might show while devouring high in air a Red-throated Lizard, swept from one of the magnificent trees of the Louisiana woods.

There was a favorite pet on board, belonging to our captain, and which was nothing more nor less than the female companion of a cock, in other words, a common hen. Some liked her because she now and then dropped a fresh egg,—a rare article at sea, even on board the Delos; others, because she exhibited a pleasing simplicity of character; others again, because, when they had pushed her overboard, it gave them pleasure to see the poor thing in terror strike with her feet, and strive to reach her floating home, which she would never have accomplished, however, had it not been for the humane interference of our Captain, Mr. Joseph Hatch of Kennebunk. Kind, good-hearted man! when, several weeks after, the same pet hen accidentally flew overboard, as we were scudding along at a furious rate, I thought I saw a tear stand in his eye, as she floated panting in our wake.—But as yet we are becalmed, and heartily displeased at old Aeolus for overlooking us.

One afternoon we caught two sharks. In one of them, a female, about seven feet long, we found ten young ones, all alive, and quite capable of swimming, as we proved by experiment; for, on casting one of them into the sea, it immediately made off, as if it had been accustomed to shift for itself. Of another, that had been cut in two, the head half swam off out of our sight. The rest were cut in pieces, as was the old shark, as bait for the dolphins, which I have already said are fond of such food.

Our captain, who was much intent on amusing me, informed me that the rudder-fishes were plentiful astern, and immediately set to dressing hooks for the purpose of catching them. There was now some air above us, the cotton sheets aloft bulged out, the ship moved through the water, and the captain and I repaired to the cabin window. I was furnished with a fine hook, a thread line, and some small bits of bacon, as was the captain, and we dropped our bait among the myriads of delicate little fishes below. Up they came, one after another, so fast in succession, that, according to my journal, we caught three hundred and seventy in about two hours. What a mess! and how delicious when roasted! If ever I am again becalmed in the Gulf of Mexico, I shall not forget the rudder-fish. The little things scarcely measured three inches in length; they were thin and deep in form, and afforded excellent eating. It was curious to see them keep to the lee of the rudder in a compact body; and so voracious were they that they actually leaped out of the water at the sight of the bait, as "sunnies" are occasionally wont to do in our rivers. But the very instant that the ship became still, they dispersed around her sides, and would no longer bite. I made a figure of one of them, as indeed I tried to do of every other species that occurred during this death-like calm. Not one of these fishes did I ever see when crossing the Atlantic, although many kinds at times come close to the stern of any vessel in the great sea, and are called by the same name.

Another time we caught a fine Porpoise, which measured about two yards in length. This took place at night, when the light of the moon afforded me a clear view of the spot. The fish, contrary to custom, was grained, instead of being harpooned; but in such a way and so effectually, through the forehead, that it was thus held fast, and allowed to flounce and beat about the bows of the ship, until the person who had struck it gave the line holding the grains to the Captain, slided down upon the bob-stays with a rope, and after a while managed to secure it by the tail. Some of the crew then hoisted it on board. When it arrived on deck, it gave a deep groan, flapped with great force, and soon expired. On opening it next morning, eight hours after death, we found its intestines still warm. They were arranged in the same manner as those of a pig; the paunch contained several cuttlefishes partially digested. The lower jaw extended beyond the upper about three-fourths of an inch, and both were furnished with a single row of conical teeth, about half an inch long, and just so far separated as to admit those of one jaw between the corresponding ones of the other. The animal might weigh about four hundred pounds; its eyes were extremely small, its flesh was considered delicate by some on board; but in my opinion, if it be good, that of a large alligator is equally so; and on neither do I intend to feast for some time. The Captain told me that he had seen these Porpoises leap at times perpendicularly out of the water to the height of several feet, and that small boats have now and then been sunk by their falling into them, when engaged with their sports.

During all this time flocks of Pigeons were crossing the Gulf, between Cuba and the Floridas; many a Rose-breasted Gull played around by day; Noddies alighted on the rigging by night; and now and then the Frigate bird was observed ranging high over head in the azure of the cloudless sky.

The directions of the currents were tried, and our Captain, who had an extraordinary genius for mechanics, was frequently employed in turning powder-horns and other articles. So calm and sultry was the weather that we had a large awning spread, under which we took our meals, and spent the night. At length we got so wearied of it, that the very sailors I thought seemed disposed to leap overboard, and swim to land. But at length, on the thirty-seventh day after our departure, a smart breeze overtook us. Presently there was an extraordinary bustle on board; about twelve the Tortugas light-house bore north of us, and in a few hours more we gained the Atlantic. Aeolus had indeed awakened from his long sleep; and on the nineteenth day after leaving the Capes of Florida, I was landed at Liverpool.

[From *Ornithological Biography*, Vol. III, pp. 520-522.]

U. S. Revenue Cutter Marion Lt. R. Day Actg Comd

Thursday May 10th 1832

Commences with clear weather and pleasant breezes from the Eastward at 2 PM saw the Tortugas light at 3.30 boarded off the tortugas the Sloop Paragon. J. Noyes Master from Key West having cleared out for New London in Ballast at the Latter port It appears he had a quantity of cotton on these Keys and ~~further~~ clearing out from Key west in Ballast he came here and took in a quantity of cotton in Bales. When he was first boarded his papers were demanded and he handed a manifest, clearance & Register he was asked if there was cargo on board his answer was none and his manifest mentioned only Ballast, After searching under hatches this cotton was found, we therefore have enclosed his papers with the following letter to the Collr of Key West—

Tortugas May 9th 1832

Sir

I hereby report to you the within named vessel the Paragon J. Noyes master was this day boarded by the Revenue Cutter Marion ~~under your direction~~ the capt being called upon to Exhibit his papers produced a false manifest as you will perceive by the enclosed papers but upon Examination of the vessel found that she was laden with cotton taken from this place She has in my Opinion violated the Revenue laws I therefore wish you to consult the District attorney and proceed as the law directs.

Yours &c

David Pinkham Esqr

Depy Collr Key West

Signed R. Day

Lieut. U. S. R. C. Marion

Appendix

LOG BOOK OF U.S. REVENUE CUTTER *MARION*
Lieut R. Day Actg Commander

The period covered in each entry extends from 12 noon (Meridian) to 12 noon. Therefore, when the entry for April 18th states that Audubon came on board at 11 a.m., the date actually was April 19th.

Tuesday April 17th 1832

Comences clear and pleasant crew employed preparing for Sea Shipped R. Gordon A Luther & O. P. Cappele. Latter part of the day employed getting off Stores.

Wednesday April 18th 1832

Comences clear and pleasant employed getting off the Stores Struck the foretopmast to put a new Sheave in the head and got him up again. J.E. Smith Carp^{t} Shipping & B. Johns are on this day. At 5 P.M. we moored Ship during the night Light airs at day light light [?] and at 11 am Mr Audobon came on board passenger. got under weigh and proceeded down at noon working down channele.

Thursday April 19th 1832

At 3 P.M. came to anchor in the roads at 8 P.M. a heavy Squall from N.W. at day light got under weigh at 7:30 crosst the bar at noon Charleston light bore N.N.W. 18 miles dist.

Friday April 20th 1832

First part of this day light winds and Smooth Sea crew employed variously Carpenter repairing boat from 4 to 8 PM very light airs at 4 called the crew to quarters—

From 8 to Midnight variable at 10 the wind freshened at midnight fine breeze.

Sounded in 15 fathoms.

from 1 to 4 AM very fine breeze and clear weather

from 4 to 8 AM moderate breezes carrying all sail off the wind.

from 8 to Meridian fine breeze & clear at Meridian Sounded in 10 1/4 fathoms.

Latt obs. 30° 52′ 30″ N.

Remarks Saturday April 21St. 1832

This day comences with clear weather and light Ely [easterly] winds at 2 PM Saw the Land at 4 PM St. Johns Light bore West. 12 miles [Jacksonville]

from 4 to 6 fine breeze & clear weather

from 6 to 8 Moderate breezes at 8 Saw Augustine light.

from 8 to Midnight very light airs and clear.

from 12 to 4 AM light airs and clear at 3 AM Let the Squaresail & light Sails

from four to 8 very very light airs.Sounded in 15 fathoms water—

from 8 to Meridian nearly calm crew employed repairing the flying Jib.

Latt obs. 29° 15′ N.

Remarks Sunday April 22nd 1832

Comences with fresh breezes & clear weather at 4 PM cloudy all Sail Let by the wind bent the flying Jib.

from 4 to 6 fresh breezes & cloudy

from 6 to 8 cloudy with Sharp lightning

from 8 to Midnight Squally with thunder at 10 heavy Squall from NW. took in all Sail Latter part of the watch calm

from 12 to 4 AM. light winds and cloudy made Sail on [illegible].

from 4 to 8am variable at 6 light breeze from Erd [Eastward] at 7 Moderate breeze Made all Sail Saw a Ship in the offing.

from 8 to Meridian moderate breeze all Sail Let accordingly.

at noon Latt Obs. 28°. 08′ N.

Remarks Monday 23rd April 1832

Comences with moderate breezes & fair weather at 2h. 30m. PM Saw the land and Jibed Ship at 4 PM running along shore

From 4 to 6 clear and pleasant at 6 took in Steering Sails—

From 6 to 8 fresh breezes at 7. took in the Square Sail—

From 8 to 12 fresh breezes and cloudy Shortened Sail accordingly. Split the Top Sail

From 12 to 4 more moderate. Made Sail—

From 4 to 8 am fair weather at daylight made the light Sails

from 8 to Meridian moderate breezes and clear til Noon

Latt Obs. 26°.32′ N.

Tuesday April 24th 1832

From 1 to 4 PM light breezes and clear weather carrying all Sail to best advantage

from 4 to 6 fresh breezes and clear at 5.30. Saw cape Florida light—

from 6 to 8 fresh breezes & at 8 the light. bore N.W.

from 8 to 12. fresh breezes Shortened Sail accordingly

From 12 to 4 am more Moderate made Sail

from 4 to 8 moderate made all light Sails

from 8 to 12 Moderate at 10.30 Saw the light boat Eeagen at Noon Key Rodrigues bore N.W. by W.

Wednesday April 25th 1832

Comences with clear pleasant weather—at 3 PM Saw Indian Key at 5 came to anchor at Indian Key. During the night fresh breezes.

Latter part of the day the crew employed fitting fore and main peak haulyd block & straps Rattling the rigging & other necessary jobs—mending the fore top Sail etc.

Thursday April 26th 1832

Comences with clear pleasant weather During the day the crew employed mending the light Sail rattling the rigging & carpenter repairing boats.

Friday April 27th 1832

Comences with thick cloudy weather and fresh S.E. winds crew employed at the rigging. Boarded Sloop Isabella. Housman from Key West a Licenced wrecker, also Schooner Thistle. Bethel from Key West. & Mary-Ann Appleby. from Do. [ditto] wrecking.

Saturday April 28th 1832

Comences with fresh breezes & cloudy during the first part of the day employed cleaning Small Arms during the night fresh breezes from the S.E. latter employed at various Jobs of rigging Tarring, etc.

Sunday April 29th 1832

Comences with fresh breezes & cloudy with rain and heavy Swell let go the best bower anchor. at 4 PM more moderate hove up the best bower found the cable very much chafed 4 fathoms from the bend cut it off and rebent it during the night fresh breezes & cloudy latter part of the night clear at 5 am got under weigh and Stood to the westward at 10 am boarded off Key Vacas [Vaca]. The Schooner Whale of N. London. Wolfe master cargo of cotton from Key West for New London at noon Squared away for Vacas harbor.

Monday April 30th 1832

Comences with fresh breezes from South at 1.30 PM came to anchor in Vacas harbor and furled Sails during the night fresh breezes & cloudy. at 5 am got under weigh at 11 am came to anchor in Key of Honda [Bahia Honda].

Tuesday May 1St 1832

Comences with clear weather and pleasant breezes all hands employed painting the larboard Side at 3 P.M. cloudy at heavy Squall from N.W. Let go the best bower during the night rain Squalls. Latter part of the day clear.

Wednesday May 2nd. 1832

Comences with clear weather and fresh Sly [southerly] breezes crew employed painting the Starboard Side at 4 P.M. finished painting During the night heavy Squals of rain latter part of the day clear.

Thursday May 3rd 1832

Comences with clear weather and light Sly breezes crew employed at various duties during the night Clear at 3 AM unmoored at 4 got under weigh and Stood out of the harbor at 10AM hove too off Looe Key and sent the boat to examine the beacon which was found to be in very bad order the Top being blown down for 4 or 5 feet below the Spindle. at noon the boat returned pulled away and Stood to the westward.

Friday May 4th 1832

Comences with light Southerly winds and clear weather crew employed working Ship at 5 PM saw Key West light at 6.30 came to anchor in the harbor furled Sails & Let the awnings—during the night fresh breezes & cloudy. Let go the best bower anchor at day light moderate hove up the bower. All the remainder of the day employed overhauling different parts of the rigging.

Saturday May 5th 1832

Comences with very fair weather and moderate breezes from SE at 4 PM unbent the topsail and repaired it During the night heavy Squalls attended with rain—latter part of the day very warm and calm filled a barrell of Water.

Sunday May 6th 1832

Comences with calm and clear weather at midnight Light Ely winds during the day fine breezes & clear weather Latter part of this day clear weather and breezes.

Monday 7th 1832

Comences with clear weather and fresh SEly winds at 9 PM let go the best bower anchor it being very Squally Latter part of this day the crew employed Scraping the Masts etc.

Tuesday May 8th 1832

Comences with clear weather and fresh breeze crew variously employed at the rigging during the night clear latter part of the day the crew cleaning Small arms.

Wednesday May 9th 1832

Comences with clear weather and moderate breezes from ESE at 5 pm hove up the best bower anchor at 7 hoisted in the barge. got Some wood from Shore and a barrell of water. at 2.30 AM. got under weigh and Stood out of the harbor. at 4.30 am Hove too off Sand Key Light house and sent the boat on Shore for M.r Thompson Ass.t Light Keeper at the Tortugas. At 5 Bore away and ran down at 8 am off the Marquis Key Boarded the Sch.r Edward Francis of N. York, J. Baker Master from Montego Bay (Jai). for New York. Cargo of Rum and Piminto.—at noon off the quicksands all Sail Let steering westward.

Thursday May 10th 1832

Comences with clear weather and pleasant breezes from the Eastward. at 2 PM saw the Tortugas light at 3.30 boarded off the Tortugas the Sloop Paragon. F. Noyes Master from Key West having cleared out for New London in Ballast at the Latter port. It appears he had a quantity of cotton on these Keys and after clearing out from Key west in Ballast he came here and took in a quantity of cotton in Bales. When he was first boarded his papers were demanded and he handed a manifest, clearance & Register. he was asked if there was cargo on board & his answer was None? and his manifest mentioned only Ballast. After searching under hatches this cotton was found, we therefore have enclosed his papers & with the following letter to the Collet.r of Key West—

Tortugas May 9th 1832

Sir

I hereby report to you the within named vessel The Evergreen F. Noyes Master was this day boarded by the Revenue Cutter Marion. Under your direction the capt being called upon to Exibit his papers produced a false manifest—as you will perceive by the enclosed papers—but upon Examination of the vessel found that She was laden with cotton taken from this place. She has in my Opinion violated the Revenue laws I therefore wish you to consult the District attorney and proceed as the Law directs.

David Pinkham Esq
Depty Colltr Key West

Yours etc.
Signed
R. Day
Lieut. U.S.C. Marion

Friday May 11th 1832

Comences with clear pleasant weather the crew variously employed latter part of the day light Sthly winds. Boarded Schnr. Pizarro Hoxie Master from Key West. Wrecking.

Saturday May 12th 1832

Comences with clear pleasant weather and light SE winds during the night calm latter part of the day light Ely winds Boarded the Sloops Spermacetti—Clift Master—Wrecking and Brilliant—Packer Master from Key West for eggs, etc. Painted the Starboard Bow—

Sunday May 13th 1832

Comences with clear weather & light SE. winds during the night cloudy latter part of the [night?] Small Showers of rain & fresh breeze from E. 2 am the Kedge & Hawser out to windward Mustered the crew, etc.

Monday May 14th 1832

Comences clear & pleasant—crew principally employed gathering Shells etc for J.J. Audubon Esq. During the night clear latter part of the day the crew employed painting the Larboard Side

Remarks Tuesday May the 15th. 1832

Comences with clear pleasant weather at 5 PM finished painting the Larboard Side. during the night clear weather and Nly winds. at 7 am M.r Thompson requested assistance to carry his boat to Key West. (The Asst. Light Keeper) gave him two men at 9 am got under weigh after having examined all the Keys. and Light house at noon all hands employed working Ship.

Wednesday May 16th 1832

Comences with clear weather and pleasant breezes at 2 PM passed east Key all Sail Set. at 5.30 Saw the Marquis [Marquesa] Key at 8 PM Saw Sand Key Light and at 10 Saw Key West Light at 10.30 being calm and the tide ebb came to anchor at 3 am got under weigh with the flood tide at 10 am came to anchor in Key West Harbor. furled Sails and Let awnings.

Thursday comences with clear weather & N.W wind crew employed watering at 4 PM severe showers of rain and Squalls of wind from NE. at 3 PM. received from the Shore *one hundred & fifty galls of water* during the night heavy Squalls. let go the best bower at day light hove up the best bower and moored with the Kedge latter part of the day clear. crew wooding watering etc. received Four-hundred & Eighty galls water.

Remarks Friday May 18th 1832

Comences with clear pleasant weather crew wooding & watering at 4 P.M. got 2 Loads of wood dry Sails 2 Men returned to duty who were about in the light house boat—During the night fresh breezes at daylight Sent boat watering and 2 hands wooding. the remainder of the crew necessarily employed etc. Received 450 galls water on board.

Saturday May 19th 1832

Comences with clear weather and pleasant breezes. crew employed wooding, etc. during the night heavy Squalls of rain. Latter part of the day clear loosed Sails to dry.

Sunday May 20th 1832

Comences with clear pleasant weather crew employed variously. during the night clear weather at 3 am. unmoored Ship. got ready for Sailing.

Monday May 21St 1832

Comences with clear weather at 3 PM. cloudy and fresh breezes during the night Squalls of rain at 3 am got under weigh and Stood out. at noon calm or nearly. So came to anchor off the Sugar Loaf [Key].

Tuesday May the 22nd 1832

Comences with clear weather crew employed variously during the night light N.E.ly. winds and clear weather at 3.30 AM. got under weigh and Stood Ely. at noon came to anchor near Newfound harbor.

Wednesday May the 23rd 1832

Comences with cloudy Weather during the night clear pleasant weather latter part of the day fresh Ely winds & clear part of the crew employed at Ship duty the remainder in the Boat.

Thursday May 24th 1832

Comences with clear pleasant weather during the night light variable winds at 7 am got under weigh and Stood to the eastward. latter part of the day light Ely winds.

Friday May 25th 1832

Comences with clear weather and light Ely winds at 1.30 came to anchor in the Bay of Honda [Bahia Honda] during the night calm. latter part of the day employed painting.

Saturday May 26th 1832

Comences with cloudy weather and light showers of rain. during the night calm and very much anoyed with mosquitoes crew employed at Ships dutys. a Boat & crew in the boat—at 6 am got under weigh and Stood out of the harbor. Then Stood eastwardly at Meridian anchored off Prickly pear Key.

Sunday May 27th 1832

Comences with clear pleasant weather during the night—clear pleasant weather—all hands employed variously at 8 am got under weigh and Stood to the Eastwardly, at noon off Duck Key.

Monday May 28th 1832

Comences with clear pleasant weather crew employed working Ship at 3 PM came to anchor off Indian Key. during the night clear weather latter part of the day crew employed worming the cable & other Ships duty. Boarded Brig Janus and Issabella. I Martin from France for N. Orleans for N. Orleans.

Tuesday May 29th 1832

Comences clear pleasant weather all hands employed variously. Boarded Sloop Brilliant—Packer a wrecker and Schr Mary Ann. Appleby a wrecker.—

Wednesday May 30th 1832

Comences with clear pleasant weather during the night fresh Breezes from N.E. All hands employed at the rigging etc. Boarded the Sloop Sarah Issabella Housman from Key West a Wrecker.

Remarks May 31 St. 1832 Thursday

Comences with clear weather and moderate breezes from the Erd at 3 pm hoisted in the barge & prepared for Sea at 4 got under weigh at 5.30 crossed the reef at 6 Indian Key bore NW By N. 9 miles dist at 6.30 took in the fore top Sail and Jib a Jib wind light & variable at 12 near calm

from 8 to 12 light wind & variable

from 12 to 4 am calm

From 4 to 8 am light airs at day light Saw 3 Sail. at 8 light breezes

Set the Jib a Jib a top Qtr

From 8 to Meridian moderate breezes & clear at noon clear

all Sail Let By the wind—

Notes

1. John James Audubon, *Ornithological Biography* (Edinburgh: Adam and Charles Black, 1832-1839), Vol. I, p. v.

2. Maria R. Audubon, *Audubon and His Journals* (New York: Dover Publications, Inc., 1960), Vol. I, p. 17.

3. Ibid., p. 18.

4. Francis Hobart Herrick, *Audubon the Naturalist* (New York: D. Appleton and Co., 1917), Vol. I, p. 198.

5. Ibid., pp. 260-261.

6. Ibid., p. 323.

7. Ibid., p. 358.

8. Ibid., p. 361.

9. Stanley Clisby Arthur, *Audubon, An Intimate Life of the American Woodsman* (New Orleans: Harmanson, 1937), p. 356.

10. John James Audubon, *Letters of John James Audubon 1826-1840* (Boston: Club of Odd Volumes, 1929), Vol. I, p. 17.

11. Arthur, p. 403.

12. Ibid., p. 369.

13. Audubon, *Letters,* Vol. I, pp. 138, 143.

14. Herrick, Vol. II, pp. 8-9, reprinted from Letter No. 1, dated St. Augustine, East Florida, Dec. 7, 1831, in *Monthly American Journal of Geology and Natural Science* I (1832): 358.

15. Audubon, *Letters,* Vol. I, pp. 151-155.

16. Ibid., pp. 159-164.

17. Herrick, Vol. II, pp. 12-14.

18. Audubon, *Letters,* Vol. I, pp. 164-165.

19. Ibid., pp. 165-168.

20. Herrick, Vol. II, p. 15.

21. Herrick, Vol. II, pp. 15-16, 17-18, 19-20, 20-21.

22. Ibid., pp. 21-22, Letter No. 3, *Monthly American Journal of Geology and Natural Science,* Vol. I (1832): 529-537.

23. Audubon, *Letters,* Vol. I, p. 171.

24. Ibid., pp. 171-172.

25. Ibid., pp. 172-176.
26. Ibid., pp. 177-179.
27. Ibid., pp. 180-181.
28. Ibid., pp. 182-183.
29. U.S. National Archives,. Record Group 45, "Naval Records Collection of the Office of Naval Records and History."
30. Personal communication from Theodore E. Leach, Library of Congress; information from National Archives, Record Group 45, "Naval Records Collection of the Office of Naval Records and History."
31. Audubon, *Letters*, Vol. I, p. 184.
32. Arthur, p. 411.
33. Ibid.
34. Audubon, *Letters*, Vol. I, pp. 184, 185.
35. Ibid., p. 187.
36. Personal communication from Dr. Ashby Hammond, University of Florida; information from National Archives, Record Group 26, "Records of the U.S. Coast Guard, Log Book of the U.S. Revenue Cutter, Marion, Lt. Day."
37. Audubon, *Letters*, Vol. I, p. 193.
38. Howard I. Chapelle, *The History of American Sailing Ships* (New York: W. W. Norton & Co., 1935), pp. 189, 200.
39. Audubon, *Ornithological Biography*, Vol. II, p. 312.
40. Reference to the melody was found in an unidentified newspaper clipping headed "Reminiscences of Key West, No. 13" by William A. Whitehead, subtitled "Wrecking Fifty Years Ago." In it the Florida Wrecker's Song is reprinted, with the notation "Air—The Garden Gate." The clipping is bound into a first edition of *A Sketch of the History of Key West, Florida* by Walter C. Maloney (Newark, N.J.: 1876) in the Florida Collection of the University of Miami Library. The Library of Congress Music Division attributes the words of "The Garden Gate" to W. Upton and the music to W. T. Parke, according to Vol. I of Sabine Baring-Gould's *English Minstrelsie* (Edinburgh, 1900). According to Baring-Gould, the song was first published in 1809 and during the nineteenth century made its way into the English folk tradition.
41. Audubon, *Ornithological Biography*, Vol. III, pp. x-xi.

Bibliography

Arthur, Stanley Clisby. *Audubon: An Intimate Life of the American Woodsman.* New Orleans: Harmanson, 1937.

Audubon, John James. *Audubon, By Himself.* Selected, Arranged, and Edited by Alice Ford. Garden City, N.Y.: Natural History Press, 1969.

Audubon, John James. *The Birds of America, from Original Drawings.* 4 vols. London: privately published by author, 1827-1838.

Audubon, John James. *The Birds of America.* Octavo Edition. 7 vols. New York: Roe Lockwood and Son, 1859.

Audubon, John James. *The Birds of America.* Introduction by William Vogt. New York: The Macmillan Co., 1937, 1953. Includes a transcript of the legends on the original plates, with notes.

Audubon, John James. *Journals of John James Audubon 1820-1821 and 1840-1843.* Edited by Howard Corning. 2 vols. Boston: Club of Odd Volumes, 1929.

Audubon, John James. *Letters of John James Audubon 1826-1840.* Edited by Howard Corning. 2 vols. Boston: Club of Odd Volumes, 1930.

Audubon, John James. *The Original Water-Color Paintings by John James Audubon for The Birds of America.* Reproduced in color from the collection at The New-York Historical Society. Introduction by Marshall B. Davidson. 2 vols. New York: American Heritage Publishing Co., Inc., 1966.

Audubon, John James. *Ornithological Biography, Or An Account of The Birds of the United States of America; Accompanied by Descriptions of the Objects Represented in the Work Entitled The Birds of America, and Interspersed with Delineations of American Scenery and Manners.* 5 vols. Edinburgh: Adam and Charles Black, 1832-1839. Vol. I was published in Philadelphia by E. L. Cary and A. Hart, Vol. II in Boston by Hilliard, Gray and Company.

Audubon, Lucy. *The Life of John James Audubon, the Naturalist.* New York: G. P. Putnam and Son, 1869.

Audubon, Maria R. *Audubon and His Journals.* 2 vols. New York: Charles Scribner's Sons, 1897. Reprint, with zoological and other notes by Elliott Coues. New York: Dover Publications, Inc., 1960.

Audubon's Birds of America. Introduction and Descriptive Captions by Ludlow Griscom. New York: Macmillan, 1950.

Audubon Watercolors and Drawings. Catalogue of Exhibition. Introduction by Edward H. Dwight. Utica, N.Y. and New York: Munson-Williams-Proctor Institute and the Pierpont Morgan Library, 1965.

Bailey, Harold H. *The Birds of Florida.* Baltimore: Williams and Wilkins Co., 1925.

Bartram, William. *The Travels of William Bartram.* New York: Macy-Masius, 1928. Several reprint editions are available.

Beard, Annie. *Our Foreign Born Citizens.* New York: Thomas Y. Crowell, 1939.

Brewer, Thomas M. "Reminiscences of John James Audubon." *Harper's* 61 (June 1880): 665-675.

Brookfield, Charles, and Griswold, Oliver. *They All Called It Tropical.* Miami: Miami Post Publishing Co., 1960.

Browne, Jefferson B. *Key West, The Old and the New.* St. Augustine, Fla.: The Record Co., 1912. Reprint, facsimile reproduction with Introduction and Index by E. Ashby Hammond, Bicentennial Floridiana Facsimile Series. Gainesville: University of Florida Press, 1973.

Buchanan, Robert. *Life and Adventures of Audubon the Naturalist.* New York: E. P. Dutton & Co., 1915.

Burroughs, John. *John James Audubon.* Boston: Small, Maynard & Co., 1902.

Cabell, James Branch, and Hanna, Alfred J. *The St. Johns: A Parade of Diversities.* New York: Farrar and Rinehart, Inc., 1943.

Charleston Courier, The, May 1839.

Charleston Mercury, The, June-July 1833.

Davis, T. Frederick. "Pioneer Florida. Indian Key and Wrecking, 1833." *Florida Historical Quarterly* 22 (July 1943): 57-61.

Dodd, Dorothy. "The Wrecking Business on the Florida Reef, 1822-1860." *Florida Historical Quarterly* 22 (April 1944): 171-199.

Dovell, Junius E. *Florida: Historic, Dramatic, Contemporary.* 4 vols. New York: Lewis Historical Publishing Co., 1952.

Fairbanks, George R. *Florida, Its History and Its Romance.* Jacksonville, Fla.: H. and W. B. Drew Co., 1904.

Federal Writers Project. *A Guide to Key West.* Rev. 2nd ed. New York: Hastings House, 1949.

Ferguson, G. E., Lingham, C. W., Love, S. K., and Vernon, R. O. "Springs of Florida." Florida Geological Survey *Bulletin* 31 (1947): 165-166.

Ford, Alice. *John James Audubon.* Norman: University of Oklahoma Press, 1964.

Gold, Pleasant Daniel. *History of Duval County: Including Early History of East Florida.* St. Augustine, Fla.: The Record Co., 1929.

Greene, Earle R. "Birds of the Lower Florida Keys (The Great White Heron Reserve)." *Journal of the Florida Academy of Sciences* 8 (September 1945).

Hammond, E. A. "Wreckers and Wrecking on the Florida Reef, 1829-1832." *Florida Historical Quarterly* 41 (January 1963): 239-273.

Harper, Francis. *Bartram's Travels, A Commentary.* New Haven, Conn.: Yale University Press, 1958.

Herrick, Francis Hobart. *Audubon the Naturalist: A History of His Life and*

Time. 2 vols. New York: D. Appleton and Co., 1917. Reprint. New York: Dover Publications, Inc., 1968.

Holder, J. B. "Dry Tortugas." *Harper's* 37 (July 1868): 260-267.

Howell, Arthur H. *Florida Bird Life*. New York: Coward McCann, 1932.

Key West Gazette, April 20, 1831-September 5, 1832.

Maloney, Walter C. *A Sketch of the History of Key West, Florida*. Newark, N.J.: Advertiser Printing House, 1876. Reprint, with Introduction by Thelma Peters, Floridiana Facsimile and Reprint Series. Gainesville: University of Florida Press, 1968.

Muschamp, Edward A. *Audacious Audubon*. New York: Brentano's, 1929.

Patrick, Rembert W., and Morris, Allen. *Florida Under Five Flags*. 4th ed. Gainesville: University of Florida Press, 1967.

Peattie, Donald C. *Audubon's America*. Boston: Houghton Mifflin Co., 1940.

Peithmann, Irvin M. *The Unconquered Seminole Indians*. St. Petersburg, Fla.: Great Outdoors, 1960.

Proby, Kathryn Hall. "Three Islands." *Muse News* 4 (June 1972): 47-50, 81.

Robertson, William B., Jr. "The Terns of the Dry Tortugas." *Bulletin of the Florida State Museum* 8 (1964).

Sprunt, Alexander, Jr. *Florida Bird Life*. New York: Coward-McCann, 1954.

Stanton, Edith P. "Ruins of the Early Plantations of the Halifax Area, Volusia County, Florida." Volusia County Historical Commission, n.d.

Tebeau, Charlton W. *A History of Florida*. Coral Gables, Fla.: University of Miami Press, 1971.

Tebeau, Charlton W. *Man in the Everglades: 2000 Years of Human History in the Everglades National Park*. 2nd rev. ed. Coral Gables, Fla.: University of Miami Press, 1968.

Washington, D.C. National Archives. Record Group 26, "Records of the U.S. Coast Guard, Logbook of the U.S. Revenue Cutter Marion, Lt. Day," April 17, 1832-May 31, 1832.

Washington, D.C. National Archives. Record Group 45, "Naval Records Collection of the Office of Naval Records and History."

Index

Birds are listed alphabetically by the common names used by Audubon. Modern common and scientific names are given only for those birds receiving major treatment. Main entries are indicated by boldface type.

MacDonald, Patricia J.

Not guilty.

DATE	BORROWER'S NAME	

DATE
BORROWER'S NAME